Taking SIDES

Clashing Views on Controversial Issues in
Human Sexuality

Fourth Edition

Taking
SIDES

Clashing Views on Controversial Issues in
Human Sexuality

Fourth Edition

Edited, Selected, and with Introductions by

Robert T. Francoeur
Fairleigh Dickinson University

The Dushkin Publishing Group, Inc.

*For my wife and daughters, Anna, Nicole, and Danielle, and other
special friends who continually force me to ask new questions.*

Photo Acknowledgments

Part 1   United Nations/John Isaac
Part 2   Sara Krulwich/The New York Times
Part 3   AP/Wide World Photos

Cover Art Acknowledgment
Charles Vitelli

Manufactured in the United States of America

Fourth Edition, Second Printing

Library of Congress Cataloging-in-Publication Data

Main entry under title:
    Taking sides: clashing views on controversial issues in human sexuality/edited, selected,
    and with introductions by Robert T. Francoeur.—4th ed.
    Includes bibliographical references and index.
    1. Sex customs—United States. 2. Sexual ethics—United States. 3. Sex. 4. Sex and law—
    United States. I. Francoeur, Robert T., *comp.*
        HQ18.U5T33   306.7'0973—dc20
        ISBN: 1–56134–249–1   93–31818

Printed on Recycled Paper

The Dushkin Publishing Group, Inc.
Sluice Dock, Guilford, CT 06437

PREFACE

In few areas of American society today are clashing views more evident than in the area of human sexual behavior. Almost daily, in the news media, in congressional hearings, and on the streets, we hear about Americans of all ages taking completely opposite positions on such issues as abortion, contraception, homosexuality, surrogate motherhood, teenage sexuality, and the like. Given the highly personal, emotional, and sensitive nature of these issues, sorting out the meaning of these controversies and fashioning a coherent position on them can be a difficult proposition. The purpose of this book, therefore, is to encourage meaningful critical thinking about current issues related to human sexuality, and the debates are designed to assist you in the task of clarifying your own personal values and identifying what society's are or should be in this area.

For this fourth edition of *Taking Sides: Clashing Views on Controversial Issues in Human Sexuality,* I have gathered 34 lively and thoughtful statements by articulate advocates on opposite sides of a variety of sexuality-related questions. For the questions debated in this volume, it is vital that you understand and appreciate the different positions other people take on these issues, as well as your own. You should respect other people's philosophical biases and religious beliefs and attempt to articulate your own. Democracies are strongest when they respect the rights and privileges of all citizens, be they conservative, liberal, or middle-of-the-road, religious or humanistic, of the majority or in the minority. Although you may disagree with one or even both of the arguments offered for each issue, it is important that you read each statement carefully and critically. Since this book is a tool to encourage critical thinking, you should not feel confined to the views expressed in the articles. You may see important points on both sides of an issue and may construct for yourself a new and creative approach, which may incorporate the best of both sides or provide an entirely new vantage point for understanding.

To assist you as you pursue the issues debated here, each issue has an issue *introduction*, which sets the stage for the debate, tells you something about each of the authors, and provides some historical background to the debate. Each issue concludes with a *postscript* that briefly ties the readings together and gives a detailed list of *suggested readings*, if you would like to further explore a topic.

Changes to this edition For this edition, I have made some significant changes. More than half the issues are new. The 10 new issues are as follows: *Are Gender Differences Rooted in the Brain?* (Issue 1); *Does Sexual Infidelity Destroy a Relationship?* (Issue 4); *Should RU 486 Be Legalized?* (Issue 6); *Should Schools Distribute Condoms?* (Issue 7); *Is There a Date Rape Crisis on College*

Campuses? (Issue 10); *Do Parental Notification Laws Benefit Minors Seeking Abortions?* (Issue 12); *Should the Policy Banning Gays from the Military Be Lifted?* (Issue 13); *Should Society Recognize Gay Marriages?* (Issue 15); *Is Sexual Harassment a Pervasive Problem?* (Issue 16); and *Has the Federal Government Spent Enough on AIDS Research?* (Issue 17). In addition, the NO article has been changed in the issue on fetal personhood (Issue 9) in order to bring a fresh perspective to the debate. In all, there are 21 new selections in this edition. I have also revised and updated the issue introductions and postscripts where necessary.

A word to the instructor An *Instructor's Manual With Test Questions* (multiple-choice and essay) is available through the publisher for the instructor using *Taking Sides* in the classroom, and a general guidebook, *Using Taking Sides in the Classroom,* which discusses methods and techniques for integrating the pro/con approach into any classroom setting, is also available.

Acknowledgments The task of tracking down the best essays for inclusion in this collection is not easy, and I appreciate the useful suggestions from the many users of *Taking Sides* across the United States and Canada who communicated with my publisher. Special thanks go to those who responded with specific suggestions for the fourth edition:

Connie C. Alexander
Tarrant County Junior
   College–Northwest

Joseph J. Byrne
Ocean County College

Ellen Cole
Prescott College

J. Kenneth Davidson, Sr.
University of Wisconsin–Eau
   Claire

Philip Hart
Plymouth State College

Gay James
Southwest Texas State University

Kelly B. Kyes
Wake Forest University

Robert H. Pollack
University of Georgia

E. N. Simons
University of Delaware

Edward Stevens
Regis College

John C. Touhey
Florida Atlantic University

I am also grateful to Herb Samuels for his insights on black sexuality, which I made use of in the Volume Introduction. Continue to write to me in care of The Dushkin Publishing Group with comments and suggestions for issues and readings.

Benjamin Franklin once remarked that democracies are built on compromises. But you cannot have healthy compromises unless people talk with each other and try to understand, appreciate, and respect their different ways of reasoning, their values, and their goals. Open and frank discussions of controversial issues is what this book is all about. Without healthy controversy and open exchange of different views, intolerance and bigotry could easily increase to the point where our democratic system could no longer function. Democracy thrives on controversy.

Robert T. Francoeur
Madison, NJ

CONTENTS IN BRIEF

CONTENTS

Doreen Kimura, a professor of psychology, describes a wide range of cognitive variations between the genders that reflect differing hormonal influences on fetal brain development. She maintains that differences between the female and the male brains help explain differences in occupational interests and capabilities between the sexes. Carol Tavris, a social psychologist, finds that scientific efforts conducted over the past century to prove gender differences originate in the brain have yielded enough conflicting views and distorted findings to invalidate such a hypothesis. She maintains that although biology is not irrelevant to human behavior, this research has consistently been used to define women as fundamentally different from and inferior to men in body, psyche, and brain.

Patrick Carnes, a therapist who has established an inpatient program for sexual dependency, argues that a significant number of people have identified themselves as sexual addicts—persons with "unstoppable" repetitive behavior patterns that are destructive to the addict and to his or her family. Sexual addiction can best be treated, he claims, by using systems theory and technigues developed by Alcoholics Anonymous, obesity clinics, and substance-abuse rehabilitation programs. Marty Klein, a sex therapist and marriage and family counselor, challenges sexual addiction as being vaguely defined and often diagnosed by nonsexologists. He claims that the symptoms of sexual addiction are arbitrary and that its promulgation promotes unhealthy, negative, and immature attitudes toward natural human sexuality.

Clinical psychologists A. Nicholas Groth and H. Jean Birnbaum argue that rape is not primarily a sexual act but one of hostility, degradation, and anger, often not resulting in sexual arousal at all. Professor Craig T. Palmer claims that the arguments that present rape as being motivated primarily by anger, rage, the need for power, or sadism are illogical, based on inaccurate definitions, untestable, or inconsistent with the actual behavior of rapists.

Frank Pittman, a family therapist and the author of *Private Lies: Infidelity and the Betrayal of Intimacy*, maintains that infidelity is the primary disrupter of families, the most dreaded and devastating experience in marriage. He identifies and refutes seven myths about adultery that are true some of the time but that are not as universal as most people think. Sandra C. Finzi, a family therapist, argues that the European approach to extramarital "arrangements" is much more realistic than the American tradition of viewing every extramarital sexual encounter as an indication of a deep flaw in the character of the "wandering" spouse or a fatal flaw in the marriage. Finzi claims that marriages in which couples learn to distinguish between the long-term solidarity of the relationship and the passing infatuation may not collapse in the wake of an extramarital affair.

Psychologist James C. Dobson, the founder and president of Focus on the Family, a publishing and broadcasting organization "dedicated to the maintenance of traditional values," feels that the U.S. Attorney General's Commission on Pornography saw and heard enough evidence to be convinced that pornography causes untold harm to adolescents and women. Philip

Nobile and Eric Nadler, two journalists who followed the U.S. Attorney General's Commission on Pornography around the nation to report on its theory and practice, solicited the opinions of 11 citizens—feminists, journalists, sex therapists, and civil libertarians—who considered the attorney general's report. This Shadow Commission, as Nobile and Nadler called the group, contends that the report has many biases and does not demonstrate a causal connection between pornography and possible harms, such as rape.

Janet Callum, former director of administrative services for the Feminist Women's Health Center, and Rebecca Chalker, an author and women's health advocate, claim that the risks of using RU 486 for abortion are exceedingly low. They argue that the ban against RU 486 should be lifted in the United States because it is less intrusive than surgical abortion, it leaves women in control, and it appears to be a safe and effective abortion alternative, which they feel women need. Janice Raymond, a professor of women's studies, Renate Klein, a lecturer in the humanities, and Lynette Dumble, a research fellow in the surgery department at the University of Melbourne, believe that feminists should not advocate a dubious and dangerous technology such as RU 486, but instead should fight to take conventional abortion methods out of the hands of physicians and promote the licensing of trained laywomen to handle most abortions.

The Center for Population Options, an organization that promotes healthy decision-making about sexuality among youth, outlines what is known about the sexual behavior and the accompanying health risks of teens today and then examines strategies for reducing these risks, specifically, encouraging abstinence and condom use. Considering all the options and all the risks, the center concludes that making condoms available to students through the schools with counseling and education is the best course of action. Professor of education Edwin J. Delattre, in opposing condom distribution in schools, notes several flaws in the argument that we have a moral obligation to distribute condoms to save lives. He dismisses the claim that this is purely a health issue, and he discusses various moral issues involved in promoting casual sexual involvement, which he believes condom distribution does.

Richard John Neuhaus, director of the Rockford Institute Center on Religion and Society, argues that the renting of wombs and buying of babies associated with surrogate motherhood exploits the lower class and raises hostilities in America and therefore should be outlawed. Professor of sociology Monica B. Morris supports the practice of surrogate mothering and maintains that it should be regulated by law to avoid widespread misuse.

The Knights of Columbus, a national organization of lay Catholics, argue that the concept of "viability" on which the case of *Roe v. Wade* was based has changed and that, in terms of the Fourteenth Amendment, ability to survive outside the mother's womb is not a proper basis for defining the word *person*. Hence, the unborn child should be protected as a person from conception on. Janet Benshoof, an associate at the Center for Reproductive Law and Policy, argues that, historically, the law has never regarded the fetus as a person. She warns that recent attempts to force legal recognition of fetal personhood have already created a frightening array of restrictions on women and their right to privacy, from court-ordered obstetrical interventions to lawsuits and legislation for feticide, fetal abuse, and fetal neglect.

Robin Warshaw, a journalist specializing in social issues, examines the data from a nationwide survey conducted by Ms. magazine and psychologist Mary P. Koss and concludes that date rape is "happening all around us." Katie Roiphe, author of *The Morning After: Sex, Fear and Feminism on Campus,* claims that feminist prophets of a rape crisis wrongfully redefine rape to include almost any sexual encounter between women and men. She argues that shifting the criteria for rape from force and coercion to male political power promotes a destructive and sexist image of women as delicate, naive, unable to express their true feelings, and incapable of resisting men.

Supreme Court justice Byron R. White, arguing the majority opinion, claims that, unlike heterosexuals, homosexuals do not have a constitutional right to privacy when it comes to engaging in oral or anal sex, even in the privacy of their homes, because of the traditional social and legal condemnation of sodomy. Supreme Court justice Harry A. Blackmun, dissenting from the majority opinion, argues that since the right to be left alone is the most comprehensive of human rights and the one most valued by civilized people, the state has no right or compelling reason to prohibit any sexual acts engaged in privately by consenting adults.

Focus on the Family, a publishing and broadcasting organization "dedicated to the maintenance of traditional values," and the Family Research Council of America, a conservative, profamily lobbying organization, argue that the state has many legitimate and compelling reasons to require parental notification and consent for teenagers seeking abortions. Such laws permit parents to deal with issues underlying adolescent pregnancy and to provide emotional and psychological support for whatever decision the pregnant minor makes. Fran Avallone, state coordinator for Right to Choose of New Jersey, favors parental involvement in a minor's abortion decision but opposes laws requiring parental notification or consent. She argues that the only real effect of such laws is to delay abortions and further traumatize pregnant minors, especially among the poor.

Randy Shilts, national correspondent for the *San Francisco Chronicle,* argues that the military's handling of the homosexual issue in World War II, the Korean War, the Vietnam War, and the Gulf War documents the hypocrisy of the policy that embraces gay men and lesbians in times of war and discharges them in times of peace. Eugene T. Gomulka, a commander in the U.S. Navy Chaplain Corps, argues that the ban must be maintained because of "widespread sexual compulsion," a high rate of suicide, and high rates of alcoholism, STDs, and HIV infection among gays, as well as "behavioral problems" and tensions that come with housing gay and heterosexual personnel together in tight quarters.

Norma Jean Almodovar, a prostitutes' rights activist and the author of *Cop to Call Girl*, argues that the real problem with prostitution lies not with some women's choice to exchange sexual favors for money but with the consequences of laws that make this exchange illegal. Charles Winick, coauthor of *The Lively Commerce—Prostitution in the United States*, argues that prostitution serves no function except to exploit women and to encourage other illegal activities and that it should therefore be eliminated entirely.

Brent Hartinger, a free-lance writer, argues that "domestic partnership" legislation and other legal strategies used by gay men and lesbians to protect their relationship rights are inadequate and actually weaken the traditional institution of marriage. Society, he argues, has a clear interest in committed, long-lasting relationships and strong family structures, whether these are heterosexual or same-gender. Legalizing gay marriages, Hartinger concludes, would promote social stability and enhance heterosexual marriage. Dennis O'Brien, president of the University of Rochester, defends deep and abiding homosexual relationships, but he is not convinced that legally recognizing these unions as marriages would accomplish anything that cannot be accomplished equally as well with existing legal strategies. The religious or moral meaning of marriage, he contends, poses an even more substantial argument against recognizing gay unions as marriages.

Catharine R. Stimpson, graduate dean at Rutgers University, claims that sexual harassment is epidemic in American society and will remain epidemic as long as males are in power and control. Although some significant progress has been made in creating resistance to sexual harassment, she believes the only way to create a harassment-free society is to redefine the historical connections between sexuality, gender, and power. Gretchen Morgenson, senior editor of *Forbes* magazine, argues that statistics on the prevalence of sexual harassment are grossly exaggerated by "consultants" who make a good livelihood instituting corporate anti-harassment programs. She argues that, in reality, the problem of sexual harassment has and will continue to become less of a problem.

Michael Fumento, a former AIDS analyst for the U.S. Commission on Civil Rights, is disturbed that the Public Health Service spent more money in 1990 for AIDS research and education than it allocated for any other fatal disease. He points out that each year many times more Americans die of heart disease and cancer than of AIDS, and he asserts that the time has come to stop spending so much money and time on the disease. Assistant professor of philosophy Timothy F. Murphy maintains that the massive funding for AIDS research and prevention is justified. He argues that a communicable, lethal disease like AIDS ought to receive priority over noncommunicable diseases like cancer and heart disease, both of which can be medically managed to allow patients to live to old age.

INTRODUCTION

Sexual Attitudes in Perspective
Robert T. Francoeur

How do we develop our attitudes, values, and stereotypes about what is proper and expected behavior for men and women? Where do we get our ideas and beliefs about the purposes of sexual intercourse, sexual behavior, the role and position of the child in the family, the role of the family in society, and countless other sexual issues?

In part, the newborn infant learns about gender roles and what is right or wrong in sexual relations through conditioning by his or her parents and by society. Sociologists call this conditioning process socialization, or social scripting. They study the processes whereby each newborn infant is introduced to the values and attitudes of his or her social group; sociologists start their examination with the family and branch out to include the broader community as well. Psychologists talk about the process of psychological conditioning and learned responses. Anthropologists speak of the process of enculturation and study how the infant becomes a person who can function within a particular culture, more or less adopting the values and attitudes characteristic of that culture. Educators talk about value-oriented education and values clarification. Religious leaders speak of divine revelations, commandments, and indoctrination with moral principles and values. Each of these perspectives gives us some clues as to how we develop as individuals with different sets of values and attitudes about sexuality and other aspects of human life.

Before we explore the contrasting views on specific controversial human sexuality issues contained in this volume, we should try to understand our own views, and those of others who take positions that are different from ours, by reviewing some key insights into our development as thinking persons. We can start with the insights of three developmental psychologists. Working from that base, we can move to a cultural perspective and consider some socioeconomic and ethnic factors that help shape our attitudes about sex. To fill out our picture, we can briefly examine two religious perspectives that play a major role in the attitudes and values we adopt and come to defend with both tenacity and emotion.

THE INSIGHTS OF DEVELOPMENTAL PSYCHOLOGY

Jean Piaget
According to the theories of Jean Piaget (1896–1980), the famous Swiss developmental psychologist, we begin life as completely amoral, totally self-

centered beings. For the first two years of life, we are only concerned with our basic survival needs. The need for food, comfort, and security make us oblivious to the values of our parents. We do not understand nor do we care about what our families or culture have to say about our future roles as males or females and the kinds of relations and behaviors we might engage in. However, our parents are already conditioning and scripting us for our future roles. Parents and other adults generally treat boy and girl infants differently.

By age two, the child enters a stage of development Piaget calls the *egocentric stage*. For the next five years or so, the child has only a very general idea of what the rules are. As the child becomes aware of these rules, he or she tries to change them to accommodate personal needs and wants. A child's world is centered on itself. The child manipulates the world outside, then adjusts to the demands and expectations of parents and others.

By age seven, the child is ready to enter a new stage of development, which Piaget calls the *heteronomous stage*. In this stage, morality and what we see as right and wrong is based on outside authorities and a morality based on rules and laws. Guided by parents and other authority figures, the child begins to assert some degree of logical and moral control over his or her behavior. Between the ages of 7 and 12, the child begins to distinguish between valid and invalid ideas. Authority becomes a dominant concern, regardless of whether it is a parent, teacher, or older child who exerts it. The child often accepts an idea, attitude, or value without question, and issues tend to be seen in terms of black and white. There is little understanding of what is moral because of the total acceptance of the morality imposed by others.

As a young person enters the early teen years, he or she begins to comprehend values and apply them in original ways. This marks a transition, a turning point before one accepts full moral responsibility for one's life.

Finally, usually sometime after age 12, the young person starts moving into what Piaget calls an *autonomous stage*. At this level of moral development, we start thinking and acting as adults. We accept personal responsibility. We think in terms of cooperation rather than constraint. Peer interactions, discussions, criticisms, a sense of equality, and a respect for others help us develop this sense of morality and values. We begin to see other perspectives on moral and ethical issues. We may question and struggle to verify rules and ideas. If we find a rule morally acceptable, we internalize it, making it an integral part of our values.

Lawrence Kohlberg

Lawrence Kohlberg, another influential developmental psychologist, built on Piaget's model of moral development and expanded it with further insights. Instead of Piaget's egocentric, heteronomous, and autonomous stages, Kohlberg speaks of preconventional, conventional, and postconventional stages. He then divides each of these stages into two substages.

On the level of *preconventional morality*, the child responds to cultural rules and the labels of good and bad. This level is divided into two stages: (1) punishment and obedience orientation and (2) instrumental relativist orientation. At this level, the child expresses a total respect for the authority figure and has only a very primitive sense of morality. On the second level of preconventional morality, the child is concerned with satisfying its own needs rather than the needs of others or of society.

When we reach the level of *conventional morality*, our sense of values is characterized by conformity to and maintenance of the moral conventions that are expected by one's family, group, or nation (stage 3)—regardless of the consequences. When we first begin to think in terms of social conventions, we are labeled a good boy or nice girl if we conform our behavior to familial and societal norms. As we reach stage 4, our understanding of conventional morality matures, and we develop a sense of law and order, focusing on fixed rules and upholding the social order. On this level, moral behavior consists of respecting authority and maintaining the social order so that society can function smoothly.

Finally, Kohlberg describes a *postconventional morality*, which is very similar to Piaget's autonomous stage. At this stage, an individual tries to define his or her own morality apart from that of authoritative figures. Stage 5, the social contract stage, is reached when an individual puts an emphasis on what is legally binding, but realizes that laws may change to meet social demands. The last stage of moral development is the level of universal ethical principle orientation. At this level, a person's conscience serves as the judge for moral dilemmas. Abstract qualities such as justice, human rights, respect for the dignity of human life, and equality become important in making decisions. For some people, adherence to an inner conscience may require them to break a law for a higher purpose.

While Kohlberg's theory is more detailed, it overlaps in many ways with Piaget's model. In a revision of his work, Kohlberg implies that a higher stage, such as stage 5 or 6, is not necessarily better than a lower stage, and that most people do not reach the sixth stage. In fact, Kohlberg's research suggests that most people seem to get "stuck" in stage 4, where law and order is the overriding orientation. What connections, if any, can you see between these two models of moral development and the value systems based on either a fixed or process world view?

Carol Gilligan
In 1982 Carol Gilligan, a Harvard psychologist, criticized Kohlberg's theory and its conclusions, and by implication the model suggested by Piaget. She suggests that these theories break down when applied to the ways in which women deal with moral issues. Studies have shown that when female solutions to hypothetical moral dilemmas are evaluated using Kohlberg's

scheme, women appear to be "stuck" at the second level, that of conventional morality, where moral decisions are made in terms of pleasing and helping others. Gilligan rejects this conclusion. She contends that women are not deficient or immature in their moral development but that the standard against which they are measured is biased. Kohlberg's model was derived from a 20-year study of moral development in 84 boys and no girls, although the model has been generalized and applied to the moral sensitivity of both men and women.

As a result of some pilot studies of moral reasoning in women, Gilligan suggests that there is another, equally valid, moral perspective besides Kohlberg's "justice and rights" framework. She calls this second perspective the "care" perspective because it emphasizes relationships and connections between people rather than an abstract hierarchy of rules and rights. This framework stresses nurturance and responsibility to and for others. For Gilligan, the justice and the care perspectives of morality are different, but neither is superior to the other. Neither is more or less mature. Both are necessary for human survival.

Gilligan points out that the two moral frameworks are gender related, but not gender specific. For the most part, women seem to be more comfortable within the care perspective, and men within the justice and rights perspective. However, in some instances, women reason from a justice/rights view and men from a care view.

SOCIAL AND ETHNIC FACTORS IN OUR VALUES

In our personal development, socioeconomic and ethnic factors play a major role in the sexual values and attitudes we incorporate into our lives.

The kinds of values and attitudes toward sex which we adopt in growing up are very much affected by our family's income level and general socioeconomic status. Studies have shown that, in general, there is more mutuality and sharing between men and women in the middle class than in the blue-collar working class. Working-class males are more reluctant to share in household duties and are more apt to segregate themselves from women at social functions. Working-class women tend toward passivity and nurturing and are more emotionally volatile than their middle-class counterparts. Studies have also indicated that one's occupation, educational level, and income are closely related to values his or her attitudes, role conceptions, child-rearing practices, and sexual identity.

Our values and attitudes about sex are also influenced by whether we are brought up in a rural, suburban, or large urban environment. Our ethnic background can be an important, if subtle, influence on our values and attitudes. In contrast to the vehement debates among white middle-class Americans about pornography, for instance, Robert Staples, a professor of sociology at the University of California, San Francisco, says that among American blacks, pornography is a trivial issue. "Blacks," Staples explains, "have traditionally had a more naturalistic attitude toward human sexuality, seeing it as the normal expression of sexual attraction between men and women. . . . Rather than seeing the depiction of heterosexual intercourse or nudity as an inherent debasement of women, as a fringe group of [white] feminists claims, the black community would see women as having equal rights to the enjoyment of sexual stimuli. . . . Since the double [moral] standard has never attracted many American blacks, the claim that women are exploited by exhibiting their nude bodies or engaging in heterosexual intercourse lacks credibility." (Quoted in Nobile and Nadler, *United States of America vs. Sex* [Minobaur Press, 1986].) While middle-class whites may be very concerned about pornography promoting sexual promiscuity, most black Americans are much more concerned about issues related to poverty and employment opportunities.

Similarly, attitudes toward homosexuality vary among white, black, and Latino cultures. In the macho tradition of Latin America, homosexual behavior is a sign that one cannot find a woman and have sexual relationships like a "real" man. In lower socioeconomic black cultures, this same judgment prevails in its own way. Understanding this ethnic value becomes very important in appreciating the ways in which blacks and Latinos respond to the crisis of AIDS and the presence of males with AIDS in their families. Often, the family will deny a son or husband has AIDS until the very end because others might interpret this admission as a confession that the son is homosexual.

Another example of differing ethnic values is the issue of single motherhood. In ethnic groups with a strong tradition of extended matrilineal families, the concept of an "illegitimate" or "illegal" child born "out-of-wedlock" may not even exist. Unmarried mothers in these cultures do not carry the same stigma often associated with single mothers in other, less-matrilineal cultures. When "outsiders" who do not share the particular ethnic values of a culture enter into such a subculture, they often cannot understand why birth control and family life educational programs do not produce any substantial change in attitudes. They overlook the basic social scripting that has already taken place.

Gender roles also vary from culture to culture. Muslim men and women who grow up in the Middle East and then emigrate to the United States have to adapt to the much greater freedom women have in the States. Similarly, American men and women who served in the armed forces in Saudi Arabia during the 1990 Gulf War found they had to adapt to a very different Mulsim culture, one that put many restrictions on the movement and dress of women, including Americans.

A boy who grows up among the East Bay Melanesians in the Southwestern Pacific is taught to avoid any social contact with girls from the age of three or four, even though he may run around naked and masturbate in public. Adolescent Melanesian boys and girls are not allowed to have sex, but boys are expected to have sex both with an older male and with a boy of his own age. Their first heterosexual experiences come with marriage. In the Cook Islands, Mangaian boys are expected to have sex with many girls after an older woman teaches them about the art of sexual play. Mangaians also accept and expect both premarital and extramarital sex.

But one doesn't have to look to exotic anthropological studies to find evidence of the importance of ethnic values. Even within the United States, one can find subtle but important differences in sexual attitudes and values among people of French, German, Italian, Polish, Spanish, Portuguese, Dutch, Scandinavian, Irish, and English descent.

RELIGIOUS FACTORS IN OUR ATTITUDES TOWARD SEX

In the Middle Ages, Christian theologians divided sexual behaviors into two categories: behaviors that were "natural" and those that were "unnatural." Since they believed that the natural function and goal of all sexual behavior and relations was reproduction, masturbation was unnatural because it frustrated the natural goal of conception and continuance of the species. Rape certainly was considered illicit because it was not within the marital bond, but since it was procreative, rape was considered a natural use of sex. The same system of distinction was applied to other sexual relations and behaviors. Premarital sex, adultery, and incest were natural uses of sexuality, while oral sex, anal sex, and contraception were unnatural. Homosexual relations, of course, were both illicit and unnatural. These religious values were based on the view that God created man and woman at the beginning of time and laid down certain rules and guidelines for sexual behavior and relations. This view is still very influential in our culture, even for those who are not active in any religious tradition.

In recent years, several analysts have highlighted two philosophical or religious perspectives that appear throughout Judeo-Christian tradition and Western civilization.[1] Understanding these two perspectives is important in any attempt to debate controversial issues in human sexuality.

Let me introduce these two distinct world views by drawing on a non-Western example from history, the Islamic or Muslim world of the Middle East and the politics of Iran and Egypt. On one side of the spectrum are Muslims who see the world as a process, an ever-changing scene in which they must struggle to reinterpret and apply the basic principles of the Koran to new situations. On the opposing side of the spectrum are fundamentalist Muslims who, years ago, overthrew the shah of Iran and then tried to return Iran and the Muslim world to the authentic faith of Muhammed and the Koran. This meant purging Iran's Islamic society of all the Western and modern customs the shah had encouraged. Anwar Sadat, the late president of Egypt, was assassinated by Muslim fundamentalists who opposed his tolerance of Muslim women being employed outside the home and wearing Western dress instead of the traditional black, neck-to-ankle chador. These fundamentalists also were repulsed by the suggestion made by Sadat's wife that Muslim women should have the right to seek divorce and alimony. Nowadays, Muslim women do have the right to divorce their husbands, but new issues that raise conflicts between the two world views continually arise in the Middle East, such as the 1993 election of Tansu Ciller as Turkey's first female prime minister.

These same two world views are equally obvious in the ongoing history of American culture. Religious fundamentalists, New Right politicians, and the various members of the American Family Association, the Family Research Council of America, Focus on the Family, and the Eagle Forum believe that we need to return to traditional values. These distinct groups often share a conviction that the sexual revolution, changing attitudes toward masturbation and homosexuality, a tolerance of premarital and extramarital sex, sex education in the schools instead of in the homes, and the legality of abortion are contributing to a cultural decline and must be rejected.

At the same time, other Americans argue for legalized abortion, civil rights for homosexuals, decriminalization of prostitution, androgynous sex roles in child-rearing practices, and the abolition of all laws restricting the right to privacy for sexually active, consenting adults.

Recent efforts to analyze the dogma behind the fundamentalist and the "changing-world" value systems have revealed two distinct world views or philosophies tenuously coexisting for centuries within the Judaic, Christian, and Islamic traditions. When Ernst Mayr, a biologist at Harvard University, traced the history of biological theories, he concluded that no greater revolution has occurred in the history of human thought than the radical shift from a fixed world view of cosmology rooted in unchanging archetypes to a dynamic, evolving cosmogenic world view based on populations and individuals. While the process or evolutionary world view may have gained dominance in Western cultures and religious traditions, the influences felt by such groups as the Moral Majority and religious New Right in the United States, the rise of Islamic fundamentalism in Iran and the Near East, and the growing vitality of orthodox Judaism provide ample evidence that the fixed world view still has clear influence in moderating human behavior.

These two world views characteristically permeate and color the way we look at and see everything in our lives. One or the other view colors the way each of us approaches a particular political, economic, or moral issue, as well as the way we reach decisions about sexual issues and relationships. However, one must keep in mind that no one is ever fully and always on one or the other end of the spectrum. The spectrum of beliefs, attitudes, and values proposed here is an intellectual abstraction. Real life is not that simple. Still, it is a useful model that can help us understand each other's positions on controversial issues provided we realize that the fixed and process world views are at the two ends of a continuum that includes a wide range of approaches to moral and sexual issues. While individuals often take a fixed position on one issue and a process position on a second issue, they generally tend to adopt one or the other approach and maintain a fairly consistent set of intertwined religious values and attitudes with respect to sexuality.

Either we view the world as a completely finished universe in which human nature was perfectly and completely created by some supreme being, unchanging in essence from the beginning, or we picture the world involved in continual change with human nature constantly evolving as it struggles to reach its fuller potential, or what is called "to become by the deity." Either one believes that the first human beings were created by God as unchanging archetypes, thus determining standards of human behavior for all time, including our fixed roles as males and females, or one believes that human nature, behavior, and moral standards have been evolving since the beginning of the human race. In the former view, a supreme being created an unchanging human nature. In the latter view, the deity created human nature, then let it transform under human influences.

Coming out of these two views of the world and human nature, one finds two distinct views of the origins of evil and sexuality. If one believes that human nature and the nature of sexual relations were established in the beginning, then one also finds it congenial to believe that evil results from some original sin, a primeval fall of the first humans from a state of perfection and grace. If, on the other hand, one believes in an evolving human nature, then physical and moral evils are viewed as inevitable, natural growth pains that come as humans struggle toward the fullness of their creation.

The Work of James W. Prescott

One paradigm in particular is worth mentioning here to emphasize the importance of the two ways people view the world and their sexual attitudes, beliefs, and values. This model resulted from years of analyzing cross-cultural data, surveys of college students' attitudes, and voting patterns in state and federal governments. James W. Prescott, a noted neuropsychologist, began by examining the effects of the lack of nurturance and somatosensory stimulation on infant monkeys raised and studied by psychologists Harry and Margaret Harlow. In the Harlow studies, some monkeys were taken from their mothers immediately after birth and raised with only a wire mesh and a nursing bottle serving as a surrogate mother. Control infants remained with their natural mothers. Without the normal touching and cuddling of a parent, the test infants quickly became antisocial, withdrawn, and often autistic in their behavior. They were terrified at the approach of other monkeys and at the possibility of being touched. Infant monkeys nurtured and cuddled by a natural mother were peaceful and socially well adjusted when they grew up. Prescott then began to wonder whether or not these effects would be consistent with human child-rearing practices.[2]

From these varied biological, developmental, and cross-cultural studies, Prescott derived a behavioral/attitudinal pattern that links somatosensory affectional deprivation or positive nurturance in infancy and childhood with adult behaviors and attitudes. His statistical analysis reveals a causal connection between parental attitudes, child-rearing values, and the subsequent social adaptation, or lack of it, in the children when they grow up. In societies or families that encourage body pleasuring and somatosensory nurturance, parents commonly share a wide variety of nonviolent values, attitudes, and behavioral patterns for which their children are neurologically scripted by a high level of nurturing touch during infancy, childhood, and adolescence.

In subsequent statistical analyses using both contemporary American, Canadian, and European data, Prescott correlated the lack of childhood nurturance with negative attitudes toward gun control laws, nudity, sexual pleasure, masturbation, premarital and extramarital sex, breast-feeding, and women. Other values consistently associated with this perspective include a glorification of war and the frequent use of alcohol and drugs. Societal factors that were correlated with a high nurturance of infants include a lack of strong social stratification, prolonged breast-feeding, a strong sense of humor, an acceptance of abortion, premarital sex, and extramarital sex, low anxiety about sex, little sexual dysfunction, a negative view of war, and satisfying peer relationships between men and women.

Religious beliefs undoubtedly affect the child-rearing practices of our parents, which in turn color the way each of us views our sexuality and our attitudes toward different sexual behaviors and relationships. These same religious beliefs affect and color our social scripting and enculturation as we grow up and move through the stages of moral development outlined by Piaget, Kohlberg, and Gilligan. Along the way, we pick up values and attitudes that are peculiar to our ethnic and socioeconomic background.

APPROACHING THE ISSUES IN THIS VOLUME

As you think over the controversial issues in this volume of *Taking Sides*, think of how your parents, family, friends, and associates have helped mold your opinions on specific issues. Try to be sensitive to how religious, racial, ethnic, and socioeconomic factors in your own background may affect the positions you take on different issues. At the same time, try to appreciate how these same factors may have influenced the people whose opinions clash with your own.

NOTES

1. Details of the perspectives offered in this introductory essay can be found in the author's chapter on "Religious Reactions to Alternative Lifestyles" in E. D. Macklin and R. H. Rubin, eds. *Contemporary Families and Alternative Lifestyles: A Handbook on Research and Theory* (Sage Publications, 1983). In that chapter, I summarize and give a complete comparison of seven models developed by researchers working independently in quite distinct disciplines. Included are: a behavioral model based on a comparison of chimpanzee, baboon, and human social behavior by the British primatologist Michael Chance; a cultural/moral model based on an

analysis of British and French arts, fashions, politics, life-styles, and social structures proposed by British science writer and philosopher Gordon Rattray Taylor; a cross-cultural comparison based on child-rearing nurturance patterns and adult life-styles by neuropsychologist James W. Prescott; a model relating life-styles and values with technological and economic structures by economist/engineer Mario Kamenetzky; a model of open and closed marriages created by George and Nena O'Neill, authors of the 1970s best-seller *Open Marriage*; and my own model of "Hot and Cool Sexual Values," which I adapted from an insight by Marshall McLuhan and George B. Leonard.

2. J. W. Prescott, "Body Pleasure and the Origins of Violence," *The Futurist* (vol. 9, no. 2, 1975), pp. 64–74.

PART 1

Biology and Behavior

Traditional views of men, women, and sexuality have undergone dramatic changes during the latter half of the twentieth century. Social critics and activists for change have raised questions about sex roles, sexual fidelity, and cultural values. Terms such as addiction, rape, *and* pornography *have been reconsidered and redefined. The causes and effects of changing social values and definitions are examined in this section.*

- Are Gender Differences Rooted in the Brain?

- Can Sex Be an Addiction?

- Is Rape Motivated by Aggression Instead of Sex?

- Does Sexual Infidelity Destroy a Relationship?

- Is Pornography Harmful?

ISSUE 1

Are Gender Differences Rooted in the Brain?

YES: **Doreen Kimura,** from "Sex Differences in the Brain," *Scientific American* (September 1992)

NO: **Carol Tavris,** from *The Mismeasure of Woman* (Simon & Schuster, 1992)

ISSUE SUMMARY

YES: Doreen Kimura, a professor of psychology, describes a wide range of cognitive variations between the genders that reflect differing hormonal influences on fetal brain development. She maintains that differences between the female and the male brains help explain differences in occupational interests and capabilities between the sexes.

NO: Carol Tavris, a social psychologist, finds that scientific efforts conducted over the past century to prove gender differences originate in the brain have yielded enough conflicting views and distorted findings to invalidate such a hypothesis. She maintains that although biology is not irrelevant to human behavior, this research has consistently been used to define women as fundamentally different from and inferior to men in body, psyche, and brain.

The question of whether women and men are essentially similar or different is often drowned in emotional responses, unspoken assumptions, and activist politics. This sometimes results in patriarchal biases that dogmatically stress differences as justification for "natural gender roles" and, hence, discrimination. But similar emotional responses, unspoken assumptions, and activist politics are just as likely to result in a different bias that maintains there are no significant differences between men and women except their sexual anatomy.

For 3,000 years Western thought viewed human development as the result of two separate, parallel, noninteracting influences. *Nature,* genes and hormones, was believed to be dominant before birth and irrelevant after birth. *Nurture,* learning and social environment, was believed to be irrelevant during the nine months of pregnancy, only to take over after birth.

In a way, this dichotomy of nature versus nurture grew out of the Western dualism of body and soul, which René Descartes, the French philosopher, popularized. Historically, this dichotomy has been used to support the superiority of spirit over body, intellect over senses, men over women, analytical thought over intuitive thought, rationality over emotionality, and spiritual pleasures over sexual pleasures.

In the twentieth century, communism ignored the nature side, maintaining that all humans are born equal and that capitalist patriarchal society is the cause of all social inequities and discrimination. German philosopher Karl Marx's solution was to create a sexless, genderless, socialist system in which all distinctions, be they sexual, gender-related, economic, or social, are rooted out and eliminated. Soviet science, in contrast, favored the theory that traits acquired during one's life could be genetically passed on to one's offspring, a theory that was originally proposed by French biologist Jean-Baptiste Lamarck. The dangers of such one-sided approaches, however, have been well demonstrated in the bankruptcy of Marxist economics, agriculture, and social policy.

In recent years the traditional Western dichotomy of nature versus nurture has been gradually supplanted by the theory that there is a lifelong developmental interaction between nature and nurture, from conception to death. In this view, the genetic constitution of each body cell (nature) continually interacts at many different critical periods in the developmental process with a wide range of environmental factors (nurture).

This new perspective of lifelong interactions between nature and nurture is essential in appreciating and understanding the question posed here, that of whether gender differences are due to nature (our genes, hormones, and neural templates) or to nurture (our learning and social environment).

In the following selections, Doreen Kimura supports the view that nature, specifically differences in the organization of the male and female brains, is the primary reason for observable differences between the sexes. Carol Tavris argues that social and environmental effects are as important as biology in determining behavior and that theories about brain differences between males and females are advanced in order to maintain patriarchal biases against women.

YES   Doreen Kimura

SEX DIFFERENCES IN THE BRAIN

Women and men differ not only in physical attributes and reproductive function but also in the way in which they solve intellectual problems. It has been fashionable to insist that these differences are minimal, the consequence of variations in experience during development. The bulk of the evidence suggests, however, that the effects of sex hormones on brain organization occur so early in life that from the start the environment is acting on differently wired brains in girls and boys. Such differences make it almost impossible to evaluate the effects of experience independent of physiological predisposition.

Behavioral, neurological and endocrinologic studies have elucidated the processes giving rise to sex differences in the brain. As a result, aspects of the physiological basis for these variations have in recent years become clearer. In addition, studies of the effects of hormones on brain function throughout life suggest that the evolutionary pressures directing differences nevertheless allow for a degree of flexibility in cognitive ability between the sexes.

MAJOR SEX DIFFERENCES IN INTELLECTUAL FUNCTION SEEM TO LIE IN PATTERNS OF ability rather than in overall level of intelligence (IQ). We are all aware that people have different intellectual strengths. Some are especially good with words, others at using objects—for instance, at constructing or fixing things. In the same fashion, two individuals may have the same overall intelligence but have varying patterns of ability.

Men, on average, perform better than women on certain spatial tasks. In particular, men have an advantage in tests that require the subject to imagine rotating an object or manipulating it in some other way. They outperform women in mathematical reasoning tests and in navigating their way through a route. Further, men are more accurate in tests of target-directed motor skills—that is, in guiding or intercepting projectiles.

Women tend to be better than men at rapidly identifying matching items, a skill called perceptual speed. They have greater verbal fluency, including the ability to find words that begin with a specific letter or fulfill some other constraint. Women also outperform men in arithmetic calculation and in recalling landmarks from a route. Moreover, women are faster at certain precision manual tasks, such as placing pegs in designated holes on a board.

Although some investigators have reported that sex differences in problem solving do not appear until after puberty, Diane Lunn, working in my laboratory at the University of Western Ontario, and I have found three-year-old boys to be better at targeting than girls of the same age. Moreover, Neil V. Watson, when in my laboratory, showed that the extent of experience playing sports does not account for the sex difference in targeting found in young adults. Kimberly A. Kerns, working with Sheri A. Berenbaum of the University of Chicago, has found that sex differences in spatial rotation performance are present before puberty.

Differences in route learning have been systematically studied in adults in laboratory situations. For instance, Liisa Galea in my department studied undergraduates who followed a route on a tabletop map. Men learned the route in fewer trials and made fewer errors than did women. But once learning was complete, women remembered more of the landmarks than did men. These results, and those of other researchers, raise the possibility that women tend to use landmarks as a strategy to orient themselves in everyday life. The prevailing strategies used by males have not yet been clearly established, although they must relate to spatial ability.

Marion Eals and Irwin Silverman of York University studied another function that may be related to landmark memory. The researchers tested the ability of individuals to recall objects and their locations within a confined space—such as in a room or on a tabletop. Women were better able to remember whether an item had been displaced or not. In addition, in my laboratory, we measured the accuracy of object location: subjects were shown an array of objects and were later asked to replace them in their exact positions. Women did so more accurately than did men.

It is important to place the differences described above in context: some are slight, some are quite large. Because men and women overlap enormously on many cognitive tests that show average sex differences, researchers use variations within each group as a tool to gauge the differences between groups. Imagine, for instance, that on one test the average score is 105 for women and 100 for men. If the scores for women ranged from 100 to 110 and for men from 95 to 105, the difference would be more impressive than if the women's scores ranged from 50 to 150 and the men's from 45 to 145. In the latter case, the overlap in scores would be much greater.

One measure of the variation of scores within a group is the standard deviation. To compare the magnitude of a sex difference across several distinct tasks, the difference between groups is divided by the standard deviation. The resulting number is called the effect size. Effect sizes below 0.5 are generally considered small. Based on my data, for instance, there are typically no differences between the sexes on tests of vocabulary (effect size 0.02), nonverbal reasoning (0.03) and verbal reasoning (0.17).

On tests in which subjects match pictures, find words that begin with similar letters or show ideational fluency—such as naming objects that are white or red—the effect sizes are somewhat larger: 0.25,

0.22 and 0.38, respectively. As discussed above, women tend to outperform men on these tasks. Researchers have reported the largest effect sizes for certain tests measuring spatial rotation (effect size 0.7) and targeting accuracy (0.75). The large effect size in these tests means there are many more men at the high end of the score distribution.

SINCE, WITH THE EXCEPTION OF THE SEX chromosomes, men and women share genetic material, how do such differences come about? Differing patterns of ability between men and women most probably reflect different hormonal influences on their developing brains. Early in life the action of estrogens and androgens (male hormones chief of which is testosterone) establishes sexual differentiation. In mammals, including humans, the organism has the potential to be male or female. If a Y chromosome is present, testes or male gonads form. This development is the critical first step toward becoming a male. If the gonads do not produce male hormones or if for some reason the hormones cannot act on the tissue, the default form of the organism is female.

Once testes are formed, they produce two substances that bring about the development of a male. Testosterone causes masculinization by promoting the male, or Wolffian, set of ducts and, indirectly through conversion to dihydrotestosterone, the external appearance of scrotum and penis. The Müllerian regression factor causes the female, or Müllerian, set of ducts to regress. If anything goes wrong at any stage of the process, the individual may be incompletely masculinized.

Not only do sex hormones achieve the transformation of the genitals into male organs, but they also organize corresponding male behaviors early in life. Since we cannot manipulate the hormonal environment in humans, we owe much of what we know about the details of behavioral determination to studies in other animals. Again, the intrinsic tendency, according to studies by Robert W. Goy of the University of Wisconsin, is to develop the female pattern that occurs in the absence of masculinizing hormonal influence.

If a rodent with functional male genitals is deprived of androgens immediately after birth (either by castration or by the administration of a compound that blocks androgens), male sexual behavior, such as mounting, will be reduced. Instead female sexual behavior, such as lordosis (arching of the back), will be enhanced in adulthood. Similarly, if androgens are administered to a female directly after birth, she displays more male sexual behavior and less female behavior in adulthood.

Bruce S. McEwen and his co-workers at the Rockefeller University have shown that, in the rat, the two processes of defeminization and masculinization require somewhat different biochemical changes. These events also occur at somewhat different times. Testosterone can be converted to either estrogen (usually considered a female hormone) or dihydrotestosterone. Defeminization takes place primarily after birth in rats and is mediated by estrogen, whereas masculinization involves both dihydrotestosterone and estrogen and occurs for the most part before birth rather than after, according to studies by McEwen. A substance called alpha-fetoprotein may protect female brains from the masculinizing effects of their estrogen.

The area in the brain that organizes female and male reproductive behavior is the hypothalamus. This tiny structure at the base of the brain connects to the pituitary, the master endocrine gland. Roger A. Gorski and his colleagues at the University of California at Los Angeles have shown that a region of the pre-optic area of the hypothalamus is visibly larger in male rats than in females. The size increment in males is promoted by the presence of androgens in the immediate postnatal, and to some extent prenatal, period. Laura S. Allen in Gorski's laboratory has found a similar sex difference in the human brain.

Other preliminary but intriguing studies suggest that sexual behavior may reflect further anatomic differences. In 1991 Simon LeVay of the Salk Institute for Biological Studies in San Diego reported that one of the brain regions that is usually larger in human males than in females—an interstitial nucleus of the anterior hypothalamus—is smaller in homosexual than in heterosexual men. LeVay points out that this finding supports suggestions that sexual preference has a biological substrate.

Homosexual and heterosexual men may also perform differently on cognitive tests. Brian A. Gladue of North Dakota State University and Geoff D. Sanders of City of London Polytechnic report that homosexual men perform less well on several spatial tasks than do heterosexual men. In a recent study in my laboratory, Jeff Hall found that homosexual men had lower scores on targeting tasks than did heterosexual men; however, they were superior in ideational fluency—listing things that were a particular color.

This exciting field of research is just starting, and it is crucial that investigators consider the degree to which differences in life-style contribute to group differences. One should also keep in mind that results concerning group differences constitute a general statistical statement; they establish a mean from which any individual may differ. Such studies are potentially a rich source of information on the physiological basis for cognitive patterns.

THE LIFELONG EFFECTS OF EARLY EXPOSURE to sex hormones are characterized as organizational, because they appear to alter brain function permanently during a critical period. Administering the same hormones at later stages has no such effect. The hormonal effects are not limited to sexual or reproductive behaviors: they appear to extend to all known behaviors in which males and females differ. They seem to govern problem solving, aggression and the tendency to engage in rough-and-tumble play—the boisterous body contact that young males of some mammalian species display. For example, Michael J. Meaney of McGill University finds that dihydrotestosterone, working through a structure called the amygdala rather than through the hypothalamus, gives rise to the play-fighting behavior of juvenile male rodents.

Male and female rats have also been found to solve problems differently. Christina L. Williams of Barnard College has shown that female rats have a greater tendency to use landmarks in spatial learning tasks—as it appears women do. In Williams's experiment, female rats used landmark cues, such as pictures on the wall, in preference to geometric cues, such as angles and the shape of the room. If no landmarks were available, however, females used geometric cues. In contrast, males did not use landmarks at all, preferring geometric cues almost exclusively.

Interestingly, hormonal manipulation during the critical period can alter these behaviors. Depriving newborn males of testosterone by castrating them or administering estrogen to newborn females results in a complete reversal of sex-typed behaviors in the adult animals. (As mentioned above, estrogen can have a masculinizing effect during brain development.) Treated females behave like males, and treated males behave like females.

Natural selection for reproductive advantage could account for the evolution of such navigational differences. Steven J. C. Gaulin and Randall W. FitzGerald of the University of Pittsburgh have suggested that in species of voles in which a male mates with several females rather than with just one, the range he must traverse is greater. Therefore, navigational ability seems critical to reproductive success. Indeed, Gaulin and FitzGerald found sex differences in laboratory maze learning only in voles that were polygynous, such as the meadow vole, not in monogamous species, such as the prairie vole.

Again, behavioral differences may parallel structural ones. Lucia F. Jacobs in Gaulin's laboratory has discovered that the hippocampus—a region thought to be involved in spatial learning in both birds and mammals—is larger in male polygynous voles than in females. At present, there are no data on possible sex differences in hippocampal size in human subjects.

Evidence of the influence of sex hormones on adult behavior is less direct in humans than in other animals. Researchers are instead guided by what may be parallels in other species and by spontaneously occurring exceptions to the norm in humans.

One of the most compelling areas of evidence comes from studies of girls exposed to excess androgens in the prenatal or neonatal stage. The production of abnormally large quantities of adrenal androgens can occur because of a genetic defect called congenital adrenal hyperplasia (CAH). Before the 1970s, a similar condition also unexpectedly appeared when pregnant women took various synthetic steroids. Although the consequent masculinization of the genitals can be corrected early in life and drug therapy can stop the overproduction of androgens, effects of prenatal exposure on the brain cannot be reversed.

Studies by researchers such as Anke A. Ehrhardt of Columbia University and June M. Reinisch of the Kinsey Institute have found that girls with excess exposure to androgens grow up to be more tomboyish and aggressive than their unaffected sisters. This conclusion was based sometimes on interviews with subjects and mothers, on teachers' ratings and on questionnaires administered to the girls themselves. When ratings are used in such studies, it can be difficult to rule out the influence of expectation either on the part of an adult who knows the girls' history or on the part of the girls themselves.

Therefore, the objective observations of Berenbaum are important and convincing. She and Melissa Hines of the University of California at Los Angeles observed the play behavior of CAH-affected girls and compared it with that of their male and female siblings. Given a choice of transportation and construction toys, dolls and kitchen supplies or books and board games, the CAH girls preferred the more typically masculine toys—for example, they played with cars for the same amount of time that normal boys did. Both the CAH girls and the boys differed from unaffected girls in their patterns of choice. Because there is every reason to think that parents would be at least as likely to encourage feminine preferences in their CAH daughters as in their unaffected daughters, these findings suggest that the toy preferences were actually altered in some way by the early hormonal environment.

Spatial abilities that are typically better in males are also enhanced in CAH girls. Susan M. Resnick, now at the National Institute on Aging, and Berenbaum and their colleagues reported that affected girls were superior to their unaffected sisters in a spatial manipulation test, two spatial rotation tests and a disembedding test—that is, the discovery of a simple figure hidden within a more complex one. All these tasks are usually done better by males. No differences existed between the two groups on other perceptual or verbal tasks or on a reasoning task.

STUDIES SUCH AS THESE SUGGEST THAT THE higher the androgen levels, the better the spatial performance. But this does not seem to be the case. In 1983 Valerie J. Shute, when at the University of California at Santa Barbara, suggested that the relation between levels of androgens and some spatial capabilities might be nonlinear. In other words, spatial ability might not increase as the amount of androgen increases. Shute measured androgens in blood taken from male and female students and divided each into high- and low-androgen groups. All fell within the normal range for each sex (androgens are present in females but in very low levels). She found that in

women, the high-androgen subjects were better at the spatial tests. In men the reverse was true: low-androgen men performed better.

Catherine Couchie and I recently conducted a study along similar lines by measuring testosterone in saliva. We added tests for two other kinds of abilities: mathematical reasoning and perceptual speed. Our results on the spatial tests were very similar to Shute's: low-testosterone men were superior to high-testosterone men, but high-testosterone women surpassed low-testosterone women. Such findings suggest some optimum level of androgen for maximal spatial ability. This level may fall in the low male range.

No correlation was found between testosterone levels and performance on perceptual speed tests. On mathematical reasoning, however, the results were similar to those of spatial ability tests for men: low-androgen men tested higher, but there was no obvious relation in women.

Such findings are consistent with the suggestion by Camilla P. Benbow of Iowa State University that high mathematical ability has a significant biological determinant. Benbow and her colleagues have reported consistent sex differences in mathematical reasoning ability favoring males. These differences are especially sharp at the upper end of the distribution, where males outnumber females 13 to one. Benbow argues that these differences are not readily explained by socialization.

It is important to keep in mind that the relation between natural hormonal levels and problem solving is based on correlational data. Some form of connection between the two measures exists, but how this association is determined or what its causal basis may be is unknown. Little is currently understood about the relation between adult levels of hormones and those in early life, when abilities appear to be organized in the nervous system. We have a lot to learn about the precise mechanisms underlying cognitive patterns in people.

Another approach to probing differences between male and female brains is to examine and compare the functions of particular brain systems. One noninvasive way to accomplish this goal is to study people who have experienced damage to a specific brain region. Such studies indicate that the left half of the brain in most people is critical for speech, the right for certain perceptual and spatial functions.

It is widely assumed by many researchers studying sex differences that the two hemispheres are more asymmetrically organized for speech and spatial functions in men than in women. This idea comes from several sources. Parts of the corpus callosum, a major neural system connecting the two hemispheres, may be more extensive in women; perceptual techniques that probe brain asymmetry in normal-functioning people sometimes show smaller asymmetries in women than in men, and damage to one brain hemisphere sometimes has a lesser effect in women than the comparable injury has in men.

In 1982 Marie-Christine de Lacoste, now at the Yale University School of Medicine, and Ralph L. Holloway of Columbia University reported that the back part of the corpus callosum, an area called the splenium, was larger in women than in men. This finding has subsequently been both refuted and confirmed. Variations in the shape of the corpus callosum that may occur as an individual ages as well as different methods of measurement may produce some of the disagreements. Most recently, Allen and Gorski found the same sex-related size difference in the splenium.

The interest in the corpus callosum arises from the assumption that its size may indicate the number of fibers connecting the two hemishperes. If more connecting fibers existed in one sex, the implication would be that in that sex the hemispheres communicate more fully. Although sex hormones can alter callosal size in rats, as Victor H. Denenberg and his associates at the University of Connecticut have demonstrated, it is unclear whether the actual number of fibers differs between the sexes. Moreover, sex differences in cognitive function have yet to be related to a difference in callosal size. New ways of imaging the brain in living humans will undoubtedly increase knowledge in this respect.

The view that a male brain is functionally more asymmetric than a female brain is long-standing. Albert M. Galaburda of Beth Israel Hospital in Boston and the late Norman Geschwind of Harvard Medical School proposed that androgens increased the functional potency of the right hemisphere. In 1981 Marian C. Diamond of the University of California at Berkeley found that the right cortex is thicker than the left in male rats but not in females. Jane Stewart of Concordia University in Montreal, working with Bryan E. Kolb of the University of Lethbridge in Alberta, recently pinpointed early hormonal influences on this asymmetry: androgens appear to suppress left cortex growth.

Last year de Lacoste and her colleagues reported a similar pattern in human fetuses. They found the right cortex was thicker than the left in males. Thus, there appear to be some anatomic reasons for believing that the two hemispheres might not be equally asymmetric in men and women.

Despite this expectation, the evidence in favor of it is meager and conflicting, which suggests that the most striking sex differences in brain organization may not be related to asymmetry. For example, if overall differences between men and women in spatial ability were related to differing right hemispheric dependence for such functions, then damage to the right hemisphere would perhaps have a more devastating effect on spatial performance in men.

My laboratory has recently studied the ability of patients with damage to one hemisphere of the brain to rotate certain objects mentally. In one test, a series of line drawings of either a left or a right gloved hand is presented in various orientations. The patient indicates the hand being depicted by simply pointing to one of two stuffed gloves that are constantly present.

The second test uses two three-dimensional blocklike figures that are mirror images of one another. Both figures are present throughout the test. The patient is given a series of photographs of these objects in various orientations, and he or she must place each picture in front of the object it depicts (These nonverbal procedures are employed so that patients with speech disorders can be tested.)

As expected, damage to the right hemisphere resulted in lower scores for both sexes on these tests than did damage to the left hemisphere. Also as anticipated, women did less well than men on the block spatial rotation test. Surprisingly, however, damage to the right hemisphere had no greater effect in men than in women. Women were at least as affected as men by damage to the right hemisphere. This result suggests that the normal differences between men and women on such rotational tests are not the result of differential dependence on the right hemisphere. Some other brain systems must be mediating the higher performance by men.

Parallel suggestions of greater asymmetry in men regarding speech have rested on the fact that the incidence of aphasias, or speech disorders, are higher in men than in women after damage to the left hemisphere. Therefore, some researchers have found it reasonable to conclude that speech must be more bilaterally organized in women. There is, however, a problem with this conclusion. During my 20 years of experience with patients, aphasia has not been disproportionately present in women with right hemispheric damage.

IN SEARCHING FOR AN EXPLANATION, I discovered another striking difference between men and women in brain organization for speech and related motor function. Women are more likely than men to suffer aphasia when the front part of the brain is damaged. Because restricted damage within a hemisphere more frequently affects the posterior than the anterior area in both men and women, this differential dependence may explain why women incur aphasia less often than do men. Speech functions are thus less likely to be affected in women not because speech is more bilaterally organized in women but because the critical area is less often affected.

A similar pattern emerges in studies of the control of hand movements, which are programmed by the left hemisphere. Apraxia, or difficulty in selecting appropriate hand movements, is very common after left hemispheric damage. It is also strongly associated with difficulty in organizing speech. In fact, the critical functions that depend on the left hemisphere may relate not to language per se but to organization of the complex oral and manual movements on which human communication systems depend. Studies of patients with left hemispheric damage have revealed that such motor selection relies on anterior systems in women but on posterior systems in men.

The synaptic proximity of women's anterior motor selection system (or "praxis system") to the motor cortex directly behind it may enhance fine-motor skills. In contrast, men's motor skills appear to emphasize targeting or directing movements toward external space— some distance away from the self. There may be advantages to such motor skills when they are closely meshed with visual input to the brain, which lies in the posterior region.

Women's dependence on the anterior region is detectable even when tests involve using visual guidance—for instance, when subjects must build patterns with blocks by following a visual model. In studying such a complex task, it is possible to compare the effects of damage to the anterior and posterior regions of both hemispheres because performance is affected by damage to either hemisphere. Again, women prove more affected by damage to the anterior region of the right hemisphere than by posterior damage. Men tend to display the reverse pattern.

Although I have not found evidence of sex differences in functional brain asymmetry with regard to basic speech, motor selection or spatial rotation ability, I have found slight differences in more abstract verbal tasks. Scores on a vocabulary test, for instance, were affected by damage to either hemisphere in women, but such scores were affected only by left-sided injury in men. This finding suggests that in reviewing the meanings of words, women use the hemispheres more equally than do men.

In contrast, the incidence of non-right-handedness, which is presumably related to lesser left hemispheric dependence, is higher in men than in women. Even among the right-handers, Marion Annett, now at the University of Leicester in the U.K., has reported that women are more right-handed than men—that is, they favor their right hand even more than do right-handed men. It may well be, then, that sex differences in asymmetry vary with the particular function being studied and that it is not always the same sex that is more asymmetric.

Taken altogether, the evidence suggests that men's and women's brains are organized along different lines from very early in life. During development, sex hormones direct such differentiation. Similar mechanisms probably operate to produce variation within sexes, since there is a relation between levels of certain hormones and cognitive makeup in adulthood.

ONE OF THE MOST INTRIGUING FINDINGS IS that cognitive patterns may remain sensitive to hormonal fluctuations throughout life. Elizabeth Hampson of the University of Western Ontario showed that the performance of women on certain tasks changed throughout the menstrual cycle as levels of estrogen went up or down. High levels of the hormone were associated not only with relatively depressed spatial ability but also with enhanced articulatory and motor capability.

In addition, I have observed seasonal fluctuations in spatial ability in men. Their performance is improved in the spring when testosterone levels are lower. Whether these intellectual fluctuations are of any adaptive significance or merely represent ripples on a stable baseline remains to be determined.

To understand human intellectual functions, including how groups may differ in such functions, we need to look beyond the demands of modern life. We did not undergo natural selection for reading or for operating computers. It seems clear that the sex differences in cognitive patterns arose because they proved evolutionarily advantageous. And their adaptive significance probably rests in the distant past. The organization of the human brain was determined over many generations by natural selection. As studies of fossil skulls have shown, our brains are essentially like those of our ancestors of 50,000 or more years ago.

For the thousands of years during which our brain characteristics evolved, humans lived in relatively small groups of hunter-gatherers. The division of labor between the sexes in such a society probably was quite marked, as it is in existing hunter-gatherer societies. Men were responsible for hunting large game, which often required long-distance travel. They were also responsible for defending the group against predators and enemies and for the shaping and use of weapons. Women most probably gathered food near the camp, tended the home, prepared food and clothing and cared for children.

Such specializations would put different selection pressures on men and women. Men would require long-distance route-finding ability so they could recognize a geographic array from varying orientations. They would also need targeting skills. Women would require short-range navigation, perhaps using landmarks, fine-motor capabilities carried on within a circumscribed space, and perceptual discrimination sensitive to small changes in the environment or in children's appearance or behavior.

The finding of consistent and, in some cases, quite substantial sex differences suggests that men and women may have different occupational interests and capabilities, independent of societal influences. I would not expect, for example, that men and women would necessarily be equally represented in activities or professions that emphasize spatial or math skills, such as engineering or physics. But I might expect more women in medical diagnostic fields where perceptual skills are important. So that even though any one individual might have the capacity to be in a "nontypical" field, the sex proportions as a whole may vary.

NO

Carol Tavris

MEASURING UP

BRAIN: DISSECTING THE DIFFERENCES

In recent years the sexiest body part, far and away, has become the brain. Magazines with cover stories on the brain fly off the newsstands, and countless seminars, tapes, books, and classes teach people how to use "all" of their brains. New technologies, such as PET scans, produce gorgeous photographs of the brain at work and play. Weekly we hear new discoveries about this miraculous organ, and it seems that scientists will soon be able to pinpoint the very neuron, the very neurotransmitter, responsible for joy, sadness, rage, and suffering. At last we will know the reasons for all the differences between women and men that fascinate and infuriate, such as why men won't stop to ask directions and why women won't stop asking men what they are feeling.

In all this excitement, it seems curmudgeonly to sound words of caution, but the history of brain research does not exactly reveal a noble and impartial quest for truth, particularly on sensitive matters such as sex and race differences. Typically, when scientists haven't found the differences they were seeking, they haven't abandoned the goal or their belief that such differences exist; they just moved to another part of the anatomy or a different corner of the brain.

A century ago, for example, scientists tried to prove that women had smaller brains than men did, which accounted for women's alleged intellectual failings and emotional weaknesses. Dozens of studies purported to show that men had larger brains, making them smarter than women. When scientists realized that men's greater height and weight offset their brain-size advantage, however, they dropped this line of research like a shot. The scientists next tried to argue that women had smaller frontal lobes and larger parietal lobes than men did, another brain pattern thought to account for women's intellectual inferiority. Then it was reported that the parietal lobes might be associated with intellect. Panic in the labs—until anatomists suddenly found that women's parietal lobes were *smaller* than they had originally believed. Wherever they looked, scientists conveniently found evidence of female inferiority, as Gustave Le Bon, a Parisian, wrote in 1879:

> In the most intelligent races, as among the Parisians, there are a large number of women whose brains are closer in size to those of gorillas than to the most developed male brains. This inferiority is so obvious that no one can contest it for a moment; only its degree is worth discussion.

We look back with amusement at the obvious biases of research a century ago, research designed to prove the obvious inferiority of women and minorities (and non-Parisians). Today, many researchers are splitting brains instead of weighing them, but they are no less determined to find sex differences. Nevertheless, skeptical neuroscientists are showing that biases and values are just as embedded in current research—old prejudices in new technologies.

The brain, like a walnut, consists of two hemispheres of equal size, connected by a bundle of fibers called the corpus callosum. The left hemisphere has been associated with verbal and reasoning ability, whereas the right hemisphere is associated with spatial reasoning and artistic ability. Yet by the time these findings reached the public, they had been vastly oversimplified and diluted. Even the great neuroscientist Roger Sperry, the grandfather of hemispheric research, felt obliged to warn that the "left-right dichotomy . . . is an idea with which it is very easy to run wild." And many people have run wild with it: Stores are filled with manuals, cassettes, and handbooks that promise to help people become fluent in "whole-brain thinking," to beef up the unused part of their right brain, and to learn to use the intuitive right brain for business, painting, and inventing.

The fact that the brain consists of two hemispheres, each characterized by different specialties, provides a neat analogy to the fact that human beings consist of two genders, each characterized by different specialties. The analogy is so tempting that scientists keep trying to show that it is grounded in physical reality. Modern theories of gender and the brain are based on the idea that the left and right hemispheres develop differently in boys and girls, as does the corpus callosum that links the halves of the brain.

According to one major theory, the male brain is more "lateralized," that is, its hemispheres are specialized in their abilities, whereas females use both hemispheres more symmetrically because their corpus callosum is allegedly larger and contains more fibers. Two eminent scientists, Norman Geschwind and Peter Behan, maintained that this sex difference begins in the womb, when the male fetus begins to secrete testosterone—the hormone that will further its physical development as a male. Geschwind and Behan argued that testosterone in male fetuses washes over the brain, selectively attacking parts of the left hemisphere, briefly slowing its development, and producing right-hemisphere dominance in men. Geschwind speculated that the effects of testosterone on the prenatal brain produce "superior right hemisphere talents, such as artistic, musical, or mathematical talent."

Right-hemisphere dominance is also thought to explain men's excellence in some tests of "visual-spatial ability"— the ability to imagine objects in three-dimensional space (the skill you need for mastering geometry, concocting football formations, and reading maps). This is apparently the reason that some men won't stop and ask directions when they are lost; they prefer to rely on their right brains, whereas women prefer to rely on a local informant. It is also supposed to be the reason that men can't talk about their feelings and would rather watch television or wax the car. Women have interconnected hemispheres, which explains why they excel in talk, feelings, intuition, and quick judgments. Geschwind and Behan's theory had tremendous scientific appeal, and it is cited frequently in research papers and textbooks. *Science* hailed it with the headline "Math Genius May Have Hormonal Basis."

The theory also has had enormous popular appeal. It fits snugly, for example, with the Christian fundamentalist belief that men and women are innately different and thus innately designed for different roles. For his radio show "Focus on the Family," James Dobson interviewed Donald Joy, a professor of "human development in Christian education" at Asbury Theological Seminary, who explained Geschwind and Behan's theory this way:

JOY: . . . this marvelous female brain, is a brain that's not damaged during fetal development as the male brain is, but the damage gives a specialization to the male brain which we don't get in the female.

DOBSON: I want to pick up on that concept of us brain-damaged males. [laughter, chuckling]

JOY: . . . It's giving a chemical bath to the left hemisphere and this connecting link between the two hemispheres that reduced the size and number of transmis-

sion passages that exist here . . . So males simply can't talk to themselves across the hemispheres in a way that a woman does.

DOBSON: So some of the sex differences that we see in personality can be tracked back to that moment.

JOY: Oh, absolutely. And when we're talking about this now, we're talking about a glorious phenomenon because these are intrinsic sex differences. . . this is glorious because we are fearfully and wonderfully differentiated from each other.

DOBSON: Let's look at 'em, name 'em.

JOY: We're, we're mutually interdependent. Every household needs both a male brain and a female brain, for example. The woman's brain works much like a computer . . . lateral transmission in her brain allows her to consult all of her past experience and give you an instant response. She can make a judgment more quickly than a male can. . . . [but how she arrives at it is] hidden even from her, because it is like a computer, all it gives is the answer, it doesn't give you the process.

The male brain, Joy added, is more like an "adding machine," in which facts are totaled and a logical solution presents itself. So males are good at logical reasoning, and females at intuitive judgments, because of the prenatal "chemical bath" that affects the male brain. . . .

Now it may be true that men and women, on the average, differ in the physiology of their brains. It may even be true that this difference explains why James Dobson's wife Shirley can sum up a person's character right away, while he, with his slower, adding-machine brain, takes weeks or months to come to the same impressions. But given the disgraceful history of bias and sloppy research designed more to confirm prejudices than to enlighten humanity, I think we would all do well to be suspicious and to evaluate the evidence for these assertions closely.

This is difficult for those of us who are not expert in physiology, neuroanatomy, or medicine. We are easily dazzled by words like "lateralization" and "corpus callosum." Besides, physiology seems so *solid*; if one study finds a difference between three male brains and three female brains, that must apply to all men and women. How do I know what my corpus callosum looks like? Is it bigger than a man's? Should I care?

For some answers, I turned to researchers in biology and neuroscience who have critically examined the research and the assumptions underlying theories of sex differences in the brain. The first discovery of note was that, just like the nineteenth-century researchers who kept changing their minds about which *lobe* of the brain accounted for male superiority, twentieth-century researchers keep changing their minds about which *hemisphere* of the brain accounts for male superiority. Originally, the left hemisphere was considered the repository of intellect and reason. The right hemisphere was the sick, bad, crazy side, the side of passion, instincts, criminality, and irrationality. Guess which sex was thought to have left-brain intellectual superiority? (Answer: males.) In the 1960s and 1970s, however, the right brain was resuscitated and brought into the limelight. Scientists began to suspect that it was the source of genius and inspiration, creativity and imagination, mysticism and mathematical brilliance. Guess which sex was now thought to have right-brain specialization? (Answer: males.)

It's all very confusing. Today we hear arguments that men have greater left-brain specialization (which explains their intellectual advantage) *and* that they have greater right-brain specialization (which explains their mathematical and artistic advantage). *Newsweek* recently asserted as fact, for instance, that "Women's language and other skills are more evenly divided between left and right hemisphere; in men, such functions are concentrated in the left brain." But [in their book *The Language of Love*, Christian fundamentalists Gary Smalley and John Trent] asserted that

> most women spend the majority of their days and nights camped out on the right side of the brain [which] harbors the center for feelings, as well as the primary relational, language, and communication skills . . . and makes an afternoon devoted to art and fine music actually enjoyable.

You can hear the chuckling from men who regard art museums and concert halls as something akin to medieval torture chambers, but I'm sure that the many men who enjoy art and fine music, indeed who create art and fine music, would not find that last remark so funny. Geschwind and Behan, of course, had argued that male specialization of the right hemisphere explained why men *excel* in art and fine music. But since Smalley and Trent apparently do not share these prissy female interests, they relegate them to women—to women's brains.

The two hemispheres of the brain do have different specialties, but it is far too simple-minded (so to speak) to assume that human abilities clump up in opposing bunches. Most brain researchers today believe that the two hemispheres complement one another, to the extent that one side can sometimes take over the functions of a side that has been damaged. Moreover, specific skills often involve components from both hemispheres: one side has the ability to tell a joke, and the other has the ability to laugh at one. Math abilities include both visual-spatial skills and reasoning skills. The right hemisphere is involved in creating art, but the left hemisphere is involved in appreciating and analyzing art. As neuropsychologist Jerre Levy once said, "Could the eons of human evolution have left half of the brain witless? Could a bird whose existence is dependent on flying have evolved only a single wing?"

These qualifications about the interdependence of brain hemispheres have not, however, deterred those who believe that there are basic psychological differences between the sexes that can be accounted for in the brain. So let's consider their argument more closely.

The neuroscientist Ruth Bleier . . . carefully examined Geschwind and Behan's data, going back to many of their original references. In one such study of 507 fetal brains of 10 to 44 weeks gestation, the researchers had actually stated that they found *no significant sex differences* in these brains. If testosterone had an effect on the developing brain, it would surely have been apparent in this large sample. Yet Geschwind and Behan cited this study for other purposes and utterly ignored its findings of no sex differences.

Instead, Geschwind and Behan cited as evidence for their hypothesis a study of *rats'* brains. The authors of the rat study reported that in male rats, two areas of the cortex that are believed to be involved in processing visual information were 3 percent thicker on the right side than on the left. In one of the better examples of academic gobbledygook yet

to reach the printed page, the researchers interpreted their findings to mean that "in the male rat it is necessary to have greater spatial orientation to interact with a female rat during estrus and to integrate that input into a meaningful output." Translation: When having sex with a female, the male needs to be able to look around in case a dangerous predator, such as her husband, walks in on them.

Bleier found more holes in this argument than in a screen door. No one knows, she said, what the slightly greater thickness in the male rat's cortex means for the rat, let alone what it means for human beings. There is at present no evidence that spatial orientation is related to asymmetry of the cortex, or that female rats have a lesser or deficient ability in this regard. And although Geschwind and Behan unabashedly used their limited findings to account for male "superiority" in math and art, they did not specifically study the incidence of genius, talent, or even modest giftedness in their sample, nor did they demonstrate a difference between the brains of geniuses and the brains of average people.

Bleier wrote to *Science*, offering a scholarly paper detailing these criticisms. *Science* did not publish it, on the grounds, as one reviewer put it, that Bleier "tends to err in the opposite direction from the researchers whose results and conclusions she criticizes" and because "she argues very strongly for the predominant role of environmental influences." Apparently, said Bleier, one is allowed to err in only one direction if one wants to be published in *Science*. The journal did not even publish her critical Letter to the Editor.

At about the same time, however, *Science* saw fit to publish a study by two researchers who claimed to have found solid evidence of gender differences in the splenium (posterior end) of the corpus callosum. In particular, they said, the splenium was larger and more bulbous in the five female brains than in the nine male brains they examined, which had been obtained at autopsy. The researchers speculated that "the female brain is less well lateralized—that is, manifests less hemispheric specialization—than the male brain for visuospatial functions." Notice the language: The female brain is *less specialized* than, and by implication inferior to, the male brain. They did not say, as they might have, that the female brain was *more integrated* than the male's. The male brain is the norm, and specialization, in the brain as in academia, is considered a good thing. Generalists in any business are out of favor these days.

This article, which also met professional acclaim, had a number of major flaws that, had they been part of any other research paper, would have been fatal to its publication. The study was based on a small sample of only fourteen brains. The researchers did not describe their methods of selecting the brains in that sample, so it is possible that some of the brains were diseased or otherwise abnormal. The article contained numerous unsupported assumptions and leaps of faith. For example, there is at present absolutely no evidence that the number of fibers in the corpus callosum is even related to hemispheric specialization. Indeed, no one knows what role, if any, the callosum plays in determining a person's mental abilities. Most damaging of all, the sex differences that the researchers claimed to have found in the size of the corpus callosum were not statistically significant, according to the scientific conventions for accepting an article for publication.

Bleier again wrote to *Science*, delineating these criticisms and also citing four subsequent studies, by her and by others, that independently failed to find gender differences of any kind in the corpus callosum. *Science* failed to publish this criticism, as it has failed to publish all studies that find no gender differences in the brain.

Ultimately, the most damning blow to all of these brain-hemisphere theories is that the formerly significant sex differences that brain theories are attempting to account for—in verbal, spatial, and math abilities—are fading rapidly. Let's start with the famed female superiority in verbal ability. Janet Hyde, a professor of psychology at the University of Wisconsin, and her colleague Marcia Linn reviewed 165 studies of verbal ability (including skills in vocabulary, writing, anagrams, and reading comprehension), which represented tests of 1,418,899 people. Hyde and Linn reported that at present in America, there simply are no gender differences in these verbal skills. They noted: "Thus our research pulls out one of the two wobbly legs on which the brain lateralization theories have rested."

Hyde recently went on to kick the other leg, the assumption of overall male superiority in mathematics and spatial ability. No one disputes that males do surpass females at the highly gifted end of the math spectrum. But when Hyde and her colleagues analyzed 100 studies of mathematics performance, representing the testing of 3,985,682 students, they found that gender differences were smallest and favored *females* in samples of the general population, and grew larger, favoring males, only in selected samples of precocious individuals.

What about spatial abilities, another area thought to reveal a continuing male superiority? When psychologists put the dozens of existing studies on spatial ability into a giant hopper and looked at the overall results, this was what they reported: Many studies show no sex differences. Of the studies that do report sex differences, the magnitude of the difference is often small. And finally, there is greater variation *within* each sex than *between* them. As one psychologist who reviewed these studies summarized: "The observed differences are very small, the overlap [between men and women] large, and abundant biological theories are supported with very slender or no evidence."

Sometimes scientists and science writers put themselves through contortions in order to reconcile the slim evidence with their belief in sex differences in the brain. The authors of a popular textbook on sexuality, published in 1990, acknowledge that "sex differences in cognitive skills have declined significantly in recent years." Then they add: "Notwithstanding this finding, theories continue to debate why these differences exist." Pardon? Notwithstanding the fact that there are few differences of any magnitude, let's discuss why there are differences? Even more mysteriously, they conclude: "If Geschwind's theory is ultimately supported by further research, we will have hard evidence of a biological basis for alleged sex differences in verbal and spatial skills." "Hard evidence" for *alleged* sex differences—the ones that don't exist!

It is sobering to read, over and over and over again in scholarly papers, the conclusions of eminent scientists who have cautioned their colleagues against generalizing about sex differences from poor data. One leader in brain-hemisphere research, Marcel Kinsbourne, observing that the evidence for sex differences "fails to convince on logical, methodological, and empirical grounds," then asked:

> Why then do reputable investigators persist in ignoring [this evidence]? Because the study of sex differences is not like the rest of psychology. Under pressure from the gathering momentum of feminism, and perhaps in backlash to it, many investigators seem determined to discover that men and women "really" are different. It seems that if sex differences (e.g., in lateralization) do not exist, then they have to be invented.

These warnings have, for the most part, gone unheeded. Poor research continues to be published in reputable journals, and from there it is disseminated to the public. Many scientists and science writers continue to rely on weak data to support their speculations, like using pebbles as foundation for a castle. Because these speculations fit the dominant beliefs about gender, however, they receive far more attention and credibility than they warrant. Worse, the far better evidence that fails to conform to the dominant beliefs about gender is overlooked, disparaged, or, as in Bleier's experience, remains unpublished.

As a result, ideas enter the common vocabulary as proven facts when they should be encumbered with "maybes," "sometimes," and "we-don't-know-yets." Scientist Hugh Fairweather, reviewing the history of sex differences research in cognition, concluded: "What had before been a possibility at best slenderly evidenced, was widely taken for a fact; and 'fact' hardened into a 'biological' dogma."

Now, it is possible that reliable sex differences in the brain will eventually be discovered. Will it then be all right for Dobson to go on the air to celebrate how delightfully but innately different men and women are? Should we then all make sure we have a male brain and a female brain in every household? Should we then worry about the abnormality of households like mine, in which the male is better at intuitive judgments and the female has the adding-machine mentality?

The answers are no, for three reasons. First, theories of sex differences in the brain cannot account for the complexities of people's everyday behavior. They cannot explain, for instance, why, if women are better than men in verbal ability, so few women are auctioneers or diplomats, or why, if women have the advantage in making rapid judgments, so few women are air-traffic controllers or umpires. Nor can brain theories explain why abilities and ambitions change when people are given opportunities previously denied to them. Two decades ago, theorists postulated biological limitations that were keeping women out of men's work like medicine and bartending. When the external barriers to these professions fell, the speed with which women entered them was dizzying. Did everybody's brain change? Today we would be amused to think that women have a brain-lateralization deficiency that is keeping them out of law school. But we continue to hear about the biological reasons that keep women out of science, math, and politics. For sex differences in cognitive abilities to wax and wane so rapidly, they must be largely a result of education, motivation, and opportunity, not of innate differences between male and female brains.

Second, the meanings of terms like "verbal ability" and "spatial reasoning" keep changing too, depending on who is using them and for what purpose. For example, when conservatives like Dobson speak of women's verbal abilities, they usually mean women's interest in and willingness to talk about relationships and feelings. But in studies of total talking time in the workplace, men far exceed women in the talk department. In everyday life, men interrupt women more than vice versa, dominate the conversation, and are more successful at introducing new topics and having their comments remembered in group discussions. What does this mean for judgments of which sex has the better "verbal ability"?

Third, the major key problem with biological theories of sex differences is that they deflect attention from the far more substantial evidence for sex similarity. The finding that men and women are more alike in their abilities and brains than different almost never makes the news. Researchers and the public commit the error of focusing on the small differences—usually of the magnitude of a few percentage points—rather than on the fact that the majority of women and men overlap. For example, this is what the author of a scientific paper that has been widely quoted as *supporting* sex differences in brain hemispheres actually concluded:

> Thus, one must not overlook perhaps the most obvious conclusion, which is that basic patterns of male and female brain asymmetry seem to be more similar than they are different.

Everyone, nevertheless, promptly overlooked it.

The habit of seeing women and men as two opposite categories also leads us to avoid the practical question: How much ability does it take to do well in a particular career? When people hear that men are better than women in spatial ability, many are quick to conclude that perhaps women, with their deficient brains, should not try to become architects or engineers. This reaction is not merely unfortunate; it is cruel to the women who *do* excel in architectural or engineering ability. The fields of math and science are losing countless capable women because girls keep hearing that women aren't as good as men in these fields.

None of this means that biology is irrelevant to human behavior. But whenever the news trumpets some version of "biology affects behavior," it obscures the fact that biology and behavior form a two-way street. Hormones affect sexual drive, for instance, but sexual activity affects hormone levels. An active brain seeks a stimulating environment, but living in a stimulating environment literally changes and enriches the brain. Fatigue and boredom cause poor performance on the job, but stultifying job conditions produce fatigue and boredom. Scientists and writers who reduce our personalities, problems, and abilities to biology thereby tell only half the story, and miss half the miracle of how human biology works.

Ruth Bleier, . . . a neuroscientist, put the whole matter in perspective this way:

> Such efforts directed at the callosum (or any other particular structure in the brain, for that matter) are today's equivalent of 19th-century craniology: if you can find a bigger bump here or a smaller one there on a person's skull, if you can find a more bulbous splenium here or a more slender one there . . . you will know something significant about their intelligence, their personality, their aspirations, their astrological sign, their gender and race, and their status in society. We are still mired in the naive hope that we can find something that we can *see* and *measure* and it will explain everything. It is silly science and it serves us badly.

POSTSCRIPT

Are Gender Differences Rooted in the Brain?

Jerome Kagan, one of the major researchers in the area of personality development, has pointed out that many Americans prefer to minimize biology and maximize nurture and the environment when it comes to discussing the origin of psychological differences and desires. This tendency, he says, owes much to the prevailing commitment Americans have to egalitarianism. If differences between individuals, between the genders, or between gender orientations are biologically based, then there is little we can do about them. If, however, differences are due to inequities in the social environment, there may be a lot we can do to reduce or eliminate the differences.

Alice Rossi, in concluding her 1983 presidential address to the American Sociological Association, pointed out that attempts to explain human behavior and therapies that seek to change behavior "carry a high risk of eventual irrelevance" if they "neglect the fundamental biological and neural differences between the sexes" and "the mounting evidence of sexual dimorphism from the biological and neural sciences." Although Rossi seems to favor Kimura's arguments, her subsequent comment touches on the issues raised by Tavris: "Diversity is a biological fact, while equality is a political, ethical, and social precept."

If the biological and neuropsychological evidence supports the existence of significant differences between females and males, then we have to be careful to view these differences as part of human diversity and not in terms of superior-inferior or good-bad. Human diversity does not deny or obstruct human equality, because human equality is a political, moral, and social issue and concern. Too often a concern for human equality conditions and influences our understanding of human diversity.

SUGGESTED READINGS

A. Fausto-Sterling, *Myths of Gender: Biological Theories About Women and Men,* 2d ed. (Basic Books, 1992).

C. Gorman, "Sizing Up the Sexes," *Time* (January 20, 1992).

C. Holden, "The Genetics of Personality," *Science* (August 7, 1987).

S. LeVay, *The Sexual Brain* (MIT Press, 1993).

A. Moir and D. Jessel, *Brain Sex: The Real Difference Between Men and Women* (Lyle Stuart, 1991).

D. Tannen, *You Just Don't Understand: Women and Men in Conversation* (Ballantine Books, 1990).

A. Walsh, *The Science of Love: Understanding Love and Its Effects on Mind and Body* (Prometheus Books, 1991).

ISSUE 2

Can Sex Be an Addiction?

YES: **Patrick Carnes,** from "Progress in Sex Addiction: An Addiction Perspective," *SIECUS Report* (July 1986)

NO: **Marty Klein,** from "Why There's No Such Thing as Sexual Addiction— And Why It Really Matters," *Annual Meeting of the Society for the Scientific Study of Sex* (November 1989)

ISSUE SUMMARY

YES: Patrick Carnes, a therapist who has established an inpatient program for sexual dependency, argues that a significant number of people have identified themselves as sexual addicts—persons with "unstoppable" repetitive behavior patterns that are destructive to the addict and to his or her family. Sexual addiction can best be treated, he claims, by using systems theory and techniques developed by Alcoholics Anonymous, obesity clinics, and substance-abuse rehabilitation programs.
NO: Marty Klein, a sex therapist and marriage and family counselor, challenges sexual addiction as being vaguely defined and often diagnosed by nonsexologists. He claims that the symptoms of sexual addiction are arbitrary and that its promulgation promotes unhealthy, negative, and immature attitudes toward natural human sexuality.

The way we define or label a particular behavior greatly affects the way people react to it. When a society labels a particular behavior, like masturbation or oral sex, as an unnatural act and the result of a narcissistic, unstable mental disorder, we "know" that people who engage in these behaviors have a psychological disorder that requires treatment by psychologists, psychiatrists, and psychotherapists. If we define the behavior as a moral disorder, or a sin, we "know" that the person needs redemption, absolution, and some kind of spiritual or moral counseling.

In recent years, our society has wavered about whether to define alcoholism and substance abuse as compulsive behaviors, addictions, or diseases. If they are diseases, then medical insurance may be available for treatment. If the *Diagnostic and Statistical Manual of Mental Disorders (DSM-III-R),* the handbook of psychiatrists, does *not* list "sexual addiction" or "obsessive-compulsive sexual behavior" as a psychosexual disorder, insurance companies may not pay for treatment.

More recently, some therapists have borrowed the label *addiction* from alcohol and substance abuse and applied it to behavior that the patient, the therapist, or society labels "promiscuous."

The debate over whether sexually compulsive behavior is an addiction or a psychosexual, obsessive-compulsive behavior disorder may sound like a quibble over words. But words, especially definitions, can be extremely powerful. Witness the major social changes that occurred when feminists in the early 1970s redefined *rape* as "an act of rage, power, and the need for control" instead of "a sexual act," as it was commonly defined before 1970. Redefining *rape* changed the treatment of both the rapist and the victim. How we define *promiscuous* or whether we label a particular case of promiscuous sex an "obsessive-compulsive psychosexual condition" or an "addiction" will have a definite impact on how we view and treat persons who exhibit this behavior.

According to Patrick Carnes, certain levels of promiscuity—namely the unstoppable practice of certain sexual behaviors—indicate an addiction that requires treatment. Marty Klein dismisses sexual addiction as popular nonsense—a political maneuver intended to increase the power of moral zealots.

YES

Patrick Carnes

PROGRESS IN SEX ADDICTION: AN ADDICTION PERSPECTIVE

Over the last fifteen years the new professional discipline of addictionology has emerged from the extensive foundations laid in both research and treatment of alcohol and drug addictions. Led by organizations like the American Academy of Addictionology and scholarly publications like the *Journal of Addictive Behaviors*, researchers have found that different addictive behaviors (e.g. compulsive eating, alcoholism, compulsive gambling, smoking) have much in common. It is not surprising that sex has only recently been added to the list, given the guilt and shame still attached to the subject. Nor should it surprise us that the professional controversy far exceeds that of other forms of addiction.

DEFINING SEXUAL ADDICTION

The fact remains that a significant number of people have identified themselves as sexual addicts: people whose sexual behavior has become "unstoppable" despite serious consequences. These consequences include the physical (self-mutilation, sexual violence, disease, unwanted pregnancy), occupational (large financial losses, job losses, sexual abuse and harassment, withdrawal of professional licenses), and familial (loss of relationships, impaired family functioning, sexual abuse, sexual dysfunction). In addition to those problems, one of the most frequent mental health complaints of sexual addicts is suicidal ideation.

Another frequent complaint of "recovering" sex addicts is that the mental health community does not acknowledge their problem. They become enraged when sexologists dismiss sexual addiction as a problem of sexual misinformation, or excessive guilt due to a cultural dissonance, or not a serious or widespread problem. I recently spoke at a Sexaholics Anonymous convention in which participants were rageful and moved to tears over statements made by professionals in a *New York Times* article. Stepping back from the intensity of their feelings, I had to reflect that compared to the

From Patrick Carnes, "Progress in Sex Addiction: An Addiction Perspective," *SIECUS Report*, vol. 14, no. 6 (July 1986). Copyright © 1986 by Sex Information and Education Council of the U.S., Inc., 130 West 42nd Street, Suite 2500, New York, NY 10036. 212/819-9770, fax 212/819-9776. Reprinted by permission.

amount of time taken to gain acceptance for the concept of alcoholism, the progress made in sexual addiction is remarkable.

My purpose here is to summarize this progress from an addictionologist's point of view and to specify further challenges which will require the close cooperation of specialists in addiction and professionals in human sexuality.

CASE STUDY

Consider the case of Larry, a 45-year-old manager of a computer programming department. Larry was arrested for exhibitionism and sent to a court-mandated group for eight sessions. The group focused on the exposing behavior, but from Larry's point of view it was merely the tip of the iceberg. He had a 15-year collection of pornography, carefully cataloged and indexed. He saw prostitutes three to four times a month and masturbated daily—sometimes five times in one day. His sexual relationship with his wife, Joan, had diminished largely due to her rage at his increasing sexual demands and his sexual affairs with other women. Part of her response was to overeat so much that she gained over 125 pounds.

Larry also used marijuana and cocaine, ironic considering his intense hatred of his dad's drinking problem, another form of substance abuse. A further irony was that his wife bought the drugs for Larry because, as she later reported, it was better to have him stoned at home than out cruising around.

Larry lived in constant fear of discovery that his children, wife, or church community would find out about the range of his activities. He hated his life and was constantly trying to cope financially to support his sexual activities and drug use.

Venereal disease created a crisis in the marriage, and with the help of their physician, Larry and Joan entered a hospital outpatient program for sexual addiction. Larry found that he was not alone in his problems. Many of the patients had the same or similar issues. In an interview with Larry two-and-a-half years later, upon completion of his treatment, he recounted that there were three main changes in his life since he began treatment. First, his sexuality had shifted dramatically. No longer was he pursuing a desire that he never seemed able to satisfy. Now he and Joan were learning and enjoying sex in different ways than they had believed possible. Second, he had time for work and play. And third, he was no longer living in constant jeopardy of being discovered or running out of money.

In *Out of the Shadows: Understanding Sexual Addiction*, I describe a model (see Figure 1, next page) in which the principle momentum for the addiction in addicts like Larry comes from a personal belief system. This belief system captures all the cultural and familial messages about sex and relationships. When these messages are very sex negative and are coupled with low self esteem, core beliefs about one's own innate shamefulness emerge. Shame is basically a problem of mastery (why is it other kids can do this and I can't?). When the shame is sexual (why is it other people seem to be in control of their sexual feelings and I am not?), the environment for obsessive behavior is at its optimum.

IMPAIRED THINKING

Through these lenses the addict's thinking becomes impaired, literally, to the point of loss of contact with reality. Ad-

Figure 1

The Addictive System

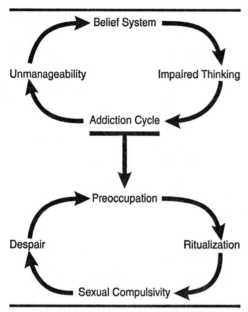

From Patrick Carnes, *Out of the Shadows: Understanding Sexual Addiction* (Minneapolis, MN: CompCare Publishers, 1983). Copyright © 1983 by Patrick Carnes, Ph.D. Reprinted by permission of CompCare Publishers.

dicts talk of entering an altered state parallel to the Jekyll-Hyde shift where even common sense considerations disappear. Denial and delusion govern their lives. One addict, for example, told of following a woman into what he thought was a restaurant only to discover himself standing in the lobby of a police station to which the woman had fled.

Because of the impaired thinking, an addiction cycle perpetuates itself through four phases:

- preoccupation in which the addict enters a trance-like obsession
- ritualization that enhances the trance
- sexual behavior that is often not rewarding

- despair that, once again, the behavior has been repeated.

One way to stave off the despair is to start the preoccupation over again. And the cycle becomes the recursive series of events which dominates the addict's life. With this process underway, the addict's life becomes more and more unmanageable, thus confirming the basic feelings of unworthiness that are the core of the addict's belief system.

Larry's secretive life was embedded in this process of shame, powerlessness, and despair. He wanted very much to stop the pain, but the only things that seemed to help were his rituals of indexing his pornography, finding a prostitute, or, when unable to pay for sex, exposing himself. Larry's addictive process presents a very common model familiar to addiction professionals. Shame is a key factor in all addictions. Sexual shame, especially in a sex-negative culture, is particularly virulent.

MULTIPLE ADDICTIONS

Other familiar factors in Larry's case are multiple addictions, both in the addict and his immediate family members. Golden Valley Health Center, a suburban Minneapolis hospital, has a twenty bed in-patient treatment program for sexual addiction called the Sexual Dependency Unit. I serve as a program consultant to that facility. Seventy-one percent of the patient population reports multiple addiction or compulsive behaviors. In fact, thirty-eight percent of the program's patients are chemically dependent; another thirty-eight percent have eating disorders. Compulsive gambling, spending, caffeine use, and smoking are also frequent complaints.

The Golden Valley Program represents, in a concrete manner, the emerging recognition among addictionologists that not only do addictions occur concurrently, but in mutually reinforcing ways. Clinicians often observe that the treatment of one addiction will result in the flourishing of another. Patients, for example, who have both alcoholism and sexual addiction often observe that their alcohol use was a way to anesthetize their pain around their out-of-control sexual behavior. They further comment that their alcoholism was relatively easy to deal with compared to their sexual acting out.

Such observations are at odds significantly with the traditional "disease" model of chemical dependency in which alcoholism and drug addiction are perceived as the primary "illness" and the sexual behavior as resulting from it. Unfortunately, there are still alcoholism treatment centers where patients are told that their sexual behavior will straighten out once they get sober.

Major progress is being made, however, in terms of understanding the relationships among the various addictions. One exciting example is the research of Milkman and his colleagues (*Advances in Alcohol and Substance Abuse*, 1983) on the psychobiological impact of hormone interactions on addiction pathology. For their research purposes, they use a matrix developed around three categories of addictions: the arousal addictions (e.g., gambling, sex, stimulant drugs, and high risk behaviors), the satiation addictions (e.g., overeating, depressant drugs, and alcohol), and the fantasy addictions (e.g., psychedelic drugs, marijuana, and mystical/artistic preoccupations). Beyond their research method of categorization, the conceptualization of models of poly-addiction will go far in broadening traditional models of addiction. They will also assist in answering the questions many practitioners have about cross-tolerance effects.

FAMILY SYSTEM THEORY

Many addiction professionals are using systems theory as a conceptual foundation for their work not only because it is an integrative paradigm but also because it is a *growth* versus *illness* model. One of the systems identified, for example, by most addiction specialists as key to the self-defeating patterns of the addiction is the family system. Note in Larry's story how other family members had their own addiction patterns (father's drinking and wife's overeating). Observe also Joan's co-participation in the illness through the purchasing of Larry's drugs. Even her weight gain was a statement about their sexuality.

As part of the etiology of the addictive system, extreme family behavior such as extreme rigidity or chaos are common to people who have dependency problems. Further, I describe in a new book now in press a survey of 300 sexual addicts and the incidence of childhood sexual abuse. Sixty-five percent of the women and forty-five percent of the men report having been sexually abused. For a number of reasons I specify in the book, I believe that this is, in fact, underreported.

As part of treatment, the family or significant others are vital to the recovery process. When Golden Valley Health Center staff conducted six-month post-treatment evaluations, they discovered only one common denominator to all the patients who suffered relapse: no family members, partners, or significant others had participated in the family week of treatment.

Systems theory also allows a more organic approach to treatment. For example, comparisons between alcoholism and sexual addiction treatment can create misperceptions about the course of treatment. A better comparison can be made by looking at eating disorders. There are 34 million obese and 14 million morbidly obese persons in the United States. Yet, like sexual addiction, we have been very slow to address this problem. In compulsive overeating, patients are not asked to give up eating, but rather to learn how to eat differently. Eating patterns, environments, foods, and rituals shift so that they enhance rather than destroy the patient's life.

Similarly, sexual addiction treatment helps patients reclaim their sexuality by a primary refocusing of their sexual behavior. Some have assumed that the abstinence focus of alcohol programs has been directly translated to sex addiction programs, and they feared that treatment in these programs would be a sex-negative experience. Of the four hospital based programs I know, treatment staff work very hard to help their patients achieve the goal of sexual enhancement. Part of review criteria for all such programs should include treatment goals that encourage healthy and varied forms of sexual expression.

TREATMENT OUTCOME

In terms of treatment outcomes, the early six-month evaluation of Golden Valley Health Center patients is encouraging. This internal study of 30 patients has all the obvious limitations of a preliminary study done on the first patient cohort to reach six months. It is also not a large

sample, nor is it conducted over a long period of time. Nor were the forms consistently completed. But the information obtained from this preliminary study is positive. For quality of life indicators, patients reported significant improvement in the following areas:

- Family Life 76%
- Job Performance 81%
- General Physical Health 80%
- Self-Image 71%

For program outcomes, patients reported:

- Having no or minimal problems maintaining recovery 86%
- Recommending program to others 100%
- Attending regular or frequent 12-step meetings 76%

The last program outcome requires some explanation. Addiction programs often rely on community support groups based on the 12 steps of Alcoholics Anonymous or as they are translated (e.g., Overeaters Anonymous, Gamblers Anonymous). In the case of sexual addiction, there are a number of groups, such as Sex Addicts Anonymous or Sexaholics Anonymous. The fact that 76 percent of Golden Valley's patients could find local groups is remarkable, given that the majority of them came from all over the United States and Canada. It is a testimony to the rapid expansion of resources for this problem.

CONCLUSION

Some professionals are mistrustful of self-help groups, especially when they have had no experience with them. The fact is they are of uneven quality. However, a good group is hard to beat in terms of helping addicts cope with their shame. The 12 steps are particularly effective with shame-based addictive disorders. Perhaps the best brief explanation of the process is Ernst Kurtz's class article "Why AA Works" (*Journal of Studies on Alcohol*, 43:38-80) for those readers with no 12-step group experience.

Definitional problems abound in sexual addiction. Eli Coleman elaborates upon them in his companion article to this piece. Questions of normalcy, cross-cultural comparisons, special populations are all familiar terrain to the addiction specialist. In fact, Jim Orford, one of the very first to articulate a theory on sexual dependency, comments in his recent book *Excessive Appetites* (1985):

> Debate over definitions in this area is intriguingly reminiscent of debates on the same subject when drugtaking, drinking, or gambling are under discussion. In none of these areas is there agreement about the precise points on the continuum at which normal behaviour, heavy use, problem behaviour, excessive behaviour, "mania" or "ism" are to be distinguished one from another. When reading of the supposed characteristics of the "real nymphomaniac," one is haunted by memories of attempts to define the "real alcoholic" or the "real compulsive gambler."

Current research trends are abandoning the traditional disease oriented typologies in favor of recognizing that natural systems are varied even in pathologies. To find the model "sex addict" that everyone can agree on will take us down a trail the professional addictionologist has been on before. There is not one kind of alcoholic but actually a variety of types who have excessive use of alcohol in common. So I believe that we will find similar patterns in sexual addiction.

The risk is that addiction specialists look skeptically at sex therapists and their lack of training in addictive delusional thought processes and relapse prevention while sexual scientists criticize addictionologists as having inadequate knowledge of sexuality. Meanwhile, people who are struggling with the issue are asking for help. And no progress will be made.

Therein is the opportunity. Some years ago the Italian psychiatrist Mara Palazolli (1981) appealed for professionals to work for what she termed "transdisciplinary" knowledge as contrasted with interdisciplinary efforts in which different specialists focused on a common problem. From her point of view "transdisciplinary" meant creating a new body of knowledge through the cooperation of different disciplines. Sexual addiction presents us with a great challenge and opportunity for addictionologists and sexual scientists to develop the new body of knowledge that Palazolli envisioned.

NO
Marty Klein

WHY THERE'S NO SUCH THING AS SEXUAL ADDICTION—AND WHY IT REALLY MATTERS

If convicted mass murderer Ted Bundy had said that watching Bill Cosby reruns motivated his awful crimes, he would have been dismissed as a deranged sociopath. Instead, Bundy said his pornography addiction made him do it—which many people treated as the conclusions of a thoughtful social scientist. Why?

There's a phenomenon emerging in America today that affects us and our profession whether we like it or not. Not caring about it, or having no opinion about it, is no longer an option for us.

I am not interested, by the way, in trashing 12-step programs. AA performs a great service every year in helping people handle their addiction to alcohol and other drugs. The two-part question that has been put to us— again, whether we like it or not—is, is the addiction model a good one for diagnosing sexual problems, and is the 12-step model a good one for treating sexual problems?

If it is, is it as appropriate for treating rapists as it is for people who masturbate too much?

HOW THE SEXUAL ADDICTION MOVEMENT AFFECTS PROFESSIONALS

*People are now self-diagnosing as "sex addicts."

They're also diagnosing their partners. Non-sexologist professionals such as ministers and doctors are diagnosing some of their clientele as sex addicts, too. As a result of these trends, many people who should be seeing therapists or sexologists are not. And many who don't need "treatment" *are* getting it.

*The sexual addiction movement is aggressively training non-sexologists, such as marriage counselors, in the treatment of sexual problems.

From the Annual Meeting of the Society for the Scientific Study of Sex, November 1989. Copyright © 1989 by Marty Klein. Reprinted by permission.

Many professionals are now taking these programs instead of those offered by sexologists. Also, some professionals now feel incompetent to treat certain systemic problems without this sexual addiction "training."

It is important to note that the content of this sexual addiction training is sexologically inadequate: there is little or no discussion of systems, physiology, diagnoses, cultural aspects, etc.

*The concept of sexual addiction affects the sexual climate of the new society in which we work—negatively.

This negativity is reflected in anti-sex education legislation, anti-pornography ordinances, homophobic industry regulations, etc.

*Sex addicts now have cachet as sex experts.

Mass murderer Ted Bundy, widely quoted as an expert on the effects of pornography, is only one example. Right-wing crusaders now routinely quote "sex addicts" to justify repressive beliefs and public policy suggestions.

DEFINING SEXUAL ADDICTION

In the literature, the sex addict is typically described as:
• Someone who frequently does or fantasizes sexual things s/he doesn't like
• Someone whose sexual behavior has become unstoppable despite serious consequences (including, according to Patrick Carnes, unwanted pregnancy)
• Someone whose sexual behavior and thoughts have become vastly more important than their relationships, family, work, finances, and health
• Someone whose sexual behavior doesn't reflect her/his highest self, the grandest part of her/his humanness

• According to the National Association of Sexual Addiction Problems, "6% or 1 out of 17 Americans are sexual addicts." That's about 14 million people.

From this literature and from meetings of groups like Sexaholics Anonymous (SA), the beliefs of people committed to the sexual addiction model appear to include:
• Sex is most healthy in committed, monogamous, loving, heterosexual relationships;
• The "goal" of sex should always be intimacy and the expression of our highest self;
• There are limits to healthy sexual expression, which are obvious (e.g., masturbation more than once a day);
• Choosing to use sex to feel better about yourself or to escape from problems is unhealthy.

CLINICAL IMPLICATIONS OF THE CONCEPT

*It sees powerlessness as a virtue.

Step 1 of the traditional "12 steps" of all AA-type groups is "we admitted we were powerless over X (alcohol, our sexual impulses, etc.) . . ."

Controlling our sexuality can be painful, not because we lack self-control or will power, but because sexual energy is powerful and demands expression. The primitive, infantile forces behind those demands often make sexuality feel like a matter of life and death—which, in the unconscious, it is.

"Sex addicts" say they are "out of control," but this is just a *metaphor*—i.e., they *feel* out of control; controlling their impulses is very painful. We've all had that experience, with sex and with other things. *Virtually everyone* has the ability to choose how to control and express their sexual impulses (we'll discuss the small group who can't later).

The concept of sexual addiction colludes with peoples' desire to shirk responsibility for their sexuality. But powerlessness is far too high a price to pay.

*It prevents helpful analysis by patients and therapists.

The concept of sexual addiction prevents any examination of the personality dynamics underlying sexual behavior. It prevents the assessment and treatment of sexual or personality problems, because identifying and dealing with the "addiction" is the goal.

By encouraging people to "admit" that they *are* powerless, the concept of sexual addiction prevents people from examining how they come to *feel* powerless—and what they can do about that feeling. This careful examination, ultimately, is the source of personality growth and behavior change.

The expression "That's my addiction talking" is creeping into the popular vocabulary. This translates into "don't confront or puncture my defenses."

*It trivializes sexuality.

The concept of sexual addiction ignores the childhood passions at the source of sexual guilt. Aggression, lust for power, and greedy demands to be pleasured are all part of normal sexuality, which every adult needs to broker in some complex fashion.

People learn to feel guilty about their sexual impulses as infants. "Sex addicts" are told they have nothing to feel guilty about, that they can learn to feel better one day at a time. But people know all the "good" reasons they have for feeling sexual guilt. By denying the dark side of normal, healthy sexuality that most peo-

ple know they have, the concept of sexual addiction *increases* guilt.

Self-identified "sex addicts" want us to remove the darkness from their sexuality, leaving only the wholesome, nonthreatening part—which would, of course, also leave them as non-adults. Rather than collude with this understandable desire, competent therapists are willing to confront this darkness. Instead of snatching it away from patients, we can help them approach it, understand it, and ultimately feel less afraid of it.

Another way to describe this is that

*It lets people split—i.e., externalize their "bad" sexuality.

Once a person describes her/himself as a "sex addict," s/he can say "*I* don't want that sexual feeling or behavior over there; *the disease* wants it." Good therapists know how to recognize splitting, how it blocks adult functioning, and how to move patients away from it.

*It makes a disease out of what is often within reasonable limits of sexual behavior.

High levels of masturbating and *any* patronage of prostitutes, for example, are typically condemned as "abnormal" and reflecting a "disease," according to SA-type groups. Which experts get to make judgments about acceptable sexual behavior? Exactly where do their criteria come from?

*It doesn't teach sexual decision-making skills, or how to evaluate sexual situations.

Rather, the concept uses a "just say no" approach. As Planned Parenthood's Faye Wattleton says, "just say no" helps people abstain from self-destructive sex about as well as "have a nice day" helps people deal with depression.

SA-type groups say that ultimately, sexual abstinence is more like abstinence from compulsive eating—that is, moderation—than it is like abstinence from compulsive drinking—that is, zero participation. On what theoretical basis has this critical judgment been made? Simple expediency.

*Where is the healthy model of sexuality?

The sexual addiction model of human sexuality is moralistic, arbitrary, misinformed, and narrow. *Excluded* from this model are using sex to feel good; having "bad" fantasies; and enjoying sex without being in love. Where is the theoretical justification for this moralistic position?

We've seen this before: the concept of sin as sickness. It has led to sincere attempts to "cure" homosexuality, nymphomania, and masturbation—by the world's leading social scientists, within our own lifetime.

It is outrageous to treat sexual problems without a healthy model of sexuality that relates to most people's experience. The sexual addiction concept shows a dramatic ignorance of the range of typical human sexuality.

At the end of competent sex therapy or psychotherapy treatment, the patient is a grown-up, able to make conscious sexual choices. Sex addiction treatment offers a patient the chance to be a recovering sex addict. Which would you rather be?

PROFESSIONAL IMPLICATIONS OF THE CONCEPT

*It reduces the credibility of sexologists.

Prospective patients are now asking therapists a new kind of question: "Are you in recovery yourself?" "Have you treated sex addicts before?" What if a

therapist is emotionally/sexually healthy and therefore *not* "in recovery"? Is s/he then disqualified as a professional?

The public, I'm afraid, is also getting a picture of us as being ivory tower types out of touch with the real—i.e., *destructive*—sexuality out on the street. They're feeling "You want to waste time discussing systems, regression, defenses, and meanwhile there are kids buying *Playboy* out there!"

*It replaces professional sexologists as relevant sex experts.

There are two groups of people behind this:
a) Addictionologists, often in recovery themselves (i.e., they have unresolved sexual and impulse control issues). They typically have little or no training in sexuality (e.g., I am told that Patrick Carnes' Ph.D. is in Counselor Education and Staff Development); and
b) 12-steppers themselves, lay people who love being in recovery. Their missionary zeal has nothing to do with science or clinical expertise. They freely generalize their own experience with sexual problems and "recovery" to all people and to human sexuality.

Both groups of people are now being quoted—and are actively portraying themselves—as sex experts.

By offering training from people with little or no sexological background, the concept suggests that all we offer is just another "theory" about sexual functioning. Just as creationists now want (and frequently get) "equal time" when scientists teach or discuss evolution, addictionologists now want—and are beginning to get—"equal time" regarding sexual functioning.

Graduates of such training programs believe that they have learned something about sexuality, when they haven't. They have learned something about *addiction*. And they are taught that they are competent to treat addiction in any form, whether its vehicle alcohol, food, gambling, love, or sex.

Addictionologists admit they lack skills in differential diagnosis. They and their 12-step programs let anyone define him/herself as a "sex addict." How many personality disorders, how much depression, how many adjustment reactions are being treated as "sex addiction"?

POLITICAL IMPLICATIONS OF THE CONCEPT

*It strengthens society's anti-sex forces.

"Sexual addiction" is the Right's newest justification for eliminating sex education, adult bookstores, and birth control clinics. They are using the same arguments to eliminate books like *The Color Purple* from school libraries. Businessman Richard Enrico, whose group Citizens Against Pornography eliminated the sale of *Playboy* magazine from all 1800 7–11 stores, did so, he says, "because smut causes sex addiction." And he was able to convince one of America's largest corporations of this complete fiction.

We should not be colluding with this destructive force.

*It emphasizes negative aspects of sex.

Sex addiction treatment is essentially creating a special interest group of people who feel victimized by their own sexuality. Not *others'* sexuality, like rape victims—their *own*. This lobby/interest group is growing as increasing numbers of people are recruited into identifying themselves as sex addicts. With the agenda of protecting people from their *own* sexuality, they are a dangerous group, easily exploited by the Right and other sex-negative points of view.

*It frightens people about the role of sexuality in social problems.

Increasingly, "sex addicts" and trainers are talking in public about how sexual impulses took over their lives and made them do things like steal money, take drugs, and see prostitutes.

This also frightens people about their ability to control their own sexuality—as if they're vulnerable to being taken over.

*It supports public ignorance about sexuality.

"Sex addicts" and trainers spread stories about how childhood masturbating to *Playboy* leads to porn addiction, and about how prostitutes become so alluring that people destroy their marriages. The public, of course, takes the additional step that this could happen to anyone—even though there is no data to support this idea.

The movement continues to spread dangerous lies about sex, even though the ultra-conservative Meese Commission was unable to find any evidence that pornography leads to child molestation, and even though no medical society in the world has ever proven that masturbation of any kind is harmful.

*It focuses on the "dignified" "purpose" of sex.

These words always seem to mean a rigid sex role system, with sex needing love to give it meaning. Sweating and moaning never seem dignified to people concerned with the dignity of sex. Ultimately, the "purpose" of sex can only be a political, rather than scientific, concept.

*It obscures the role of society in distorting our sexuality.

Sexologists understand that our moralistic American society constricts healthy sexual expression. We all know the sexual and intimacy problems this creates; in fact, we are now beginning to understand how such distortion even helps create sex offenders.

But the sexual addiction movement only sees society as encouraging promiscuity, instead of discouraging pleasure and healthy sexuality. This simplistic analysis cannot see how the media and other institutions make guilt-free sex almost impossible.

The sexual addiction concept attempts to heal society's sexual pain while keeping its economic, political, and social foundations intact. This is not only naive and ineffective, but dangerous.

WHY IS THE SEXUAL ADDICTION CONCEPT SO POPULAR?

*It distances personal responsibility for sexual choices.

As Dr. Domeena Renshaw says, "my illness makes me have affairs" is a very popular concept.

The concept seems to allow sexual expression without the punishment our infantile side fears. This is a great childhood fantasy. But the price is too high.

*It provides fellowship.

SA-type meetings provide structure and relaxed human contact for people who have trouble finding these in other ways.

The program also allows alcoholics in AA to work the steps again. This is one of the single biggest sources of self-described "sex addicts." In fact, Patrick Carnes claims that 83% of all sex addicts have some other kind of addiction.

*It provides pseudo-"scientific" support for the intuitive belief that sex is dangerous.

In doing so it legitimizes sex-negative attitudes, and supports sexual guilt.

*It lets people self-diagnose.

This is very American, very democratic. People like to feel they are taking charge of their lives, and self-diagnosing gives them the illusion that they are.

*It encourages people to split.

When people are troubled by their sexuality, it is comforting to imagine the problem "out there" rather than "in here." A striking example is Jimmy Swaggart, who railed against immorality out in the world, while behaving in the very ways he was condemning.

It also encourages a kind of splitting among *non*-"sex addicts." In answering the defensive question "how can people be sexual like *that*?," it makes people who behave in certain ways essentially *different* (they're "addicted") from us "normal" folk. Basically, people use the concept of sexual addiction as a projection of their fear about their own sexuality. Its very existence is sort of an exorcism of sexuality on a societal level.

*It helps people get distance from their sexual shame.

Most of us have deep shame about our sexuality—either our overt behavior, or the more primitive urges and images left over from childhood that we've never accepted. This profound sense of shame is what people would really like to get rid of; the behavioral symptoms they're supposedly addicted to are just a symbol of that shame.

SA-type groups reframe this shame into a positive thing. It becomes a badge for membership; it lets "addicts" know they're heading toward a solution; it affirms that a sex-crazed society is victimizing them; and it suggests they're being too hard on themselves.

Good therapy does the opposite. It helps people feel their shame, relate it to an even deeper pain, and temporarily feel worse—before helping them resolve it.

WHY DO SO MANY PEOPLE CLAIM TO GET RELIEF FROM SEXUAL ADDICTION PROGRAMS?

First, we should keep in mind that simply because people claim that something gives them emotional relief doesn't mean it works in the way they claim. Astrology apparently helped reduce Nancy Reagan's anxiety about Ron's career; but that doesn't mean it actually helped him make better decisions.

*The recovery process can be emotionally reassuring for many people.

It offers structure, goals, fellowship, and an accepting social environment. In fact, since most of the talk at SA-type groups is about sex and relationships, it's a relatively easy place to meet people for dating. And that *does* go on.

Conversation at SA-type meetings is exclusively about material that each individual is already focusing on. Thus, *all* conversation feels like it's about the individual "addict," and so participants can feel connected with others without having to abandon their own narcissistic focus. This feels intimate, and gives the illusion that an individual is making progress.

And, of course, virtually everyone gets to hear stories of people who are worse off than they are, and so they feel better.

*People enjoy feeling like they're heading somewhere.

While "addicts" learn to enjoy the *process* of recovery, they also learn they're never going to fully *get* there. So they set their sights lower—and *do* accomplish never being cured.

Because the sexual addiction movement is not interested in personality change, it can offer symptom relief without any ethical conflicts. In many cases people do get that relief—although it's at the expense of the rest of their character structure.

Finally, as "addicts" continue learning how to distance themselves from their "bad" sexuality, they feel an increasing sense of direction and relief.

*Addicts transfer some of their compulsivity to the SA-type group meeting itself.

For many "sex addicts," meetings (sometimes many times per week) are the most important part of the week. In a predictable setting and way, with comforting regularity, they get to listen to and talk about sexual feelings and behavior they dislike.

This feeling is perfectly conveyed by a "sex addict" quoted in *Contemporary Sexuality*. He notes that "Every Thursday night for the past year and a half I have repeated that statement [about his so-called "addiction"] to my 12-step support group." By itself this is a trivial point; in the context of a program supposed to heal compulsive behavior, it is troubling.

WHAT ABOUT SEXUAL COMPULSIVITY?

Most self-described sex addicts aren't out of control; they are relatively "normal" neurotics for whom being in control is *painful*. In fact, as the National Association of Sexual Addiction Problems says, "most addicts do not break the law, nor do they satisfy their need by forcing themselves upon others."

Those who are *really* sexually compulsive are typically psychotic, sociopathic, character-disordered, etc. Some of these people have impaired reality testing. Others have absolutely no concern about the consequences of their behavior. Dr. Renshaw states that "undifferentiated sexual urgency is a symptom of manic-depression."

These people don't need help laying off one day at a time. They need deep therapy, medication, structured behavioral interventions, or other intensive modalities. Dr. Eli Coleman, for example, reports treatment success with lithium, comparable to the clinical results lithium produces with other compulsives.

It is absolutely indefensible to suggest that the same mechanism is operating in the rapist and the guy who masturbates "too often." The concept of sexual addiction does nothing to diagnose serious problems, assess danger, discuss beliefs about sex, take a history, or change personality. There are no treatment statistics on *true* obsessive-compulsives via the sexual addiction model.

We must also, and this is much harder, continue to resist and interpret society's demand for simple answers and easy solutions about sex offenders.

Sexual energy scares people; distorted expressions of that energy terrify people. We need to continually educate policymakers and the public as to why the treatment of sex offenders is so complex and difficult, and why quick-fix solutions are worse than partial solutions. We must find a way to say "I don't know" or "We're still working on it" without apologizing. Cancer researchers, for example, have done a good job of making partial answers—like early detection and quitting smoking—acceptable.

SUMMARY

The concept of "sex addiction" really rests on the assumption that sex is dangerous. There's the sense that we frail humans are vulnerable to the Devil's temptations of pornography, masturbation, and extramarital affairs, and that if we yield, we become "addicted."

Without question, being a sexual person is complex, and we *are* vulnerable—to our sex-negative heritage, shame about our bodies, and conflict about the exciting sexual feelings we can't express without risking rejection. Sexuality per se, however, is not dangerous—no matter how angry or frightened people are.

Professional sexologists should reject any model suggesting that people must spend their lives 1) in fear of sexuality's destructive power; 2) being powerless about sexuality; 3) lacking the tools to relax and let sex take over when it's appropriate.

Addictionologists have cynically misled the public into thinking that "sexual addiction" is a concept respected and used by professional therapists and educators. Even a brief look at our literature, conferences, and popular writing shows how rarely this is true. But addictionologists don't care about sexual truth or expertise—only about addiction.

The sexual addiction movement is not harmless. These people are missionaries who want to put everyone in the missionary position.

In these terrible anti-sex times, one of our most important jobs is to reaffirm that sexuality—though complicated—is precious, not dangerous. Now more than ever, our job is to help people just say yes.

POSTSCRIPT

Can Sex Be an Addiction?

One of the most basic and hotly debated questions in human sexuality is: "What is normal sexual behavior?" Carnes assumes that his judgment of what is normal sexual behavior is shared by the majority of Americans. But even if Carnes's assumption of normal behavior is correct, Klein denies that this subjective judgment justifies labeling those who do not accept this social norm as "addicts."

Definitions and labels can be powerful instruments of social control. For example, if homosexuality is labeled an "abnormal, unnatural, and psychologically disordered behavior pattern," then society can legitimately make laws punishing such behavior, and religious groups can oppose legislation that would protect the civil rights of gay males and lesbians. If a human being exists from the first moment of conception, then abortion of an embryo or fetus at any time after fertilization can be properly defined as "homicide," and society can take whatever steps it finds necessary to protect the "inalienable rights" of the unborn person in the womb. Likewise, defining certain behaviors or relationships as "addictions" brings into consideration important personal, social, and medical consequences.

The recent flurry of popular books on addictions to relationships, love, romance, and sex suggests that Americans, for whatever reasons, are fascinated by the subject and perhaps looking for answers. Deciding where a healthy behavior ends and addiction begins can be a difficult undertaking.

SUGGESTED READINGS

S. Bakos, "How Much Sex (Even Just Thinking About It) Is Too Much?" *Cosmopolitan* (August 1992).

A. L. Bardach, "A Fever in the Blood," *Vanity Fair* (January 1991).

R. J. Barth and B. R. Kinder, "The Mislabeling of Sexual Compulsion," *Journal of Sex and Marital Therapy* (1987).

P. J. Carnes, *Don't Call It Love* (Bantam Books, 1992).

E. Coleman, "Sexual Compulsion vs. Sexual Addiction: The Debate Continues," *SIECUS Report* (July 1986).

J. Diamond, *Looking for Love in All the Wrong Places: Overcoming Romantic and Sexual Addictions* (Putnam Publishing Group, 1988).

B. Dolan, "Do People Get Hooked on Sex?" *Time* (June 4, 1990).

M. P. Levine and R. R. Troiden, "The Myth of Sexual Compulsivity," *Journal of Sex Research* (1987).

E. Rapping, "Hooked on a Feeling," *The Nation* (March 5, 1990).

E. Rapping, "Exchange of Views," *The Nation* (May 21, 1990).

A. M. Schaef, *Escape from Intimacy: Untangling the "Love" Addictions: Sex, Romance, Relationships* (Harper & Row, 1989).

ISSUE 3

Is Rape Motivated by Aggression Instead of Sex?

YES: A. Nicholas Groth and H. Jean Birnbaum, from *Men Who Rape: The Psychology of the Offender* (Plenum Press, 1979)

NO: Craig T. Palmer, from "Twelve Reasons Why Rape Is Not Sexually Motivated: A Skeptical Examination," *Journal of Sex Research* (November 1988)

ISSUE SUMMARY

YES: Clinical psychologists A. Nicholas Groth and H. Jean Birnbaum argue that rape is not primarily a sexual act but one of hostility, degradation, and anger, often not resulting in sexual arousal at all.

NO: Professor Craig T. Palmer claims that the arguments that present rape as being motivated primarily by anger, rage, the need for power, or sadism are illogical, based on inaccurate definitions, untestable, or inconsistent with the actual behavior of rapists.

In the past 20 years, the feminist movement has radically changed society's image of rape. Today, the treatment of rape victims by the police, courts, and general public is fairer and more humane as compared to past practices. Rape victims are no longer viewed as inviting their rapes. Women are much more aware of how they can avoid rape situations and defend themselves when confronted. The reality of marital rape is now legally recognized. Rape is no longer a joke. In all these changes, the efforts of feminists have been crucial.

In the process, feminism has also changed the way the rapist and what motivates him are viewed. Prior to the early 1970s, most researchers of rape assumed that the primary motive behind rape was sexual. Feminists challenged this view, arguing that rape is unrelated to male sexuality. Rape, they claimed, is an act of violence and domination that is characteristic of American patriarchal and sexist traditions. In the early 1970s, this view was pioneered by Kate Millet, Susan Griffin, and Germaine Greer. It soon became a focal point of feminist theory. In 1975, Susan Brownmiller's book *Against Our Will: Men, Women and Rape* popularized the "not for sex" explanation of rape. In the aftermath of Brownmiller's book, the "not for sex" explanation of rape was widely adopted by feminists and nonfeminists alike.

As an act of violence and domination, rape was said to express the rapists' anger and rage: they used sex to gain control and power over women. And in the extreme case of sadistic rape, men used sexual pain to achieve pleasure. In 1979 A. Nicholas Groth, currently the director of the Sex Offender Treatment Program at the Wyoming State Honor Farm, provided evidence for the "not for sex" explanation with clinical data on convicted rapists. In subsequent years, Groth and H. Jean Birnbaum's book *Men Who Rape* became the bible of those working with rapists and their victims. The "not for sex" explanation was repeated in all the literature on sexual assaults. By 1980, according to C. Warner (*Rape and Sexual Assault: Management and Intervention* [Aspen, 1980]), it was "generally accepted by criminologists, psychologists, and other professionals working with rapists and rape victims that rape is not primarily a sexual crime, it is a crime of violence."

But not all researchers were entirely convinced by the "not for sex" explanation. In recent years, some researchers have continued to endorse the feminist explanation but imply that sex might be a factor in some rapes.

In the following selections, A. Nicholas Groth and H. Jean Birnbaum, in support of the "not for sex" theory, describe three categories of rape that they feel illustrate the aggression model. Craig T. Palmer maintains that motivation for rape is untestable; he then offers rebuttal to several of the "not for sex" theory's supporting arguments.

YES

A. Nicholas Groth
and H. Jean Birnbaum

ANGER, POWER, AND SADISM ARE THE PRIMARY MOTIVES FOR RAPE

One of the most basic observations one can make regarding men who rape is that not all such offenders are alike. They do not do the very same thing in the very same way or for the very same reasons. In some cases, similar acts occur for different reasons, and in other cases, different acts serve similar purposes. From our clinical experience with convicted offenders and with victims of reported sexual assault, we find that in *all* cases of forcible rape, three components are present: power, anger, and sexuality. The hierarchy and interrelationships among these three factors, together with the relative intensity with which each is experienced and the variety of ways in which each is expressed, vary from one offender to another. Nevertheless, there seems to be sufficient clustering within the broad spectrum of sexual assault so that distinguishable patterns of rape can be differentiated based on the descriptive characteristics of the assault and the dynamic characteristics of the offender.

Rape is always and foremost an aggressive act. In some offenses, the assault appears to constitute a discharge of anger; it becomes evident that rape is the way the offender expresses and discharges a mood state of intense anger, frustration, resentment, and rage. In other offenses, the aggression seems to be reactive; that is, when the victim resists the advances of her assailant, he retaliates by striking, hitting, or hurting her in some way. Hostility appears to be quickly triggered or released, sometimes in a clear, consciously experienced state of anger or, in other cases, in what appears to be a panic state. In still other offenses, the aggression becomes expressed less as an anger motive and more as a means of dominating, controlling, and being in charge of the situation—an expression of mastery and conquest. And in a fourth viscissitude, the aggression itself becomes eroticized so that the offender derives pleasure from both controlling his victim and hurting her/him—an intense sense of excitement and pleasure being experienced in this context whether or not actual sexual contact is made. These variations on the theme of aggression are not mutually exclusive, and, in any given instance of rape, multiple meanings may be expressed in regard to both the sexual and the aggressive behaviors.

In every act of rape, both aggression and sexuality are involved, but it is clear that sexuality becomes the means of expressing the aggressive needs and feelings that operate in the offender and underlie his assault. Three basic patterns of rape can be distinguished in this regard: (1) the *anger rape*, in which sexuality becomes a hostile act; (2) the *power rape*, in which sexuality becomes an expression of conquest; and (3) the *sadistic rape*, in which anger and power become eroticized.

Rape is complex and multidetermined. It serves a number of psychological aims and purposes. Whatever other needs and factors operate in the commission of such an offense, however, we have found the components of anger, power, and sexuality always present and prominent. Moreover, in our experience, we find that either anger or power is the dominant component and that rape, rather than being primarily an expression of sexual desire, is, in fact, the use of sexuality to express these issues of power and anger. Rape, then, is a pseudosexual act, a pattern of sexual behavior that is concerned much more with status, hostility, control, and dominance than with sensual pleasure or sexual satisfaction. It is sexual behavior in the primary service of nonsexual needs.

ANGER RAPE

In some cases of sexual assault, it is very apparent that sexuality becomes a means of expressing and discharging feelings of pent-up anger and rage. The assault is characterized by physical brutality. Far more actual force is used in the commission of the offense than would be necessary if the intent were simply to overpower the victim and achieve sexual penetration. Instead, this type of offender *attacks* his victim, grabbing her, striking her, knocking her to the ground, beating her, tearing her clothes, and raping her. He may use a blitz style of attack, a violent surprise offensive, in which the victim is caught completely off guard. Or he may use a confidence-style approach to gain access to the victim and then launch a sudden, overpowering attack. In the former situation, the offender approaches the victim directly by hitting her. In the latter situation, victims often relate that at first the assailant seemed pleasant enough, but that at some point he changed. Suddenly and without warning he became mean and angry. His later behavior was in sharp contrast to the initial impression:

Listening to how the victims described me in court, the impression that I got was almost a Jekyll and Hyde. I approached all of my victims in a very acceptable manner, but then I seemed to change suddenly. When I went into these bars, I was looking for someone that would be comfortable. I was looking for people to talk to, and these women were willing to talk to me. But during the course of sitting and talking, something would happen inside of me, the anger would erupt. The assault with intent to rape wasn't it—I was trying to kill them!

The rape experience for this type of offender is one of conscious anger and rage, and he expresses his fury both physically and verbally. His aim is to hurt and debase his victim, and he expresses his contempt for her through abusive and profane language. If his primary motive is one of anger, and if he is not sexually motivated, why doesn't this offender confine his assault to a battering of the victim? Why does he also rape her? The answer seems to be that such a man considers rape the ultimate offense he can commit against another person. Sex becomes his weapon, and rape constitutes the ultimate expression of his anger:

> I wanted to knock the woman off her pedestal, and I felt rape was the worst thing I could do to her.

Often this type of offender forces the victim to submit to or to perform additional sexual acts that he may regard as particularly degrading, such as sodomy or fellatio. In some cases, contempt for the victim is expressed by urinating or by masturbating and ejaculating onto her.

Characteristically, this type of offender does not report being in a state of sexual excitement or arousal. In fact, he may be initially impotent during the assault and able to achieve an erection only by masturbating himself or having the victim perform oral sex on him. Sexuality itself is typically regarded by this type of offender as something basically "dirty" and offensive at some level of his subjective experience, and, therefore, it becomes a weapon, a means by which he can defile, degrade, and humiliate his victim. The anger rapist typically finds little or no sexual gratification in the rape—in fact, his subjective reaction to the sexual act itself is frequently one of revulsion and disgust. Satisfaction and relief result from the discharge of anger rather than from sexual gratification:

> I was enraged when I started out. I lost control and struck out with violence. After the assault I felt relieved. I felt I had gotten even. There was no sexual satisfaction; in fact, I felt a little disgusted. I felt relieved of the tension and anger for a while, but then it would start to build again, little things, but I couldn't shake them off.

Typically, such an offender reports that he did not anticipate committing a rape. It was not something he fantasized or thought about beforehand—it was, instead, something that happened on the spur of the moment. Sometimes he will say that he felt "something was going to happen" but could not identify or anticipate what course of action his feelings would lead to. Even during the offense itself the offender may psychologically dissociate himself from the assault as if he were in a trance or were more an observer than a participant; the event is experienced as unreal, and the offender may not fully appreciate the extent of his aggression:

> It wasn't until afterwards, it wasn't until after I had been able to get rid of all the anger and all the feelings that I had inside of me that I could in some ways come back to the real situation and to what I had done. And, in that way, I did in a sense sort of feel like I became an animal, and it was only then that I felt very upset by what I had done.

Relatively speaking, such attacks tend to be of short duration. The offender strikes, assaults, and flees. Such assaults appear to be more impulsive or spontaneous than premeditated, and the offender finds it difficult to account for his assault, when he cannot deny it, except to rationalize that he was intoxicated or on drugs, or that he just "flipped out":

My offense was pretty bad. I believe I was flipped out at the time. I have no defense at all. I was drunk. I was standing on the corner and—I don't know. I don't know what the hell happened. I just was standing around, and I saw this girl pull up in her car, and I didn't see her face or anything. I just saw her pull up to the stoplight, and I walked up to the car, opened the door, pushed her over to the passenger side, and I took off with her in the car. And I can't be sure why I did it, but, anyway, I took off with her and got her to an area that I thought was a good place, and I got out of the car and hit her. I hit her right in the eye, and I still don't know why I raped her.

In describing the evolution of the assault, the offender typically reports being in an upset and distressed frame of mind at the time of the offense. His predominant mood state appears to be a combination of anger, distress, frustration, and depression, and the offense itself is typically preceded by some upsetting event, often, but not invariably, involving some significant woman in the assailant's life. The assault is in response to some identifiable precipitating stress. For example, some offenders reported a serious dispute with their wives prior to the offense. These arguments revolved around a number of marital issues, such as the wife's threatening to or, in fact, leaving him, arguments over his drinking, complaints about her housekeeping skills, suspicions of infidelity, and the like. Others felt aggravated with their parents for imposing unfair restrictions on their activities or unjust punishments for their misbehavior. Some offenders

cited conflicts with their girlfriends, such as being stood up, rejected, taunted, or sexually frustrated. Others reported feeling upset over such things as being rejected from military service, being fired, being burdened by financial debts, or being harassed in some fashion by other people. The common theme appeared to be one in which the offender felt that he had been wronged, hurt, put down, or treated unjustly in some fashion by some individual, situation, or event. Rape served to discharge the resulting anger, resentment, and frustration. In this fashion, the anger rapist revenges himself for what he perceives to be wrongs done him by others, especially women.

The anger rapist's relationships to important persons in his life are frequently fraught with conflict, irritation, and aggravation. The anger, resentment, hostility, and frustration engendered in these relationships is often displaced onto other individuals, and, therefore, the victim may be a complete stranger to the offender, someone who has been unfortunate enough to be in his presence at the point at which his controls begin to fail and his rage erupts. Although she has done nothing to warrant it, she becomes the target of his revenge—not revenge in a calculated, planned fashion but, instead, the recipient of an impulsive reaction precipitated by a situation she has had no part in. . . .

POWER RAPE

In another pattern of rape, power appears to be the dominant factor motivating the offender. In these assaults, it is not the offender's desire to harm his victim but to possess her sexually. Sexuality becomes a means of compensating for underlying feelings of inadequacy and serves to express issues of mastery, strength, control, authority, identity, and capability. His goal is sexual conquest, and he uses only the amount of force necessary to accomplish this objective. His aim is to capture and control his victim. He may accomplish this through verbal threat ("Do what I say and you won't get hurt!"), intimidation with a weapon ("I came up behind her and put a knife to her throat and told her to come with me"), and/or physical force ("I told her to undress, and when she refused I struck her across the face to show her I meant business"). Physical aggression is used to overpower and subdue the victim, and its use is directed toward achieving sexual submission. The intent of the offender usually is to achieve sexual intercourse with his victim as evidence of conquest, and to accomplish this, he resorts to whatever force he finds necessary to overcome his victim's resistance and to render her helpless. Very often, the victim is kidnapped or held captive in some fashion, and she may be subjected to repeated assaults over an extended period of time.

Such offenders entertain obsessional thoughts and masturbatory fantasies about sexual conquest and rape. The characteristic scenario is one in which the victim initially resists the sexual advances of her assailant; he overpowers her and achieves sexual penetration; in spite of herself, the victim cannot resist her assailant's sexual prowess and becomes sexually aroused and receptive to his embrace:

The fantasies began with going out to a nightclub or bar and picking up a girl, and these changed to increasingly more drastic attempts. I'd think about either going to big parking lots or to a quiet

area where there might be girls walking and confronting them. I began to have the thought that perhaps sometime if I did this, that the woman would agree or perhaps almost attack me—perhaps just my appearance or whatever would just turn her on and she would almost literally attack me in a complete state of sexual excitement, that she would rape me as if I were just what she had been waiting for. I would fantasize about confronting a girl with a weapon, a knife or a gun, and that she would tell me that I didn't need it and that she wanted me, and that she wanted me sexually. She would say, "No, you don't need it, you don't need a gun, you don't need any of this, you're enough."

Since it constitutes a test of his competency, the rape experience for this type of offender is a mixture of excitement, anxiety, anticipated pleasure, and fear:

I don't know how to explain the feeling I got. My heart just started to pound, and I got sort of a funny feeling in the pit of my stomach, sort of like the feeling I had the first time I ever had sexual intercourse, and I felt that I had to go out and get her. I didn't have an erection at all; I just had the feeling and desire to have a woman.

In reality, the offender tends to find little sexual satisfaction in the rape. The assault is disappointing, for it never lives up to his fantasy:

It never came down the way I imagined it would. In the fantasy, after the initial shock of the attack, I thought the victim would be more accepting and responsive, but, in reality, that was not the case. I did not have the good feelings I fantasized about. I felt let down. I didn't experience the same feelings in the actual assault that I had expected to feel. Everything was pleasurable in the fantasy, and there was acceptance, whereas in the reality of the situation, it wasn't pleasurable, and the girl was scared, not turned on to me.

Whatever he may tell himself to explain the situation, at some level of experience he senses that he has not found what he is looking for in the offense—something he cannot clearly identify or define is missing or lacking. He does not feel reassured by either his own performance or his victim's response to the assault, and, therefore, he must go out and find another victim, this time "the right one." His offenses become repetitive and compulsive, and he may commit a whole series of rapes over a relatively short period of time:

I felt I needed something more. I just felt that there was something more, and that I had to have it. I really felt a compulsion, I mean a strong . . . something. It's funny. Even when these assaults happened, my life, my wife, my responsibilities, my parents, and so forth would flash in front of my mind, but it seemed to be of no consequence. I mean, I just had to no matter what. The crime itself just frustrated me more. I wasn't sexually aroused. I had to force myself. I felt some relief coming off because there was some tension release, but very shortly afterwards the feelings were worse. I blamed the victim and felt it was her fault and that a different girl would give me the satisfaction I craved, so I went out looking for another victim.

The amount of force used in the assaults may vary depending in part on situational factors, but there may be an increase in aggression over time as the offender becomes more desperate to achieve that indefinable experience that continues to elude him:

Somehow I felt that I had not accomplished what I wanted to. The first three victims I approached resisted in some way or other—they just sort of laughed in my face—so the next time I went out, I took a knife with me. And even when I succeeded in committing a rape, the fantasies didn't go away; they just intensified, and I got more and more aggressive.

The offenses themselves are either premeditated (the offender goes out in search of a victim with the clear intent of sexual assault) or opportunistic (a situation presents itself in which the offender unexpectedly finds that he has access to a victim and this access activates his propensity for sexual assault).

The victim of the power rapist may be of any age but generally tends to be within the same age range as the offender or younger. The choice of a victim is predominantly determined by availability, accessibility, and vulnerability. As one offender put it, "I always looked for a victim who was smaller than me."

Although the power rapist may report that his offense was prompted by a desire for sexual gratification, careful examination of his behavior typically reveals that efforts to negotiate the sexual encounter or to determine the woman's receptiveness to a sexual approach are noticeably absent, as are any attempts at lovemaking or foreplay. Instead, the aim of the offender is to capture, conquer, and control his victim. Sexual desire, in and of itself, is not the primary or paramount issue operating in this assailant. If it were, there are a number of opportunities available in our society for consensual sex. In fact, sexual assaults always coexist with consenting sexual relations in the life of the offender. In no case have we ever found that rape was the first or only sexual experience in the offender's sexual history, or that he had no other alternatives or outlets for his sexual desires. To the question, "If what you wanted was sex, why didn't you just go to a prostitute?" the power rapist is likely to reply, "A real man never pays for it," revealing that one of the dynamics in the assault is reaffirmation of his manhood. Such offenders feel insecure about their masculinity or conflicted about their identity. . . .

One of the key issues in working with victims of power rapes is their anger at themselves and self-blame for being victimized and not being able to escape the assault. It is important to help them realize that no strategy would necessarily have been more effective than the one they tried. What deters one assailant only encourages another, but frequently the victim feels that if she had said or done something different, she could have discouraged the assault. And it is this feeling of not having achieved her primary goal—that of escaping the offender—that affects the victim and retards her recovery from the trauma of sexual assault.

SADISTIC RAPE

In a third pattern of rape, both sexuality and aggression become fused into a single psychological experience known as *sadism*. There is a sexual transformation of anger and power so that aggression itself become eroticized. This offender finds the intentional maltreatment of his victim intensely gratifying and takes pleasure in her torment, anguish, distress, helplessness, and suffering. The assault usually involves bondage and torture and frequently has a bizarre or ritualistic quality to it. The offender may subject his victim to curious actions, such as clipping her hair, washing or cleansing her body, or forcing her to dress in some specific fashion or behave in some specified way. Such indignities are accompanied by explicitly abusive acts, such as biting, burning the victim with cigarettes, and flagellation. Sexual areas of the victim's body (her breasts, genitals, and buttocks) become a specific focus of injury and abuse. In some cases, the rape may not involve the offender's sexual organs. Instead, he may use some type of instrument or foreign object, such as a stick or bottle, with which to penetrate his victim sexually:

> My intention from the outset was to give my victims an enema and follow it with anal sex, but in most cases I "came off" during the enema without requiring anal entry. I have found as much pleasure, if not more, reaching a climax with masturbation during the administration of the enema—sodomy or coitus being unnecessary.

In extreme cases—those involving sexual homicide—there may be grotesque acts, such as the sexual mutilation of the victim's body or sexual intercourse with her corpse. Eric, an infamous sex killer, committed four grisly murders in the span of one summer. As described in the pathologist's report, each victim had been dismembered into five parts. The skin was peeled off the breasts and vagina. On the legs and buttocks, there were multiple stab wounds and punctures. Stab wounds were also present in the anterior chest wall. Sperm were found in both the vagina and the rectum of the body, and findings were consistent with its having been deposited postmortem. . . .

MULTIPLE MOTIVES UNDERLYING RAPE

Regardless of the pattern of the assault, rape is a complex act that serves a number of retaliatory and compensatory aims in the psychological functioning of the offender. It is an effort to discharge his anger, contempt, and hostility toward women—to hurt, degrade, and humiliate. It is an effort to counteract feelings of vulnerability and inadequacy in himself and to assert his strength and power—to control and exploit. It is an effort to deny sexual anxieties and doubts and reaffirms his identity, competency, and manhood. It is an effort to retain status (in gang rape) among male peers, and it is an effort to achieve sexual gratification. Rape is equivalent to symptom formation in that it serves to defend against anxiety, to express a conflict, and gratify an impulse. It is symptomatic of personality dysfunction, associated more with conflict and stress than with pleasure and satisfaction. Sexuality is not the only—nor the primary—motive underlying rape. It is, however, the means through which conflicts surrounding issues of anger and power become discharged. Rape is always a combination of anger, power, and sexuality, and each of these components must be examined in evaluating the offender and assessing the impact of the assault on the victim and the nature of her trauma.

NO
Craig T. Palmer

TWELVE REASONS WHY RAPE IS NOT SEXUALLY MOTIVATED: A SKEPTICAL EXAMINATION

The first step in evaluating the "not sex" explanation of rape is to establish exactly what the debate is over. Thanks to the feminist movement, no one any longer defends the dangerous claim that rape is a sexually arousing or sought-after experience on the part of the *victim*. Neither does anyone deny that male sex organs are necessarily involved in the act. The debate is over the motivation of the rapist in using his sex organs in a way that constitutes rape. Motivation refers to the purpose or goal of a behavior. Proponents of the "not sex" explanation hold that the occurrence of rape cannot be accounted for by the hypothesis that sexual stimulation is the *goal* of rapists. These authors hold that the occurrence of rape can only be explained by the hypothesis that sex is just a *means* used to attain the goals of power, control, domination, and violence.

Unfortunately, motivation is a covert entity, existing solely in the minds of individuals (either consciously or unconsciously). The problem with viewing motivation as covert is that such an entity is not externally identifiable. Statements about motivation *in this sense* are completely untestable. No data of any kind could falsify a statement about such a "motivation."

Vague semantics have also clouded the issue of whether sex is a "means" or an "end" for rapists. For example, Bercovitch et al. state that "Human rape seems to be an outcome of status assertive by males which acts as a form of power domination used to copulate with a female who could not be attained with conventional methods" (Bercovitch et al., in press). This statement appears to imply that sex (i.e., "copulation") is the sought-after goal of rape, since "power" is "used to" accomplish this goal. However, the authors use this statement to support the claim that "Rape is probably not primarily a sexually motivated phenomenon" (ibid.).

While the literature of rape motivation is often clouded by vague semantics and uncheckable claims, the issue "is an important one, and how the

From Craig T. Palmer, "Twelve Reasons Why Rape Is Not Sexually Motivated: A Skeptical Examination," *Journal of Sex Research*, vol. 25, no. 4 (November 1988), pp. 512–530. Copyright © 1988 by *Journal of Sex Research*. Reprinted by permission.

verdict is rendered determines whether fundamental matters are obfuscated or come into more useful analytical light" (Geis & Huston, 1980, p. 187). Consequently, the present paper attempts to resolve this controversy by examining 12 arguments given to support the "not sex" explanation.

SUPPORTING ARGUMENTS FOR THE "NOT SEX" EXPLANATION

Argument 1

> When they say sex or sexual, these social scientists and feminists mean the *motivation*, moods, or drives associated with honest courtship and pair bonding. In such situations, males report feelings of tenderness, affection, joy and so on. . . . It is this sort of pleasurable motivation that the socioculturists (and feminists) denote as sexuality. . . . (Shields & Shields, 1983, p. 122; original emphasis)

The validity of this argument depends on the accuracy of its definition of "sex," and there appears to be considerable evidence that this definition of sex is unduly limiting. First,

> it is abundantly self evident . . . that a large percentage of males have no difficulty in divorcing sex from love. Whistles and wolf-calls, attendance at burlesque shows, patronizing of call girls and prostitutes—all of these are probably manifestations of a sexual urge totally or largely bereft of romantic feelings. (Hagen, 1979, pp. 158-159)

More fundamentally, the word "sexual" (but not "tenderness," "affection," or "joy") is routinely used to refer to the motivation of non-human animals involved in reproductive acts.

Argument 2

> Rape is not sexually motivated because of the "fact that most rapists have stable sexual partners." (Sanford & Fetter, 1979, p. 8)

This widely mentioned argument (Brownmiller, 1975; Finkelhor & Yllo, 1985; Groth, 1979a; Groth & Hobson, 1983; Medea & Thomson, 1974; Queen's Bench Foundation, 1978; Rada, 1978a; Rodabaugh & Austin, 1981; Shields & Shields, 1983) hinges on the assumption that a male's sexual desire is exhausted by a single "outlet." Symons points out that this does not appear to be true: "Most patrons of prostitutes, adult bookstores, and adult movie theatres are married men, but this is not considered evidence for lack of sexual motivation" (Symons, 1979, p. 280).

Argument 3

> Rape is not sexually motivated because rapes are often "premeditated." (See Brownmiller, 1975; Griffin, 1971)

The fact that many rapes are premeditated does not nullify that many rapes are also spontaneous. However, this argument presumes that all sexually motivated behavior is spontaneous. Obviously, this is untrue since there are many kinds of consenting sexual acts (affairs, rendezvous, seductions) which are highly planned and still considered to be sexually motivated (see Symons, 1979, p. 279).

Argument 4

> The age distribution of rapists demonstrates that rape is a crime of violence and aggression instead of sex:
> the violence prone years for males extend from their teenage years into their late forties, this is the age range into which most

rapists fall. *Unlike sexuality*, aggression does diminish with age and, therefore, a male's likelihood of committing a rape diminishes with the onset of middle age. (Groth and Hodson, 1983, p. 161; my emphasis)

It is unfortunate that the authors of this argument do not cite the basis for their claim that the human male sexual drive does *not* decrease with age. There is abundant evidence that numerous types of male sexual activity peak in the late teens and then slowly diminish (Kinsey, Pomeroy, & Martin, 1948; Goethals, 1971). Not only does the age of most rapists fail to disprove that rape is sexually motivated, the general correlation between the age distribution of rapists and the general level of sexual activity of males is very consistent with the view that rape *is* sexually motivated.

Argument 5

The common occurrence of rape in war shows that rape is motivated by hostility instead of sex. (See Brownmiller, 1975, pp. 23-118; Shields & Shields, 1983)

The prevalance of rape during war has indeed been well documented by Brownmiller and others. However, the writers who see this as evidence of a lack of sexual motivation are often the same ones who stress that vulnerability is a critical variable in victim selection (see Shields & Shields, 1983). Females in war situations are vulnerable to an exceptional degree. While hostility may be involved in any rape, the tremendously high degree of female vulnerability is both a sufficient and more parsimonious explanation of the high frequency of rape in war situations. Thus, the high frequency of rape during war is not evidence for the absence, or even unimpor-

tance, of sexual motivation. In fact, Brownmiller herself implies the importance of sexual motivation by reporting that: "In some of the camps, pornographic movies were shown to the soldiers, 'in an obvious attempt to work the men up' " (Brownmiller, 1975, p. 83; see also Medea & Thompson, 1974, p. 32).

Argument 6

Instead of being a sexually motivated act, rape is a form of "social control" because it is used as a form of punishment in some societies. (See Brownmiller, 1975, p. 319)

Symons clearly demonstrates the problem with this argument by pointing out that the use of rape as a punishment "does not prove that sexual feelings are not also involved, any more than the deprivation of property as punishment proves that the property is not valuable to the punisher" (Symons, 1979, p. 280).

Argument 7

"Men have been asked why they raped and many have said it was not out of sexual desire but for power and control over their victims." (Dean & de Bruynkopps, 1982, p. 233; citing evidence from Groth, 1979a; see also Shields & Shields, 1983, p. 121)

This might appear to be the simplest way to decide the issue—just ask rapists. However, such an approach requires the problematical assumption that one clearly experiences, remembers, and truthfully reports his motives. Such an assumption is especially troublesome when the subjects in question are convicts: "It is difficult to avoid the conclusion that the men's conscious attempts to emphasize their correct attitudes and to minimize their sexual impulsiveness were to some extent calculated to foster the impression that they no longer constituted a threat" (Symons, 1979, p. 283).

Even if the truthfulness of rapists' statements could be assumed, there is still the problem of *interpretation*. Symons (1979, pp. 282-283) cites several questionable interpretations present in the literature at that time (also see the Queen's Bench Foundation, 1978). This problem became particularly crucial with the subsequent publication of Groth's influential book *Men Who Rape*. Not only did Groth's interpretations go against other findings such as those by Smithyman (1978, p. iv) in which 84% of the rapists cited sexual motivation "solely or in part" as the cause of their acts (see also Ageton, 1983; Geis, 1977; Katz & Mazur, 1979; Rada, 1978a; Russell, 1975; Sussman & Bordwell, 1981), but even the examples Groth selected to support his argument make his interpretations questionable. One rapist explains his behavior by saying, "She stood there in her nightgown, and you could see right through it—you could see her nipples and breasts and, you know they were just waiting for me, and it was just too much of a temptation to pass up" (Groth, 1979a, p. 38). Another rapist reported that "I just wanted to have sex with her and that was all" (Groth, 1979a, p. 42; see also Groth, 1979a, pp. 50, 55, 93, 159, 161, 181, and 183).

Groth's reasons for not considering such statements as evidence for sexual motivation being primary in rape are interesting in light of some of the previously discredited arguments:

Although the power rapist [by far the most common type in Groth's classification] may report that his offense was prompted by a desire for sexual gratification, careful examination of his behavior typically reveals that efforts to negotiate the sexual encounter or to determine the woman's receptiveness to a sexual approach are noticeably absent, as are any attempts at lovemaking or foreplay. (Groth, 1979a, p. 28)

Here again we see an attempt to redefine "sex." This time it must include concern for the other person's arousal to "really" be sexual. Even if this was true, some of Groth's own examples show evidence of negotiation and foreplay (Groth, 1979a, p. 29). Other studies on victims have found that many rapes, particularly "date rapes," often involve extensive negotiation and foreplay (e.g., Ageton, 1983; Katz & Mazur, 1979; Kirkpatrick & Kanin, 1957; Rada, 1978a). It appears that the data gathered from the statements of convicted rapists are inconclusive at best. Such "evidence" does not demonstrate the absence of sexual motivation in rape.

Argument 8

"The high incidence (1 out of 3 cases) of sexual dysfunction is further evidence for the relative unimportance of sexual desire in the act of rape." (Groth & Hobson, 1983, p. 171; see also Groth, 1979a; Harding, 1985)

The evidence of dysfunction during rape has been subject to questionable definitions (see Thornhill & Thornhill, 1983) and varies greatly between different studies (see Rada, 1978a). Hence, despite the claims of Harding (1985), sexual dysfunction in rape has not been conclusively shown to be significantly higher in rapes than in consenting acts. Even if a higher rate of actual dysfunction was conclusively demonstrated, it could be easily accounted for by the adverse circumstances under which rape often occurs. Symons (1980) points out that even the most sexually motivated rapist might experience dysfunction due to anxiety over the possibility of severe punishment and the existence of conflicting emotions. There is also the fact that offenders are often under the influence of drugs. Groth reports that 50% of the rapists in his study were drunk or on drugs at the time of the assault (1979a, p. 96). Smithyman reports that 32% of the rapists in his study were intoxicated in some way (1978, p. 60). The Queen's Bench Foundation found that 61.6% of the rapists had consumed alcohol before the rape (1978, p. 773).

Argument 9

Rape is motivated by aggression instead of sex because "changes in number of rapes and assaults showed similar seasonal patterns, suggesting that rape comprised a subcategory of aggressive behavior" (Michael & Zumpe, 1983, p. 883; cited as evidence of the unimportance of sexual motivation in rape by Bercovitch et al., in press).

Rape and non-sexual assault both appear to occur most frequently in the summer months (Michael & Zumpe, 1983). The conclusion that this is evidence for a lack of sexual motivation in rape is seriously flawed in a number of ways. First, it ignores numerous alternative explanations of why rape might occur most frequently in the summer, such as greater social interaction and greater visual cues, which are quite compatible with the assumption that sex is an important motivation in rape (see Chappell et al., 1977). Second, if seasonality of occurrence is an indicator of motivation, then all aggressive behaviors should follow the same pattern. The same study that reports a correlation between assault and rape reports a dramatic differ-

ence in the seasonal pattern of rape and murder (Michael & Zumpe, 1983). Finally, this argument ignores the drastic differences in other patterns of assault and rape. Many of these patterns, especially the age and sex of victims, are much more likely to be related to the motivation of the offenders than is seasonality (see Thornhill & Thornhill, 1983).

Argument 10

The real motivation in rape is violence instead of sex because castrated rapists just find other ways of doing violence to women. (See Cohen et al., 1971; Dusek, 1984; Groth, 1979a, p. 10; Katz & Mazur, 1979; LeGrand, 1973; MacDonald, 1971; Rada, 1978a)

All data on the effects of castration must be viewed skeptically because of the many uncontrolled variables involved (Greene, 1979). Existing data suggest that castrated sex offenders have significantly lower recidivism rates in regard to *sexual* offenses (Bremer, 1959; MacDonald, 1971; Rada, 1978b; Sturup, 1960, 1968). Proponents of the "not sex" argument have refused to see this as evidence of rape being sexually motivated. This is because "Those who view rape as primarily an aggressive offense do not believe that castration will cure the rapist's aggressive impulses" (Rada, 1978b, p. 143). People holding this view would predict that castrated offenders would simply replace their "sexual" assaults with "non-sexual" assaults.

Argument 11

Rape is clearly an act of aggression. McCahil et al. (1979) in their study of 1,401 rape victims show that: (1) a majority of victims (64%) reported being pushed or held during the incident, (2) victims are often slapped (17%), beaten (22%), and/or choked (20%), and (3) 84% of victims experienced some kind of nonphysical force during the incident (threat of bodily harm, etc.). (Thornhill & Thornhill, 1983, p. 163)

To determine the significance of data on rapist violence and victim injury, it is crucial to make the distinction between instrumental force used to accomplish the rape (and possibly to influence the female not to resist and/or not to report the rape), and excessive violence that appears to be an end in itself. This distinction is necessary because only excessive force is a possible indication of violent motivation on the part of the rapist.

Harding makes the following claim: "In many cases of rape in humans, assault seems to be the important factor, not sex. . . . [because] . . . In most cases the use of force goes beyond that necessary to compel the victim's compliance with the rapist's demands" (Harding, 1985, p. 51). However, existing evidence, including that cited by Harding (1985, p. 51), indicates that excessive force is actually only used in a minority of cases. Consistent with the previously cited figures by McCahil, Meyer and Fischman (1979), Chappell and Singer found only 15 to 20 percent of rape victims required hospital treatment for physical injuries (1977). Katz and Mazur also report the following: "Although most rape victims encountered some form of physical force, few experienced severe lasting [physical] injuries" (1979, p. 171; see also Burgess & Holmstrom, 1974; Schiff, 1971). Amir even found that "In a large number of cases (87%), only temptation and verbal coercion were used to subdue the victim" (Amir, 1975, p. 7).

Other evidence also indicates that it is only in a minority of cases that violence and injury are even one of the goals of a rapist.

Argument 12

"IT IS NOT A CRIME OF LUST BUT OF VIOLENCE AND POWER [because] . . . RAPE VICTIMS ARE NOT ONLY THE 'LOVELY YOUNG BLONDS' OF NEWSPAPER HEADLINES—RAPISTS STRIKE CHILDREN, THE AGED, THE HOMELY—ALL WOMEN." (Brownmiller, 1975, back cover; original emphasis)

It is fitting that Brownmiller chose this argument to place in bold type on the cover of her milestone book. Whether rapists prefer sexually attractive victims, or only select victims who are most vulnerable, forms a major argument of those on both sides of the debate (e.g., Alcock, 1983; Brownmiller, 1975; Dean & de Bruyn-kopps, 1982; Denmark & Friedman, 1985; Groth, 1979a; Groth & Hobson, 1983; Rodabaugh & Austin, 1981; Symons, 1979).

The argument that rape is not sexually motivated because rapists allegedly do not prefer attractive victims begins with the accurate observation that "Any female may become a victim of rape" (Brownmiller, 1975, p. 388). This is then taken as evidence that sexual attractiveness of victims is unimportant: "I already knew that the rapist chooses his victim with a striking disregard for conventional 'sex appeal'—she may be seventy-four and senile or twelve and a half with braces on her teeth" (Brownmiller, 1975, p. 376). This alleged unimportance of attractiveness is then understandably assumed to demonstrate the unimportance of sexual motivation in the act of rape: "Only young attractive women are raped. This myth is another that stems from the belief that rape is a crime of passion and sex rather than what it is: a crime of violence" (Dean & de Bruyn-kopps, 1983, p. 36; see also Brownmiller, 1975, pp. 131-132).

The weak link in this argument is the assumption that the rape of unattractive females implies that rapists lack a preference for attractive victims. This conclusion is unjustified because it ignores the fact that rape victims are not a representative cross-section of all women. It also ignores the possibility that victim selection is based on *both attractiveness and vulnerability*.

Perhaps the most consistent finding of studies on rape, and one not likely to be merely the result of reporting bias (see Hindelang, 1977), is that women in their teens and early twenties are vastly over-represented among rape victims (Amir, 1971; Hindelang & Davis, 1977; Kramer, 1987; MacDonald, 1971; Miyazawa, 1976; Svalastoga, 1962; Thornhill & Thornhill, 1983). This fact is crucial because age can be used as at least a rough indicator of female attractiveness: "Physical characteristics that vary systematically with age appear to be universal criteria of female physical attractiveness; Williams (1975), in fact, remarks that age probably is the most important determinant of human female attractiveness" (Symons, 1979, p. 188). It also appears reasonably certain that "Judgments of female physical attractiveness will correspond in females closely to the age of maximum reproductive value or fertility, which peaks in the mid-teens and early 20's respectively and drops off sharply in the late 30's" (Buss, 1987, p. 342; see also Shields & Shields, 1983; Symons, 1979, 1987; Thornhill & Thornhill, 1983; Wil-

liams, 1975). This means there is a strong correlation between attractiveness and the likelihood of becoming a rape victim.

The existence of such a correlation would appear to be conclusive evidence that rapists prefer attractive victims (see Alcock, 1983; Symons, 1979). However, backers of the "not sex" explanation continue to claim that rapists do not prefer attractive victims.

The high vulnerability of the elderly is indeed reflected in their high susceptibility to a number of types of violent crimes (Hindelang, 1977). However, contrary to the claims of Katz and Mazur (1979), the age distribution of rape victims is vastly different from the age distributions of victims of nonsexual violent crimes (Lennington, 1985; Thornhill & Thornhill, 1983). In fact, the age distributions are so different that studies, including Groth's own study, consistently find that *less than five percent of rape victims are over the age of fifty*. The fact that elderly women are very rarely raped *despite* being "particularly vulnerable" is strong evidence that rapists have a very definite preference for younger (and therefore more attractive) victims.

This does not mean that vulnerability is irrelevant to victim selection. It only means that vulnerability must be combined with attractiveness in order to account for the age distribution of rape victims.

CONCLUSION

Public awareness of the violence and horror of the act of rape *as experienced by the victim* has been crucial to facilitating social change. However, at present, the evidence does not justify the denial of sexual motivation on behalf of the *rapist*. This point is significant since adherence to the "not sex" explanation may have the unintended consequence of hindering attempts to prevent rape. For example, the effectiveness of instruction manuals on how to avoid rape (see Crook, 1980), treatment programs for rapists (see Brecher, 1978), and public policy perspectives are potentially compromised by the denial of the sexual aspect of the crime.

Although there may be evidence of the unimportance of sexual motivation in the act of rape, such evidence cannot be unskeptically adopted. Rape is prevented by accurate knowledge about its causes, and accurate knowledge can only be obtained by the objective examination of evidence and the skeptical evaluation of conclusions based on that evidence. The preceding twelve arguments have gone unquestioned for nearly twenty years, suggesting that skepticism has been noticeably absent from recent research on rape.

Perhaps the reason for this lack of skepticism and accurate knowledge about rape is that "rape" the behavior has become obscured by the politics of "rape" the "master symbol of women's oppression" (Schwendinger & Schwendinger, 1985, p. 93). An objective and accurate approach to the prevention of rape requires that the subject of rape be "de-politicized." Unfortunately, many researchers on rape fear such an objective approach: "To use the word *rape* in a de-politicized context functions to undermine ten years of feminist consciousness-raising" (Blackman, 1985, p. 118; original emphasis). Surely such fears are unfounded. "Consciousness-raising" is the act of falsifying unsupported dogma. Adherence to unsupported dogma like the "not sex" explanation of rape not only prohibits true "consciousness-rais-ing" but potentially does so at the expense of an increased number of rape victims.

POSTSCRIPT

Is Rape Motivated by Aggression Instead of Sex?

No one would deny the important and positive advances that the feminist "not for sex" explanation has brought in the treatment of rape victims and rapists. At the same time, however, the political considerations and insights that led to the explanation raise questions about its continued usefulness and, more important, its validity.

David Finkelhor, in *Child Sexual Abuse* (Free Press, 1984), concludes, "The debate about the sexual motivation of sexual abuse is something of an unfortunate red herring. . . . The goal should be to explain how the sexual component fits in."

But the majority of researchers remain committed to the "not for sex" explanation. This is understandable because the interpretation of rape as an expression of anger and rage, as a compulsive need for power, or as a means to obtain sadistic pleasure has led criminologists and those working with rapists to develop programs that apparently have some positive effects on the social rehabilitation of sexual assaulters. If we admit that the desire for sexual pleasure is a significant factor in many rapes and a primary factor in some rapes, then we would be forced to reexamine the treatment and rehabilitation of rapists. We would also need to reexamine our education programs for rape prevention and defense.

The question is, is the "not for sex" explanation the full story and are we willing to reexamine it critically?

SUGGESTED READINGS

S. Brownmiller, *Against Our Will: Men, Women and Rape* (Simon & Schuster, 1975).

D. Finkelhor, *Child Sexual Abuse* (Free Press, 1984).

D. Finkelhor and K. Yllo, *License to Rape: Sexual Abuse of Wives* (Holt, Rinehart & Winston, 1985).

D. Gelman, "The Mind of the Rapist," *Newsweek* (July 23, 1990).

ISSUE 4

Does Sexual Infidelity Destroy a Relationship?

YES: Frank Pittman, from "What Price Camelot?" *The Family Therapy Networker* (May/June 1989)

NO: Sandra C. Finzi, from "Così Fan Tutte: 'So Does Everyone,' " *The Family Therapy Networker* (May/June 1989)

ISSUE SUMMARY

YES: Frank Pittman, a family therapist and the author of *Private Lies: Infidelity and the Betrayal of Intimacy*, maintains that infidelity is the primary disrupter of families, the most dreaded and devastating experience in marriage. He identifies and refutes seven myths about adultery that are true some of the time but that are not as universal as most people think.

NO: Sandra C. Finzi, a family therapist, argues that the European approach to extramarital "arrangements" is much more realistic than the American tradition of viewing every extramarital sexual encounter as an indication of a deep flaw in the character of the "wandering" spouse or a fatal flaw in the marriage. Finzi claims that marriages in which couples learn to distinguish between the long-term solidarity of the relationship and the passing infatuation may not collapse in the wake of an extramarital affair.

When marriage is mentioned, many of us think of two particular passages from the traditional marital vows: "forsaking all others" and "until death do us part." Lifelong romance coupled with sexual-emotional exclusivity is the ideal of American marriage. Yet, the reality belies this myth because the average marriage in the United States lasts only seven years. With over half of all marriages ending in divorce, serial monogamy—divorce and remarriage—is more common than lifelong marriage. And with extramarital sex occurring in at least half of all marriages, less than a quarter of American marriages meet the standards of lifelong and sexually exclusive.

Western religious leaders extol sexually exclusive monogamy—one spouse and sexual partner for life—as the highest form of marriage. They see exclusive monogamy as the highest level of social evolution, a mark of an advanced civilization. But some of the most primitive cultures are much more strictly monogamous than some highly advanced cultures are, many of which have shifted to a form of "flexible monogamy" in response to increasing life expectancy, affluence, leisure, mobility, and contraception, as well as lower birthrates and increasing numbers of women in the work force. Sociologists Clelland Ford and Frank Beech studied 185 contemporary cultures around the world and found that only 29 of them—less than 16 percent—restrict men and women to a single sexual partner for life. Moreover, less than a third of the 29 monogamous cultures completely disapprove of both premarital and extramarital relations.

For centuries, marriage was a dynastic affair, arranged by parents and families whose main motives were economics, social status, and the extension of family alliances. In the Middle Ages, the concept of courtly love—a passionate love for an unattainable woman, usually the wife of a nobleman—spawned two major new patterns of marriage. In Spain, Italy, and much of France, the traditional, family-arranged, economically based marriage was joined with the courtly love code, a conventionalized code prescribing the conduct of ladies and their lovers, resulting in the proliferation of extramarital affairs. Since divorce was not possible in the dominant Catholic tradition, social customs evolved that protected marriage and childrearing but accommodated the wanderlust of both husbands and wives.

In northern Europe, the emerging middle class was uneasy with the Mediterranean accommodation and acceptance of affairs. The solution was to shift the object of a man's desire from the unattainable wife of another man to a single woman and then to his own wife. In this second pattern, love and marriage were combined, and adultery was viewed as a lethal threat to marriage. However, divorce was available as a remedy for infidelity.

In American culture, the northern European pattern became dominant. In both the liberal Protestant and Jewish traditions, increasing life expectancy and other social changes led to a modification of the "until death do us part" ideal. Despite the high incidence of extramarital sex, sexual exclusivity remains the American ideal, even if it results in serial monogamy. Hence, it is common for a person to become involved in two, three, or more marriages, each of which is sexually exclusive while it lasts.

In the following selections, Frank Pittman and Sandra C. Finzi debate the effects of infidelity on a marriage. For Pittman, the northern European model of exclusive serial monogamy is preferable to a lifelong, loving, but not sexually exclusive marriage. Although Finzi uses the tired stereotypes of the "Hero" (H), his "Good Old Wife" (GOW), and the "Pretty Young Assistant" (PYA), her description and defense of the Mediterranean model of flexible marriage can easily be applied to wives and husbands who decide to have a more flexible style of nonexclusive marriage. While Finzi's stereotypes seem to assume a dysfunctional, unhappy marriage, many happily married couples have agreed to include in their stable, mature, lifelong marriages the possibility of sexual intimacy with others. See if you can identify other dimensions not mentioned by Pittman and Finzi.

YES

Frank Pittman

WHAT PRICE CAMELOT?

The way I define it, infidelity is a breach of the trust, a betrayal of a relationship, a breaking of an agreement. There are many kinds of infidelity, but here we are talking about a sexual infidelity in monogamous marriage or a relationship that is tantamount to marriage. Most couples agree to strict sexual exclusivity within the marriage, permitting masturbation and whatever fantasies each would like to have, but insisting that the genitals stay out of the hands, or whatever, of outsiders. Different couples may have different codicils to their agreement, and most of those have to be negotiated as they go along.

In the pre-AIDS era, I saw couples who worked out their own set of rules about what is and what is not an infidelity. I've seen prostitutes, male and female, who were granted sexual exception when it was done for business, but not for pleasure. Swingers have encouraged mate swapping and orgies as long as the sex was public, but have been outraged over private intimacies. Traveling people have been granted permission to be unfaithful when outside the city limits, or, in one case,"more than a four-hour drive from home." A few couples have decided that homosexual behavior outside the marriage would be acceptable, while heterosexual behavior would be disapproved. And there are some marriages in which men are permitted to have affairs while women are not. Couples have justified this arrangement by insisting that men can have affairs casually, while women are in danger of becoming romantically involved. Conversely, I have seen at least one couple who decided that the woman could have affairs, but the husband couldn't because he might be expected to spend money on the other women, which would create problems with the family budget.

In hindsight, these arrangements seem less benign to me than they did at the time, and might be unsupportable in the era of AIDS. Open adultery may not be nearly as dangerous as secret infidelity, but it is still far from safe. Whatever the agreement (if it really *is* an agreement), that is the accepted ideal for this couple in this marriage. The infidelity is in the breaking of the agreement.

From Frank Pittman, "What Price Camelot?" *The Family Therapy Networker* (May/June 1989). Adapted from Frank Pittman, *Private Lies: Infidelity and the Betrayal of Intimacy* (W. W. Norton, 1990). Copyright © 1990 by Frank Pittman. Reprinted by permission of W. W. Norton, Inc.

WHILE WORDS IN OUR CASUAL LANGUAGE don't seem to retain specificity, we might make a distinction between infidelity and adultery. Adultery might be considered the religious and legal concern, in which certain acts are sinful or unlawful in themselves, independent of the relationship between the marriage partners. I'm not much concerned with adultery if all partners consent to it. If it is lied about or kept secret, or done over the partner's objection, then it is an infidelity, a betrayal of the marital agreement that the couple would keep their sexual activities within the relationship, within whatever guidelines the two of them—having an equal voice in the matter—have agreed to.

A familiar example of a conflict over the definition of infidelity would be the situation that occurs when one partner has engaged in flirtation, clandestine meetings, or furtive sex play with a co-worker or social acquaintance, but insists that nothing that has taken place has been "wrong," since there was no intercourse. The partner, seeing the direction of things, feels a threat to the security of the marriage and would feel more comfortable distancing the flirtation partner. Even more common, couples might have to debate the wisdom of having lunch with a former affair partner, or a former spouse. The effort to avoid discussing the matter might well be a betrayal of the honesty of the relationship. If one partner bullies the other into agreeing to tolerate a friendship with so much sexual tension or sexual history, there has been a betrayal of respect for the current partner's feelings in the matter.

So when a man asks me whether something is or is not an infidelity, I suggest that he ask his wife. When a woman asks me if she has done something wrong in a certain situation, I reply that if she kept it secret from her husband, she might think so.

We might define adultery as a sexual act outside the marriage, while we might define infidelity as a sexual dishonesty within the marriage. Adultery may be against the law or against God's will, but infidelity is against the marriage and is thus a more relevant and more personal danger.

Infidelity may not be the worst thing that one marriage partner can do to another, but it may be the most confusing and disorienting and therefore the most likely to destroy the marriage—not necessarily because of the sex, but because of the secrecy and the lies. . . .

INFIDELITY IS THE PRIMARY DISRUPTER OF families, the most dreaded and devastating experience in a marriage. It is the most universally accepted justification for divorce. It is even a legally accepted justification for murder in some states and many societies. The crises that follow infidelities fill the offices of family therapists, lawyers, and plastic surgeons. I doubt if there is any problem on which we all devote more energy. At the beauty parlor or the health club, it is a major topic of conversation. Yet the subject is fraught with misinformation and mythology.

There is a lot of nonsense in the popular mythology about extramarital affairs. There are some ideas that are fallacious, yet universally accepted as true. From all the socially accepted fallacies about infidelity, what causes it, and how to handle it, seven myths stand out as especially misleading. These myths show up in adulterous families, in "Dear Abby," in popular magazines, and even in the literature on family and marriage (where thick books on marriage therapy often bypass the problem entirely.)

They are:

1. Everybody is unfaithful; it is normal, expectable behavior.

2. Affairs are good for you; an affair may even revive a dull marriage.

3. The infidel must not "love" the cuckold; the affair proves it.

4. The affairee must be "sexier" than the spouse.

5. The affair is the fault of the cuckold, proof that the cuckold has failed the infidel in some way that made the affair necessary.

6. The best approach to the discovery of a spouse's affair is to pretend not to know and thereby avoid a crisis.

7. If an affair occurs, the marriage must end in divorce.

All of these ideas, like the proverbial stopped clock, are right some of the time. Many people are unfaithful, occasionally a marriage is better after an affair or some other crisis, people who don't define themselves as being "in love" with a spouse are at greater risk for infidelity, some people do choose affair partners for purely sexual qualities, a few people do encourage their mates to have affairs, many marriages have not developed tolerance for openness, and the divorce rate in adulterous marriage is high. But these observations, even at times when they are true, are misleading.

Myth #1: *Everybody has affairs.* The data on the frequency of infidelity is fairly consistent. About half do and half don't. Traditionally, more men than women have been adulterous, but the women seem to be catching up. Surveys in the last few years tell us that about 50 percent of husbands have been unfaithful, while 30–40 percent of wives have been.

The younger generation of women is more likely to be unfaithful than the older generation was at that age or is now. In the very youngest groups, the husbands and wives are equally unfaithful, while among the oldsters, infidelity is largely a male activity. As the percentage of adulterous wives goes up, the percentage of adulterous husbands may actually have been going down.

If infidelity of some sort takes place in over half of all marriages, that's a lot of infidelity. The figures are misleading, though. Many adulterers have had only one affair, most only a few. Much of the infidelity takes place (as cause or effect) in the last year of a dying marriage. Intact, continuing marriages are far less adulterous. Marital fidelity remains the norm, in that most marital partners are faithful most of the time. The same surveys that show most marriages as adulterous also show that the vast majority of people believe strongly in marital fidelity, certainly for their spouse and generally for themselves. It remains the ideal, even if it is not always achieved. I notice that people who screw around tend to assume that everyone else does too, while those who don't screw around assume extramarital sex is unusual behavior. Maybe people choose friends who share their values, and their hobbies. Quite obviously, people who grew up in families in which the adults had affairs are more likely to see this as normal behavior and do it themselves.

Infidelity takes several different forms. Some of it is out of character, unplanned, occurring under unique or unusual circumstances. I call it Accidental Infidelity. It can happen to anyone who is a little careless, but is more likely to happen to those whose values and commitments are tenuous. The most disruptive infidelity is Falling In Love, an intense, passionate alliance that threatens the marriage and closes out other reality. These are Romantic Affairs. They may be bizarrely inappropriate, but usually burn out quickly. They tend to occur at crisis points in life. People who fall in love and run away from home seem to be threatened by too much reality. Falling in love is much like a manic episode.

Some adultery can become part of the marriage arrangement, and may even be overt. People who live in such marital arrangements are often stuck, reluctant to be totally inside or totally outside a marriage. They prefer to limit intimacy, and may not be good at negotiating conflict. These arrangements are hardest on the marital aides who serve as the semipermanent affair partners.

Continuous, compulsive, secret infidelity (philandering) is a well-known macho pattern, but it may occur in no more than 20 percent of intact marriages. Of course, some open marital arrangements are accommodations to philanderers, and some romances are efforts to escape them. Philanderers are mostly men who fear female control and are in love with their masculinity. They believe there is a gender war going on, and they want to be on the winning team, so they score with each woman in turn, tag her, and discard her. They aren't good at marriage, since it requires honesty and equality with a female partner.

It would seem inappropriate to consider any of this "normal."

Myth #2: *Affairs are good for marriage.* Somehow the idea has been foisted upon us that affairs can revive dull marriages. I've found that idea expressed in *Playboy* and in *Cosmopolitan* magazine, which sell sexy fantasies, but I've also heard it from marriage and family therapists, which is frightening. People must like believing this, though all the evidence points to the contrary. I've seen only a handful of divorces in established first marriages that were strictly monogamous. Adulterous marriages don't always end in divorce, but marriages that stay faithful nearly always stay together—even if they'd be better off apart.

For most people and most marriages, infidelity is dangerous. . . . To have an affair in order to trigger a crisis from which the marriage might eventually benefit is truly a screwball, convoluted approach to problem solving. . . .

Myth #3: *Affairs prove that love has gone from the marriage.* The reasons for affairs are rich and varied. Most of the reasons have to do with the ego state of the person having the affair rather than the person against whom the infidelity is being committed. The reasons can range all the way from "hobby" (the infidel belongs to a club in which they do this weekly) to "politeness" (the infidel stumbled into an awkward situation in which it would have been rude not to commit an infidelity). Even if someone did not love the spouse, an infidelity would be a rather complicated and indirect way to say so, and an inefficient way to approach the problems in the marriage. The feelings one spouse has for another are complicated from the beginning. The degree of complexity of the emotions in long-standing marriages is staggering. To reduce this complexity to a question as adolescent as the presence or absence of "love" is idiocy of the highest order. That question is best left to the petals of daisies. . . .

It is routine for a frantic cuckold to ask the question "Do you love him/her?" There is something so romantic and innocent in reducing these complex matters to such a simple yes or no question. Affairs may be driven by hate as often as by love. Certainly, I've seen more affairs in which friendship is the primary emotion than those based on being in love. Many affairs begin as friendship, and continue as friendships until the sex occurs. Once the sex occurs, the friendship then goes through a period of growing more intense and complicated, until it finally makes the friendship too uncomfortable to continue. What is so sad, and seems so foolish about affairs, is that many of them might have been wonderful, utterly unthreatening friendships had they not been so naively sexualized by people who are overly preoccupied with gender differences, and just don't know how to have a friendship with someone of a different gender.

Myth #4: *The affairee was sexier than the spouse.* Since an affair involves sex, it is often assumed that the affair is about sex and the object of the affair is a champion sexual athlete. Of course, that is sometimes the case. But in my practice, I've noticed that it is about as common for the infidel to acknowledge that sex was better at home. And affairs may not involve very much sexual activity at all. Most affairs seem to involve a little bad sex, and a lot of time on the telephone.

Affair partners are not chosen because they are the winners of some objective sex contest. They are chosen for all manner of strange and usually nonsexual reasons. Affair choices are usually far more neurotic than marriage choices. When one is chosen to be an affair partner, one should not feel complimented. . . .

Myth #5: *The affair is the fault of the cuckold.* The irresponsible belief "You made me do it" is often accepted by both the betrayer and the betrayed. Despite all the therapeutic effort that goes into teaching patients that they are responsible for their behavior, many therapists believe that affairs are an exception, and they can only be brought about by collusion between the marital partners. . . .

It is certainly easy for one marital partner to make the other wish to be somewhere else, or to be with someone else. But the unhappy partner could choose divorce, murder, an argument, therapy, or whatever instead. The dissatisfaction in a marriage may or may not be a joint effort, but the decisions about how to deal with an intolerable situation are clearly individual. When adulterous couples come in to therapy, the one doing the betraying may be complaining that the one being betrayed has, in some way, caused the affair, but this may be the first time the problems have been emphasized. Even when the problems have been argued about for years and blamed for the affair, there may be considerable reluctance to solve them during the affair.

The relationship between the affair and the problems blamed for the affair becomes increasingly confusing. It is often difficult to believe there is any relationship. It may well be that the decision that there is a problem in the marriage is made after the affair begins. This decision has one useful result—the cuckold can't withdraw into a position of moral superiority. . . .

It is very difficult for people to work on a marriage in which an affair is going on. Affairs usually stop once they are revealed. Sometimes, though, the affair comes out into the open and still continues despite all efforts to stop it. The continuation of the affair proves that it has an existence independent of anything about the marriage. Affairs, once begun, have a life of their own, and it seems foolhardy for the betrayed spouse to pretend to have any influence over it. Efforts to stop an ongoing affair seem only to strengthen the attachment.

In general, I don't find it helpful for a betrayed spouse to take responsibility for any part of the affair. The one being betrayed can't make affairs happen, can't make the betrayer stop, and can only make him or herself available for solving whatever problems there might be in the marriage, though those are going to be grotesquely distorted and exaggerated as long as the affair is continuing or being defended.

Myth #6: *There is safety in ignorance of a spouse's affair.* Affairs are complicated and have a certain message value. One message might be that the betrayer wants out of the marriage but doesn't want to take responsibility for that position, so would like to offend the one being betrayed into threatening divorce. I have encountered an occasional marriage in which one partner seems to be saying, "If you object to my behavior in any way, then leave me or I will leave you." . . .

Ignorance of affairs puts people in the position of not having to acknowledge problems or do anything to solve them. If the affair ends, the sexual, emotional, functional, and intimate relationship will be between husband and wife. Many— sometimes I think most—people prefer not to be happily married, to retain some limits on the intimacy and "togetherness." They work at maintaining just the right distance in the relationship. Al-

though the spouse's affair may create an undesirable state of distance, the end-of-the-affair reunion and postaffair problem solving might produce an even less desired state of excessive closeness. The danger of bringing an affair into the open is not that the infidel becomes more likely to leave, but that the infidel becomes more likely to *stay*, and try to get close.

. . . The power of any affair may be in its secrecy. The weakness of the marriage may be in its avoidance of issues.

Myth #7: *After an affair, divorce is inevitable.* Certainly, an affair is a crisis in a marriage. After any crisis, the marriage may become better and it may become worse. There are people of such distrusting, perfectionist, or romantic natures that they find it difficult to live in a blemished marriage, or elsewhere in a real, imperfect world. Once some defect has been discovered in their world, they can suffer indefinitely, whether the adulterous spouse stays or goes. There are marriages in which the betrayer remains on probation or under punishment for decades after the affair. . . .

Whatever the problems in the marriage before a crisis of infidelity, the problems after the affair are quite different and far more serious. The affair brings its own problems, God knows, but also brings urgency to the preexisting problems. In my experience, in my practice, couples therapy is crucial after an affair, and can reverse the prognosis for the marriage. . . .

Once the affair is over and out in the open, the process can begin of redeveloping the intimacy. If the affair is kept secret, the intimacy has been betrayed, and can't be restored. The marriage tends to decay from inside, and after more affairs, finally dies.

Honestly, it is safe to talk openly about affairs. It saves lives and marriages to do so. So I would substitute a quite different set of generalizations about infidelity:

1. Infidelity is not normal behavior, but a symptom of some problem.

2. Affairs are dangerous and can easily, and inadvertently, end marriages.

3. Affairs can occur in marriages that, prior to the affair, were quite good.

4. Affairs involve sex, but the sex is not usually the purpose of the affair.

5. No one can drive someone else to have an affair.

6. Affairs are fueled by secrecy and threatened by exposure.

7. Marriages can, with effort, survive affairs if the affairs are exposed.

NO

Sandra C. Finzi

COSÌ FAN TUTTE:
"SO DOES EVERYONE"

There is an acceptance of the extramarital "arrangement" in European society that one rarely encounters in this country. Most Europeans I know were amused at the moralistic frenzy that accompanied the disclosure of Gary Hart's infidelities during the last presidential campaign. For them it was another example of Americans' naivete. They could not understand what made a politician's infidelities so surprising that they became front-page news. Nor could they fathom what being unfaithful to a spouse had to do with being qualified to be a national leader. Rather than viewing infidelities as an indication of a deep character flaw, most Europeans are far more relaxed with the idea that acting on sexual longing depends more on availability of opportunity than the state of one's marriage or the condition of one's psyche. It was this attitude that Mozart immortalized when he wrote his great opera "Così fan tutte" ("So does everyone").

Perhaps because of my cultural bias—I was born in Italy and moved to the United States only after I was married—I have always taken a less problematic view of infidelity than most of my American colleagues. When couples caught up in the emotional whirlwind triggered by the revelation of an extramarital affair come to see me, I usually start by saying, "Even if your relationship were perfect—and of course it is not—the affair could have happened anyway." I never begin by assuming that an infidelity demonstrates the awful state of marriage.

The most common scenario for the affair that I have encountered in my practice, which is made up largely of European and Latin American academics and diplomats, features three players. There is the Hero (H), once a shy, bookish, unprepossessing young man who has become in middle age rather important in his field. He has been comfortably attached to his Good Old Wife (GOW), the woman with whom he had his first serious relationship. Middle aged and usually quite attractive, GOW is cautiously returning to the career that she postponed to raise her family.

I believe that women as well as men can have adventures that would not necessarily interfere with marital affection. Yet so far I have treated very few couples in which the wife has had the affair.

Suddenly, overwhelmingly, H discovers the eternal feminine in the person of Pretty Young Assistant (PYA), a student, a secretary, a research assistant, a younger colleague. Awed by his professional and intellectual achievements, she was drawn to his work before they ever met. Almost miraculously, it seems to them both, she helps him rediscover that he is a physical as well as mental being; she awakens the forgotten adventurer, the unknown playboy in him.

PYA, on her part, has suffered many disappointments in love, and cannot believe that the Boss, the Venerated Professor, this god-like eminence, has condescended to become human for her. He is even willing to jeopardize some of the very qualities she had admired in the first place: his seriousness of purpose, his dedication to work, his devotion to his family.

The Hero is amazed by the intensity of his feelings. He has never seen himself as an adventurer. He wasn't seeking excitement, but now excitement has seized him by the throat. "There must be a reason for all this," he reflects, puzzled and shaken. Perhaps he married the wrong woman, perhaps he devoted his energies to the wrong pursuits. He begins to feel that his entire life up to now has been a charade, a false front hiding his true self. Now, he feels, he is at last experiencing real life. This woman, he

decides, is the one whom he should have met 20 years ago, and this is the way he wants to live from now on.

DURING THIS UPHEAVAL, ALL IS NOT QUIET on the home front. The Hero has not learned to lie casually and adroitly, or to gloss over, even to himself, troublesome inconsistencies in thought and behavior. So he either throws himself into an orgy of self-revelation, telling everything as fast as he can or withdraws completely from family life, hiding behind a wall of total silence. If he tells all, the whole adventure comes rushing out, no glowing details omitted, leaving GOW stunned and shattered. Sometimes the children are called in as astonished, unwilling witnesses to the parental melodrama. On the other hand, if he chooses to withdraw, he seems to regard even the most innocent questions as an unwarranted intrusion into his personal concerns. He becomes a silent guest in his own house, responding to his puzzled family with glassy-eyed stares and incomprehensibly long hesitations. Even so, sooner or later his secret is revealed, perhaps through a casual remark by a friend, a letter found in a pocket, his own unexpected flare of emotion when he blurts out to GOW, "You do not know what I am giving up for you!"

Now GOW is deluged by her own flood of almost unbearably intense emotions. After years of unarticulated, but (she thought) implicitly understood communication, when excitement over published papers or concern about the children were about all she and her husband ever openly discussed, now her predictable and peacefully absent-minded companion has begun opening his soul to her. And his soul contemplates beatific vistas of romance, passion, fulfill-ment—an imaginary landscape that she herself has longed for but never seen. All that has been missing from her life, GOW realizes—just as she contemplates her impending physical decline—is suddenly there, but not for her!

Her own panic comes as a profound shock to her. She had never imagined losing her own composure, the tranquility that has sustained her through all the crises of marriage and childrearing. She too now questions all the life choices she has made. Was she too available or not available enough to her husband? Should she have pursued a career more actively? Perhaps this would never have happened, she mourns, had she been a more seductive, affectionate wife, a more devoted mother, a better companion, a superior woman all around. Of course, this catastrophe proves what she had sensed all along but could never quite say: her marriage has been a charade, a comfortable arrangement, an illusion.

Anguished, confused, and terrified, H and GOW face each other in the most painful encounter they have ever experienced. In the turmoil they forget the daily concerns, the comfortable ups and downs of a quiet life together, to focus exclusively on their pain and fear.

IF THEY ARE NOT HELPED TO GENTLY QUES-tion their conclusions, emotions may run so high that something irreparable may happen. He may leave, she may hire a lawyer or have a nervous breakdown. Even if there is no explosion, no dramatic break, the slow dying of emotions may leave a deadly trace: H may give up his dream, unable to bear causing GOW such devastating suffering. He will say

good-bye to his PYA, close and shutter the windows overlooking the dangerous, thrilling chasm that so drew him. Grudgingly, he will make the Supreme Sacrifice, still furious that he must give up his dream for the dreary, impoverished life he sees stretching in front of him.

GOW will stay too, though interpreting every forlorn absent look on H's face as evidence of his underground longing for freedom. Deep down she may remain convinced that he has stayed only out of loyalty, attachment to his children, and a desire to protect his reputation and public image. The short period of deep, if painfully intense communication will pass. And from time to time, she will wonder about the romance that he had but that she never will.

"Plaisir d'amour ne dure qu'un moment, chagrin d'amour dure toute la vie" (The pleasure of love lasts but a moment, the pain of love lingers all one's life) runs an old French song. But must it always work out this way?

Not necessarily. The therapist can make a difference in the foregoing scenario, not as a moral arbiter but as someone who helps people question their extreme emotions and learn less automatic responses. The first time we ski we instinctively draw back toward the mountain and only with diligent practice do we learn the skill of leaning forward away from the safety of the hill. So when I coach couples through the aftermath of an affair, I focus away from the vivid drama of the pain, betrayal, gory details, and strong passions, and ask them to look at the silent world of companionship, understanding, affection, and solidarity in their relationship. At times, of course, we find that these emotional resources are lacking and these marriages end because they are empty, not because of the affair.

IN MOST OF THESE CASES I HAVE FOUND that when the protagonists learn to distinguish between long-term, unshakable solidarity and passing infatuations, when they stop expecting passion from the person who has seen them before breakfast for 20 years, the marriage becomes more solid, based less on charged feelings—that change from moment to moment—and more on the solid ground of shared experience and compatibility tested by the years. But my practice has taught me that weathering the marital storm in this way does not necessarily make the couple "affair-proof." What does change, however, are the attitudes with which each partner regards the drama of the affair.

I have repeatedly met Heroes years after therapy was over at a party or some social occasion. Sometimes during the evening he will discreetly thank me for helping him not to trade the gold of his affection for GOW for the glitter of a very strong sexual attraction. "A playboy would have been more likely to fall for such a trade," he jokes. He is not yet a playboy, he smiles, but he suggests he has had other strong attractions. But we are not in a therapy session and I do not ask whether he has acted on them. Almost confirming my silent thought, he confesses that he no longer takes sudden, intense attractions as evidence that his marriage has been a great mistake, any more than he takes a sudden craving for a Big Mac as a negation of wholesome home cooking. He may have tried other highs after the affair, but he has learned to put his fantasy of the One Right Woman to rest and enjoy the pleasures of being with the world's expert on his fragilities, his quirks, his memories, the whole panorama of what his life has been about.

IT IS SEVEN YEARS AFTER THE AFFAIR AND GOW tells me that she has become less centered on her husband. She feels less guilty now for devoting more time to her own pursuits. She trusts the good moments they have together more than his chastity. She notices the way he talks about current co-workers and spends some moments wondering about him whenever he goes to a convention or away on a business trip, but she does not need to know. She has decided that she does not need to envy the women for whom he must put on the Hero's mask. She makes a point of waving him a fond good-bye when he leaves and feels a genuine pleasure when he returns. She knows that nobody can take away what they have built together over the years, and she figures they will need to work at it, for the rest of their lives, "But together, not by myself as before." She feels less "all-giving" than she once was. She has not had her romance ("Yet," she winks). But she has taken vacations by herself and with friends.

So to those therapists who ringingly declare, "I am for fidelity," I answer, "Yes, I agree of course. And I am also for honest politics and immortality." Middle-age extramarital sexual longings, whether acted upon or not, are just about as avoidable as adolescent sexual longings, and there is no more point in denying or ignoring the former than the latter. This demon is ubiquitous, for those who are not too frightened to face up to it. As therapists, we might begin to consider the possibility that it is our fearful, primordial *reactions* to the threat of mid-life, extramarital sexuality rather than infidelity itself, that often makes it difficult for us to guide our clients through the emotional turmoil that follows an affair. We must make sure that our attempted therapeutic "solutions" do not wind up compounding our clients' problems.

POSTSCRIPT

Does Sexual Infidelity Destroy a Relationship?

How "natural" is lifelong sexually exclusive pair-bonding?

For 2,000 years Christian moralists have cited the lifelong pair-bonding and sexual exclusivity among ducks, swans, and other animals as examples of the true nature of marriage. Biologists long believed that up to 94 percent of bird species were monogamous, with one mother and one father sharing the burden of rearing their chicks. Recently, however, biologists compared the DNA of chicks with the DNA of their assumed parents and discovered that, on average, 30 percent or more of the offspring had been fathered by another male rather than the resident male. Even mammals have been found to be only 2 to 4 percent sexually exclusive. The new evidence from many different animal species clearly indicates that both males and females commonly engage in sex with partners other than their apparent pair-bond mates.

In one variation of the debate about marriage and sexual exclusivity, published several years ago in *Forum* magazine, Lisa Davis maintained that sexually exclusive monogamy is the most satisfying long-term relationship because it provides a sense of continuity, promotes personal growth, and ultimately makes true intimacy possible. On the other side of the debate, Phyllis Raphael argued that the American style of exclusive monogamy is an unnatural and unattainable ideal that cripples personal development.

These variations go beyond Finzi's stereotyped "Hero," "Good Old Wife," and "Pretty Young Assistant" to show a society in which marital diversity is increasingly obvious and acknowledged. In our society, men and women need to examine their emotional needs and expectations as they move into married relationships and as they live those marriages over many years.

SUGGESTED READINGS

D. M. Anapol, *Love Without Limits: The Quest for Sustainable Intimate Relationships* (IntiNet Resource Center, 1992).

N. Angier, "Mating for Life? It's Not for the Birds and Bees," *The New York Times* (August 21, 1990).

N. Branden, *The Psychology of Romantic Love* (Jeremy P. Tarcher, 1980).

A. Chapman, *Man-Sharing: Dilemma or Choice* (William Morrow, 1987).

S. Davis, *Future Sex* (Personal Enhancement Press, 1991).

H. E. Fisher, *Anatomy of Love: The Natural History of Monogamy, Adultery, and Divorce* (W. W. Norton, 1992).

H. Goldberg, *The New Male-Female Relationship* (William Morrow, 1983).

A. Karlen, *Threesomes: Studies in Sex, Power, and Intimacy* (William Morrow, 1990).

G. Leonard, *Adventures in Monogamy* (Jeremy P. Tarcher, 1983).

R. Nearing, *The New Faithful: A Polyfidelity Primer* (Polyfidelitous Educational Productions, 1989).

J. Ramey, *Intimate Friendships* (Prentice Hall, 1976).

R. Walters, *Sexual Friendships: A New Dynamics in Relationships* (Libra, 1988).

ISSUE 5

Is Pornography Harmful?

YES: James C. Dobson, from *Final Report of the Attorney General's Commission on Pornography* (July 1986)

NO: Philip Nobile and Eric Nadler, from *United States of America vs. Sex: How the Meese Commission Lied About Pornography* (Minotaur Press, 1986)

ISSUE SUMMARY

YES: Psychologist James C. Dobson, the founder and president of Focus on the Family, a publishing and broadcasting organization "dedicated to the maintenance of traditional values," feels that the U.S. Attorney General's Commission on Pornography saw and heard enough evidence to be convinced that pornography causes untold harm to adolescents and women. **NO:** Philip Nobile and Eric Nadler, two journalists who followed the U.S. Attorney General's Commission on Pornography around the nation to report on its theory and practice, solicited the opinions of 11 citizens—feminists, journalists, sex therapists, and civil libertarians—who considered the attorney general's report. This Shadow Commission, as Nobile and Nadler called the group, contends that the report has many biases and does not demonstrate a causal connection between pornography and possible harms, such as rape.

What is the role of pornography? Why does so much pornography depict violent sex and the degradation and victimization of women? Is novelist and literary critic Marilyn French on target when she contends in her 1992 book *The War Against Women* that pornography is a major weapon in the cultural war against women because it presents women "as mainly sexual, indeed heterosexual, beings who have no life apart from men"? Is pornography a symptom of a sick society, or is it a healthy safety valve in a society that is basically uncomfortable with sexuality? If society were more accepting of sexuality and had a more positive view of sex that allowed it a natural place in daily life, would pornography continue to sell?

How do we define *pornography*? A married couple who rents a sexually explicit film to view on their VCR to inspire variety in their lovemaking does not necessarily consider such a film pornographic or obscene. Others, however, could denounce the same videotape as obscene, degrading to women, or even an inducement for males to rape.

Pat Califia, a lesbian feminist, points out an example of this problem of defining what is pornographic or obscene in her critique of the position taken by Women Against Violence in Pornography and the Media (WAVPM), vocal opponents of sexism and violence in pornography:

> [For WAVPM], pornography can include a picture of a woman whose body is smeared with honey, a woman stabbing a man in the back, or a woman dressed in leather towering over two men as well as films showing various sex acts. This vague definition allows them to support their contention that pornography objectifies and demeans women, since any image that is objectifying or demeaning is called pornographic. This allows them to claim that they are fighting against sexist stereotypes of women, not sexually explicit material, and serves as a basis for claiming that misogyny [hatred of women] is more prevalent and pernicious in pornography than in any other type of media.
>
> Their definition of violence is equally broad. It includes any kind of sex with a minor, consensual sadomasochism, bondage, watersports, prostitution, . . . casual sex and anal sex as well as rape and assault. . . . They make no distinction between a photograph of a woman's genitals, gang rape, an advertisement for spike heels, child abuse, a photograph of a woman who was tied up, and wife-beating.

In her controverisal 1987 book *Intercourse,* writer and social critic Andrea Dworkin argues that sexual "intercourse is the pure, sterile, formal expression of men's contempt for women." Men use intercourse, Dworkin claims, to "occupy," "violate," "invade," and "colonize" women's bodies. She concludes that because this is a world ruled by men who hate women, women cannot freely consent to any act of sexual intercourse. Dworkin's position has disturbed many, including feminists who readily recognize the reality of misogyny and rape but who are unpersuaded by her view of sexual intercourse. In the context Dworkin sets up, any literature, picture, video, or film that celebrates a heterosexual encounter is pornographic because no woman can give informed consent to being "violated, invaded, colonized, and occupied, or raped."

While most definitions of sexual violence and pornography are not this broad or this extreme, the use of these terms often lacks clarity, and you may want to spend some time considering what these terms mean to you or how you may have seen them defined elsewhere.

In the following selections, James C. Dobson affirms the Meese commission's findings that pornography in any form causes definite harm to the viewer, to the "victims" involved in its production, and to the whole of society. Philip Nobile and Eric Nadler, citing the opinions of various informed citizens, attack the commission's conclusions as unscientific, predetermined, and inconclusive regarding any causal relationship between pornography and violence.

YES

James C. Dobson

PORNOGRAPHY HARMS SOCIETY

Now that the work of the Attorney General's Commission on Pornography has come to an end, I look back on this fourteen-month project as one of the most difficult . . . and gratifying . . . responsibilities of my life. On the down side, the task of sifting through huge volumes of offensive and legally obscene materials has not been a pleasant experience. Under other circumstances one would not willingly devote a year of his life to depictions of rape, incest, masturbation, mutilation, defecation, urination, child molestation, and sadomasochistic activity. Nor have the lengthy and difficult deliberations in Commission meetings been without stress. But on the other hand, there is a distinct satisfaction in knowing that we gave ourselves unreservedly to this governmental assignment and, I believe, served our country well.

I now understand how mountain climbers must feel when they finally stand atop the highest peak. They overcome insurmountable obstacles to reach the rim of the world and announce proudly to one another, "we made it!" In a similar context, I feel a sense of accomplishment as the Commission releases its final report to the President, the Attorney General and the people. For a brief moment in Scottsdale last month, it appeared that our differing philosophies would strand us on the lower slopes. And of course, we were monitored daily by the ACLU, the pornographers, and the press, who huddled together and murmured with one voice, "they are doomed!" But now as we sign the final document and fling it about to the public, it does not seem pretentious to indulge ourselves in the satisfaction of having accomplished our goals. By George, I think we made it!

Let me indicate now, from the viewpoint of this one commissioner, what the final report *is* and *is not*. First, it is not the work of a biased Commission which merely rubber stamped the conservative agenda of the Reagan administration. A quick analysis of our proceedings will reveal the painstaking process by which our conclusions were reached. If the deck were stacked, as some have suggested, we would not have invested such long, arduous hours in debate and compromise. Serving on the Commission were three attorneys, two psychologists, one psychiatrist, one social worker, one

From *Attorney General's Commission on Pornography, Final Report*, July 1986, pp. 71–87. Washington, DC: Government Printing Office, 1986. (158–315)

city council member, one Catholic priest, one federal judge, and one magazine editor. Some were Christians, some Jewish, and some atheists. Some were Democrats and some Republicans. All were independent, conscientious citizens who took their responsibility very seriously. Our diversity was also evident on strategic issues about which society itself is divided. Our voting on these more troublesome matters often split 6–5, being decided by a swing member or two. Some whitewash! So the characterization of this seven-man, four-woman panel as an ultraconservative hit squad is simply poppycock. Read the transcripts. You will see.

Second, the final report does not do violence to the First Amendment to the Constitution. The *Miller* standard,* by which the Supreme Court clearly reaffirmed the illegality of obscene matter in 1973, was not assaulted during any of our deliberations. No suggestion was made that the Court had been too lenient . . . or that a constitutional Amendment should lower the threshold of obscenity . . . or that the Justices should reconsider their position. No. The *Miller* standard was accepted and even defended as the law of the land. What *was* recommended, to the consternation of pornographers, was that government should begin enforcing the obscenity laws that are already on the books . . . criminal laws that have stood constitutional muster! Considering the unwillingness of our elected representatives to deal with this issue, that would be novel, indeed.

Third, the hearings on which this report was based were not manipulated to produce an anti-pornography slant. *Every*

* [Dobson refers to the case of *Miller v. California* (1973).—Ed.]

qualified libertarian and First Amendment advocate properly requesting the right to testify was granted a place on the agenda, limited only by the constraints of time. A few individuals and organizations on *both* sides of the issue were unable to testify because the demand far exceeded available opportunities. However, objective procedures were established to deal fairly with those wishing to be heard, and complaints alleging bias were, I believe, unfounded. In fact, several organizations were asked to speak on behalf of sexually explicit materials but either declined or failed to appear. It *is* true that more witnesses testified against pornography than those who favored it, but that was a function of the disproportionate requests that were received by the executive director. Furthermore, I think it also reflects a disproportionate number of American citizens who oppose the proliferation of obscenity.

Looking now at the other side of the coin, let me express what the final report is and what I believe its impact is likely to be. First, the Commission expressed an unmistakable condemnation of sexually explicit material that is violent in nature. We were unanimous in that position throughout our deliberations. There is no place in this culture for material deemed legally obscene by the courts which depicts the dismemberment, burning, whipping, hanging, torturing, or raping of women. The time has come to eradicate such materials and prosecute those who produce it. There was no disagreement on that point.

Second, we were also unanimous in our condemnation of sexually explicit materials which depict women in situations that are humiliating, demeaning, and subjugating. I can still recall photographs of nude young women being penetrated by broom handles, smeared with feces, urinated upon, covered in blood or kneeling submissively in the act of fellatio. Most American citizens have no idea that such gruesome scenes are common in the world of obscene publications today. When asked to describe pornography currently on the market, they think in terms of airbrushed centerfolds in the popular "men's magazines." But steady customers of pornography have long since grown tired of simple heterosexual nudity. Indeed, a visit to an adult bookstore quickly reveals the absence of so-called "normal" sexuality. The offerings today feature beribboned 18- to 20-year-old women whose genitalia have been shaved to make them look like little girls, and men giving enemas or whippings to one another, and metal bars to hold a woman's legs apart, and 3-foot rubber penises, and photographs of women sipping ejaculate from champagne glasses. In one shop which our staff visited on Times Square, there were 46 films for sale which depicted women having intercourse or performing oral sex with different animals . . . pigs, dogs, donkeys, and horses. This is the world of pornography today, and I believe the public would rise up in wrath to condemn it if they knew of its prominence.

Finally, our Commission was unanimously opposed to child pornography in any form. Though categorically illegal since 1983, a thriving cottage industry still exists in this country. Fathers, stepfathers, uncles, teachers, and neighbors find ways to secure photographs of the children in their care. They then sell or trade the pictures to fellow pedophiles. I will never forget a particular set of photographs shown to us at our first hearing in Washington, D.C. It focused on a cute, nine-year-old boy who had fallen into the hands of a molester. In the first picture, the blond lad was fully clothed and smiling at the camera. But in the second, he was nude, dead, and had a butcher knife protruding from his chest. I served for 14 years as a member of a medical school faculty and thought I had seen it all. But my knees buckled and tears came to my eyes as these and hundreds of other photographs of children were presented . . . showing pitiful boys and girls with their rectums enlarged to accommodate adult males and their vaginas penetrated with pencils, toothbrushes, and guns. Perhaps the reader can understand my anger and disbelief when a representative for the American Civil Liberties Union testified a few minutes later. He advocated the free exchange of pornography, *all* pornography, in the marketplace. He was promptly asked about material depicting children such as those we had seen. This man said, with a straight face, that it is the ACLU's position that child pornography should not be produced, but once it is in existence, there should be no restriction on its sale and distribution. In other words, the photographic record of a child's molestation and abuse should be a legal source of profit for those who wish to reproduce, sell, print, and distribute it for the world to see. And that, he said, was the intent of the First Amendment to the Constitution!

Speaking personally, I now passionately support the control of sexually explicit material that is legally obscene, whether it relates to children or adults. Though the Commission has dealt at some length in its report with specific "harms" associated with pornography, I would like to list the dangers here from my own point of view. Our critics have alleged that the Commission wishes to usher in a new era of sexual repression . . . that we favor governmental interference in America's bedrooms and even in our thoughts. That is nonsense. On the other hand, I have seen enough evidence in the past year to convince me of the devastation inflicted on victims of pornography. It is on their behalf that we must intervene. Here, then, are the harms as I perceive them.

(1) Depictions of violence against women are related to violence against women everywhere. Though social research on this subject has been difficult to conduct, the totality of evidence supports the linkage between illustration and imitation. Furthermore, pornography perpetrates the so-called "rape myth" whereby women are consistently depicted as wanting to be assaulted even when they deny it. They are shown as terrified victims in the beginnings of rape scenes, but conclude by begging for more. Men who want to believe that women crave violent sex can find plenty of pornographic evidence to support their predilections.

(2) For a certain percentage of men, the use of pornographic material is addictive and progressive. Like the addiction to drugs, alcohol, or food, those who are hooked on sex become obsessed by their need. It fills their world, night and day. And too often, their families are destroyed in the process.

(3) Pornography is degrading to women. How could any of us, having heard Andrea Dworkin's moving testimony, turn a deaf ear to her protest? The pornographic depictions she described are an affront to an entire gender, and I would take that case to any jury in the land. Remember that men are the purchasers of pornography. Many witnesses testified that women are typically repulsed by visual depictions of the type therein described. It is provided primarily for the lustful pleasure of men and boys who use it to generate excitation. And it is my belief, though evidence is not easily obtained, that a small but dangerous minority will then choose to act aggressively against the nearest available females. Pornography is the theory; rape is the practice.

(4) It appears extremely naive to assume that the river of obscenity which has inundated the American landscape has not invaded the world of children. This seven-billion-dollar industry pervades every dimension of our lives. There are more stores selling pornographic videos than there are McDonald hamburger stands. More than 800,000 phone calls are made each day to dial-a-porn companies in New York (180,000,000 in 1984), many placed by boys and girls still in elementary school. Furthermore, recent clinical observations by Dr. Victor Cline and others have indicated that a growing number of children are finding their parents' sexually explicit videos and magazines, and are experimenting with what they have learned on younger children. The problem is spreading rapidly. Obviously, obscenity cannot be permitted to flow freely through the veins of society without reaching the eyes and ears of our children. Latchkey kids by the millions are watching porn on Cable TV and reading their parents' adult magazines. For 50 cents, they can purchase their own pornographic tabloids from vendor machines on the street. Or they can hear shocking vulgarities for free on their heavy metal radio stations. At an age when elementary school children should be reading Tom Sawyer and viewing

traditional entertainment in the spirit of Walt Disney, they are learning perverted facts which neither their minds nor bodies are equipped to handle. It is my belief, accordingly, that the behavior of an entire generation of teenagers is being adversely affected by the current emphasis on premarital sexuality and general eroticism seen nightly on television, in the movies, and in the other sources of pornography I have mentioned. It is not surprising that the incidence of unwed pregnancy and abortions has skyrocketed since 1970. Teens are merely doing what they've been taught, that they should get into bed, early and often. And to a large degree, pornography has done this to them.

(5) Organized crime controls more than 85 percent of all commercially produced pornography in America. The sale and distribution of these materials produces huge profits for the crime lords who also sell illegal drugs to our kids and engage in murder, fraud, bribery, and every vice known to man. Are we to conclude that the 7 billion (or more) tax-free dollars that they receive each year from the pornography industry is not harmful to society? Is malignant melanoma harmful to the human body?

(6) Pornography is often used by pedophiles to soften children's defenses against sexual exploitation. They are shown nude pictures of adults, for example, and are told, "See. This is what mommies and daddies do." They are then stripped of innocence and subjected to brutalities that they will remember for a lifetime.

(7) Outlets for obscenity are magnets for sex-related crimes. When a thriving adult bookstore moves into a neighborhood, an array of "support-services" typically develops around it. Prostitution, narcotics, and street crime proliferate. From this perspective, it is interesting that law enforcement officials often claim they do not investigate or attempt to control the flow of obscenity because they lack the resources to combat it. In reality, their resources will extend farther if they first enforce the laws relating to pornography. The consequent reduction in crime makes this a cost-effective use of taxpayer's funds.

The City of Cincinnati, Ohio, has demonstrated how a community can rid itself of obscenity without inordinate expenditures of personnel and money.

(8) So-called adult bookstores are often centers of disease and homosexual activity. Again, the average citizen is not aware that the primary source of revenue in adult bookstores is derived from video and film booths. Patrons enter these 3-by-3 foot cubicles and deposit a coin in the slot. They are then treated to about 90 seconds of a pornographic movie. If they want to see more, they must continue to pump coins (usually quarters) in the machine. The booths I witnessed on New York's Times Square were even more graphic. Upon depositing the coin, a screen was raised, revealing two or more women and men who performed live sex acts upon one another on a small stage. Everything that is possible for heterosexuals, homosexuals, or lesbians to do was demonstrated a few feet from the viewers. The booths from which these videos or live performers are viewed become filthy beyond description as the day progresses. Police investigators testified before our Commission that the stench is unbearable and that the floor becomes sticky with semen, urine, and saliva. Holes in the walls between the booths are often provided to permit male homosexuals to

service one another. Given the current concern over sexually transmitted diseases and especially Acquired Immune Deficiency Syndrome (AIDS), it is incredible that health departments have not attempted to regulate such businesses. States that will not allow restaurant owners or hairdressers or counselors or acupuncturists to operate without licenses have permitted these wretched cesspools to escape governmental scrutiny. To every public health officer in the country I would ask, "Why?"

(9) Finally, pornography is a source of significant harm to the institution of the family and to society at large. Can anything which devastates vulnerable little children, as we have seen, be considered innocuous to the parents who produced them? Raising healthy children is the primary occupation of families, and anything which invades the childhoods and twists the minds of boys and girls must be seen as abhorrent to the mothers and fathers who gave them birth. Furthermore, what is at stake here is the future of the family itself. We are sexual creatures, and the physical attraction between males and females provides the basis for every dimension of marriage and parenthood. Thus, *anything* that interjects itself into that relationship must be embraced with great caution. Until we *know* that pornography is not addictive and progressive . . . until we are *certain* that the passion of fantasy does not destroy the passion of reality . . . until we are *sure* that obsessive use of obscene materials will not lead to perversions and conflict between husbands and wives . . . then we dare not adorn them with the crown of respectability. Society has an absolute obligation to protect itself from material which crosses

the line established objectively by its legislators and court system. That is not sexual repression. That is self-preservation.

If not limited by time and space, I could describe dozens of other harms associated with exposure to pornography. Presumably, members of Congress were also cognizant of these dangers when they drafted legislation to control sexually explicit material. The President and his predecessors would not have signed those bills into criminal laws if they had not agreed. The Supreme Court must have shared the same concerns when it ruled that obscenity is not protected by the First Amendment—reaffirming the validity and constitutionality of current laws. How can it be, then, that these carefully crafted laws are not being enforced? Good question! The refusal of federal and local officials to check the rising tide of obscenity is a disgrace and an outrage. It is said that the production and distribution of pornography is the only unregulated industry remaining today . . . the last vestige of "free enterprise" in America. Indeed, the *salient* finding emerging from 12 months of testimony before our commission reflected this utter paralysis of government in response to the pornographic plague. As citizens of a democratic society, we have surrendered our right to protect ourselves in return for protection by the State. Thus, our governmental representatives have a constitutional mandate to shield us from harm and criminal activity . . . including that associated with obscenity. It is time that our leaders were held accountable for their obvious malfeasance. Attorney General Meese, who has courageously supported other unpopular causes, has been reluctant to tackle this one. He is reportedly awaiting the final report from the Commission before mobilizing the Department of Justice. We will see what happens now. . . .

[It] is my hope that the effort we invested will provide the basis for a new public policy. But that will occur only if American citizens demand action from their government. Nothing short of a public outcry will motivate our slumbering representatives to defend community standards of decency. It is that public statement that the pornographers fear most, and for very good reason. The people possess the power in this wonderful democracy to override apathetic judges, disinterested police chiefs, unmotivated U.S. Attorneys, and unwilling federal officials. I pray that they will do so. If they do not, then we have labored in vain.

NO

Philip Nobile and Eric Nadler

THE SHADOW COMMISSION

BARRY LYNN

Fathers Who Know Best

I spent much of the last year stalking the pornography commission, commenting regularly on their inadequacies and criticizing the civil liberties dangers posed by many of their proposals. The zaniness of the pornography commission was, of course, so inspired that it will provide the grist for a lifetime of my censorship lectures. Who can forget the FBI agent detailing the photographs he seized in his career, including the terrifying one of a "woman surrounded by a vagina"? How about the commissioner discussing a recently viewed bestiality slide of a man and a chicken and who queried, after noting it was but a "small point," whose penis was in whom (or what)? When the laughter ends, though, the real tragedy of the commission starts to become visible.

This body was not encumbered with the need to accept Supreme Court-articulated limitations on the availability of sexual material. They were writing on a clean slate and could have chosen to repudiate, as did their predecessor commission, the archaic constraints of "obscenity" law and let consenting adults see what they choose, regardless of whether their neighbors would be offended by it.

Instead, they tried to breathe new life into "obscenity" regulation. They applauded the most dangerous reasoning of all to suppress speech—that it generates bad "attitudes." I'm convinced that much pornography does generate bad attitudes, along with much in cartoon shows, floor-wax advertising and network sitcoms. But when in this battle against "bad attitudes" we abandon what we view as affirmative alternative speech and turn instead to use of governmental censorship or moral mob rule, we are all the losers.

The commission could not really discover much more than a smidgen of science to bolster the claims of real-life sexual violence caused by pornography. No matter. They simply filled in the gaps of science with the legion of their own preconceptions and intuitions buttressed with some Gestalt derived from the sometimes plaintive, sometimes pathetic, voices of alleged "victims" of pornography.

Many of their "victims" were obsessed "addicts," one of whom claimed to have seen a deck of pornographic playing cards and then became obsessed with stealing *Playboy* and, finally took to sexually abusing the family dogs; and the rapists who sought to explain away their crime and guilt by scapegoating a medium more contemporary than comic books and more plausible than the Twinkies which drive Dan White to murder. The *victims* also included women so mired in abusive relationships steeped in pathology, substance abuse and family crisis that claimed causality from pornography was so tangential as to be nearly an invisible afterthought.

They could have endorsed things which would have made a difference to real "victims" of the rampant abuses of a still sexist culture—strengthening sexual harassment laws; removing spousal immunity in sexual-assault cases; providing real help to those actually coerced into pornography. And then to prevent the creation of future "victims," they could wholeheartedly have embraced a serious sex-education program in our schools. Instead, they launched a national crusade against dirty pictures, as if they had some magical powers to corrupt the young, obliterate the values taught by the other institutions in our culture and preserve a dying patriarchy. I am underwhelmed by pornography's power to do any of these.

They were, on balance, quintessential censors, sharing all the arrogance of censors throughout the world and throughout our history. They truly believed that they knew best what all should see about sex—and most even knew how all should "behave" sexually as well. Moreover, although they have wallowed in the worst of pornographic muck for a year and been apparently unaffected, they remain convinced that the average American would be led down the path to criminality or deviance by his or her chosen encounters with the same material.

Here is a group that says it would be "socially harmful" if people picketed the bookseller hawking [James Joyce's] *Ulysses*—a book nearly as unreadable as the turgid prose of the commission's report—but embraces with all their hearts the boycotters of stores which hustle *Penthouse* from behind the counter. Let the elite read; keep the masses from even looking. Historically, there was no "obscenity" law before the printing press finally gave average people a chance to see the sexually explicit material previously available only to the wealthy and powerful, who undoubtedly thought only they could handle it.

The 1,000-page report they wrote was so predictable, it could have been drafted the day after the commission convened and saved the taxpayers a good $500,000. But the particular way it was styled is clever to a fault, slippery enough to be cast [aside] if it becomes too much of a personal or professional embarrassment. It sometimes reads like a scientific discourse and occasionally like a legal treatise. Mostly, though, it crows like some elephantine moral tract passed out at the bus station. . . .

I believe it was the commission which ultimately neutralized itself—its methods for gathering evidence, evaluating it and finally reporting it were so intellectually indefensible that it sank from its own irrelevance and irresponsibility.

Barry Lynn is the legislative counsel for the American Civil Liberties Union.

DR. JOHN MONEY

A Conspiracy Against Women

The Meese commission report purports to be a modern-day Saint George, slaying the evil dragon of pornography to protect women from its violent and degrading effects. But the real intent of the report is not to protect women, but to exploit them. By adopting the militant-feminist rhetoric of Catharine MacKinnon and Andrea Dworkin, the Meese commission affirms that women have no right to be sexual. They are obliged only to be loving wives committed to their men, whom they must treat not as sex, but as status and success, objects.

The Meese report turns out to be a conspiracy against women—the most furtively sexist and antifeminist document of our time. It declares that women are so morally delicate that they may not partake with men of the explicit depiction of the frankly erotic. Can you believe it? Even the sexual normalcy of the naked human body and of healthy, happy people having joyful sexual intercourse must be suppressed, lest it lead the viewer downward on the ladder of degeneracy to the warped and pathological sex of violence and degradation.

With women excluded, men will not, of course, relinquish pornography, for by nature's decree they are dependent on their eyes more than women are to get turned on sexually. As they did with alcohol under Prohibition, men will simply take pornography back to where it used to be, distributed commercially by bootleggers on the nontaxable underground market and seen in locker rooms and at stag parties restricted to men only. Women once again will be divided into Madonnas and whores, lust belonging only to the whores, not to the sexually neutered Madonnas. The deceptive purpose of the Meese report is to deny women's equality with men; and to put women back in their traditional place, unliberated, dependent on men and under men's patriarchal protection.

It is not surprising that the commission split, 9–2, and that the two dissenting voices are those of two of the four women commissioners. Ellen Levine and Judith Becker had the wit to perceive the overall effect of the report in subjugating women, and the wisdom to recognize that it is just plain foolish to attribute all the injustices of women's inequality in society to dirty pictures.

That does not mean that the two dissenting voices condone the kind of pornography which the report classifies as violent and degrading and which medicine and science classify as paraphilic and pathological. This kind of pornography is erotically useless to people who do not have the particular paraphilia that it depicts. The report singles out for special mention urophilia, the paraphilia in which a man or a woman is turned on and climaxes sexually not in the usual way, but by being urinated upon and drinking urine. People who are not urophiliacs could be locked in a viewing room and forced to watch 50 hours—or 500 hours—of urophilic movies, but they would not be turned into urophiliacs as a result of the experience. If you don't believe that statement, then try the experiment.

Paraphilias are not contagious. They are not caught from books, films or videotapes. The contagion theory is as old as the theory of witchcraft. Less than three centuries ago, people, mostly women, were being burned at the stake because of it. Today they are imprisoned—at exorbitant taxpayer expense, one should be reminded. The commission was given expert testimony on the falsity of the contagion theory, but it elected to disregard the evidence of its own experience. If the contagion theory were correct, then the commissioners should by now all be imprisoned as sex criminals, for they have been exposed to large quantities of all varieties of pornography, violent, degrading and otherwise.

By clinging to the ancient falsehood of the contagion theory, the report evades what should have been its major responsibility, namely, finding out how to prevent the development of paraphilias, especially those that it classified as violent or degrading, in the generation of children now growing up. A boy does not need to look at pornography to know what turns him on sexually. Nature presents him with his own personal pornography in his wet dreams. Developmentally, the sequence is from wet dreams and masturbation fantasies to homemade pornography that copies the dream content and possibly, as he grows older, to commercial pornography—but only if he finds the type of commercial pornography that matches his own wet-dream and masturbation fantasies. Any other type, no matter how much it may stimulate someone else, will leave him cold.

Girls at puberty do not have the same dramatic experience of seeing pornography vividly and visually as the accompaniment of a wet dream. Only a few girls have explicit sexual dreams with orgasm, at the time of puberty. This is one reason, and a very powerful one, why females, by and large, do not understand the male's interest in and arousal by visually explicit pornography. Women's pornography is different. It is more verbal, more romantic and centered more on cuddling, hugging, kissing and the sense of touch.

Children who grow up sexually healthy develop a healthy, usually heterosexual, mental "lovemap" in their brains (see J. Money, *Lovemaps*, New York, Irvington, 1986). They become the future purchasers of normal, healthy pornography. Children, especially boys, who fail to develop a healthy lovemap are those who are sexually traumatized while growing up. The greatest single source of traumatization is the brutal punishment and humiliation of children who are discovered playing with their own genitals or engaging in normal sexual rehearsal play with playmates. Traumatic punishment of children for obeying nature's way of preparing for healthy sexuality in maturity vandalizes the lovemap and either destroys it or turns it into a paraphilic one. Not unexpectedly, brutal punishment of childhood sexual rehearsal play introduces brutality and violence into the lovemap, thus creating a person who will grow up to be dependent on violence for sexual arousal and climax. This is the person who becomes a patron of violent pornography.

Because the commission does not address the issue of the origins of pornographic imagery, and because it advocates an escalation of punishment related to pornography, its report will prove to be self-defeating. Instead of protecting women, the report will have the long-range effect of actually producing an ever-expanding epidemic of violence and degradation presently evident not only in pornography, but also in reality. The next generation, and the next, will hold us all accountable.

Dr. John Money is a professor of medical psychology and pediatrics at the Johns Hopkins University and Hospital.

DR. BERNIE ZILBERGELD
Porn as Therapy

Pornography has one great value that is often overlooked—its use in enhancing marital sex. Pornography can help to strengthen not only individual marriages, but perhaps the very institution of marriage itself. The importance of satisfaction in a good marriage is supported by scientific research and is recognized by many Christian ministers. Millions of ordinary married Americans benefit from erotica and will suffer if it is taken away from them.

Why do so many people refuse to admit that keeping sex interesting, exciting and satisfying in a long relationship is not easy? Couples have to work at it, using whatever aids they can find. Vacations without children, sharing fantasies and open communication are reliable ways to rejuvenate a marriage. Equally valuable is the sharing of erotic materials. It would be tragic if this loving opportunity were denied them.

Dr. June Reinisch, director of the Kinsey Institute, frequently gets letters like this: "My wife and I belong to the church, have three children and do everything right. But once a week we like to spice up our private lives with an erotic video. Why are people trying to take them away from us?" I hear similar things all the time from clients and others who talk to me about sex.

Many people in traditional marriages have turned to erotic films, books and magazines to enhance their sex lives. These people recognize that it is no easy matter to keep ennui at bay over a long period. Before turning to erotica, these spouses made love infrequently, found it either boring or unexciting and realized that much of their sexual desire was directed at people other than their partner. But they did not want to have affairs. Rather they preferred to rekindle passion for their own spouse.

Such couples often report that watching an erotic film, usually on a VCR in their own bedrooms, or reading sexual letters and articles in magazines like *Penthouse* or *Playboy,* leads to more frequent and more intense sex.

Obviously, erotic materials are not for everybody. Some people are turned off by them rather than on. I simply want to emphasize the popularity of erotica among many traditional couples.

Other benefits of pornography include learning specific sexual techniques and getting ideas about how and where to have sex with their partners.

Exposure to sexually explicit materials also leads to more open communication about sex. "I've always wanted to try that," or "Have you ever fantasized anything like this?" are common reactions to viewing pornography. Such honest conversations usually lead to increased closeness and better sex. I have found that exposure to erotica is one of the best ways to improve sexual communication between a man and a woman. Even if a person's initial reaction is "I could never imagine doing that," a useful dialogue often results. It's a scientifically proven fact that talking about sex plays an important part in a good sex life.

Most of what I have learned about the benefits of erotica comes from middle-aged churchgoers who believe strongly in monogamy and family. Some acknowledge that they would be tempted to have affairs if they failed to put some zest into their marital sex. Contrary to what the critics of erotica maintain, these people are using pornography to strengthen their marriages. But all the negative publicity about pornography causes them to be apologetic or embarrassed about discussing it. Even though they know its value in their own lives, they still feel that perhaps it indicates a defect in their personalities or in their love for one another.

Therapists who work with couples' sex problems are also familiar with the benefits of erotica. It's probable that more than half of all sex therapists recommend explicit sexual materials to their clients. A fair amount of research indicates that exposure to sexual materials increases both a couple's tolerance of the sexual behavior of others and desire for one another.

Personally I find the vast bulk of erotica to be poorly presented and boring. But I cannot deny the rewards it has brought to many American couples. It is sad to think that this gift may be taken away.

Dr. Bernie Zilbergeld is a psychologist and the author of Male Sexuality.

DR. LARRY BARON
AND DR. MURRAY A. STRAUS

Two False Principles

In 1970 the President's Commission on Obscenity and Pornography concluded that there was no evidence demonstrating that sexually explicit materials caused sex crimes. In the intervening years, those who wanted to limit pornography claimed that sex magazines and movies had become increasingly explicit and violent and that new research has invalidated the finding of the 1970 president's report. On the basis of this assumption, Attorney General Meese mandated his 11-member commission to study a wide variety of pornographic materials, document adverse effects and devise new strategies to curb its proliferation. True to its assignment, the Meese commission concluded that pornography is harmful and urged law-enforcement agencies to crack down on those engaged in the production and sale of obscene materials.

Ironically, the new and more sophisticated research reviewed by the commission makes a causal connection between sexually explicit materials and rape even *less* plausible than it was when the 1970 commission was examining this issue. How then could the Meese commission come to this conclusion? The answer is fairly clear. It is based on two principles.

The first principle is that explicit depiction of sex is offensive and harmful in and of itself. Based on this principle, there is no way of coming to any other conclusion than that pornography should be forbidden. Although the two commissioners (Judith Becker and Ellen Levine) who dissented from the final report lamented that the commission was not granted sufficient time and money with which to properly assess the testimony and reports made available to them, in light of the principle that sexually explicit materials are inherently offensive, more time and money would not have made much of a difference.

The second principle underlying the commission's conclusions and its recommendations to vigorously prosecute those who produce and sell obscene materials is to base conclusions on the "totality of evidence." This is a code phrase which means that the commission gave as much credence to the testimony of fundamentalist preachers, police officers, antipornography zealots and putative victims of pornography as it did to the results of carefully conducted social research. The "totality of evidence" also gave the commission an escape hatch to disregard the warnings and interpretations of researchers whenever they suggested that the findings do not support a causal connection between pornography and rape. In fact, that was the fate of our own research at the hands of the Meese commission.

We found that rape rates are higher in states with a large readership of sexually explicit magazines. That impressed the commissioners. However, they were not impressed by our explanation that this correlation was most likely the result of a common factor which underlies both sex-magazine-readership rates and rape, nor by our recent demonstration that when appropriate statistical controls are introduced, the correlation between sex-magazine-readership rates and rape rates no longer holds.

There are many such "spurious" (i.e., noncausal) correlations. For example, there is a very high correlation between the reading ability of children and their shoe size, but having big feet does not cause children to read better. The underlying factor is the child's age—older children read better and also have bigger feet. If age is statistically controlled, then the correlation between shoe size and reading ability does not hold. Similarly, we pointed out that there are underlying social and demographic factors which cause both high rape rates and high sex-magazine readership. How does the

commission report deal with such information? By ignoring our warnings and arguing that: "The absence of evidence should by no means be taken to deny the existence of the causal link." The commission is so bent on showing harmful effects that when the research shows none, they argue that harm simply has not yet been uncovered.

Our view of the totality of the *scientific* evidence is that it shows no causal relationship between pornography and rape. Indeed, Donnerstein's experimental studies show a *reduction* in aggression following exposure to pornography without violent content; and Berle Kutchinsky's recent studies of nations that have removed restrictions on pornography shows either no increase in the rape rate for the years after the legalization of pornography, or a decrease in the rape rate. Of course, there are aggressive and violent people who use sex as a means of expressing aggression, but images of sex do not cause such violence.

The commission probably began its inquiry assuming that the research conducted since the 1970 pornography report would support its belief in the harmfulness of pornography. Instead it was confronted by evidence which shows that the roots of violence are to be found in violence, not in sex, no matter how explicit or "offensive" it may be. The commission ignored or distorted that evidence because, in our opinion, it was more concerned with censoring sexual depictions than with eliminating violence against women.

Dr. Larry Baron is a lecturer of sociology at Yale University. Dr. Murray Straus is a professor of sociology and the chair of the Family Research Laboratory at the University of New Hampshire.

DR. ROBERT STAPLES

The Black Response

As the black member of the "shadow commission," I am indebted to the opponents of sexual fascism for giving me a chance to express the black view on pornography—an opportunity denied by the government-formed commission. Although we represent 35 million American citizens or one in nine inhabitants of this country, the attorney general did not see fit to include one of us among his carefully selected commission. This is hardly surprising considering that Ed Meese is a known adversary of the black community. Perhaps he thought blacks were too perverse to ever agree that porn debased women, destroyed the family and caused violent rapes and sexual promiscuity. More likely he realized that it would be difficult to find a black representative of his/her community who viewed porn as a major issue. In one sense, we were relieved that Meese's attention was diverted from restoring us to our nineteenth-century status and that instead he had decided to concentrate on regulating what all Americans can do in the privacy of their own homes. To that extent, he has become an equal-opportunity enforcer of the denial of human rights to all members of this society.

Most blacks would agree with Dr. Morris Lipton, one of the experts on the 1970 presidential report on pornography, that "given the major issues of the day, pornography is a trivial issue." Blacks would add to that analysis the caveat that porn is a white man's problem—a particular kind of white man's problem. The presidential commission Dr. Lipton served on found that the typical consumer of porn was a white male and that blacks were underrepresented among the purveyors of erotica. However, blacks were not total abstainers from porn consumerism. Nor did they harbor any particular antipathy toward it. Indeed, many today do buy sex videocassettes, purchase *Penthouse* and enjoy risqué jokes, cartoons, etc. But as a group that earns only 56 percent of the income whites do, they often do not have the discretionary income with which to purchase erotica.

As for the black position on porn, it would certainly differ from that arrived at by the Meese commission. Meese and his minions reflect a particular white worldview that there is something inherently damaging and sinful about sexual activity and interest outside the marital bedroom, and that any participation in other kinds of sexual behavior should produce enormous amounts of guilt in the errant individual. Blacks have traditionally had a more naturalistic attitude toward human sexuality, seeing it as the normal expression of sexual attraction between men and women. Even in African societies, sexual conduct was not the result of some divine guidance by God or other deities. It was secularly regulated and encompassed the tolerance of a wide range of sexual attitudes and behaviors. Sexual deviance, where so defined, was not an act against God's will but a violation of community standards.

Rather than seeing the depiction of heterosexual intercourse or nudity as an inherent debasement of women, as a fringe group of feminists claims, the black community would see women as having equal rights to the enjoyment of sexual stimuli. It is nothing more than a continuation of the white male's traditional double standard and paternalism to regard erotica as existing only for male pleasure and women only as sexual objects. Since that double standard has never attracted many American blacks, the claim that women are exploited by exhibiting their nude bodies or engaging in heterosexual intercourse lacks credibility. After all, it was the white missionaries in fourteenth century Africa who forced African women to regard their quasi-nude bodies as sinful and placed them in clothes. This probably accounts for the rather conspicuous absence of black women in the feminist fight against porn. Certainly black men were unlikely to join with the likes of lunatic feminists such as Catharine MacKinnon and Andrea Dworkin, who treat pornography as discrimination against women.

The black community represents organic evidence against some of the assumptions of the Meese commission on pornography. If porn is alleged to lead to male sexual aggression, that is, rape, why are the lowest consumers of porn (blacks) so overrepresented among those arrested for and convicted of rape? A porn commission without a political axe to grind might have concluded that when other expressions of manhood such as gainful employment and economic success are blocked, those men will express their frustration and masculinity against women. In other words, it is the denial of economic rights, not porn, that is in large part responsible for rape in this country. Such a conclusion would not go down well with the Reagan administration, whose policies have led to the burgeoning number of unemployed black males.

As for the Meese commission view that porn is related to sexual promiscuity, it is almost a laughable finding in the black community. One man's sexual promiscuity is another man's definition of sexual freedom. In most cases it refers to keeping women in their sexual straitjackets so that sexual pleasure remains a male domain. The black community has exhibited a lusty sexual appetite while obeying certain rules of common sense and propriety in its sexual conduct. The kinds of kinky sex favored by a small minority of whites is almost unknown among the black population. Group sex, and sexual crimes other than rape, were and are rare among us. And a recent survey commissioned by the National Institutes of Health found that sexually active black women were more likely to be involved in long-term "serious" relationships than were sexually active white women, and that their serious relationships lasted longer than the relationships of white women.

Still, it is one of the ironies of American life that the one racial group in the U.S. whose image is so strongly linked to sexuality in the public mind should be excluded from a commission dealing with the sexual aspects of human behavior. Ranging from the thousands of lynchings of black men for the dubious sin of lusting after white women to the segregation of races in the South to prevent interracial sexual contact, we now have the more recent variation on the theme of black immorality.

While there may be cause for concern over the high rate of out-of-wedlock births occurring among black women in their teenage years, the Meese commission refused to endorse the best weapon against teenage pregnancy—sex education. The same National Institutes of Health survey discovered that twice as many single black women as white women are having sex through their 20s without contraceptives. Nationally, a majority of all out-of-wedlock births occur among black women. Ultimately, blacks suffer more and are the chief victims of white sexual guilt. They are denied sex education in the public schools because a white-controlled bureaucracy either denies it to the school system or forces it to contain a largely moral content. However, in those few public schools that have decided to provide contraceptive services to their students, only schools with a predominantly black student body have chosen to do so. Using black high-school students as the first guinea pigs in these experiments is akin to the same kind of white colonialism that tested birth-control products on Puerto Rican women to see if they would be safe for white women.

Teenage pregnancy is a problem in the black community because the unwed mothers keep their children and many become dependent on public assistance. The N.I.H. survey found that half of the white women surveyed and only one-tenth of the black women aborted their first pregnancies. Young black women seldom resort to shotgun weddings, because their pool of potential husbands largely consists of young and unemployed black males. Were they to be provided a sound sex education or safe contraceptives, many would never face this dilemma.

The kinds of morals that Ed Meese and Ronald Reagan understand are related to nineteenth-century notions of sin. . . .

Their past record is one of supporting racial segregation and black deprivation. Therefore blacks can only hope they will cease to interfere with the private lives of American citizens and adopt a real moral posture toward the conditions of poverty, nuclear disarmament and the conduct of government. Permitting pov-erty to exist and escalating the nuclear-arms race are the real sins and major issues of today.

Dr. Robert Staples is professor of sociology at the University of California, San Francisco.

POSTSCRIPT

Is Pornography Harmful?

The issues raised by the 1986 Meese commission about whether or not pornography poses a threat to society continue to run through current debates over the role of pornography in our culture and its impact on personal relationships. But time has added some new dimensions to the debate about whether or not there exists a connection between sex and violence.

Ellen Willis, a feminist, zeros in on one important new dimension when she points out that violence, conquest, submission, vulnerability, power, and messy passion are natural and inescapable dimensions of sex for both men and women. She argues:

> [T]he view of sex that most often emerges from talk about erotica is as sentimental and euphemistic as the word itself: lovemaking should be beautiful, romantic, soft, nice, and devoid of messiness, vulgarity, impulses to power, or indeed aggression of any sort. . . . This goody-goody concept of eroticism is not feminist but feminine. . . . [Women are not] supposed to admit that we, too, have sadistic impulses, that our sexual fantasies may reflect forbidden urges.

Marilyn French, also a feminist, disagrees and claims that the heart of the problem is that sex and pornography are both about power and control. As long as males hold the power in society, she claims, they will tolerate pornography's hatred of and violence toward women, even as they condemn all expressions of hatred and violence based on race or ethnic origin:

> One cannot *prove* that violence against women in pornography leads to violence against women in life any more than one can *prove* that the disparagement of blacks and Jews pervasive in nineteenth-century culture *caused* the horrors of African colonialism and the Holocaust. The mere suspicion of a connection is considered sufficient reason to refuse to legitimate hatred of groups. Only when it comes to women does our culture suspend this restraint.

SUGGESTED READINGS

M. French, *The War Against Women* (Ballantine Books, 1992).

D. L. Mosher, "Misinformation on Pornography: A Lobby Disguised as an Educational Organization," *SIECUS Report* (May 1986).

D. E. Mould, A Critical Analysis on Recent Research on Violent Erotica," *Journal of Sex Research* (1988).

K. E. O'Grady, "Donnerstein, Malamuth, and Mould: The Conduct of Research and the Nature of Inquiry," *Journal of Sex Research* (1988).

E. Willis, "Feminism, Moralism, and Pornography," in David Steinberg, ed., *The Erotic Impulse: Honoring the Sensual Self* (Jeremy P. Tarcher/Perigee Books, 1992).

PART 2

Issues in Reproduction and Health

As medical technology progresses, and as physicians and scientists become better able to manipulate the human body, social and moral awareness changes. Because such procedures as embryo transplant and abortion are now performed with relative ease—indeed, the chemical abortifacient RU 486 may revolutionize abortion—we must consider the legal, historical, and humanistic implications, as well as the effects on prevailing views of gender roles. In addition, the increasing health threat of sexually transmitted diseases, especially AIDS, raises questions on how to best protect one of the fastest-growing at-risk groups: teenagers.

■ Should RU 486 Be Legalized?

■ Should Schools Distribute Condoms?

■ Should Surrogate Motherhood Be Outlawed?

■ Abortion and the "Pro-Life" *v.* "Pro-Choice" Debate: Should the Human Fetus Be Considered a Person?

ISSUE 6

Should RU 486 Be Legalized?

YES: Janet Callum and Rebecca Chalker, from "RU 486: Yes," *Ms.* (March/April 1993)

NO: Janice Raymond, Renate Klein, and Lynette Dumble, from "RU 486: No," *Ms.* (March/April 1993)

ISSUE SUMMARY

YES: Janet Callum, former director of administrative services for the Feminist Women's Health Center, and Rebecca Chalker, an author and women's health advocate, claim that the risks of using RU 486 for abortion are exceedingly low. They argue that the ban against RU 486 should be lifted in the United States because it is less intrusive than surgical abortion, it leaves women in control, and it appears to be a safe and effective abortion alternative, which they feel women need.

NO: Janice Raymond, a professor of women's studies, Renate Klein, a lecturer in the humanities, and Lynette Dumble, a research fellow in the surgery department at the University of Melbourne, believe that feminists should not advocate a dubious and dangerous technology such as RU 486, but instead should fight to take conventional abortion methods out of the hands of physicians and promote the licensing of trained laywomen to handle most abortions.

In 1982, Dr. Etienne-Emile Baulieu discovered a "muscular little molecule that blocks the hormonal messages crucial in allowing the fertilized egg to implant in the uterine lining and in maintaining a pregnancy." This discovery was the basis of the early abortifacient RU 486. Since then, RU 486 has fast become a classic example of how medical progress can revolutionize our lives and, at the same time, create a maelstrom of ethical, religious, political, and feminist conflict.

Early on, antiabortion forces in France joined the Roman Catholic church in threatening to boycott all products manufactured by the French pharmaceutical company Roussel-Uclaf if they marketed RU 486. After considerable debate, the French minister of health intervened, ordering the state-owned company to make RU 486 available to French women.

In subsequent years, RU 486 has been received variously by other countries. Germany, for example, has refused to allow marketing of RU 486 in order to avoid "the risk of being accused of mass murder"; the countries of Scandinavia and the United Kingdom have embraced the pill; and whether or not RU 486 will be accepted in Italy, China, and elsewhere remains to be determined.

In the United States, RU 486 has been a point of controversy in the pro-life versus pro-choice debate for over a decade. In the 1980s, fundamentalist Protestants, the Catholic hierarchy, and conservative male politicians formed an alliance with the Reagan and Bush administrations to stop all RU 486 research at the National Institutes of Health (NIH), which eventually resulted in the prevention of any importation of the drug even for experimental testing and research. At the same time, the threat of a boycott against all the products of any company that would consider marketing RU 486 in the United States scared off all potential sponsors.

Meanwhile, in Europe, important secondary uses of RU 486 were being discovered and documented. RU 486 has been used to limit the growth of brain tumors and to relieve the symptoms of life-threatening Cushing's syndrome, which is caused by an excess of adrenal gland hormone. RU 486 has also been used in other countries to treat breast cancer and endometrial (uterine) cancer.

The election of President Clinton signaled a change in the U.S. government's position on RU 486, and early in 1993 testing of the drug began in the United States. This suggests that RU 486 may soon be available to American women, at least on a limited basis.

Globally, RU 486 may become a major weapon in controlling population growth. In most Third World countries, Eastern Europe, China, and Southeast Asia, contraceptives are in short supply and very few people opt for voluntary sterilization. An estimated 500 million couples and individuals could benefit from RU 486 being made available. RU 486 could also benefit the millions of women who turn to illegal abortions in the absence of facilities for legal abortions, as well as the estimated 200,000 women who die annually from botched conventional abortions.

In the following selections, Janet Callum and Rebecca Chalker argue in favor of legalizing RU 486 for these and other reasons. Janice Raymond, Renate Klein, and Lynette Dumble call the drug "dubious reproductive technology" and encourage women's groups to abandon the push for RU 486.

YES

Janet Callum and
Rebecca Chalker

RU 486: YES

Given real and potential abuses of rapidly advancing reproductive technology, vigilance is necessary if women are to have control over their reproductive lives. Examples of such abuse include inadequate testing of oral contraceptives before marketing, suppression of critical information that would have prevented the marketing of the Dalkon Shield, aggressive sterilization of women without full informed consent, widespread use of diethylstilbestrol (DES) during pregnancy without adequate testing, and lack of reasonable legal protection for surrogate mothers. Given this history, it is important that, as with any new drug with application to women's reproductive rights, we question RU 486. However, we believe the suggestion that surgical abortion is preferable to abortion done with RU 486 is based on an incomplete understanding of the parameters of surgical abortion and that its analysis is seriously flawed.

"A Drug Cocktail" It is true that the RU 486 drug regimen includes other drugs: specifically, a prostaglandin injection or suppository and, if needed, an antinausea drug and pain medication, as well as antibiotics if an infection develops. [Prostaglandins are a type of local action hormones that stimulate smooth muscle fibers. An injection of prostaglandin can stimulate contractions of the uterus as well as the muscles of the heart and digestive tract.] However, women who have early-termination surgical abortions may also take a variety of drugs, including a preprocedure tranquilizer, local or general anesthetic, pain medication for postabortion cramping, Methergine or Pitocin for postabortion bleeding, and because of instrumentation of the uterus, antibiotics for postabortion infection. In both cases, women take a variety of drugs, some required, some optional.

Residual Effects RU 486 is an antiprogestin, a drug that blocks progesterone in the uterus, thus causing the embryo to be sloughed off. But it appears to do little else. It metabolizes quickly and is almost entirely cleared from the body within 48 hours. Currently there are no known residual effects of using RU 486 on a one-time or occasional basis. In the case of an incomplete abortion, the effects on the fetus are less certain. Because of this, we do acknowledge, as does the manufacturer, Roussel-UCLAF, that once RU 486 has been taken, a woman experiencing an incomplete abortion should seek surgical termination of her pregnancy.

Prostaglandins (PGs) do have a number of serious, sometimes violent, side effects. Alone they have been used to cause abortions, but because of the severe side effects, PGs have never become an important abortifacient. Most of the side effects women experience with RU 486, including nausea, headaches, dizziness, diarrhea, and hemorrhage, are attributable to the PG booster necessary to make RU 486 highly effective. However, the dose is only one fifth of that used in prostaglandin-only abortions, and these effects are transitory in most women.

Heavy Bleeding Following an RU 486 abortion, bleeding can last up to 35 or 40 days, with an average of eight to ten days. This is markedly similar to bleeding that occurs after an early-termination surgical abortion. Bleeding with RU 486 in total ranges from 14ml to 400 ml, similar to that of an early-termination suction abortion or, for that matter, heavy menstruation.

Complications As has been pointed out, several women who had RU 486 abortions had heart attacks or strokes, and that subsequently, one death has occurred. To date, these have been the only major complications reported with RU 486. The unfortunate death, that of a 31-year-old heavy smoker, could have been avoided if established screening protocols had been followed. Thus, to date, there has been one reported death in 100,000 women who have had RU 486 abortions. In the U.S., there is one death for every 200,000 abortions. Because only 100,000 RU 486 abortions have been done, it is not possible to compare the risk of death with that of early-termination abortion, except to note that such risk from either is exceedingly low, comparable to taking a single does of penicillin.

Incomplete Abortions With skilled practitioners, the initial aspiration procedure of early-termination abortion is successful 98 to 99 percent of the time. However, with less skilled practitioners, reaspiration rates may be as high as 3 percent, making surgical abortion not that different from RU 486, which has a second intervention rate of 4 to 6 percent. In either case, women are apprised of the symptoms of incomplete abortions and instructed to contact their practitioners if any symptoms develop. And in "developed" countries, incomplete abortions are often not considered a serious complication.

Medical Supervision It has been suggested that RU 486 abortions are too supervision-intensive, requiring up to four visits to a medical facility. The French standard does require four visits: the first for a pregnancy test and declaration of the intention to have an abortion; the second for the RU 486 pills; the third for the PG injection and abortion, and the fourth for followup. (In theory, it is possible to combine visits one and two, making a total of three visits.) In the U.S., early-termination surgical abortions can require two or three visits: the first for a pregnancy test, at which time the abortion is scheduled; the second for the abortion itself; and the third for a post-abortion checkup. Often the first two are combined, and a woman makes only two visits. But the number of required visits for either type of abortion does not appear to be burdensome for most women living in "developed" countries.

Early Termination In the U.S., surgical abortions are not generally done until seven weeks from the last menstrual period. One notable benefit of RU 486 is that it can be appropriately administered at five weeks from the last period, which would allow many women to have safe, complete abortions two weeks earlier than the current standard now allows.

In the "Developing" World In places where sterilization of instruments is difficult, and trained medical personnel are overburdened, RU 486 may ultimately prove to be safer and less labor-intensive. Furthermore, in "developing" countries, self-induced abortions *by any means available* are pandemic, and poorly trained practitioners, who typically operate under unsanitary conditions, are frequently employed. In many countries, infection from unsafe, incomplete procedures is one of the primary causes of hospital admission. But anecdotal evidence from Brazil suggests that the unsupervised use of over-the-counter supplies of Cytotec, as a prostaglandin abortion inducer, has decreased complications from self-induced abortions significantly. Even under less than ideal conditions, RU 486 could save many lives.

Privacy and Control The opposition contends that RU 486 does not, in fact, provide women with more private, less medicalized abortions. Granted, given both options, some women will still choose the traditional vacuum aspiration method. In 1989, Janet Callum went to France and interviewed women who were having RU 486 abortions. Some felt that because there was no instrumentation, RU 486 was gentler and less intrusive, and they also appreciated not having to disrobe and lie down before a stranger. Women were observed sitting quietly in a room together, reading mag-azines and talking. Occasionally one would excuse herself, walk into the bathroom and within about five minutes, emerge, her abortion completed. All expressed a profound appreciation of being "in control." These women left the hospital within ten to 15 minutes after their abortions, which is not that different from the 30-minute norm for non-anesthetized, early-termination suction procedures.

Summary We feel that it is essential to keep RU 486 in perspective. RU 486 is not a magic potion that will end all unwanted pregnancies and eliminate the need for surgical abortions. Nor will it, as the antiabortion zealots fear, bring the capability of abortion to every bedroom. Furthermore, it is essential that careful tracking of RU 486 be undertaken, particularly as it is introduced in the "developing" world to populations of women who are, on the whole, poorer and less healthy than are the women who have used this method thus far. RU 486 could prove to be less successful among women with fewer resources and poorer health. But given the information that we have, RU 486 appears to provide a safe and effective abortion alternative for many women at a time when we need more, not fewer, abortion options.

NO

Janice Raymond, Renate Klein, and Lynette Dumble

RU 486: NO

It is vital that U.S. women understand that some international women's groups have been far more critical of chemical abortion than have their U.S. counterparts. The Sixth International Women and Health Meeting, held in the Philippines in 1990, issued a resolution opposing the introduction of RU 486/PG, especially in "developing" countries, as did the Feminist International Network of Resistance to Reproductive and Genetic Engineering (FINRRAGE) Conference in Brazil.

We are concerned that the amount of resources and energy spent on lobbying for the introduction of RU 486 may detract from the necessary fight to maintain (and expand) safe conventional abortion facilities. We believe that women's health activists must continue to put pressure on lawmakers and abortion providers to ensure that safe, low-tech abortion is increasingly made available to women. We already have abortion methods that can be performed *safely* by skilled (lay) practitioners. We do not need "a drug cocktail" fraught with unknown consequences for women's short- and long-term health. It is distressing that others do not recognize the dangers inherent in RU 486 abortion, and instead welcome it as a new "choice" for women, calling our analysis "seriously flawed" and "based on an incomplete understanding of the parameters of surgical abortion." Only now in the promotion of RU 486 is conventional abortion referred to as "surgical," a description that bears little resemblance to low-tech (manual) vacuum aspiration.

"A Drug Cocktail" To state that both "surgical" abortion and RU 486 abortion involve the widespread use of drugs misses the point. The former can be performed with minimal drug use—a local anesthetic—whereas the latter is a medication-dependent abortion consisting of a drug cocktail: RU 486 and PG.

Residual Effects The antiprogesterone activity of RU 486 is not as localized as proponents claim. For example, it acts as an antiglucocorticosteroid blocker and can affect the central nervous system, and create

From Janice Raymond, Renate Klein, and Lynette Dumble, "RU 486: No," *Ms.* (March/April 1993). Copyright © 1993 by *Ms.* magazine and The Institute on Women and Technology, North Amherst, MA. Reprinted by permission.

unexpected and unnoted disturbances in metabolism. Evidence indicates that the drug's half-life is much greater than originally estimated; figures range from ten to 14 days. The implications of this are serious, given possible adverse effects on a woman's future health, including infertility through exposure of immature eggs to RU 486.

Despite its "serious side effects," until 1983 the use of PG alone as an abortion method *was* suggested as a safe procedure. It was the European women's protests and resistance to PG that led to its gradual abandonment.

Heavy Bleeding One should not trivialize the number of women who experience heavy bleeding with RU 486. To do so fails to address the implications this poses for women with fibroids, hypertension, or diabetes, as well as the large number of women with endemic anemia in "developing" countries. Heavy bleeding with conventional abortion usually occurs in a controlled setting, but the time and place of RU 486/PG-induced bleeding is *not* predictable. This can jeopardize a woman's life if she is unable to reach a medical center in time.

Complications Citing heart attacks or strokes as "the only major complications" trivializes the consequences of RU 486/PG failure, which then involves a second conventional abortion procedure; and may require blood transfusion, which carries its own risk. Furthermore, to say that the one death and the cardiovascular accidents could have been avoided "if established screening protocols had been followed" is incorrect. Screening procedures may have little value in predicting a fatal outcome, as evidenced by the death, following a PG-induced termination, of a 26-year-old woman who had no prior history of

cardiac or neurological disorder as evidenced from her EKG and EEG.

True, it is not possible to compare the death rate from conventional abortion (one per 200,000 in the U.S.) to that of present RU 486 figures (one per 100,000) because only 100,000 RU 486/PG abortions have been performed. But the crucial difference is that the vast majority of RU 486 abortions were performed under strict trial conditions, and accidents are more likely to happen in this less controlled general use.

Incomplete Abortions To claim that a 3 percent failure rate in conventional abortions done by less skilled practitioners is not that different from the RU 486 rate of 4 to 6 percent misses the point. Conventional abortion *can* be made safe whereas, because of the nature of these drugs once they have entered a woman's body, the risks of chemical abortion defy control.

Medical Supervision To receive the PG, it is mandatory to visit a center that has resuscitation equipment and medication. Given the virtual nonexistence of such centers in many rural areas, as well as in the "developing" world, it will be very troublesome, if not impossible, for many women to return not just once, but importantly yet another time to make sure (often with ultrasound) that the embryo has been completely expelled. This is *very* different from conventional abortion where the checkup can be done by a paramedic, and few women need postabortion treatment at high-tech clinics.

Early Termination We consider the timing of RU 486 one of its major drawbacks, for the following reasons: Teenage pregnancies, in particular, often go undetected until well into the first trimester. Because up to 30 percent of fertilized eggs are spontaneously aborted, large numbers of women may be unnecessarily exposed to RU 486/PG drugs. And finally, given the "ease" of RU 486/ PG administration *for medical personnel*— and its disputable "ease" for women—it is not too farfetched to imagine a future where it would be the only available abortion method as a result of legislation or the lack of skilled personnel to perform conventional abortions. This would reduce choice for women whose pregnancies are further advanced, and would play right into the hands of the antiabortion movement: surely a serious and unintentional consequence of RU 486 advocacy!

In the "Developing" World We have never claimed that all currently available abortion services are satisfactory, but to suggest that under less than ideal conditions RU 486 could "save lives" is unrealistic. The fact that 50 to 60 percent of women suffer some complication during RU 486/PG abortion in well-controlled trials in predominantly industrialized countries makes us fear that many more women will be seriously damaged under less than "ideal" conditions. And women deserve better than a second-rate solution.

As to the use of Cytotec, a number of studies have documented that half of the women who took it had incomplete abortions. Apart from the disastrous consequences for women from the continuation of unwanted pregnancies, uterine infections, or other health hazards, there is also the risk of severe fetal malformation.

Privacy and Control Given that in France the majority of abortions are performed under general anesthetic, RU 486 may indeed be seen as "more natural." But would women consider it superior to safe, compassionate, conventional abortion by skilled abortion providers? Second, it is wrong to say that a woman would emerge from the bathroom at the clinic, "her abortion completed," and leave the clinic "within ten to 15 minutes after the abortion just as she would for nonanesthetized, early-termination suction procedures." The bleeding induced by RU 486/PG does not necessarily mean that the embryo has been expelled. Even if it has, tissue may remain in the endometrium and the vagina, causing infection and bleeding and possibly requiring a conventional abortion procedure.

Summary We disagree with the statement that "RU 486 appears to provide a safe and effective abortion alternative." We do agree, however, that it "could prove to be less successful among women with fewer resources and poorer health." Abortion is one of the simplest of presently medicalized gynecological procedures, requiring less expertise, training, and skill than attending births. Trained paramedics in "Third World" countries perform abortions safely and competently. Why then cannot trained laywomen do abortions safely and competently in Western contexts? Rather than advocating for one more dubious reproductive technology such as RU 486/PG, feminists should be fighting for demedicalizing conventional abortion methods, and doctors and family planning groups should be joining suit.

POSTSCRIPT

Should RU 486 Be Legalized?

The fundamental question raised by RU 486 is much broader than the focused debate of these two essays. The crucial issue is whether the availability of RU 486 (if it comes to pass) will be controlled by male-dominated fundamentalist groups or whether RU 486 will be recognized as the moral property of women who have the right to decide and control their own reproductive capacities.

Dr. Baulieu, the discoverer of RU 486, says that the future of the drug will not be decided by legislators, morality, or religion. The future of RU 486 will be determined by the pressure of consumer demands in the marketplace, just as the future of the hormonal birth control pill was decided in the 1970s by consumer demand. It will not be easy for opponents of RU 486 to resist the market pressure, even though they have stalled introduction of the pill into the United States for over a decade. Two realities of the American marketplace are obvious: 46 percent of American women will have an abortion in their lifetime, and 83 percent of all counties in the United States have no facilities for legal abortions.

Add to these factors the number of abortions being performed worldwide, the explosive world population growth, and the growing poverty and starvation of far too many children, and it is obvious that the debate over RU 486 is plunging into its crucial phase.

SUGGESTED READINGS

E. Baulieu and M. Rosenblum, *The "Abortion Pill": RU 486, A Woman's Choice* (Simon & Schuster, 1992).

J. Brown, J. LeJeune, and R. Marshall, *RU 486: The Human Pesticide* (American Life League).

J. Hoffman, "The Morning-After Pill: A Well-Kept Secret," *The New York Times Magazine* (January 10, 1993).

M. Klitsch, "Antiprogestins and the Abortion Controversy: A Progress Report," *Family Planning Perspectives* (November/December 1991).

L. Lader, *RU 486: The Pill That Could End the Abortion Wars and Why American Women Don't Have It* (Addison-Wesley, 1991).

Reproductive Health Technologies Project, *The Case for Antiprogestins: A Report* (1992).

J. Smolowe, "New, Improved and Ready for Battle," *Time* (June 14, 1993).

D. Van Biema, "But Will It End the Abortion Debate?" *Time* (June 14, 1993).

ISSUE 7

Should Schools Distribute Condoms?

YES: Center for Population Options, from *Condom Availability in Schools: A Guide for Programs* (1993)

NO: Edwin J. Delattre, from "Condoms and Coercion: The Maturity of Self Determination," *Vital Speeches of the Day* (April 15, 1992)

ISSUE SUMMARY

YES: The Center for Population Options, an organization that promotes healthy decision-making about sexuality among youth, outlines what is known about the sexual behavior and the accompanying health risks of teens today and then examines strategies for reducing these risks, specifically, encouraging abstinence and condom use. Considering all the options and all the risks, the center concludes that making condoms available to students through the schools with counseling and education is the best course of action.

NO: Professor of education Edwin J. Delattre, in opposing condom distribution in schools, notes several flaws in the argument that we have a moral obligation to distribute condoms to save lives. He dismisses the claim that this is purely a health issue, and he discusses various moral issues involved in promoting casual sexual involvement, which he believes condom distribution does.

Seventy-two percent of American high school seniors have engaged in sexual intercourse. This percentage is likely higher in large cities and their suburbs.

With the highest rate of teenage pregnancy and abortion in North America and Europe, and with young people rapidly becoming the highest risk group for HIV (human immunodeficiency virus) infection, American parents, educators, and health care professionals have to decide how to deal with these problems. Some advocate teaching abstinence and saying nothing about contraceptives and other ways of reducing the risk of contracting sexually transmitted diseases (STDs) and HIV infections. Others advocate educating and counseling: "You don't have to be sexually active, but if you are, this is what you can do to protect yourself." But in some schools, the problem is so serious, some advocate offering students free condoms. School boards in New York, Baltimore, Chicago, Los Angeles, San Francisco, Philadelphia, Miami, and other cities have opted to allow school nurses and school-based health clinics to distribute free condoms to students, usually without requiring parental notification or permission.

Dr. Alma Rose George, president of the National Medical Association, opposes schools giving condoms to teens without their parents knowing about it: "When you give condoms out to teens, you are promoting sexual activity. It's saying that it's all right. We shouldn't make it so easy for them." Faye Wattleton, former president of the Planned Parenthood Federation of America, approves of schools distributing condoms and maintains that "mandatory parental consent would be counterproductive and meaningless."

Some detect overtones of racism in condom distribution programs. "When most of the decisions are made, it's by a White majority for schools predominantly Black," says Dolores Grier, noted black historian/author and vice chancellor of community relations for the Catholic Archdiocese of New York. "They introduce a lot of Black and Hispanic children to this like they're animals. I consider it racist to give condoms to children." Elijah Mohammed, founder of the Black Nation of Islam, has condemned condom distribution as racist genocide.

This debate requires the consideration of several distinct issues, as the two selections here clearly reveal. We have to take a position on the morality, implied endorsement, and/or encouragement of premarital sex. We have to decide on the roles of the school and those of the parents in dealing with the evident and growing risks of STDs and HIV infection. We have to consider the psychological, emotional, and social issue of "how early is too early" for initiating sexually intimate relationships. And we need to reach a general agreement on the timing, content, philosophy, and objectives of sex education in the schools. That is no easy task, but the issue and our answers will affect the lives of millions of young people.

YES

Center for Population Options

MAKING THE CASE

I. YOUTH AT RISK

Confronted with rising levels of adolescent pregnancy and the growing incidence among adolescents of sexually transmitted diseases (STDs), including the HIV virus that cause AIDS, most adults agree these threats to young people's health have reached crisis proportions. Strong interventions are needed to protect adolescents.

For many teens, schools are the primary source of accurate information about STDs: almost all states encourage or require HIV/AIDS prevention education in their schools. Comprehensive health and sexuality programs can also help teens delay initiation of sexual intercourse. But while education is critical for changing attitudes, it does not, alone, change the behaviors that put sexually active teens at risk of infection and unintended pregnancy. Teens also need to be provided the means to protect themselves and to be taught effective ways of discussing protection with their partners.

Many school personnel, public health officials and policymakers are suggesting that high schools make latex condoms available to sexually active students. They reason that schools are uniquely positioned to provide two-part health and sexuality programs that include education and access to barrier methods that protect against disease and unintended pregnancy.

Through these programs, those charged with educating adolescents hope to empower them to change their risk-taking, and sometimes life-threatening, sexual behavior.

A. Behaviors and Risks of Sexually Active Adolescents
Adolescents have a sense of omnipotence and invulnerability as they move toward independence. Their fearlessness can lead to dangerous behaviors, such as using drugs (including alcohol and tobacco) and having sex without contraception and/or protection. . . .

Large Numbers of Adolescents Engage in Sexual Activity. Surveys of adolescent sexual behavior indicate that young people are engaging in sexual intercourse at early ages. Seventy-seven percent of females and 86 percent of males are sexually active by age 20.

Sexually Active Adolescents Are at Risk for Unintended Pregnancy. Over one million teenage girls—one in 10—become pregnant every year. Four out of 10 teenagers will become pregnant before turning 20. At least 82 percent of teen pregnancies are unintended. One out of four adolescents does not use an effective means of contraception.

Adolescents Are at Risk for STDs. For reasons related to their physiological development, adolescent women are more vulnerable to infection when exposed to STDs than are adult women. Rates of chlamydia, gonorrhea and syphilis for adolescent women are higher than for adult women. Over three million sexually active adolescents are infected with an STD annually, representing one-fifth of all STD cases in the nation. The American Medical Association estimates that one out of four teens will have an STD before high school graduation. The estimate is even higher for youth who are not in school.[1] Left untreated, STDs can cause pelvic inflammatory disease, which is a cause of infertility and increases vulnerability to HIV.

Adolescents Are Also at Risk of Contracting HIV. Adolescents are just as vulnerable to contracting HIV as adults, and perhaps more so. Individuals already infected with an STD may have breakdowns of skin and mucosal barriers and thus are more vulnerable to HIV infection. Currently, almost 20 percent of people diagnosed with AIDS in the United States are in their 20s. Because the latency period between HIV infection and onset of symptoms is about 10 years, many were probably exposed to HIV as adolescents. From 1990 to 1992,

the number of youth ages 13 to 24 who were diagnosed with AIDS increased by 77 percent.[2] . . .

II. STRATEGIES FOR REDUCING THE RISK

A. Encouraging Abstinence

Only complete abstinence from risky sexual behaviors and judgement-impairing substances—such as alcohol and drugs—entirely eliminates the risk of pregnancy and STD infection. Comprehensive health education or HIV/AIDS prevention programs encourage young people to abstain from or delay sexual intercourse, and suggest substituting other forms of non-risky sexual activity.

Research has shown that some programs are effective in helping teens postpone intercourse. The "Postponing Sexual Involvement" (PSI) program developed at Grady Memorial Hospital in Atlanta, has been shown to increase the percentage of students who had not yet initiated intercourse by the end of the ninth grade from 61 percent (in the control group) to 76 percent (among program participants). By the end of eighth grade, students who did not participate in the program were as much as five times more likely to have initiated sexual intercourse than were PSI participants.[3] In contrast, the program demonstrated little, if any, impact on the behavior of teens who were already sexually active.

The Grady program uses the "social inoculation" model of outreach. This model assumes that young people engage in negative behaviors partly because of social influences and pressures, arising both generally and from their peers. Such programs use activities that help participants identify the origin of these pressures and develop skills to respond to them positively and effectively. Such programs also rely on peers—slightly older teens—to present information, lead group activities and discuss issues and problems.

Another program using social inoculation is "Reducing the Risk" (RTR), implemented and evaluated at 13 California high schools. RTR stresses that students should avoid unprotected intercourse—either through abstinence or contraception. RTR also encourages parent-child communication on subjects such as birth control and abstinence. The program significantly increased participants' knowledge of abstinence and contraception, and their communication about these topics with their parents. Participants who had not yet initiated intercourse indicated a significantly-reduced likelihood that they would have had intercourse 18 months later. Further, a survey of parents found broad support for RTR, as well as a belief that the program had had positive effects.[4]

Some adults believe teens should not be taught or shown methods of contraception and protection, and that sexuality education should focus exclusively on abstinence for unmarried adolescents. Numerous "abstinence-only" curricula are being promoted for use in schools that present opinion as fact, convey insufficient, inaccurate or biased information, rely on scare tactics, reinforce gender stereotypes and are insensitive to cultural and economic differences. These programs have not been adequately evaluated and should not be confused with the curricula mentioned here that have demonstrated a measure of success. . . .

There is little evidence that programs which promote abstinence alone are effective with adolescents who have already initiated sexual intercourse. Evaluations of even the most promising abstinence-based curricula reveal that substantial proportions of participants continue to engage in intercourse. These adolescents are at risk of pregnancy and STDs, including HIV.

Even the more successful abstinence-based curricula promote the delay of sexual activity but seldom prevent sexual intercourse until marriage. Most adolescents will eventually become sexually active. Therefore, all students must be taught the information and skills necessary to make healthy decisions and to accept personal responsibility.

B. Encouraging Condom Use

A majority of teens are sexually active. According to the CDC's 1990 Youth Risk Behavior Survey, 39.6 percent of ninth graders, 47.6 percent of tenth graders, 57.3 percent of eleventh graders and 71.9 percent of twelfth graders report they have had intercourse. Programs must help sexually active teens reduce the potential for negative consequences associated with unprotected intercourse.

Next to abstinence, latex condoms are the most effective method for reducing STDs and the sexual transmission of HIV infection. When properly used, latex condoms are also effective at reducing the risk of pregnancy. Promoting correct and consistent condom use by sexually active teens is an important strategy in curbing the national epidemics of HIV, other STDs and too-early childbearing.

The National Research Council, in its landmark 1987 report, *Risking the Future: Adolescent Sexuality, Pregnancy and Childbearing*, recommended "the development, implementation and evaluation of condom distribution programs."

An important U.S. National Health Promotion and Disease Prevention Objective is to increase the use of condoms at last intercourse by sexually active females aged 15–19 from 25 percent in 1988 to 60 percent by the year 2000. For sexually active males ages 15–19, the year 2000 target is 75 percent.[5]

III. BARRIERS TO CONDOM ACCESS AND USE

Adolescents have a legal right to purchase condoms. Ensuring a minor's right to contraception does not, however, translate into easy access. Condoms may appear to be widely available, but a number of factors inhibit young people's ability to acquire and effectively use them.

Surveys have found that lack of availability is one of the most frequently cited reasons sexually active adolescents fail to use condoms. Furthermore, adolescents' desire for confidentiality often overshadows their concerns for health. While fear that others will learn they are sexually active does not keep teens from having intercourse, it does apparently inhibit them from purchasing condoms. Other factors, many of which are associated with low self-esteem, that teens perceive as barriers to regular condom use include:

- peer or partner pressure
- fear of loss of relationship
- fear of decreased sexual pleasure
- cultural expectations for gender-related behavior and roles
- denial of sexual activity
- alcohol and drugs which impair judgement, often contribute to risky behavior and failure to use condoms properly or at all
- anxiety about being seen by parents, friends or neighbors when purchasing condoms

- cost

A 1988 survey by members of the Center for Population Options (CPO) Teen Council examined the accessibility of contraception in drugstores and convenience stores in Washington, D.C. and found that:

- One-third of the stores kept condoms behind the counter, forcing teens to ask for them.
- Only 13 percent of the stores had signs that clearly marked where contraceptives were shelved.
- Adolescent girls asking for assistance encountered resistance or condemnation from store clerks 40 percent of the time.

For adolescents, these obstacles are significant barriers to contraceptive access. Evidence from other parts of the country suggests that D.C. is not unique.

Even in areas where health departments or family planning clinics provide condoms free of charge and without appointments, school or work obligations may combine with clinic schedules to make it difficult or impossible for adolescents to take advantage of these services. Rural youth, in particular, have concerns about transportation and privacy—being seen at the drug store or clinic by someone they or their parents know is more likely in a small town or rural community.

IV. FACTORS THAT INCREASE LATEX CONDOM USE

Logistical barriers to condom use can be addressed by making condoms widely and freely available; however, successful strategies to help teens use latex condoms properly and consistently must address *both* physical and psychological access. Psychological and emotional barriers to condom use are embedded in the culture and are harder to address. Access is enhanced with increased knowledge, social and physical skills, perception of personal risk and perceived peer and societal norms.

Among the factors specifically cited by teens that would tend to increase condom use are condoms' acceptability among peers and a perception that they are easy to use and permit spontaneity. Teens who believe condoms help prevent HIV transmission are also more likely to report consistent use.[6] Another survey of teenagers found that providing condoms free of cost and making them easy to obtain are crucial elements in increasing adolescent use.

V. A PREVENTION STRATEGY THAT MAKES SENSE

Condoms are currently available to teens from a variety of sources: drugstores, family planning clinics, health clinics, supermarkets, convenience stores and vending machines. Making condoms available within schools does not introduce an otherwise unobtainable commodity to students. Rather, it expands the range of sources and facilitates teens' access to an important health aid. Adults understand that social endorsement by adults and society is a critical factor in normalizing condom use, and large majorities support giving teens access to condoms in school.

By making condoms available to students who choose to engage in sexual activity, schools let students know the community cares about their health and well-being. School programs reinforce that there are adults who will address adolescent sexual behavior, rather than deny it is a reality. While adults may prefer that young people refrain from sexual intercourse, it is important to help

According to a 1988 Harris poll, 73 percent of adults favor making contraceptives available in schools. A 1991 Roper poll found that 64 percent of adults say condoms should be available in high schools. According to a Gallup poll released in August, 1992, adult support for condom availability has grown to 68 percent.[7] In April, 1992, a National Scholastic Survey also found that 81 percent of high school seniors felt condoms should be available; 78 percent felt condom availability programs do not encourage sexual activity.

those teens who do not to avoid the negative consequences of HIV and other STDs, as well as unplanned pregnancy.

Condom availability programs eliminate some of the most significant barriers to condom use, including lack of access. By making condoms available in schools, caring adults can reach at-risk adolescents in a familiar and comfortable setting. Furthermore, programs can be designed specifically to reduce other barriers to condom use.

Several studies have shown that sexually active teens are more likely to use condoms if they believe their peers are using them. Condom availability in schools promotes positive and open attitudes toward condoms, increasing the likelihood that teens not only will acquire the condoms they need to protect themselves, but will also use them.

Schools are in a unique position to help teens address issues that are clearly associated with inappropriate risk-taking behaviors. Schools can provide opportunities for students to increase self-esteem and to practice decision-making, negotiation and conflict-resolution skills. Thus, school condom availability programs supported by comprehensive life skills training are uniquely able to help students gain and practice the skills necessary for successful condom use.

Despite fears to the contrary, research clearly demonstrates that students in schools which make condoms and other contraceptives available through school-based health centers are no more likely to be sexually experienced than students in schools without these services available. In fact, at some schools with centers making contraception available, teens' mean age at first intercourse was older—and already sexually active teens' frequency of intercourse was lower—than at schools without contraception availability.[8]

VI. CONDOM AVAILABILITY AS PART OF A COMPREHENSIVE PROGRAM

It is important to remember that condom availability can be most effective only if it is part of a comprehensive health, sexuality education, HIV/AIDS and pregnancy prevention program. To affect adolescent behavior it is necessary to address teens' attitudes and knowledge of reproductive health issues, as well as their ability to access and use condoms and contraceptives effectively. Strategies must also seek to improve teens' capacity to abstain from or delay sexual intercourse. Outreach to at-risk teens, education, counseling and follow-up are all necessary components of a program. As a result, school condom availability programs typically involve collaborative efforts among schools, health agencies, youth-serving organizations and community members.

A surprising but important benefit of the debate over condom availability is the way the issue has engaged entire communities and increased public awareness. Schools are conducting surveys of teenagers to determine their level of risk-taking behavior. Students themselves are speaking out on the issue, sometimes being heard for the first time. Parents and community members are becoming more involved in the early stages of the debate and are helping to design these programs. Schools and communities are also taking the opportunity to evaluate whether the health education programs that already exist are comprehensive and teach decision-making skills as well as impart information.

The complex strands of cultural influence, socio-economic status, environment and individual personality that determine why people do the things they do are not easily disentangled. No single approach—sexuality education, condom availability or abstinence programs—can alone eliminate STDs and too-early childbearing among adolescents. These components combined can help teens to develop attitudes, skills and behavior patterns that will protect them from unnecessary risks throughout their lives.

NOTES

1. Janet Gans, Ph.D. et al. *America's Adolescents: How Healthy Are They?* (Chicago, IL: The American Medical Association, 1990).

2. U.S. House of Representatives, Select Committee on Children, Youth and Families, *A Decade of Denial: Teens and AIDS in America* (Washington, DC: U.S. Government Printing Office, April 12, 1992).

3. Marion Howard and Judith Blamey McCabe, "Helping Teenagers Postpone Sexual Involvement," *Family Planning Perspectives* 22:1 (January/February 1990).

4. Douglas Kirby et al., "Reducing the Risk: Impact of a New Curriculum on Sexual Risk-Taking," *Family Planning Perspectives*, 23:6 (November/December 1991).

5. U.S. Department of Health and Human Services, Public Health Service. *Healthy People 2000* (Washington, DC: U.S. Government Printing Office, 1990) p. 503.

6. Ralph DiClemente et al., "Determinants of Condom Use Among Junior High School Students in a Minority, Inner-City School District," *Pediatrics* 89:2 (February 1992).

7. Stanley E. Ealm, Lowell C. Rose and Alex M. Gallup, "24th Annual Gallup Poll/Phi Delta Kappa Poll of the Public's Attitudes Towards the Public Schools" (September 1992).

8. Doug Kirby, Cindy Waszak and J. Ziegler, *An Assessment of Six School-Based Clinics: Services, Impact and Potential* (Washington, DC: The Center for Population Options, 1989). See also: L. S. Zabin et al., "Evaluation of a Pregnancy Prevention Program for Urban Teenagers," *Family Planning Perspectives* 18:3 (May/June, 1986).

NO

Edwin J. Delattre

CONDOMS AND COERCION: THE MATURITY OF SELF DETERMINATION

We [are] told . . . by condom distribution advocates that school distribution of condoms is not a moral issue but rather an issue of life and death. We [are] told, by the same people, that we have a moral obligation to do everything in our power, at all times, to save lives. The incoherence—indeed, contradiction—between these claims reflects the failure of condom distribution advocates to perceive the fact that *all* life-and-death issues are morally consequential; that questions of what schools have the right and the duty to do in the interest of their students are irreducibly moral questions; and that *how* schools should endorse and sustain the honorable conduct of personal life is a moral issue of the most basic and profound sort.

The plain fact is that if our only moral duty were to save lives—at whatever cost to other ideals of life—on statistical grounds, we would have to raise the legal age for acquiring a driver's license to at least twenty-five; we would have to reduce interstate highway speed limits to 35 mph or less; we would have to force everyone in America to undergo an annual physical examination; we would have to outlaw foods that contribute to bad health; we would have to prohibit the use of tobacco and advertisements for it, and spend huge resources to enforce those laws; we would have to eliminate rights of privacy in the home in order to minimize the possibility of domestic violence; we would have to establish laws to determine who can safely bear children, and therefore who is allowed to become pregnant; we would have to make AIDS and drug testing mandatory for all citizens at regular intervals; we would have to do away with the rights of suspects to due process in order to eliminate open-air drug marketplaces in our cities; we would have to incarcerate, on a permanent basis, all prostitutes who test HIV positive; we would have to announce publicly the name of every person who tests HIV positive in order to safeguard others from possible exposure through sexual activity. And so on.

From Edwin J. Delattre, "Condoms and Coercion: The Maturity of Self Determination," *Vital Speeches of the Day,* vol. 58, no. 13 (April 15, 1992). Copyright © 1992 by Edwin J. DeLattre. Reprinted by permission.

Saving lives is not the only moral concern of human beings. The prevention of needless suffering among adults, youths, children, infants and unborn babies; the avoidance of self-inflicted heartache; and the creation of opportunities for fulfilling work and for happiness in an environment of safety and justice all merit moral attention as well. And even if saving lives were our only moral concern, there is no reason to believe that distributing condoms in schools is the best way to save lives. Certainly, the distribution of condoms is an unreliable substitute for the creation of a school environment that conveys the unequivocal message that abstinence has greater life-saving power than any piece of latex can have.

Furthermore, even if condoms were the best means of saving lives, there would be no compelling reason for schools rather than parents to distribute condoms; no reason for schools to be implicated in the distribution of condoms when others are willing and eager to do so; no reason for schools to assent to the highly questionable claim that *if* they distribute condoms, they will, in fact, save lives.

We have a duty to make clear to our students . . . the implications of sexual involvement with other people who are ignorant of the dangers of sexual transmission of diseases or uncaring about any threat they may pose to the safety of the innocent. Our students need to grasp that if any one of us becomes sexually involved with someone and truly needs a condom or a dental dam because neither we nor the other person knows how much danger of exposure to AIDS that person may be subjecting us to, then we are sleeping with a person who is either staggeringly ignorant of the dangers involved or else is, in principle, willing to kill us. Such a person has not even the decency to wait long enough for informative medical tests to be conducted that would have a chance of disclosing an HIV positive condition; not even the decency to place saving our lives, or anyone else's, above personal gratification. Obviously, if we behave in this way, we, too, are guilty of profound wrongdoing.

This is so inescapably a moral issue—about saving lives—that its omission by condom distribution advocates astounds the imagination. They have said nothing about the kinds of people who are unworthy of romantic love and personal trust, who conceal or ignore the danger they may pose to another's life, even with a condom. These considerations prove yet another fundamental fact of human life: the only things casual about casual sex are its casual indifference to the seriousness of sexual life, its casual dismissal of the need for warranted trust between one individual and another, and its casual disregard and contempt for our personal duty to protect others from harm or death.

We have a duty to explain to students that there is no mystery about discovering and saying what is morally wrong. It is morally wrong to cause needless suffering, and it is morally wrong to be indifferent to the suffering we may cause by our actions. On both counts, sexual promiscuity is conspicuously wrong.

Sexual promiscuity, casual sexual involvement, whether in youth or adulthood, is an affront to all moral seriousness about one's own life and the lives of others. Exposing oneself and others to possible affliction with sexually transmitted diseases is itself morally indefensible, but even where this danger is not present, sexual promiscuity reveals a grave failure of personal character.

A person who is sexually promiscuous inevitably treats other people as mere objects to be *used* for personal gratification, and routinely ignores the possibility of pregnancies that may result in unwanted children whose lot in life will be unfair from the beginning. This is morally wrong; it is an affront to the dignity of human beings, an affront to their right to be treated with concern for their feelings, hopes, and happiness, as well as their safety.

Where promiscuity is shrewdly calculated, it is crudely exploitative and selfish; where promiscuity is impulsive, it is immature and marks a failure of self-control. In either case, promiscuity is incompatible with moral seriousness, because wherever there is promiscuity, there is necessarily an absence of the emotional and spiritual intimacy that anchor genuine love among human beings, love that is healthfully expressed among morally mature people in nonpromiscuous sexual intimacy.

Those who are sexually promiscuous—or want to become promiscuous by successfully persuading others to gratify their desires—routinely seek to exert peer pressure in favor of sexual indulgence, as surely as drug users seek to impose peer pressure in favor of drug and alcohol consumption. Anyone who believes that such persons will not try to overcome resistance to sexual involvement by insisting that the school distributes condoms; that the Health Center says condoms increase your safety, or at least make sex "less dangerous"; that sexual activity is *only* a health issue and not a moral issue, and that condoms eliminate the health problem—anyone so naive ignores entirely, or does not

know, the practices of seduction, the manipulativeness among people who treat others as objects to be used for their own pleasure, or the coercive power of adverse peer pressure.

We also have a duty to describe to our students the very real dangers of promiscuity even with condoms. According to research conducted by Planned Parenthood, condoms have a vastly greater rate of failure in preventing pregnancy when used by young unmarried women—36.3 percent—than has been reported by condom distribution advocates. The Family Research Council stresses that this figure is probably low where condom failure may involve possible exposure to AIDS, since the HIV virus is $1/450$ the size of a sperm and is less than $1/10$ the size of open channels that routinely pass entirely through latex products such as gloves.

The behavior of health professionals with respect to "less dangerous" sex ought to be described to students as well. As reported in the Richmond, Virginia, *Times-Dispatch* ten days ago:

"Dr. Theresa Crenshaw, a member of the national AIDS Commission and past president of the American Association of Sex Education, Counselors, and Therapists, told a Washington conference of having addressed an international meeting of 800 sexologists: 'Most of them,' she said, 'recommended condoms to their clients and students. I asked them if they had available the partner of their dreams, and knew that person carried the virus, would they have sex, depending on a condom for protection? No one raised their hand. After a long delay, one timid hand surfaced from the back of the room. I told them that it was irresponsible to give advice to others that they would not follow themselves. The point is, putting a mere balloon between a healthy body and a deadly disease is not safe.' " [January 4, 1992, p. A-10]

These reasons of principle and of fact ought to be sufficient to show the hazards. . . . But there is more to the moral dimension of school distribution of condoms, and those who have claimed otherwise deserve a further account with respect to sexual life itself.

In being forced to distribute condoms . . . to children and adolescents whose emotional and intellectual maturity remain, for the most part, in the balance—we are made to convey to the young the false message that we do not know these things about basic decency, about safety, about the high price of putting everything at risk for instant pleasure. And we are also giving youths whose judgment is still being formed the impression that we do not particularly care about the moral dimensions of sexual life, and that there is no particular reason for them to do so either.

Remember: we have been told . . . by adults and youths alike that there *is* no moral issue at stake. The acquiescence of the School . . . in condom distribution tacitly affirms that pronouncement. Their message betrays fidelity to high standards of ethics in education and sensitivity to more comprehensive dimensions of respect for justice, self-control, courage, and regard for persons in the articulation of institutional policy and the conduct of personal life.

Those who have told us that we are not faced with a moral issue transparently lack understanding of the fundamentals of moral maturity and character excellence. Their judgement, shallow as it is, betrays the young to a supposed, but implausible, expediency.

We will be told that all this will be covered by conscientious counseling of youths who request condoms. But, despite the best efforts of our well-intentioned health care professionals, it will not be adequately covered—and it will certainly not be covered for the students, and their former classmates who have dropped out of school, who are subject to peer pressure but never seek condoms themselves.

Condom distribution in the schools, even under the most carefully considered conditions, lends itself to the theme we have heard here: that profound dimensions of moral life, including decent treatment of others, have nothing to do with morality. It is not simply that this position is morally incompetent; it is also cruel in its licensing of peer pressure to become sexually active, peer pressure that can be, and often is, selfish, intolerant, even downright vicious.

The School . . . has sanctioned such peer pressure and has thereby given approval to forms of behavior and manipulation that cause, among the young, enormous suffering. Condom distribution advocates behave as though they know nothing of human nature and nothing of the unfair pressures to which the young are routinely subjected. The School['s] decision has now implicated us in teaching the young that we, too, are ignorant of these facts of life as they apply in youth.

The reply of condom distribution advocates to my reasoning is predictable. Sexual activity among the young is inevitable, they will say, even natural, and for reasons of birth control, avoidance of unwanted teenage pregnancies and protection from sexually transmitted diseases, including AIDS, it is better that students should use condoms than not.

They will insist that the availability of condoms does not increase the likelihood of sexual activity and that, in any case, many students who use the condoms will be selectively active rather than promiscuous.

The counterarguments are equally straightforward. If we teach the young that sexual activity is what we expect of them, at least some of them will come to expect it of themselves. We have no right to exhibit, or to have, such low expectations—especially toward those whose decisions about whether to become sexually active remain in the balance or who hope to live in an environment where restraint is not only respected but genuinely admired.

And for those who *are* sexually promiscuous—for whatever motives—whether they act in this way to aggrandize themselves; or to exert power over others; or to gain prestige, or physical pleasure, or peer approval; whether they are sexually active because of a desperate and doomed hope of securing affection and attention; or from failure to grasp alternatives; or from ignorance of consequences of promiscuity; or from a mistaken belief that intercourse and intimacy are the same— for all of them, if it is better that they should use condoms than not, how does it follow that *we* should give them the condoms *in* the High School?

In logic—and in fact—it does *not* follow. Even if it is true that promiscuity with condoms and dental dams is physically less dangerous than promiscuity without them, this ostensible fact in no way suggests or implies that *we* should be in the business of distributing condoms—as surely as the fact that filtered cigarettes are less harmful than unfiltered ones does not imply that we should be distributing free filtered cigarettes in the . . . Public Schools. We should instead be standing on the side of peer pressure against casual sex, and we should be providing resolute support for such peer pressure because it is morally right and because it has a distinctive and irreplaceable power to save lives.

Some condom distribution advocates insist that because we now have a health clinic in the High School, we are obliged to defer to the judgment of experts in health care on this subject. They claim that these experts do not try to tell us what we should do as educators, and we should not tell them what to do in matters of health and health-related services.

This artificial and illusory bifurcation of education and health is based on the false premise that what health officials do in the High School contains no educational lessons and teaches nothing about institutional policy or the decent conduct of personal life.

In this particular matter, health experts have clearly attempted to teach the public—including students—that the High School is an appropriate condom distribution site, while dismissing as irrelevant questions of educational mission and duty; and social service agency leaders have advocated that policy by pandering to and proselytizing for the view naively expressed by the students that there are no moral issues implicit in the policy. They have exceeded their competence in questions of morals.

Furthermore, it is well understood by all of us that condoms are fallible. We have not adequately addressed problems of potential legal liability for . . . the City . . . , the . . . Public Schools, and the School Committee. Yet both health professionals and social service personnel have . . . explicitly dismissed as trivial the prospect of legal liability for our institutions, as though they were qualified not only in matters of ethics but also in matters of law. In both respects, they have acted as educators—miseducators.

In doing so, they have potentially undermined the achievement of healthy levels of self-assertion by students, putting that achievement at risk from dangerous peer pressure. They have likewise jeopardized the achievement of self-respect among students by teaching them that even a questionable expediency is more important than mature judgment, personal restraint, and respect for the well-being of other people.

These are the facts of our present situation. We have been brought to a moment with we are no longer able to do what we ought to do in the High School, but are forced to do what is educationally wrong. We have been driven to this condition by a collection of flawed arguments about educational policy, about ethical life, and about law.

POSTSCRIPT

Should Schools Distribute Condoms?

Obviously, contraception is a sensitive issue where young people are concerned. In Saint Clair Shores, Michigan, five students were suspended from school for wearing buttons promoting condom use. In Seattle, Washington, activists handing out condoms and risk-reduction pamphlets at local high schools have been threatened with arrest for public obscenity.

In addition, sex-related health problems among adolescents continue to grow. One quarter of all Americans who currently have AIDS (acquired immunodeficiency syndrome) were infected during their teen years. In some areas, the rate of HIV infection among teens is doubling every 16 to 18 months. In some schools, the rate of STD infection is over 20 percent. And pregnancies in the fifth grade are not unheard of.

By mid-1993 the debate over distributing condoms in the schools as a way of reducing teenage pregnancy, STDs, and HIV infections was further complicated by debates in a dozen states about schools providing students with the five-year contraceptive implant, Norplant. Seen by some as a panacea for the problem of teenage pregnancy, school distribution of Norplant is feared by others because it may reduce the effectiveness of condom programs aimed at reducing the risk of STDs and HIV infection. Students may choose to accept free condoms and then decide whether or not to use them. Making Norplant available in the schools raises the stakes because it is surgically implanted under the woman's skin and can only be removed by a physician.

SUGGESTED READINGS

D. Allensworth and L. Kolbe, "The Comprehensive School Health Program: Exploring an Expanded Concept," *Journal of School Health* (December 1987).

T. Moore, "Should Schools Give Students Condoms Without Parents' Consent?" *Jet* (vol. 81, no. 17).

J. Seligmann, "Condoms in the Classroom," *Newsweek* (December 9, 1991).

"Unsuitable for Children," *National Review* (October 21, 1991).

B. Wright and K. Cranston, "Condom Availability in a Small Town: Lessons from Falmouth, Massachusetts," *SIECUS Report* (October/November 1992).

ISSUE 8

Should Surrogate Motherhood Be Outlawed?

YES: Richard John Neuhaus, from "Renting Women, Buying Babies and Class Struggles," *Society* (March 1988)

NO: Monica B. Morris, from "Reproductive Technology and Restraints," *Society* (March 1988)

ISSUE SUMMARY

YES: Richard John Neuhaus, director of the Rockford Institute Center on Religion and Society, argues that the renting of wombs and buying of babies associated with surrogate motherhood exploits the lower class and raises hostilities in America and therefore should be outlawed.

NO: Professor of sociology Monica B. Morris supports the practice of surrogate mothering and maintains that it should be regulated by law to avoid widespread misuse.

Early descriptions of surrogate motherhood can be found in the Bible: When the patriarch Abraham's wife Sarah was unable to bear him a child, Abraham had a child by Sarah's Egyptian slave girl, Hagar. Jewish tradition accepted this early custom of surrogate motherhood, and the practice of infertile upper-class couples hiring a peasant woman as a "baby maker" was common.

Natural surrogate motherhood took a twist in 1776 when artificial insemination was developed by the Italian embryologist Lazzaro Spallanzani. The first instance of artificial insemination occurred in 1800. Human sperm were first frozen without damage in 1942. By the mid-1970s, artificial insemination with fresh or frozen semen from the husband or a donor was widely used as a remedy for some kinds of infertility. Surrogacy technology gained another option when Louise Joy Brown, the world's first documented test-tube baby (produced by fertilization in laboratory equipment), was born in Cambridge, England, on July 25, 1978. Since then, more than 1,000 test-tube babies have been born, including over 50 sets of twins, a dozen sets of triplets, and several sets of quadruplets. In most cases, a woman's eggs are harvested and fertilized with her husband's sperm in tissue culture before the resulting embryo is transferred back to the woman's uterus. But the embryos can also be transferred to the womb of a surrogate mother.

At first, the technique of embryo transplant seemed to offer a way of reducing the risk of an artificially inseminated surrogate mother's changing her mind and seeking custody of her child, as Mary Beth Whitehead, in the widely known "Baby M" case, as well as other surrogates have done. One goal of embryo transplant was to reduce the role of the surrogate mother from that of gestating surrogate to that of nine-month prenatal wet nurse, whose only role is to gestate the embryo that results from test-tube fertilization of a wife's egg by her husband's sperm.

Various voices have challenged these uses of surrogate mothers. Members of the Feminist International Network on the New Reproductive Technologies advocate outlawing surrogate motherhood because it is a patriarchal exploitation of poor women and a new form of prostitution. Others argue that women should be able to decide on their own how they will make use of their reproductive capacities.

In the following selections, Richard John Neuhaus supports this view of surrogate mothering as lower-class exploitation and calls for declaring the practice illegal. Monica B. Morris labels surrogate mothering as "miraculous" but feels that regulation is required to prevent its abuse.

YES

Richard John Neuhaus

RENTING WOMEN, BUYING BABIES AND CLASS STRUGGLES

Quite suddenly, it seems, we have a new form of trade in human beings. It is called surrogate motherhood, and several states have already declared it legitimate by establishing regulations for the trade. Voices have been raised to oppose the baby traders before their business becomes a fait accompli. It may already be too late for that. The *New York Times* has editorially pronounced that regulation is the only way to go since, after all, "the business is probably here to stay." Numerous objections of a moral, legal, and common-sensical nature have been raised to surrogate motherhood. One aspect that has not been sufficiently explored is the way in which the baby trade so rudely rips the veil off class divisions and hostilities in American life.

SURROGATING TODAY AND YESTERDAY

The most celebrated, or notorious, case of surrogate motherhood is the one that has swirled around "Baby M" in a New Jersey courtroom. Some of the details are by now well known. Mr. William Stern, a biochemist married to Dr. Elizabeth Stern, a pediatrician who thought pregnancy might be bad for her health, contracted with Mrs. Mary Beth Whitehead to have his baby in return for $10,000 plus an equal amount in expenses. Mrs. Whitehead and her husband Richard, a sanitation worker, agreed. The surrogate contract is not uninteresting, including as it does provisions for amniocentesis and obligatory abortion if Mr. Stern did not like the results of the test. Also, Mrs. Whitehead would not receive the $10,000 but only a small payment for her troubles "in the event the child is miscarried, dies, or is stillborn." The Sterns were taking no chances. But they could not prevent Mary Beth Whitehead from changing her mind. "It's such a miracle to see a child born," she said. "The feeling is overwhelming. All the pain and suffering you've gone through is all gone." Within five minutes she is breastfeeding the baby, the bonding is effected, she runs away to avoid having to turn the baby over to the Sterns, the Sterns hire detectives to snatch the baby, and it all ends up in a court trying to decide who gets to keep the baby.

The liberal Catholic journal, *Commonweal*, observes: "Surrogate motherhood is a simple idea. It has become a critical issue today not because of the breakthrough in technology but because of a breakdown in moral understanding— namely, the understanding that human reproduction should be firmly placed in the matrix of personal sexuality, marital love, and family bonds." The point is an important one. Also in religious circles today, there is much prattle about changing moral rules because of technological advances and new discoveries about sexuality. It is highly doubtful that we know anything very significant about sexuality that, say, Saint Augustine did not know. As to surrogate motherhood, long before the dawn of modern science human males had mastered the technique of impregnating women other than their wives. Genesis 16 tells how Sarah and Abraham chose Hagar to be the surrogate mother of Ishmael. That too turned out badly, although Hagar did get to keep the child. Hagar, of course, was a slave.

Today it is at least gauche to speak of buying or renting women. The Sterns got over that awkwardness by hiring a Manhattan clinical psychologist who testified, "In both structural and functional terms, Mr. and Mrs. Stern's role as parents to Baby M was achieved by a surrogate uterus and not a surrogate mother." The contract did not call for Mrs. Whitehead to get involved. In fact *she* was supposed to stay out of this deal altogether. Mary Beth's problem, it would seem, is that she was not able to disaggregate herself from her uterus. She did not understand that she could rent out her uterus just as the Manhattan doctor could rent out his certified expertise. The capable lawyers hired by the Sterns had

made it all very clear, and for a while she thought she understood, but then somehow the whole thing began to seem surreal. (Not being an educated person, she did not say it seemed surreal. She said it just seemed wrong.)

TAKING ADVANTAGE

True, there are those who argue that there is nothing new in the rich renting of the nonrich, whether in whole or in part. A servant or employee, they say, is in effect a rented person. It is hard to argue with people who say such things. More often than not, they are the kind of people who also say that property is theft and tolerance is oppression. One can point out that the employee is free to quit, that a person's work "belongs" to him even if he is paid to do it, that the worker may find fulfillment in the work, and so forth. But such wrongheaded people do have one undeniable point: with respect to the negotiation of worldly affairs, rich people do generally have the advantage of nonrich people. That said, one can only hope it will be acknowledged that there is something singular about the connections between a woman, her sexuality, and her procreative capacity. It is not the kind of acknowledgment people can be argued into, and those to whom it must be explained probably cannot understand. Proabortion proponents of a woman's "reproductive rights" regularly appeal to the uniquely intimate relationship between a woman and her body. Strangely enough, many of them also approve surrogate motherhood as a further step in rationalizing sexual relationships and liberating society from the oppression of traditional mores. The recently discovered constitutional doctrine of "privacy," it would seem, is absolute—unless you have accepted money to have it violated. The inviolably intimate sphere of sexuality is one thing, but a deal is a deal.

As with abortion, there is another party involved. As is not the case with abortion, everyone here recognizes the other party involved. Baby M, having passed the quality-control tests, is certified as a Class-A member of the species. The question is who owns this valuable product. Presumably ownership is fifty-fifty between Mrs. Whitehead and Mr. Stern. Mr. Stern's case is that Mrs. Whitehead had agreed to sell her share of the baby for $10,000 and then reneged on the deal. A Solomonic decision may be required, except Solomon's proposed solution would likely be found unconstitutional. Mary Beth is perplexed by the ownership conundrum. The following is from a taped telephone conversation admitted in evidence: "WHITEHEAD: I gave her life. I did. I had the right during the whole pregnancy to terminate it, didn't I? STERN: It was your body. WHITEHEAD: That's right. It was my body and now you're telling me that I have no right. STERN: Because you made an agreement . . . you signed an agreement." It is not that nothing is sacred anymore. It is simply that the sacred has been relocated, away from realities such as life and motherhood and placed in a contract signed and sealed by money. Some simplistic types who have not kept up with the demands of cultural change find this repugnant. For example, William Pierce, president of the National Committee for Adoption, flatly says: "If you regulate surrogate motherhood, that is making a public statement that it's all right. We decided a hundred years ago we didn't want people bought and sold in this country."

That is not the question, says the judge in the Baby M case. The question, the only question, is what is "in the best interest" of Baby M. In other words, who can offer Baby M the better prospect for the good things in life, the Whiteheads or the Sterns? Here, although the word is never used, the question of class takes center stage in the courtroom drama. The relative stability of American society is due in part to our kindly veiling of class distinctions and hostilities. People making $20,000 and people making $100,000 or more have tacitly agreed to say they are middle class. In fact, some are rich and some are not rich and some are poor. In terms of income, the Sterns are upper-middle or upper class, the Whiteheads are low-low-middle class and have at times been poor. Perhaps more important than the criterion of income, the Sterns and their allies in the New Jersey courtroom represent the new knowledge class. The disputes are over symbolic knowledge; that is to say, over how to establish the "meaning" of ideas such as parenthood, love, stability, life opportunity, and psychological well-being. In the symbolic knowledge show-down, Mary Beth Whitehead is pitifully outgunned. She has never even heard of the transvaluation of values, which is what the Baby M trial is all about.

CLASS STRUGGLE

It is not simply that the Sterns can hire a battery of lawyers, detectives, psychological experts and social workers, while Mary Beth must get along with a lawyer three years out of school whose main experience has been in liability cases. No, the greater disparity is that the Sterns, their hired experts, the judge, and almost everyone else involved represents the new class arrayed against the world of the Whiteheads who represent the bottom side of the working class. In the class war being waged in the courtroom, the chief weapon of the new class is contempt for the world of their cultural inferiors, a world so blatantly represented by the Whiteheads. Mrs. Whitehead must be criticized for her decision to enter into the agreement in the first place. But that is not a criticism employed in the courtroom to discredit Mrs. Whitehead, for it might reflect unfavorably on the other party to the agreement, even suggesting that perhaps Mr. Stern took advantage.

Rather, Mary Beth Whitehead is to be discredited and declared an unfit mother because the world of which she is part is unfit for Mr. Stern's baby, or at least not nearly so fit as the world of the Sterns. So extensive evidence is presented that the Whiteheads have had a hard time of it financially, even living in a house trailer for a time. More than that, Mrs. Whitehead received welfare payments for a few months and her husband underwent a bout with alcoholism some years ago. The mandatory new class attitude under usual circumstances is that there is absolutely no stigma whatsoever attached to welfare or alcoholism. But that is under usual circumstances. In the class war being fought in the New Jersey courtroom such things are sure evidence of moral turpitude and the Whiteheads' "unsuitability" as parents for the 50 percent wellborn Baby M. In addition, a team of mental health experts has testified that Mrs. Whitehead shows definite signs of "distress," and one psychiatrist bluntly says she is suffering from "mixed personality disorder." That presumed illness is defined as "traits from several personality disorders but not all the criteria of any one disorder." It is a kind of catchall category in which, one fears, most human beings might be caught. Yet another psychiatrist in the new class alliance attempts to come up with harder evidence. Dr. Judith Brown Greif said that Mrs. Whitehead "often is unable to separate out her own needs from the needs of the baby." Well, there you have it. Mary Beth, in her pathetic ignorance, probably thought that was a sign of being a good mother. Little does she know about the need-fulfilling autonomy of the psychologically mature.

In order to get empirical support for their class biases, a group of mental health and child development experts visited "for several hours" in the Whitehead and Stern homes to observe firsthand how Baby M "related" to the respective parties. At the Whiteheads, Baby M seemed very happy, but their other two children, ages eleven and twelve, were vying for her attention and Mrs. Whitehead exhibited "an inflated sense of self." This, according to Dr. Marshall Schechter, psychiatrist at the University of Pennsylvania, was revealed in her making "an assumption that because she is the mother that the child, Baby M, belongs to her. This gives no credence to or value to the genetic contribution of the birth father." Things were different at the quiet and spacious Stern home. There were no other children to interrupt and, as Dr. and Mr. Stern sat on the living room floor chatting with their mental health visitors, Baby M gave every sign of relating very well to Mr. Stern. Of Mr. Stern one psychiatrist reported, "He is a thoughtful, sensitive man with a deep sense of responsibility and a respect for privacy." He did not need to add that none of those nice things could be said of Mrs. Whitehead.

Another expert (the one who contributed the distinction between renting the woman and renting the uterus), unequivocally declared that the Sterns are "far and away more capable of meeting the baby's needs than the Whiteheads." This includes of course his professional evaluation of Dr. Elizabeth, the wife. She is also, the experts told the court, very good at relating. In Dr. Stern's extensive court testimony, according to the *Times*, "she spoke of her delights at home with the baby and her disdain for Mrs. Whitehead." Often, she testified, she takes the baby shopping. "She's the cutest thing around. She's always pulling at the clothes in Bloomingdale's, trying to get them off the rack." At Bloomies, of course. You can bet that Mary Beth Whitehead probably doesn't even know where it is.

We Americans have a way of declaring something outrageous, repugnant, odious, and beyond the pale—and then concluding that we should regulate it. Surrogate motherhood should not be regulated, it should be outlawed. Some think the buying and selling of human beings was outlawed with the abolition of slavery, and the renting of women with laws against prostitution. But those big questions are bypassed if one agrees with the court, that the only question is, "What is in the best interest of the child?" Then enters the ugly factor of naked class advantage. If "interest" is defined by material well-being, life opportunities, professionally certified mental and emotional health, and a "lifestyle" approved by the new knowledge class, then clearly the baby must go to the Sterns. By the criteria which Mary Beth Whitehead is declared an unsuitable mother, millions of (dare we use the term?) lower-class women are unsuitable mothers. (One waits to see whether the court would take her other two children into custody.) By the criteria by which the Sterns are found to be "far, and away more capable of meeting the baby's needs," people of recognized achievement and approved attitudes have a right to the best babies that money can buy.

NO

Monica B. Morris

REPRODUCTIVE TECHNOLOGY AND RESTRAINTS

We are on the edge of a biotechnical revolution as profound in its implications as was the Industrial Revolution—and we are as unprepared for this one as we were for that. To believe we can outlaw surrogate parenting is to believe with the Luddites that the Industrial Revolution could be stopped by wrecking the machinery that made it possible.

Many thinkers, including Richard John Neuhaus, are adamant that surrogate motherhood should be outlawed. The reasons they give are many and, for the most part, sensible and humane. For Neuhaus, the main objection to surrogate motherhood is that it is a form of trade in which those with money exploit poor, or poorer, women and that, in the United States, in deciding matters like the Baby M case, money speaks louder than morality, ethics, or compassion.

As we spill gallons of ink on paper in discussion of social class and exploitation in the Baby M case, technological advances continue and the topic widens and deepens to include a dozen more issues, so that the "problem" becomes not one but many, so densely interwoven that solutions become ever more elusive. The speed of new discoveries and of refinements to existing technology becomes apparent when the kind of arrangement between Mary Beth Whitehead and the Sterns is referred to in a recent edition of the television program, "Nova," as "traditional surrogacy." This "traditional" surrogacy has been going on for over a decade. . . .

[Today's] biotechnical achievements are miraculous, offering hope to couples who long to have children but who, until now, have not been successful. Estimates of infertility vary between one in seven and one in five couples, and one must feel compassion for those who want children and cannot have them. Those so placed talk of their suffering, their pain, their "obsession," with having a baby. Women give up jobs, careers, to devote all their time to fertility treatments. There has even been a play on the subject, David Rudkin's bitter *Ashes*, that depicts one infertile couple's obsessive and, ultimately, fruitless efforts to procreate.

Published by permission of Transaction Publishers from *Society*, vol. 25, no. 3. Copyright © 1988 by Transaction Publishers.

Human-made miracles appear to offend some who believe that only God can work miracles. Yet, since its beginning, technology has attempted to conquer nature and make it work for us rather than against us. Scientific discoveries, from the time of Copernicus on, have been strongly resisted as against the will of God or as sacrilegious. According to the scriptures, women are to bring forth offspring in "sorrow"; science has eased our sorrow, and it has reduced the dangers that came "naturally" before we understood enough to wash our hands before plunging them into the bodies of women delivering babies.

Science, as has been repeatedly, and often passionately, argued, cannot determine morality. Given the large numbers of couples in despair over their infertility, the deep pool of poor women who might be recruited as surrogate mothers or as egg donors, and the skill of entrepreneurs in generating "needs" as yet unrealized, the potential for misuse of the reproductive technology, and for the abuse and exploitation of all parties, is vast. It raises disturbing questions about how we are to manage our technological marvels. How can we assure they are used for good? What, indeed, is "good," and for whom is it good?

BEST INTERESTS OF THE CHILD

The United States is not the only country grappling with these problems. A widely reported surrogacy case was ruled upon in Great Britain at about the same time as the Baby M case was going through the New Jersey Courts. On March 12, 1987, a surrogate mother was granted custody of six-month-old twins, a boy and a girl, conceived by artificial insemination. Like Mary Beth Whitehead, after the birth the surrogate refused to hand the babies over to the father and his wife. The judge, Sir John Arnold, said he had heard nothing that "might be taken to outweigh the advantages to these children of preserving the link to the mother to whom they are bonded and who has exercised a satisfactory degree of maternal care." Sir John saw nothing shameful in the arrangements between the parties but that "ultimately, the welfare of the children is the first and paramount consideration which the court must, by statute, take into account and that is what I do." Unlike Judge Sorkow, in deciding the best interest of the child, Sir John did not weigh the wealth of the father as important. The birth mother was unmarried and on social security; one reason she offered herself as a surrogate mother was to raise money to bring up her seven-year-old son. At last report, the mother was seeking child support for the twins from their father who, under present legislation may have to pay maintenance costs until the twins are sixteen years old, even though he has no parental rights. Appeals by the father may set precedents in this hitherto uncharted area.

Although both Judge Arnold and Judge Sorkow stated their concerns with the children in these custody cases and what would be best for them, each ruled differently. For Judge Arnold, the best interest of a child lies in preserving the link to its mother. For Judge Sorkow, the close bonding of Mary Beth Whitehead to her child was dismissed as irrelevant. Under the terms of the contract, she should not have allowed herself to become emotionally involved. Yet, in discussing custody of children in adoption cases, when birth mothers change their minds and want to keep their babies, adoption and child-development experts, as well as judges, have seen some risk of long-term emotional disturbance to a child who is taken from the care of one woman and given into the care of another at between six months and two-and-a-half years of age. The adult most suited to making a child feel wanted is the one with whom the child has already had, and continues to have, an affectionate bond. This would seem to apply to Baby M, whose mother nursed her from birth and who was with her for most of the first several months of her life.

Given the Baby M case and, perhaps, similar cases to follow, how can we determine the best interest of the child. In the United States, will the Ph.D. always win out over the high-school dropout? One problem is that we do not yet have children of these arrangements who are old enough to be studied. The best we can do is consider "scholarly" opinions as well as extrapolate from what we know about children who have grown up in other unusual or nontraditional circumstances; these might include adopted children, children of gay parents, and children born to mothers, including unmarried mothers, who chose artificial insemination by a donor.

Looking again at Great Britain, the British Medical Association (BMA) has flipped, then flopped, then flipped again on surrogate motherhood, most recently considering the practice not in the best interests of the children. In February, 1984, the association recommended that doctors not become involved in any "rent-a-womb" surrogacy scheme, whether the surrogate is paid or not and regardless of whether the baby was conceived by artificial insemination or in vitro and is genetically the couple's child. It seemed not to object to the use of in vitro fertilization to allow another woman to donate an egg for a couple with an infertile wife.

In December, 1985, the British Medical Association voted to support surrogate motherhood under "careful controls," but the May 7, 1987, report by the association's Board of Science and Education states that the baby born to a surrogate mother is "doomed to second best from the start by being deliberately deprived of one of its natural parents," and that the practice should not be supported. The report concluded that the interests of such children cannot be guaranteed and their welfare is more important than the wishes of infertile couples. This may not be the last word on surrogacy from the BMA, and its vacillation is not surprising given how little is known about surrogacy's effects on its products.

Information is sparse, too, on children resulting from artificial insemination by a donor. Researchers have found it difficult to follow the progress of such children largely because the legal parents have resisted study. As with traditional adoption, secrecy has generally been the rule. Some children of these arrangements, discovering their unorthodox origins—and estimates indicate about half of such children are later told or find out—have been vocal in expressing their anger. One, Suzanne Rubin, has been particularly visible on television talk shows and in magazine articles. She, like others in her situation, is dismayed at the lack of information available to her about her father's genetic background. She expresses horror that men like her father are able to sell their sperm without any responsibility for the lives they will help create. Discovering their origins in adolescence or in adulthood has the effect of destroying all their past lives as unreal, as fictional. These days, single women choosing artificial insemination by a donor are more likely to speak out about their decision and, presumably, will tell their offspring as much as they know about the donor. Openness is now thought to be desirable in attuning the children to their condition and in helping them accept it with minimum trauma.

Adoption agencies, too, have been recommending more openness between birth mothers and adopting couples than once was the rule. Agency research indicates that many adopted children have suffered substantial emotional anguish at their inability to trace their biological mothers, an anguish that has discolored their lives. One of my students, J, a married man with several children of his own, told me of his desperation to find his "real" mother and father, despite the great love and appreciation he felt for his adoptive parents. Records had been sealed, but after years of effort and with much ingenuity and some guile, J did trace his mother, long-married and with other children, to a city on the other side of the country. His father, also married and with grown children, was also tracked down. The father, angry at first, refused to see J. Successful in business and fearful of schemes that might deprive his legitimate children of their inheritance, he resisted. J, risking arrest, pushed his way into his father's office and confronted him. In time, J's wife and children were accepted by the families of both his biological parents. "I can't tell you what it meant," he said, "to look into my mother's face and see my little daughter's face there! And to find all those brothers and sisters I never knew I had!" Biological ties can be important, it

seems, and while William Stern's "compelling need" appears to have been in continuing his family "blood line," neither the feelings of Mary Beth Whitehead's older children at losing their sister, nor the existence of Baby M's older siblings and the meaning of their loss to her life have been considered of significance in the Baby M case. Baby M also has a "blood line," independent of her father's. . . .

My own explorations into what it feels like to be the child of older parents, prompted by the current trend toward deferred parenting, also indicates the difficulties children face when they are different in any way from most of their peers. Having one's parents mistaken for one's grandparents, or realizing that Dad is not able to play catch with the lads like the other guys' dads may not seem terrible hardships, but to the children involved they can cause embarrassment and sadness. The fear of losing parents while one is still a child is real. The now-adult subjects offered suggestions about how today's older parents might ease the problems for their children. These included being open with children about such worrying matters as the possibility of early responsibility for ailing, elderly parents, and about the likelihood of being left without parents, especially without fathers, sooner than most of their peers. The need for openness is emphasized in all kinds of nontraditional or less-than-usual family patterns. Children of older parents also emphasized their need for their parents' time. Those whose parents had been generous in discussion and in time and attention were far less likely to be troubled in any way by their parents' ages than those whose parents were less open and less available. That older parents are more likely to be financially comfortable than younger ones was noted by several subjects as an advantage, but one that is outweighed by many other factors. . . .

The requirement for subjects in my research was that their mothers were at least thirty-six-years-old when the subjects were born; the fathers' ages ranged from thirty-five to over fifty. Although little has been said about the matter, it cannot be overlooked that the Sterns are older parents, each forty or forty-one when Baby M was born, making her an ideal candidate for my research later on—were she not weighted down with a passel of problems unrelated to her parents' age.

Parents' age is seen as important in, for instance, the choice of adoptive parents for infants. Adoption counselors in three different agencies have told me, unofficially—officially they do not discriminate on the basis of age—that, given a choice of adoptive parents for an infant, they would probably not give the child to a couple aged forty or over. One reason among several is that while the couple might be energetic in their forties, by the time the baby was a teenager, they would be in their mid-fifties or older and perhaps less able to cope with stresses and strains of adolescence than would younger parents.

REPRODUCTIVE TECHNOLOGY TODAY AND TOMORROW

In the matter of Baby M, all the participants have been hurt, and they may never be entirely free of pain. We cannot assess how Baby M's life will be colored or, rather, discolored by her origins and by the publicity arising from the case for her custody. In light of the repugnance generated by talk of rented wombs and the commercialization of birth, of baby-selling, of children as commodities to be contracted for, and the outrage felt by many that an infant can be wrested from its birth mother against her will because of a bill of sale, it is not unreasonable for Neuhaus and others to call for an end to surrogate mothering. But, even were it possible to stop surrogacy completely, it would be a mistake. It is possible and, given the doubts about the future well-being of the offspring, of vital importance that it be very tightly controlled and used only in special circumstances which should be clearly specified.

Why should we not outlaw surrogacy? The technology involved is a vital step toward solving other problems. Surrogate mothering, artificial insemination by a donor, in vitro fertilization, embryo suctioning and transplanting, embryo freezing, have been developed by researchers as part of the quest not only to help infertile couples but also to diminish life-long suffering of children with serious genetic conditions. For some time, we have been able to perform certain surgical procedures on fetuses in utero; now, an embryo suctioned after a few days of gestation can be examined for genetic flaws before replanting in its mother's uterus. These techniques, while still experimental, may become routine. Instead of waiting until the second trimester of pregnancy for amniocentesis, a pregnant woman may know within days of conception if the embryo will develop normally. The choice to abort is rarely easy; it is particularly difficult at sixteen or eighteen weeks of gestation. . . .

Why must we regulate surrogacy and other procedures? Regulation is needed, not only to control exploitation of poor women but also to avoid the widespread misuse of these technologies. Neuhaus is right to deplore using one class of women for the benefit of those of another social class. This exploitation will know no bounds if allowed free rein. The ability to transplant a couple's own embryo into the uterus of a third party means that the third party need not be of the same race or ethnicity as the embryo. A black woman could bear a white child who has no genetic relationship to its "incubator." Gena Corea, author of *The Mother Machine*, raises the possibility that women in the Third World could be induced to provide baby-bearing services for far less money than American women, making the procedure attractive to couples who could not otherwise afford it. Rather than expressing horror at this idea, the studio audience of the Donahue show on which Corea appeared on August 7, 1987, as well as the rest of the panel, dismissed her as radical and shrill. Women in the audience, and those who called in, were attracted to the idea of surrogate mothering. One caller wanted to know how she could become a surrogate. A member of the audience suggested that a computerized list of would-be surrogates be made nationally available for couples to choose from. Another regarded surrogacy as "a wonderful option" for people who marry late and want children. This latter statement drew hearty applause from an audience that could gain little understanding of the implications of what they applauded from the superficial handling of the topic on a television talk show. These kinds of entertainments stir up enthusiasm and create markets. Manufacturers have not been slow to turn to workers in the Third World to keep labor costs down; entrepreneurs in the baby business will seize the same opportunities if they are cost-effective—and if they are allowed to do so.

LACK OF REGULATION

Unlike those of several other countries, the United States government has been slow to fund—and hence to regulate—research in reproductive technologies. It has been slow, too, to regulate the "private" areas of family and procreation, leaving both research and surrogacy wide open for commercial exploitation. Without regulations, lawyers and businessmen have been able to raise capital—even to sell public stock—to operate sperm banks, reproduction and fertility clinics, surrogacy agencies, and to promote the idea of "franchises" that will use patented techniques. This means that royalties would be paid to the patent holders every time a particular tool—a specialized catheter, for instance—were used. A company spokesman for Fertility and Genetic Research, Incorporated, in a sales pitch to stockbrokers, spoke of plans to tap the affluent market for egg donation. Market researchers, hired to survey the availability of women willing to serve as regular donors for $250 a procedure, discovered that "Donor women exist in cost-effective abundance." Another entrepreneur, lawyer Noel P. Keane, whose infertility center made the match between Mary Beth Whitehead and the Sterns, has a thriving business finding surrogates. His fee is about $10,000 for each match; this is apart from the fee paid to the surrogate and the cost of prenatal care and delivery, all of which is paid by the negotiating couple. It is reported that Keane is now expanding his services to include a pool of egg donors as well as surrogate mothers. The donors are available, as is a ready market of affluent couples willing to do almost anything to have children. Why not put the two together and make everybody, especially the money men, happy? It is the American way.

Indeed, Americans have not shown any great dismay or disgust with the profiting from these arrangements. Seventy-five percent of those polled by the Roper organization felt Judge Sorkow's ruling to give Baby M to the Sterns was right. "After all," people responded, "A contract is a contract." Business, in fact, is business. Only 20 percent of the personal sympathy of those polled lay with Mary Beth Whitehead. The contract for a woman to bear a child to give to another couple was viewed as no different from any other exchange of services for money.

A small part of this reasoning may be due to some, not all, feminists' insistence that women are to be treated under the law exactly as men are treated, that women should have control over their own bodies, including the right to use them to make money, and that to suggest that women's biological makeup might affect their emotions is to be sexist and paternalistic. Since the Baby M case, feminist thinking has converged and several prominent feminists, including Gloria Steinem, Betty Friedan, Phyllis Chesler, and Marilyn French, have joined with other groups to file an amicus curiae brief arguing that the commercialization of surrogate parenthood violates the Constitution and the dignity of women.

In making this distinction between surrogacy and commercial surrogacy, the feminists are following the guidelines of already established regulations in some other countries. As one example, under the Surrogacy Arrangements Act of 1985, Great Britain outlaws surrogacy agencies. It outlaws third-party intervention of any kind between a couple and the woman who is to bear a baby for them. Advertising for surrogacy arrangements is a criminal offense by the publisher or the distributor. Commercial surrogacy, then, is against the law, and although it is legal for a woman to be paid for bearing a child for someone else, contracts between the parties are not legally enforceable.

It is fascinating to watch how those profiting from surrogacy have attempted to subvert, or find loopholes, in the British law. The London *Sunday Times* reports that British women are being sought by one Washington-based agency to travel to the United States to serve as surrogate mothers for British couples, also being recruited, who are prepared to pay as much as £20,000 (approximately $32,000) for a child, thus removing the entire transaction from the United Kingdom. It may well be, as Patrick Steptoe, the pioneer in in vitro fertilization, has said, that we need international, rather than local, legislation.

REGULATING REPRODUCTIVE TECHNOLOGY

Guidelines on regulating surrogate mothering and all the other techniques are urgently needed. The lag between our technology and our social policy grows wider by the moment. At the very least, prospective parents should meet the criteria for eligibility to adopt a child under the current laws. Couples should not be able to arrange for a child, as they might arrange for an entertainment center or a BMW, simply because they want one and can afford it. Certainly, the doctrine of informed consent should prevail. That is, all parties should recognize and accept the risks and benefits involved and enter voluntarily, free of any kind of coercion. The psychological as well as the physical risks of childbearing must be understood by all and it should also be acknowledged that the emotional involvement in carrying a fetus to term and delivering it is of a different order from that involved in milking sperm into a jar. Informed consent is no simple matter; people do not always know in advance of an event how they will feel about it when it occurs.

We do not have to start with a blank sheet. We can look to countries more advanced than ours for guidelines to legislation. Britain, as already mentioned, has outlawed commercial surrogacy; the Australian state of Victoria, in The Infertility (Medical Procedures) Act of 1984 has also set firm limits, both on who is eligible for the procedures and on just how far the scientists may go. Control is firmly in government hands. Among other criteria, patients must have been under treatment for infertility for at least twelve months to assure they are seeking a "last resort" and that there is no other possibility of a pregnancy, or that the woman seeking treatment could pass on a hereditary disorder. The law prohibits any kind of payment for sperm, eggs, or embryos, other than travel or medical expenses incurred by the donor. It sets strict rules on the use by scientists of embryos in experiments, and makes it an offense, punishable by up to two years in prison, to give or receive payment for acting as a surrogate mother. Like the British law, it forbids advertising for surrogates or for offering to act as one and it declares void all contracts between the parties. . . .

The Luddites' fear of the machine was well founded. Industrialization eventually raised the standard of living for millions, providing them with shoes and dishes and clothing and other goods of a quality once reserved for the rich; but at the beginning the factory system and the shift from rural to urban areas brought untold misery. Men, women, and children were hideously exploited, separated from their roots, forced to work long hours for little pay in filthy, backbreaking, and dangerous conditions. In many parts of the world, where they remain unregulated, working conditions and pay are still appalling. Regulation of surrogacy does not necessarily "make a public statement that it is all right." Good laws and regulations protect those who are least able to protect themselves or who are unaware of the implications of their actions. They also serve to protect a society from its own folly.

POSTSCRIPT

Should Surrogate Motherhood Be Outlawed?

Whether surrogate motherhood is outlawed or regulated, new reproductive technologies will continue to raise perplexing dilemmas in the 1990s.

As society learns to cope with surrogacy, surrogate mother contracts may be forced to follow the trend now occurring with open adoptions, in which the biological mother and the adoptive parents recognize the interrelationship that exists among the child, its gestational mother, and its adoptive parents. In the case of surrogacy, the child, not the court or adoptive parents, may acquire the right to decide whether or not to recognize his or her biological mother as the child grows to adulthood.

In early 1990, Mark and Crispina Calvert hired Anna Johnson as surrogate mother for their child, the product of Crispina's ovum fertilized *in vitro* (outside the body) with Mark's semen. In October, after Johnson decided she wanted to keep the child, a California court ruled that Mark and Crispina should have full custody of their genetic child. The court decided that Anna's carrying the fetus for nine months constituted little more than service as a prenatal wet nurse. In addition, the court proposed that it would be confusing and disastrous for a child to have two natural mothers.

No court decisions thus far have completely resolved the dilemmas of contract law when applied to surrogate motherhood. Legal tradition allows that when a contract is violated or not fulfilled as specified, the injured party can either seek damages or compel the defaulting party to perform the work agreed to under the contract. But if a surrogate mother decides she wants to keep her child instead of giving it up for adoption as she is contracted to do, the genetic father and his wife are usually not going to be satisfied by receiving monetary damages from the surrogate when what they really want is "their" infant. On the other hand, if the surrogate mother decides she does not want to go through with the pregnancy and wants to seek an abortion, enforcing the contract and compelling the services of the surrogate's body is also a troubling scenario. Clearly, society is far from resolving all the complications and questions raised by surrogate technology.

SUGGESTED READINGS

M. Field, *Surrogate Motherhood* (Harvard University Press, 1990).

B. K. Rothman, *Recreating Motherhood: Ideology and Technology in a Patriarchal Society* (W. W. Norton, 1990).

C. Shalev, *Birth Power: The Case for Surrogacy* (Yale University Press, 1989).

M. B. Whitehead, *A Mother's Story* (St. Martin's Press, 1989).

V. A. Zelizer, "From Baby Farms to Baby M," *Society* (March 1988).

ISSUE 9

Abortion and the "Pro-Life" *v.* "Pro-Choice" Debate: Should the Human Fetus Be Considered a Person?

YES: Knights of Columbus, from *Amicus Curiae, William L. Webster, Attorney General of Missouri, et al. v. Reproductive Health Services et al.*, U.S. Supreme Court (October 1988)

NO: Janet Benshoof, from "Fetal 'Personhood' and the Law," in Edd Doerr and James W. Prescott, eds., *Abortion Rights and Fetal "Personhood"* (Centerline Press, 1989)

ISSUE SUMMARY

YES: The Knights of Columbus, a national organization of lay Catholics, argue that the concept of "viability" on which the case of *Roe v. Wade* was based has changed and that, in terms of the Fourteenth Amendment, ability to survive outside the mother's womb is not a proper basis for defining the word *person*. Hence, the unborn child should be protected as a person from conception on.

NO: Janet Benshoof, an associate at the Center for Reproductive Law and Policy, argues that, historically, the law has never regarded the fetus as a person. She warns that recent attempts to force legal recognition of fetal personhood have already created a frightening array of restrictions on women and their right to privacy, from court-ordered obstetrical interventions to lawsuits and legislation for feticide, fetal abuse, and fetal neglect.

In every culture and time, people have puzzled over how animals and humans reproduce. In ancient Greece, Hippocrates and his students believed that the whole animal or human was preformed in the female egg and that the male's role in reproduction was only to stimulate the egg to unfold and develop. Aristotle, a fine embryologist for his time, argued that human development was a gradual process of differentiation: a basically vegetative mass in the uterus developed until it achieved an animal form and life principle that were superseded by a human form and life principle—about 40 days after conception in male embryos and 80 days after conception in female embryos. Medieval theologians, including Thomas Aquinas, adopted

Aristotle's view and held that the human fetus was not fully human until quickening, the stage of gestation at which fetal motion is felt.

In the 1600s scientists used the newly invented microscope to study eggs and sperm. Imagination led some to claim they could see a miniature human curled up in the egg or sperm. For the next 100 years, scientists and theologians argued over the implications of these "preformed" humans. Some argued that since the human form was present in the egg or sperm, a true human person was present at conception.

In 1759 Caspar Wolff disproved all forms of the preformation theory. Protestant theologians generally accepted his scientific evidence and revived the views of Aristotle and the medieval theologians, arguing that the human fetus was not a person at conception but that it only achieved full human status sometime during pregnancy. Catholic theologians generally stayed with the preformation theory and continued to argue that from the moment of conception the fetus, whether preformed or not, was fully human and a person.

This debate continues in the 1990s, when the question of fetal "personhood" is a critical element in the abortion debate. In the following selections, the Knights of Columbus maintain that what the scientists call a zygote, an embryo, or fetus is in reality a person fully endowed with the right to protection under the commandment "Thou shall not kill" and the Fourteenth Amendment to the U.S. Constitution. Janet Benshoof argues that framing abortion laws in terms of the rights of the fetus ultimately restricts the rights and equality interests of women.

YES

Knights of Columbus

THE RIGHTS OF THE UNBORN CHILD SHOULD BE PROTECTED

SUMMARY OF ARGUMENT

The present case is an appropriate vehicle for overruling *Roe v. Wade* even if the case could be decided under the *Roe* framework.

As a practical matter, *Roe*'s analytical framework is flawed beyond repair because it rests on "viability"—the point at which an unborn child can survive outside of the womb with artificial aid—to determine when a state may protect the life of "the developing young in the human uterus." As Justice O'Connor has pointed out, because viability is almost solely defined by ever-progressing technology, it is a constantly moving point that cannot be a neutral and stable basis for long-term constitutional adjudication.

More fundamentally, viability is an invalid benchmark for construing the meaning of "person" in the Fourteenth Amendment because it has nothing to do with attributes of personhood, or a particularized state of being, but only the state of medical technology. Viability's true utility lies in its insight that a viable infant is certainly a person and that only limitations on technology prevent all unborn children from being viable. If a "viable" unborn child is a person, then so are all unborn children, viable or not.

Roe's justifications for excluding the unborn from the Fourteenth Amendment are unpersuasive. Before *Roe*, in equity, property, crime, and tort, the law recognized the unborn as persons of legal consequence, reckoning that consequence in terms of the particular circumstances of the unborn. Upon examination, neither the Constitution's other uses of the word "person," the punishment provided for abortion, the traditional status of the mother of the aborted child as a victim, not an accomplice, nor 19th century abortion practices provides any principled basis on which to exclude the unborn from the protections of the Fourteenth Amendment.

From *William L. Webster, Attorney General of Missouri, et al. v. Reproductive Health Services et al.*, 109 S. Ct. 3040 (1989). Notes and case citations omitted.

In view of the logic and history of the Amendment, and this Court's traditional liberal construction of constitutional protections for personal rights, the only reasonable reading of the word "person" is one that includes an unborn child. The framers of the Amendment explicitly intended to extend its protections to "every human being." Their expansive design for the Amendment, combined with the predominant anti-abortion sentiment and legislation of the time in which it was proposed and ratified, inexorably leads to inclusion of the unborn as "persons" under the Fourteenth Amendment.

Indeed, this Court's understanding of the word "person" has been flexible enough to hold business corporations to be Fourteenth Amendment "persons." If the word can extend the fundamental protections of law to "beings" that are mere legal constructs, no rule of interpretation or principle of law can justify excluding unborn human beings.

ARGUMENT

I. THIS CASE IS AN APPROPRIATE VEHICLE FOR OVERRULING *ROE*, EVEN IF THE MISSOURI STATUTE AT ISSUE COULD ITSELF BE UPHELD UNDER *ROE'S* ANALYSIS.

This case provides the Court with an appropriate vehicle for overruling *Roe v. Wade*. Indeed, the present case would provide the Court with such a vehicle even if appellants did not ask the Court to overrule *Roe*, and even if the case could be decided under the framework of *Roe* itself. When faced with similar circumstances in the past, the Court has overruled similar precedents.

II. *ROE'S* ANALYTICAL FRAMEWORK IS FLAWED BEYOND REPAIR.

Roe v. Wade is both inherently unworkable, and inherently wrong. Its analytical framework rests on two judgments. First, that beginning "at approximately the end of the first trimester," a state may reasonably regulate abortion in the interest of motherhood health. *Id.* at 163. This is so, *Roe* explains, because in 1973 "until the end of the first trimester mortality in abortion may be less than mortality in normal childbirth." *Roe's* second judgment is that, for "the stage subsequent to viability," the State may proscribe all abortions, except those necessary for the life or health of the mother. Viability is the demarcation, *Roe* announces, because "the fetus then presumably has the capability of meaningful life outside the mother's womb."

That analytical system, even if it were otherwise valid, could never serve as the basis for long-term constitutional analysis.

> The *Roe* framework . . . is clearly on a collision course with itself. As the medical risks of various abortion procedures decrease, the point at which the State may regulate for reasons of maternal health is moved further forward to actual childbirth. As medical science becomes better able to provide for the separate existence of the fetus, the point of viability is moved further back toward conception. Moreover, it is clear that the trimester approach violates the fundamental aspiration of judicial decisionmaking through the application of neutral principles "sufficiently absolute to give them roots throughout the community and continuity over significant periods of time. . . . "

More fundamentally, however, *Roe's* use of viability as a constitutional benchmark could never be valid. As Justice White has noted, a viability standard has almost nothing to do with attributes of personhood, or a particularized state of being, and everything to do with the "state of medical practice and technology" that allows an unborn child to survive at an ever earlier point in gestation.

Moreover, the quality of medical technology varies not only with time, but also with locale. Many unborn children who are "viable" on any given day in a major metropolitan center would not be viable in a more rural setting. If constitutional personhood were pegged to the quality of medical technology in a given state, it would lead to the absurd result of the same unborn child being a "person" in some states, but not in others. Such an unborn child would then periodically gain, lose, and regain constitutional "personhood" whenever his or her mother traveled across state boundaries.

To be sure, the idea of "viability" does have some analytical utility, but a utility completely at odds with the result in *Roe*. Referring to the point at which an unborn child could survive outside the womb, "albeit with artificial aid," viability provides a standard by which to find when an unborn child becomes "equal" to a child already born. And no one would seriously argue that an infant—even one born prematurely—was not a "person" whose right to life was protected by the Fourteenth Amendment.

Viability's value, however, lies not in its ability to draw the line at when one "becomes" a person, but rather in its insight that a viable infant is certainly a person, and that only limitations on technology prevent all unborn children from being viable. In short, if a "viable" unborn child is a person then so are all unborn children, viable or not.

A. There Is No Principled Basis by Which to Exclude the Unborn from the Protections Given to Persons by the Fourteenth Amendment.

Nevertheless, "the unborn," *Roe* announced, "have never been recognized in the law as persons in the whole sense." This point is, at the same time, both mistaken and irrelevant. Women and blacks were not treated as persons "in the whole sense" for significant periods of Anglo-American legal history, yet that fact hardly disqualifies them from personhood. Minors are not legally capable "in the whole sense" and often have legal interests that are contingent on future events, notably coming of age. Yet they most assuredly are persons.

Roe is, moreover, simply mistaken. Contrary to the *Roe* majority's belief otherwise, "[i]n equity, property, crime, and tort the unborn has received and continues to receive a legal personality." And as Dean Ely has observed, even "[t]o the extent they are not entirely conclusive, the bodies of doctrine to which the Court adverts respecting the protection of fetuses under general legal doctrine tend to undercut rather than support its conclusion." In the law of property, for example, an unborn child is considered a person in being for all purposes that are to his or her benefit, including taking by will or descent. Equally noteworthy is the extension in equity of *parens patriae* protection to unborn children regardless of gestational age illustrated by cases compelling blood transfusions for pregnant women to protect their unborn children.

Roe's discussion of tort law is also "largely inaccurate." Far from exhibiting *Roe*'s skepticism, the "ideological history of prenatal injury law, and the more recent development of prenatal death law has consistently moved toward the affirmation of the unborn as a 'person' in the law. . . . " Even in 1973, it was well established that a child born alive could recover for prenatal injury. Moreover, the trend in tort is towards permitting recovery for prenatal injury when the child is stillborn. Again, at the time of *Roe*, of the jurisdictions that had addressed the issue, 17 allowed such recovery, while 12 did not.

In short, the "sense" in which the law has recognized the unborn outside of the abortion context is as persons of legal consequence, reckoning that consequence in terms of the particular circumstances of the unborn. That sense is not only consistent with the status of persons under the Fourteenth Amendment, but, given the broad scope of the Amendment, requires inclusion of the unborn within its protections.

Ultimately, however, *Roe*'s conclusion that "the word 'person,' as used in the Fourteenth Amendment, does not include the unborn" was premised on three more precise notions: first, that no other use of the word "person" in the Constitution has a "prenatal application"; second, that aspects of "the typical abortion statute," such as permitting abortion to save the life of the mother, are inconsistent with "Fourteenth Amendment status"; and third, that "throughout major portion of the 19th century prevailing legal abortion practices were far freer than they are today." None of these propositions compels *Roe*'s conclusion. The first is irrelevant; the second and third, simply mistaken.

1. The Constitutional Text Does Not Exclude the Unborn.

As *Roe* noted, neither the Constitution as a whole nor the Fourteenth Amendment

in particular defines the word "person." Reviewing the uses of that word elsewhere in the Constitution, however, the *Roe* majority pronounced that the word nowhere else admitted of any prenatal application. And that, the majority inferred, meant that the word "person" did not embrace the unborn within the meaning of the Fourteenth Amendment. That inference is transparently unwarranted.

It is now a common criticism of this analysis that most of the provisions of the Constitution noted by the Court plainly had adults in mind when employing the word "person." This does not mean that children are not persons under the Fourteenth Amendment. The Twenty-Second Amendment, for another example, prohibits any "person" from being elected to the Office of President more than twice. Such a use of the word hardly precludes application of "person" in the Fourteenth Amendment to a human being who is not a natural-born citizen and not yet 35. Clearly, "[i]n the clauses mentioned by the Court, the concept of 'person' was broad and undefined and the function of the specific constitutional clause was to limit the broader class of persons for a particular purpose."

Perhaps more strikingly, few of the usages cited by the *Roe* Court have any application to corporations. Yet the Fourteenth Amendment's "person" is expansive enough to encompass the business corporation, an entity that exists solely in the imagination of the law. And in the words of two commentators, when *Roe* is considered in the light of *Santa Clara*, it takes on a "hauntingly Orwellian" character: "something that can be a person without being human, and can be human without being a person." If the word "person" can be extended to embrace a corporation, it surely must include living human beings, like the unborn, whom it meets along the way. . . .

B. The Letter and Intent of the Fourteenth Amendment Mandate Protection of the Unborn as Persons.

The text of the Fourteenth Amendment itself sets out only two classes of individual: "citizens," who must be born or naturalized in the United States and for whom the privileges and immunities of citizenship are assured, and "persons," a broader class not circumscribed by any specified criteria and for whom the fundamental rights of life, liberty, and property are guaranteed. U.S. Const. amend. XIV, § 1. Lacking any affirmative command to exclude unborn human children from the Fourteenth Amendment's guarantee of the right to life, the Court should apply "the rule that constitutional provisions for the security of person and property should be liberally construed," and give the word "person" in the Fourteenth Amendment the broadest possible reading. *Cf. Levy v. Louisiana* (1968) ("We start from the premise that illegitimate children are not 'nonpersons.' They are humans, live, and have their being. They are clearly 'persons' within the meaning of the Equal Protection Clause of the Fourteenth Amendment."); *Glona v. American Guar. & Liab. Ins. Co.* (1968) ("To say that the test of equal protection should be the 'legal' rather than the biological relationship [of illegitimate children to their parents] is to avoid the issue. For the Equal Protection Clause necessarily limits the authority of a State to draw such 'legal' lines as it chooses.").

Moreover, such a construction of the word "person" in Section 1 of the Fourteenth Amendment is consistent with the intent of the Amendment's framers and ratifiers. Congressman John Bingham, the sponsor of Section 1 in the House of Representatives, intended it to have "universal" application (1866), guaranteeing the rights of "any human being." The Amendment would thus extend the protections of the law to "common humanity" (1868). Bingham's test for the law's coverage was straightforward: "the only question to be asked of the creature claiming its protection is this: Is he a man?" (1867). Similarly, the Amendment's Senate sponsor, Senator Jacob Howard, felt that it would apply to the "humblest, the poorest, the most despised of the human race" (1866). Congress contemplated the broadest scope for the word "person" in the due process and equal protection clauses, postulating neither a class of humans that could be excluded nor any governmental power to make such exclusions.

To be sure, the legislative history of the Amendment makes no explicit reference to the unborn or to abortion. Yet by its adoption in 1868, every state used its criminal law to regulate abortion, and generally regarded the unborn as legal persons. In that legal milieu, the Amendment's authors, if asked, would almost certainly have considered the word "person" to include an unborn child. At a minimum, the expansive language its framers used both in the Amendment and in their explanations of what they were trying to accomplish suggests the opposite of an intent to exclude any particular class of persons from coverage, much less to overturn in one stroke newly-tightened state abortion laws. On the contrary, the anti-abortion feeling of the period in which the Fourteenth Amendment was proposed and ratified is hard to overstate. "[N]ot one statement by any nineteenth-century commentator can be found which was in any way sympathetic to women desiring abortions."

Ultimately, then, *Roe*'s effort to build an analytical framework on an unborn child's "capability of meaningful life outside the mother's womb," *Roe*, injects into judicial decisionmaking an analysis alien to the Fourteenth Amendment. When a human life becomes "meaningful," or when it loses its "meaning," are subjective questions of value that look beyond the physical existence of a human being. However illuminating such philosophical inquiry may be, the framers embodied in the Fourteenth Amendment a more fundamental threshold of value that must be applied by the courts and that is not subject to *adhoc* modifica-tion under the influence of such extrinsic value systems.

Securing the interest of the unborn in life on the same Fourteenth Amendment foundation as the right to life of all human beings would return this Court to the neutral and balanced framework of adjudication provided by the Constitution. It would harmonize this Court's understanding of human beings and of Fourteenth Amendment "persons." And it would do so on the strength of a simple insight: if a being is human, as an unborn child is, he is a person protected by the terms of the Fourteenth Amendment.

CONCLUSION

For the foregoing reasons, the Eighth Circuit should be reversed, and *Roe v. Wade* should be overruled.

NO

Janet Benshoof

FETAL "PERSONHOOD" AND THE LAW

Historically the fetus has never been treated as a separate person or a person at all. Legal rights, if any, have come into play only after a live birth. Certainly the Founding Fathers never considered fetuses as citizens or persons. By contrast, although black people and women certainly suffered legal disability under the law, their basic legal personhood was already fixed in the common law.

The characterization of a fetus as a person or as an entity that has legal status has been changing in the last ten years to what I believe to be an alarming degree, insofar as women's rights are concerned. Even though the rights of a woman versus that of a fetus in a nonabortion context have not been constitutionally adjudicated by the Supreme Court, one nonetheless sees discussions of the legal status of the fetus all across the legal landscape. I believe that it is worth noting these developments in the legal culture and looking at some of their underlying causes.

A perusal of recent legal literature reveals the following:

Actions for the wrongful death of a fetus in the womb have moved beyond simply compensating the woman for the loss of her pregnancy and begun to characterize the fetus as a human life; there has been increased recognition of the legal status of the fetus in the criminal law. For example, in 1986, Massachusetts was the first state to hold that the vehicular homicide statute applied also to fetuses. Therefore, the person who caused the accident was criminally charged not only with the death of the pregnant woman but with the death of the fetus, as well. This move, unprecedented at the time, has spawned would-be imitators; there is an increasing recognition of the fetus set over and against the pregnant woman carrying it, as we see cases of authorities forcing caesareans, forcing blood transfusions, or even going so far as criminally charging a woman because she did not follow the proper prenatal care.

The notion of fetal personhood has begun to appear even so far afield as the workplace, in the context of occupational safety. While the federal government has steadily relaxed regulations on companies and failed to enforce strict occupational safety laws, it has at the same time encouraged discriminatory application of these laws by subjecting women to strict regulation in the workplace because of their pregnancy or their potential pregnancy. For example, a few years ago, the ACLU [American Civil Liberties Union] represented five women in Virginia who had been sterilized against their will in order to keep their jobs at the American Cyanamid Company. And the company's rationale was that in order for them to keep their jobs they would either have to show that they were sterile or become sterilized, because the jobs involved potential harm to a fetus. As unions have begun to sue to stop the use of pesticides and other dangerous chemicals, one can envision a judge who has allowed limited use of, say, a pesticide order that pregnant women could not be workers. Thus, instead of cleaning up the workplace for all people, men and women, government may simply choose to exclude pregnant women or potentially pregnant women from certain jobs because of possible harm to the fetus, reminiscent of the stringent requirements and restrictions that barred women from access to the workplace 100 years ago.

There are several reasons why these developments are taking place right now. One reason is the activity of the Right to Life movement. Those who want to outlaw abortion or to pass a "human life" amendment to the Constitution realize as a strategic matter that the more humanness that can be attributed to the fetus, the more legal status can be accorded the fetus in child custody law and inheritance law and in negligence law and tort law, the better

chance there may be to ultimately pass a "human life" amendment.

A second reason is that the language of tort law cannot keep pace with its own doctrinal development. The fact that fetuses have been granted more legal rights results in part from sloppy legal conceptualization by judges who fail to realize the implications of how they write their decisions, even if those decisions are coming out with a result that people of good will would all support.

A third reason is that technology plays an increasingly major role in defining relationships, as it varies the number of ways of having children and the increased number of parents a child could have. Looking at surrogacy, for example, the fetus does become somehow separate from the mother because of the contract involved, particularly now that the technique of embryo transplant has been perfected, where the embryo is put in a woman who is not the genetic parent at all. In other words, we have a situation where the egg comes from the mother and the sperm from the father, and the resulting embryo is put into yet a third party, the woman who will carry the fetus to term. Those kinds of techniques separate the fetus from the woman in a way that makes it more possible for people to visualize and for the law to conceptualize the two separate persons.

At the same time, the logic of technological development and scientific discovery that drives doctors and scientists is animated by the operative belief that if it is possible to do something, one should do it, sometimes with unexpected and frightening results. For example, some states have begun to disallow the use of so-called "living wills" (which grant a loved one the authority to choose to terminate life support systems in the event of a coma or profound disability) by pregnant women. In other words, if you are injured in a car accident and you are pregnant, the state can take over and keep you alive forever. What this means is that becoming pregnant can cost a woman her right to have a medical surrogate carry out her wishes. In other words, you're not treated as a competent adult if you're a woman and potentially could become pregnant. This simply would not be the case were it not for recent advances in life-sustaining technology. Recently, I had a revealing exchange with a physician, who is also an ethicist heading the ethics department in a major teaching hospital in New Jersey, who talked about the fact that they were now keeping alive women who were in accidents up to 30 weeks of pregnancy and then attempting a caesarean. And he said that no matter what kind of living will the woman had signed, they would ignore it, that this advance in technology was wonderful, and besides, what does it matter what the unconscious woman wanted when she was conscious?

Hand in hand with technological development, there is also a sort of gung-ho cultural context that doctors operate in, that if they can do it, they must do it, and they want to do it. I do not think that many of those same doctors would treat a man who had a car accident that way and take out his heart immediately because they could now do heart transplants. On the contrary, they would be very careful to see that he signed an organ donation card. They would be much more respectful of that, but somehow a woman who has a fetus inside her is different and no matter how or why she became pregnant—maybe it was involuntary, maybe she was raped—her living will is inoperative.

Since *Roe v. Wade* is the touchstone of legal discussion in this area, I would like to close with some reflections on what *Roe v. Wade* means, and on the tensions that are now in the Supreme Court over where *Roe* is going.

First of all, *Roe v. Wade* said that the fetus was not a person for the purpose of constitutional rights. Beyond that, the Court said it was not competent to make the decision about whether or not a fetus was a person, and took note of the religious and moral debate around the status of the fetus. This does not mean that the Court was unaware of the biological facts of fetal development. Rather, the Court recognized that biology as such does not stand alone, that biology has whatever value we attribute to it, notwithstanding attempts by the anti-abortion movement to end discussion by invoking biological facts when in truth that is where discussion only begins. The Court recognized that what we were dealing with are questions of religion, of conscience, and not just biology, and that by not saying that the fetus was a person, it was leaving it for individual people to make their own conscientious decisions.

Roe v. Wade did not say that women have the right of privacy across the board and that they can have an abortion at any point in pregnancy under any conditions. Justice Blackmun, who wrote the opinion, did talk about the fetus as such in that he said that in the third trimester, or after viability (that is, when the fetus could live on its own), a state could, if it wanted to, outlaw abortion, but even then a woman's life or health prevailed. Now presumably under all the definitions of health the Supreme Court has used, even after viability a woman can get an abortion if her mental or physical health may be impaired. The interesting thing is that while roughly half the states in the country do limit post-viability abortions and roughly half the states do not, there is absolutely no difference in the incidence of late abortions between these two groups, absolutely none. Our research, and research by the Centers for Disease Control in Atlanta, yield the result that virtually no abortions are being performed after the fetus has reached viability.

Nevertheless, the thought of post-viability abortions makes a lot of people queasy even though they can find none in practice. I have learned from experience that the kinds of abortion one finds even near the time of viability are the most heartbreaking. They are women who found adverse results from amniocentesis, or teenagers who are trying to get the money because Medicaid doesn't pay for abortions—situations of that sort, even at around the twentieth week of pregnancy, and 99% of all the abortions in this country are done before 20 weeks of pregnancy. Now the Supreme Court's language in recognizing that after viability a state could choose to prohibit abortion in some circumstances, has led judges to extend that reasoning to the nonabortion context. This is an especially dangerous development. For example, in New York State, a judge recently ordered a blood transfusion for a woman who was a Jehovah's Witness and felt that was against her religion, when she was 18 weeks pregnant, well before viability, and the whole basis of his reasoning was *Roe v. Wade*. He said that if the state can prohibit abortion after viability because of its compelling interest in the fetus, then even before viability it can order something, albeit not as intrusive as prohibiting abortion,

such as a forced transfusion. In fact, the two contexts are wholly different, and in fact it is constitutionally threatening to adopt the *Roe* reasoning into the nonabortion context because that opens up a whole Pandora's Box.

Within the judicial community, there seem to be some pro-choice judges who are still very adamant about keeping the fetal status in the third trimester and retaining the viability concept. For example, in 1983, in *Planned Parenthood v. Ashcroft*, the Supreme Court upheld a law requiring that a second physician to help the fetus be present during a late abortion. This was definitely done for the fetus, not for the woman. Also, although we have so far won cases that restrict the kind of abortion a woman can have late in pregnancy, the Supreme Court has indicated that if you could perform an abortion that would save the fetus without additional harm to the woman it would probably uphold that as constitutional, but it has yet to confront that question in practice.

In the final analysis, I believe that the concept of viability is both dangerous and ultimately misguided. Abortion rights should be framed in terms of women's privacy and equality interests. In that light, anti-abortion laws violate rights to liberty and bodily integrity, which have a long history in this country. Ultimately, we all have to look at anti-abortion laws as real impediments to women's equality. If women are not going to be defined by biology, then biology cannot be used against them in anti-abortion legislation.

POSTSCRIPT

Abortion and the "Pro-Life" *v.* "Pro-Choice" Debate: Should the Human Fetus Be Considered a Person?

In the past few decades, researchers, embryologists, and obstetricians have developed many different ways of observing human reproduction. Today they can watch the sperm travel through the male reproductive system—from the testes to ejaculation in the vagina. Using miniaturized, computer-enhanced fiber optics, scientists can watch the sperm negotiate the cervical canal and uterine cavity and enter the fallopian tube. They can watch the sperm fertilize an egg. They can watch the fertilized egg, the zygote, burrow into the lining of the uterus five days after fertilization. On color television physicians can watch the embryo developing in the uterus. They can see the human form take shape and monitor the whole nine months of human development with amniocentesis, chorionic villi sampling, fetoscopy, and ultrasonography.

But what does all this visualization of the fetus tell us about the issue of fetal "personhood"? If the fetus looks human, is it necessarily human? Ethicist and philosopher Joseph Fletcher warns that the powerful visual images of the fetus in the uterus seduce many into a proleptic fallacy; that is, in their anticipation of the future birth, they describe the fetus as a person and attribute personhood to it as if it had already been born.

Antiabortion advocates claim the terms *baby* and *child* are proper descriptions for the developing human from conception on. Abortion, then, is logically murder.

Obviously, the issue of fetal "personhood" is crucial and perplexing, with no easy answer.

SUGGESTED READINGS

L. Blumberg, "Why Fetal Rights Must Be Opposed," *Social Policy* (Fall 1987).

E. Doerr and J. W. Prescott, eds., *Abortion Rights and Fetal "Personhood,"* 2d ed. (Centerline Press, 1990).

R. T. Francoeur, *Utopian Motherhood: New Trends in Human Reproduction*, 3rd ed. (A. S. Barnes, 1977).

R. T. Francoeur, "Transformation in Human Reproduction," in L. A. Kirkendall and A. E. Gravatt, eds., *Marriage and the Family in the Year 2020* (Prometheus Press, 1984).

R. T. Francoeur, "Reproductive Technologies: New Alternatives and New Ethics," *SIECUS Report* (1985).

R. T. Francoeur, "From Then to Now: The Evolution of Bioethical Decision Making in Perinatal Intensive Care," in C. C. Harris and F. Snowden, eds., *Bioethical Frontiers in Perinatal Intensive Care* (Northwestern State University Press, 1985).

C. A. Gardner, "Is the Embryo a Person?" *The Nation* (November 13, 1989).

S. J. Heaney, "Aquinas and the Humanity of the Conceptus," *Human Life Review* (Winter 1989).

S. Holm, "New Danish Law: Human Life Begins at Conception," *Journal of Medical Ethics* (June 1988).

K. Pollitt, "A New Assault on Feminism," *The Nation* (March 26, 1990).

PART 3

Legal and Social Issues

According to the democratic ideal, the government should make only those laws that are absolutely necessary to preserve the common good. Unless government can demonstrate a "compelling need," it should not infringe on the privacy and personal rights of individual citizens.

This principle raises some perplexing questions when applied to the sexual behavior of consenting adults, the personal decision-making of adolescents, and the rights of gay men and lesbians. This section examines some of those questions and explores the implications of two recent social concerns, date rape and sexual harassment. The final issue debates whether or not the federal government spends a disproportionate amount on AIDS research as compared to other fatal diseases.

- Is There a Date Rape Crisis on College Campuses?

- Does Government Have a Constitutional Right to Prohibit Certain Kinds of Sexual Conduct?

- Do Parental Notification Laws Benefit Minors Seeking Abortions?

- Should the Policy Banning Gays from the Military Be Lifted?

- Should Prostitution Be Decriminalized?

- Should Society Recognize Gay Marriages?

- Is Sexual Harassment a Pervasive Problem?

- Has the Federal Government Spent Enough on AIDS Research?

ISSUE 10

Is There a Date Rape Crisis on College Campuses?

YES: Robin Warshaw, from *I Never Called It Rape: The* Ms. *Report on Recognizing, Fighting, and Surviving Date and Acquaintance Rape* (Harper & Row, 1988)

NO: Katie Roiphe, from "Date Rape's Other Victim," *The New York Times Magazine* (June 13, 1993)

ISSUE SUMMARY

YES: Robin Warshaw, a journalist specializing in social issues, examines the data from a nationwide survey conducted by *Ms.* magazine and psychologist Mary P. Koss and concludes that date rape is "happening all around us."
NO: Katie Roiphe, author of *The Morning After: Sex, Fear and Feminism on Campus,* claims that feminist prophets of a rape crisis wrongfully redefine rape to include almost any sexual encounter between women and men. She argues that shifting the criteria for rape from force and coercion to male political power promotes a destructive and sexist image of women as delicate, naive, unable to express their true feelings, and incapable of resisting men.

In 1969, just as the latest sexual revolution was peaking in the United States, sociologist Eugene Kanin published a paper in the *Journal of Sex Research* reporting on aspects of male aggression that affected couples. In 1975, in her book *Against Our Wills: Men, Women, and Rape,* feminist pioneer Susan Brownmiller gave a name to one particular type of male aggression briefly examined by Kanin. "Date rape," forced sexual assault by an acquaintance when on a date, was thus introduced.

The term *date rape,* however, seemed to limit this form of male aggression to couples actually going together in some kind of ongoing courtship. A broader designation was needed to cover situations in which the aggressor and victim were not courting or dating but knew each other or went out casually and occasionally as a couple. So we now have date rape and the broader term *acquaintance rape.*

Date and acquaintance rape came into public view with a 1985 *Ms.* magazine survey, directed by Professor Mary P. Koss and funded by the

National Institute of Mental Health. In 1988 Robin Warshaw's slim volume *I Never Called It Rape: The* Ms. *Report on Recognizing, Fighting, and Surviving Date and Acquaintance Rape,* which examines data from the survey, became a national best-seller. It also generated prevention workshops and therapy groups for date rape victims on college campuses across the nation.

Prior to this new conception, rape had been understood to involve a man using or threatening to use a weapon or physical strength to force some sexually intimate act on an unwilling woman. Date and acquaintance rape have introduced the more nebulous and vaguely defined factor of "psychological force," or "coercion," to the concept of rape.

Individual perceptions of what differentiates psychological coercion (emotional force) from seduction and persuasion in a dating relationship or a casual friendship often differ, depending both on one's gender and one's social class. With men and women today often engaging in casual sex for fun, relaxation, or curiosity, it is difficult to spell out clearly when and why some forms of persuasion are acceptable at one time in one relationship and unacceptable (and worthy of being labeled "rape") at another time in another relationship. The issue becomes even more complicated the morning, 1 year, or 10 years after a casual sexual experience, when recollection and reflection can give the experience new interpretations.

It is little wonder that both women and men are confused today about the signals they send and receive in dating and acquaintance situations. The following selections by Robin Warshaw and Katie Roiphe highlight this confusion, which frequently turns into resentment and anger.

YES

Robin Warshaw

THE REALITY OF ACQUAINTANCE RAPE

Women raped by men they know—acquaintance rape—is not an aberrant quirk of male-female relations. If you are a woman, your risk of being raped by someone you know is *four times greater* than your risk of being raped by a stranger.

A recent scientific study of acquaintance rape on 32 college campuses conducted by *Ms.* magazine and psychologist Mary P. Koss showed that significant numbers of women are raped on dates or by acquaintances, although most victims never report their attacks.

Ms. SURVEY STATS

- 1 in 4 women surveyed were victims of rape or attempted rape.
- 84 percent of those raped knew their attacker.
- 57 percent of the rapes happened on dates.

Those figures make acquaintance rape and date rape more common than left-handedness or heart attacks or alcoholism. These rapes are no recent campus fad or the fantasy of a few jilted females. They are real. And they are happening all around us.

THE EXTENT OF "HIDDEN" RAPE

Most states define rape as sexual assault in which a man uses his penis to commit vaginal penetration of a victim against her will, by force or threats of force or when she is physically or mentally unable to give her consent. Many states now also include unwanted anal and oral intercourse in that definition and some have removed gender-specific language to broaden the applicability of rape laws.

In acquaintance rape, the rapist and victim may know each other casually—having met through a common activity, mutual friend, at a party, as neighbors, as students in the same class, at work, on a blind date, or while traveling. Or they may have a closer relationship—as steady dates or former sexual partners. Although largely a hidden phenomenon because it's the least reported type of rape (and rape, in general, is the most underreported crime against a person), many organizations, counselors, and social researchers agree that acquaintance rape is the most prevalent rape crime today.

Only 90,434 rapes were reported to U.S. law enforcement agencies in 1986, a number that is conservatively believed to represent a minority of the actual rapes of all types taking place. Government estimates find that anywhere from three to ten rapes are committed for every rape reported. And while rapes by strangers are still underreported, rapes by acquaintances are virtually nonreported. Yet, based on intake observations made by staff at various rape-counseling centers (where victims come for treatment, but do not have to file police reports), 70 to 80 percent of all rape crimes are acquaintance rapes.

Those rapes are happening in a social environment in which sexual aggression occurs regularly. Indeed, less than half the college women questioned in the *Ms.* survey reported that they had experienced *no* sexual victimization in their lives thus far (the average age of respondents was 21). Many had experienced more than one episode of unwanted sexual touching, coercion, attempted rape, or rape. Using the data collected in the study . . . the following profile can be drawn of what happens in just one year of "social life" on America's college campuses:

Ms. SURVEY STATS

In one year 3,187 women reported suffering:
- 328 rapes (as defined by law)
- 534 attempted rapes (as defined by law)
- 837 episodes of sexual coercion (sexual intercourse obtained through the aggressor's continual arguments or pressure)
- 2,024 experiences of unwanted sexual contact (fondling, kissing, or petting committed against the woman's will)

Over the years, other researchers have documented the phenomenon of acquaintance rape. In 1957, a study conducted by Eugene J. Kanin of Purdue University in West Lafayette, Indiana, showed that 30 percent of women surveyed had suffered attempted or completed forced sexual intercourse while on a high school date. Ten years later, in 1967, while young people donned flowers and beads and talked of love and peace, Kanin found that more than 25 percent of the male college students surveyed had attempted to force sexual intercourse on a woman to the point that she cried or fought back. In 1977, after the blossoming of the women's movement and countless pop-culture attempts to extol the virtues of becoming a "sensitive man," Kanin found that 26 percent of the men he surveyed had tried to force intercourse on a woman and that 25 percent of the women questioned had suffered attempted or completed rape. In other words, two decades had passed since Kanin's first study, yet women were being raped by men they knew as frequently as before.

In 1982, a doctoral student at Auburn University in Auburn, Alabama, found that 25 percent of the undergraduate women surveyed had at least one experience of forced intercourse and that 93 percent of those episodes involved acquaintances. That same year, Auburn psychology professor and acquaintance-rape expert Barry R. Burkhart conducted a study in which 61 percent of the men said they had sexually touched a woman against her will.

Further north, at St. Cloud State University in St. Cloud, Minnesota, research in 1982 showed 29 percent of women surveyed reported being physically or psychologically forced to have sexual intercourse.

In 1984, 20 percent of the female students questioned in a study at the University of South Dakota in Vermillion, South Dakota, said they had been physically forced to have intercourse while on a date. At Brown University in Providence, Rhode Island, 16 percent of the women surveyed reported they were raped by an acquaintance and 11 percent of the men said they had forced sexual intercourse on a woman. And another study coauthored by Auburn's Burkhart showed 15 percent of the male respondents reporting having raped a date.

That same year, the study of acquaintance rape moved beyond the serenity of leafy college quadrangles into the hard reality of the "dangerous" outside world. A random sample survey of 930 women living in San Francisco, conducted by researcher Diana Russell, showed that 44 percent of the women questioned had been victims of rape or attempted rape—and that 88 percent of the rape victims knew their attackers. A Massachusetts Department of Public Health study, released in 1986, showed that two-thirds of the rapes reported at crisis centers were committed by acquaintances.

These numbers stand in stark contrast to what most people think of as rape: that is, a stranger (usually a black, Hispanic, or other minority) jumping out of the bushes at an unsuspecting female, brandishing a weapon, and assaulting her. The truth about rape—that it usually happens between people who know each other and is often committed by "regular" guys—is difficult to accept.

Most people never learn the truth until rape affects them or someone they care about. And many women are so confused by the dichotomy between their acquaintance-rape experience and what they thought rape really was that they are left with an awful new reality: Where once they feared strange men as they were taught to, they now fear strange men *and* all the men they know. . . .

RAPE IS RAPE

Rape that occurs on dates or between people who know each other should not be seen as some sort of misguided sexual adventure: Rape is violence, not seduction. In stranger rape *and* acquaintance rape, the aggressor makes a decision to force his victim to submit to what he wants. The rapist believes he is entitled to force sexual intercourse from a woman and he sees interpersonal violence (be it simply holding the woman down with his body or brandishing a gun) as an acceptable way to achieve his goal.

"All rape is an exercise in power," writes Susan Brownmiller in her landmark book *Against Our Will: Men, Women and Rape.* Specifically, Brownmiller and others argue, rape is an exercise in the imbalance of power that exists between most men and women, a relationship that has forged the social order from ancient times on.

Today, that relationship continues. Many men are socialized to be sexually aggressive—to score, as it were, regardless of how. Many women are socialized to submit to men's wills, especially those men deemed desirable by society at large. Maintaining such roles helps set the stage for acquaintance rape.

But despite their socialization, most men are not rapists. That is the good news.

The bad news, of course, is that so many are.

Ms. SURVEY STAT

1 in 12 of the male students surveyed had committed acts that met the legal definitions of rape or attempted rape.

BLAMING THE ACQUAINTANCE-RAPE VICTIM

Without question, many date rapes and acquaintance rapes could have been prevented by the woman—if she hadn't trusted a seemingly nice guy, if she hadn't gotten drunk, if she had acted earlier on the "bad feeling" that many victims later report they felt but ignored because they didn't want to seem rude, unfriendly, or immature. But acknowledging that in some cases the woman might have prevented the rape by making a different decision does not make her responsible for the crime. Says a counselor for an Oregon rape-crisis agency: "We have a saying here: 'Bad judgment is not a rapeable offense.' "

As a society, we don't blame the victims of most crimes as we do acquaintance-rape survivors. A mugging victim is not believed to "deserve it" for wearing a watch or carrying a pocketbook on the street. Likewise, a company is not "asking for it" when its profits are embezzled; a store owner is not to blame for handing over the cash drawer when threatened. These crimes occur because the perpetrator decides to commit them.

Acquaintance rape is no different. There are ways to reduce the odds, but, like all crimes, there is no way to be certain that it will not happen to you.

Yet acquaintance-rape victims are seen as responsible for the attacks, often more responsible than their assailants. "Date rape threatens the assumption that if you're good, good things happen to you. Most of us believe that bad things don't happen out of the blue," says psychologist Koss, chief investigator of the *Ms.* study, now affiliated with the department of psychiatry at the University of Arizona Medical School in Tucson, Arizona. Society, in general, is so disturbed by the idea that a "regular guy" could do such a thing—and, to be sure, many "regular guys" are made uncomfortable by a concept that views their actions as a crime—that they would rather believe that something is wrong with the woman making such an outlandish claim: She is lying, she has emotional problems, she hates men, she is covering up her own promiscuous behavior. In fact, the research in the *Ms.* survey shows that women who have been raped by men they know are not appreciably different in any personal traits or behaviors than women who are not raped.

Should we ask women not to trust men who seem perfectly nice? Should we tell them not to go to parties or on dates? Should we tell them not to drink? Should we tell them not to feel sexual? Certainly not. *It is not the victim who causes the rape.*

But many persist in believing just that. An April 1987 letter to syndicated columnist Ann Landers from a woman who had been raped by two different men she dated reportedly drew heavy negative reader mail after Landers responded supportively to the woman. "Too bad you didn't file charges against those creeps," Landers wrote. "I urge you to go for counseling immediately to rid yourself of the feeling of guilt and rage.

You must get it through your head that you were not to blame."

So far, so good, but not for long. Three months later, Landers published a letter from an irate female reader who noted that the victim said she and the first man had "necked up a storm" before he raped her. Perhaps the raped woman hadn't intended to have intercourse, the reader said, "but she certainly must accept responsibility for encouraging the guy and making him think she was a willing partner. The trouble starts when she changes her mind after his passions are out of control. Then it's too late."

Landers bought this specious argument—a variant on the old "men can't help themselves" nonsense. In her reply to the follow-up letter she wrote, "Now I'm convinced that I must rethink my position and go back to telling women, 'If you don't want a complete sexual experience, keep a lively conversation going and his hands off you.' "

In other words, if you get raped, it's your own fault.

DATE RAPE AND ACQUAINTANCE RAPE ON COLLEGE CAMPUSES

Despite philosophical and political changes brought about by the women's movement, dating relationships between men and women are still often marked by passivity on the woman's part and aggression on the man's. Nowhere are these two seen in stronger contrast than among teenagers and young adults who often, out of their own fears, insecurity, and ignorance, adopt the worst sex-role stereotypes. Such an environment fosters a continuum of sexual victimization— from unwanted sexual touching to psychologically coerced sex to rape—that is tolerated as normal. "Because sexually

coercive behavior is so common in our male-female interactions, rape by an acquaintance may not be perceived as rape," says Py Bateman, director of Alternatives to Fear, a Seattle rape-education organization. . . .

Not surprising, then, that the risk of rape is four times higher for women aged 16 to 24, the prime dating age, than for any other population group. Approximately half of all men arrested for rape are also 24 years old or younger. Since 26 percent of all 18- to 24-year-olds in the United States attend college, those institutions have become focal points for studying date rape and acquaintance rape, such as the *Ms.* research.

Ms. SURVEY STAT

For both men and women, the average age when a rape incident occurred (either as perpetrator or victim) was 18½ years old.

Going to college often means going away from home, out from under parental control and protection and into a world of seemingly unlimited freedoms. The imperative to party and date, although strong in high school, burgeons in this environment. Alcohol is readily available and often used in stultifying amounts, encouraged by a college world that practically demands heavy drinking as proof of having fun. Marijuana, cocaine, LSD, methamphetamines, and other drugs are also often easy to obtain.

Up until the 1970s, colleges adopted a "substitute parent" attitude toward their students, complete with curfews (often more strict for females than males), liquor bans, and stringent disciplinary punishments. In that era, students were punished for violating the three-feet-on-the-floor rules during coed visiting hours in dormitories or for being caught with alcohol on college property. Although those regulations did not prevent acquaintance rape, they undoubtedly kept down the number of incidents by making women's dorms havens of no-men-allowed safety.

Such regulations were swept out of most schools during the Vietnam War era. Today, many campuses have coed dorms, with men and women often housed in alternating rooms on the same floor, with socializing unchecked by curfews or meaningful controls on alcohol and drugs. Yet, say campus crisis counselors, many parents still believe that they have properly prepared their children for college by helping them open local bank accounts and making sure they have enough underwear to last until the first trip home. By ignoring the realities of social pressures at college on male and female students—and the often catastrophic effects of those pressures—parents help perpetuate the awareness vacuum in which date rape and acquaintance rape continue to happen with regularity.

"What's changed for females is the illusion that they have control and they don't," says Claire P. Walsh, program director of the Sexual Assault Recovery Service at the University of Florida in Gainesville. "They know that they can go into chemical engineering or medical school and they've got their whole life planned, they're on a roll. They transfer that feeling of control into social situations and that's the illusion."

When looking at the statistical results of the *Ms.* survey, it's important to remember that many of these young people still have years of socializing and dating ahead of them, years in which they may encounter still more acquaintance rape. Students, parents of college

students, and college administrators should be concerned. But many are not, lulled by the same myths that pervade our society at large: Rape is not committed by people you know, against "good" girls, in "safe" places like university campuses.

THE OTHER VICTIMS OF ACQUAINTANCE RAPE

Date rape and acquaintance rape aren't confined to the college population, however. Interviews conducted across the country showed that women both younger and older than university students are frequently acquaintance-rape victims as well.

A significant number of teenage girls suffer date rape as their first or nearly first experience of sexual intercourse . . . and most tell no one about their attacks. Consider Nora, a high school junior, who was raped by a date as they watched TV in his parents' house or Jenny, 16, who was raped after she drank too much at a party. Even before a girl officially begins dating, she may be raped by a schoolmate or friend.

Then there are the older women, the "hidden" population of "hidden" rape victims—women who are over 30 years old when their rapes occur. Most are socially experienced, yet unprepared for their attacks nonetheless. Many are recently divorced and just beginning to try the dating waters again; some are married; others have never married. They include women like Helene, a Colorado woman who was 37 and the mother of a 10-year-old when she was raped by a man on their third date, and Rae, who was 45 when she was raped by a man she knew after inviting him to her Oklahoma home for coffee.

"I NEVER CALLED IT RAPE"

Ms. SURVEY STAT
Only 27 percent of the women whose sexual assault met the legal definition of rape thought of themselves as rape victims.

Because of her personal relationship with the attacker, however casual, it often takes a woman longer to perceive an action as rape when it involves a man she knows than it does when a stranger assaults her. For her to acknowledge her experience as rape would be to recognize the extent to which her trust was violated and her ability to control her own life destroyed.

Indeed, regardless of their age or background, many women interviewed . . . told no one about their rapes, never confronted their attackers, and never named their assaults as rape until months or years later.

NO

Katie Roiphe

DATE RAPE'S OTHER VICTIM

One in four college women has been the victim of rape or attempted rape. One in four. I remember standing outside the dining hall in college, looking at a purple poster with this statistic written in bold letters. It didn't seem right. If sexual assault was really so pervasive, it seemed strange that the intricate gossip networks hadn't picked up more than one or two shadowy instances of rape. If I was really standing in the middle of an "epidemic," a "crisis"—if 25 percent of my women friends were really being raped— wouldn't I know it?

These posters were not presenting facts. They were advertising a mood. Preoccupied with issues like date rape and sexual harassment, campus feminists produce endless images of women as victims—women offended by a professor's dirty joke, women pressured into sex by peers, women trying to say no but not managing to get it across.

This portrait of the delicate female bears a striking resemblance to that 50's ideal my mother and other women of her generation fought so hard to leave behind. They didn't like her passivity, her wide-eyed innocence. They didn't like the fact that she was perpetually offended by sexual innuendo. They didn't like her excessive need for protection. She represented personal, social and intellectual possibilities collapsed, and they worked and marched, shouted and wrote to make her irrelevant for their daughters. But here she is again, with her pure intentions and her wide eyes. Only this time it is the feminists themselves who are breathing new life into her.

IS THERE A RAPE CRISIS ON CAMPUS? MEASURING RAPE IS NOT AS STRAIGHTFORWARD as it might seem. Neil Gilbert, a professor of social welfare at the University of California at Berkeley, questions the validity of the one-in-four statistic. Gilbert points out that in a 1985 survey undertaken by Ms. magazine and financed by the National Institute of Mental Health, 73 percent of the women categorized as rape victims did not initially define their experience as rape; it was Mary Koss, the psychologist conducting the study, who did.

One of the questions used to define rape was: "Have you had sexual intercourse when you didn't want to because a man gave you alcohol or

From Katie Roiphe, "Date Rape's Other Victim," *The New York Times Magazine* (June 13, 1993). Adapted from Katie Roiphe, *The Morning After: Sex, Fear and Feminism on Campus* (Little, Brown, 1993). Copyright © 1993 by Katie Roiphe. Reprinted by permission of Little, Brown & Company.

drugs?" The phrasing raises the issue of agency. Why aren't college women responsible for their own intake of alcohol or drugs? A man may give her drugs, but she herself decides to take them. If we assume that women are not all helpless and naïve, then they should be held responsible for their choice to drink or take drugs. If a woman's "judgment is impaired" and she has sex, it isn't necessarily always the man's fault; it isn't necessarily always rape.

As Gilbert delves further into the numbers, he does not necessarily disprove the one-in-four statistic, but he does clarify what it means—the so-called rape epidemic on campuses is more a way of interpreting, a way of seeing, than a physical phenomenon. It is more about a change in sexual politics than a change in sexual behavior. Whether or not one in four college women has been raped, then, is a matter of opinion, not a matter of mathematical fact.

That rape is a fact in some women's lives is not in question. It's hard to watch the solemn faces of young Bosnian girls, their words haltingly translated, as they tell of brutal rapes; or to read accounts of a suburban teen-ager raped and beaten while walking home from a shopping mall. We all agree that rape is a terrible thing, but we no longer agree on what rape is. Today's definition has stretched beyond bruises and knives, threats of death or violence to include emotional pressure and the influence of alcohol. The lines between rape and sex begin to blur. The one-in-four statistic on those purple posters is measuring something elusive. It is measuring her word against his in a realm where words barely exist. There is a gray area in which one person's rape may be another's bad night. Definitions become entangled in passionate ideological battles. There hasn't been a remarkable change in the number of women being raped; just a change in how receptive the political climate is to those numbers.

The next question, then, is who is identifying this epidemic and why. Somebody is "finding" this rape crisis, and finding it for a reason. Asserting the prevalence of rape lends urgency, authority to a broader critique of culture.

In a dramatic description of the rape crisis, Naomi Wolf writes in "The Beauty Myth" that "Cultural representation of glamorized degradation has created a situation among the young in which boys rape and girls get raped *as a normal course of events*." The italics are hers. Whether or not Wolf really believes rape is part of the "normal course of events" these days, she is making a larger point. Wolf's rhetorical excess serves her larger polemic about sexual politics. Her dramatic prose is a call to arms. She is trying to rally the feminist troops. Wolf uses rape as a red flag, an undeniable sign that things are falling apart.

From Susan Brownmiller—who brought the politics of rape into the mainstream with her 1975 best seller, "Against Our Will: Men, Women and Rape"—to Naomi Wolf, feminist prophets of the rape crisis are talking about something more than forced penetration. They are talking about what they define as a "rape culture." Rape is a natural trump card for feminism. Arguments about rape can be used to sequester feminism in the teary province of trauma and crisis. By blocking analysis with its claims to unique pandemic suffering, the rape crisis becomes a powerful source of authority.

Dead serious, eyes wide with concern, a college senior tells me that she believes one in four is too conservative an estimate. This is not the first time I've heard this. She tells me the right statistic is closer to one in two. That means one in two women are raped. It's amazing, she says, amazing that so many of us are sexually assaulted every day.

What is amazing is that this student actually believes that 50 percent of women are raped. This is the true crisis. Some substantial number of young women are walking around with this alarming belief: a hyperbole containing within it a state of perpetual fear.

"ACQUAINTANCE RAPE: IS DATING DANgerous?" is a pamphlet commonly found at counseling centers. The cover title rises from the shards of a shattered photograph of a boy and girl dancing. Inside, the pamphlet offers a sample date-rape scenario. She thinks:

"He was really good looking and he had a great smile. . . . We talked and found we had a lot in common. I really liked him. When he asked me over to his place for a drink I thought it would be O.K. He was such a good listener and I wanted him to ask me out again."

She's just looking for a sensitive boy, a good listener with a nice smile, but unfortunately his intentions are not as pure as hers. Beneath that nice smile, he thinks:

"She looked really hot, wearing a sexy dress that showed off her great body. We started talking right away. I knew that she liked me by the way she kept smiling and touching my arm while she was speaking. She seemed pretty relaxed so I asked her back to my place for a drink. . . . When she said 'Yes' I knew that I was going to be lucky!"

These cardboard stereotypes don't just educate freshmen about rape. They also educate them about "dates" and about sexual desire. With titles like "Friends Raping Friends: Could It Happen to You?" date-rape pamphlets call into question all relationships between men and women. Beyond warning students about rape, the rape-crisis movement produces its own images of sexual behavior, in which men exert pressure and women resist. By defining the dangerous date in these terms—with this type of male and this type of female, and their different expectations—these pamphlets promote their own perspective on how men and women feel about sex: men are lascivious, women are innocent.

The sleek images of pressure and resistance projected in rape education movies, videotapes, pamphlets and speeches create a model of acceptable sexual behavior. The don'ts imply their own set of do's. The movement against rape, then, not only dictates the way sex *shouldn't be* but also the way it *should be*. Sex should be gentle, it should not be aggressive; it should be absolutely equal, it should not involve domination and submission; it should be tender, not ambivalent; it should communicate respect, it shouldn't communicate consuming desire.

In "Real Rape," Susan Estrich, a professor of law at the University of Southern California Law Center, slips her ideas about the nature of sexual encounters into her legal analysis of the problem of rape. She writes: "Many feminists would argue that so long as women are powerless relative to men, viewing a 'yes' as a sign of true consent is misguided. . . . Many women who say yes to men they know, whether on dates or on the job, would say no if they could. . . . Women's silence sometimes is the product not of passion and desire but of pressure and fear."

Like Estrich, most rape-crisis feminists claim they are not talking about sex; they're talking about violence. But, like Estrich, they are also talking about sex. With their advice, their scenarios, their sample aggressive male, the message projects a clear comment on the nature of sexuality: women are often unwilling participants. They say yes because they feel they have to, because they are intimidated by male power.

The idea of "consent" has been redefined beyond the simple assertion that "no means no." Politically correct sex involves a yes, and a specific yes at that. According to the premise of "active consent," we can no longer afford ambiguity. We can no longer afford the dangers of unspoken consent. A former director of Columbia's date-rape education program told New York magazine, "Stone silence throughout an entire physical encounter with someone is not explicit consent."

This apparently practical, apparently clinical proscription cloaks retrograde assumptions about the way men and women experience sex. The idea that only an explicit yes means yes proposes that, like children, women have trouble communicating what they want. Beyond its dubious premise about the limits of female communication, the idea of active consent bolsters stereotypes of men just out to "get some" and women who don't really want any.

Rape-crisis feminists express nostalgia for the days of greater social control, when the university acted in loco parentis and women were protected from the insatiable force of male desire. The rhetoric of feminists and conservatives blurs and overlaps in this desire to keep our youth safe and pure.

By viewing rape as encompassing more than the use or threat of physical violence to coerce someone into sex, rape-crisis feminists reinforce traditional views about the fragility of the female body and will. According to common definitions of date rape, even "verbal coercion" or "manipulation" constitute rape. Verbal coercion is defined as "a woman's consenting to unwanted sexual activity because of a man's verbal arguments not including verbal threats of force." The belief that "verbal coercion" is rape pervades workshops, counseling sessions and student opinion pieces. The suggestion lurking beneath this definition of rape is that men are not just physically but also intellectually and emotionally more powerful than women.

Imagine men sitting around in a circle talking about how she called him impotent and how she manipulated him into sex, how violated and dirty he felt afterward, how coercive she was, how she got him drunk first, how he hated his body and he couldn't eat for three weeks afterward. Imagine him calling this rape. Everyone feels the weight of emotional pressure at one time or another. The question is not whether people pressure each other but how our minds and our culture transform that pressure into full-blown assault. There would never be a rule or a law or even a pamphlet or peer counseling group for men who claimed to have been emotionally raped or verbally pressured into sex. And for the same reasons—assumption of basic competence, free will and strength of character—there should be no such rules or groups or pamphlets about women.

In discussing rape, campus feminists often slip into an outdated sexist vocabulary. But we have to be careful about using rape as metaphor. The sheer physical fact of rape has always been loaded with cultural meaning. Throughout history, women's bodies have been seen as property, as chaste objects, as virtuous vessels to be "dishonored," "ruined," "defiled." Their purity or lack of purity has been a measure of value for the men to whom they belonged.

"Politically, I call it rape whenever a woman has sex and feels violated," writes Catharine MacKinnon, a law professor and feminist legal scholar best known for her crusade against pornography. The language of virtue and violation reinforces retrograde stereotypes. It backs women into old corners. Younger feminists share MacKinnon's vocabulary and the accompanying assumptions about women's bodies. In one student's account of date rape in the Rag, a feminist magazine at Harvard, she talks about the anguish of being "defiled." Another writes, "I long to be innocent again." With such anachronistic constructions of the female body, with all their assumptions about female purity, these young women frame their experience of rape in archaic, sexist terms. Of course, sophisticated modern-day feminists don't use words like honor or virtue anymore. They know better than to say date-rape victims have been "defiled." Instead, they call it "post-traumatic stress syndrome." They tell the victim she should not feel "shame," she should feel "traumatized." Within their overtly political psychology, forced penetration takes on a level of metaphysical significance: date rape resonates through a woman's entire life.

Combating myths about rape is one of the central missions of the rape-crisis movement. They spend money and energy trying to break down myths like "She asked for it." But with all their noise about rape myths, rape-crisis feminists are generating their own. The plays, the poems, the pamphlets, the Take Back the Night speakouts, are propelled by the myth of innocence lost. . . .

As long as we're taking back the night, we might as well take back our own purity. Sure, we were all kind of innocent, playing in the sandbox with bright red shovels—boys, too. We can all look back through the tumultuous tunnel of adolescence on a honey-glazed childhood, with simple rules and early bedtimes. We don't have to look at parents fighting, at sibling struggles, at casting out one best friend for another in the Darwinian playground. This is not the innocence lost; this is the innocence we never had.

The idea of a fall from childhood grace, pinned on one particular moment, a moment over which we had no control, much lamented, gives our lives a compelling narrative structure. It's easy to see why the 17-year-old likes it; it's easy to see why the rape-crisis feminist likes it. It's a natural human impulse put to political purpose. But in generating and perpetuating such myths, we should keep in mind that myths about innocence have been used to keep women inside and behind veils. They have been used to keep them out of work and in labor. . . .

PEOPLE HAVE ASKED ME IF I HAVE EVER BEEN date-raped. And thinking back on complicated nights, on too many glasses of wine, on strange and familiar beds, I would have to say yes. With such a sweeping definition of rape, I wonder how many people there are, male or female, who haven't been date-raped at one point or another. People pressure and manipulate and cajole each other into all sorts of things all of the time. As Susan Sontag wrote, "Since Christianity upped the ante and concentrated on sexual behavior as the root of virtue, everything pertaining to sex has been a 'special case' in our culture, evoking peculiarly inconsistent attitudes." No human interactions are free from pressure, and the idea that sex is, or can be, makes it what Sontag calls a "special case," vulnerable to the inconsistent expectations of double standard.

With their expansive version of rape, rape-crisis feminists are inventing a kinder, gentler sexuality. Beneath the broad definition of rape, these feminists are endorsing their own utopian vision of sexual relations: sex without struggle, sex without power, sex without persuasion, sex without pursuit. If verbal coercion constitutes rape, then the word rape itself expands to include any kind of sex a woman experiences as negative.

When Martin Amis spoke at Princeton, he included a controversial joke: "As far as I'm concerned, you can change your mind before, even during, but just not after sex." The reason this joke is funny, and the reason it's also too serious to be funny, is that in the current atmosphere you can change your mind afterward. Regret can signify rape. A night that was a blur, a night you wish hadn't happened, can be rape. Since "verbal coercion" and "manipulation" are ambiguous, it's easy to decide afterwards that he manipulated you. You can realize it weeks or even years later. This is a movement that deals in retrospective trauma.

Rape has become a catchall expression, a word used to define everything that is unpleasant and disturbing about relations between the sexes. Students say things like "I realize that sexual harassment is a kind of rape." If we refer to a whole range of behavior from emotional pressure to sexual harassment as "rape," then the idea itself gets diluted. It ceases to be powerful as either description or accusation.

Some feminists actually collapse the distinction between rape and sex. Catharine MacKinnon writes: "Compare victims' reports of rape with women's reports of sex. They look a lot alike. . . . In this light, the major distinction between intercourse (normal) and rape (abnormal) is that the normal happens so often that one cannot get anyone to see anything wrong with it."

There are a few feminists involved in rape education who object to the current expanding definitions of sexual assault. Gillian Greensite, founder of the rape prevention education program at the University of California at Santa Cruz, writes that the seriousness of the crime "is being undermined by the growing tendency of some feminists to label all heterosexual miscommunication and insensitivity as acquaintance rape." From within the rape-crisis movement, Greensite's dissent makes an important point. If we are going to maintain an *idea* of rape, then we need to reserve it for instances of physical violence, or the threat of physical violence.

But some people want the melodrama. They want the absolute value placed on experience by absolute words. Words like "rape" and "verbal coercion" channel the confusing flow of experience into something easy to understand. The idea of date rape comes at us fast and coherent. It comes at us when we've just left home and haven't yet figured out where to put our new futons or how to organize our new social lives. The rhetoric about date rape defines the terms, gives names to nameless confusions and sorts through mixed feelings with a sort of insistent consistency. In the first rush of sexual experience, the fear of date rape offers a tangible framework to locate fears that are essentially abstract.

When my 55-year-old mother was young, navigating her way through dates, there was a definite social compass. There were places not to let him put his hands. There were invisible lines. The pill wasn't available. Abortion wasn't legal. And sex was just wrong. Her mother gave her "mad money" to take out on dates in case her date got drunk and she needed to escape. She had to go far enough to hold his interest and not far enough to endanger her reputation.

Now the rape-crisis feminists are offering new rules. They are giving a new political weight to the same old no. My mother's mother told her to drink sloe gin fizzes so she wouldn't drink too much and get too drunk and go too far. Now the date rape pamphlets tell us: "Avoid excessive use of alcohol and drugs. Alcohol and drugs interfere with clear thinking and effective communication." My mother's mother told her to stay away from empty rooms and dimly lighted streets. In "I Never Called It Rape," Robin Warshaw writes, "Especially with recent acquaintances, women should insist on going only to public places such as restaurants and movie theaters."

There is a danger in these new rules. We shouldn't need to be reminded that the rigidly conformist 50's were not the heyday of women's power. Barbara Ehrenreich writes of "re-making love," but there is a danger in re-making love in its old image. The terms may have changed, but attitudes about sex and women's bodies have not. Rape-crisis feminists threaten the progress that's been made. They are chasing the same stereotypes our mothers spent so much energy escaping.

One day I was looking through my mother's bookshelves and I found her old battered copy of Germaine Greer's feminist classic, "The Female Eunuch." The pages were dogeared and whole passages marked with penciled notes. It was 1971 when Germaine Greer fanned the fires with "The Female Eunuch" and it was 1971 when my mother read it, brand new, explosive, a tough and sexy terrorism for the early stirrings of the feminist movement.

Today's rape-crisis feminists threaten to create their own version of the desexualized woman Greer complained of 20 years ago. Her comments need to be recycled for present-day feminism. "It is often falsely assumed," Greer writes, "even by feminists, that sexuality is the enemy of the female who really wants to develop these aspects of her personality. . . . It was not the insistence upon her sex that weakened the American women student's desire to make something of her education, but the insistence upon a *passive* sexual *role* [Greer's italics]. In fact, the chief instrument in the deflection and perversion of female energy is the denial of female sexuality for the substitution of femininity or sexlessness."

It is the passive sexual role that threatens us still, and it is the denial of female sexual agency that threatens to propel us backward.

POSTSCRIPT

Is There a Date Rape Crisis on College Campuses?

Social developments and revolutions are inescapably two-edged swords, loaded with ambiguities, costs, and benefits.

Twenty years ago Midge Decter suggested that the rise of the women's liberation movement in the late 1960s masked a covert rejection of and disgust with the sexual revolution. Initially, the contraceptive pill, legalized abortion, and the sexual revolution appeared to give heterosexual women the freedom to enjoy and express their sexual needs as much as men traditionally had. Growing social tolerance also allowed bisexual and lesbian women the freedom to do the same.

Women and men could accept the new freedom of the sexual revolution with its inherent defects. Women and men could "challenge the old definition of sex as a physical act," with its "single-mindedness and phallocentrism." Men and women could insist "on a broader, more playful notion of sex, more compatible with women's broader erotic possibilities, more respectful of women's needs," to quote feminists Barbara Ehrenreich, Elizabeth Hess, and Gloria Jacobs. This approach is obvious today in the music videos of Madonna and the writings of Camille Paglia.

For some, however, the new freedom and sexual revolution created an uncomfortable dilemma. Some people have labeled the sexual revolution just another episode in a long history of male conspiracies to degrade and dominate women. This view, however, inevitably leads to the conclusion that all heterosexual intercourse is rape unless it is totally initiated and controlled by the woman. Norman Podhoretz sees the date rape crisis as a less radical but equally effective way to avoid the consequences of the sexual revolution. He argues that to avoid the consequences of the sexual revolution, "it becomes necessary to delegitimize any instance of heterosexual coupling that starts with male initiative and involves even the slightest degree of female resistance at any stage along the way."

The problem, then, is integrating the new freedom women and men can enjoy in their sexual relations and redefining those relations in broader terms, while at the same time dealing with date and acquaintance rape without falling into old antisexual traps.

SUGGESTED READINGS

S. Brownmiller, *Against Our Wills: Men, Women, and Rape* (Bantam Books, 1976).

A. Dworkin, *Intercourse* (Free Press, 1988).

A. Parrot and L. Bechhofer, eds., *Acquaintance Rape: The Hidden Crime* (John Wiley, 1991).

N. Podhoretz, "Rape in Feminist Eyes," *Commentary* (October 1991).

K. Roiphe, *The Morning After: Sex, Fear and Feminism on Campus* (Little, Brown 1993).

ISSUE 11

Does Government Have a Constitutional Right to Prohibit Certain Kinds of Sexual Conduct?

YES: Byron R. White, from Majority Opinion, *Michael J. Bowers, Attorney General of Georgia, v. Michael Hardwick, and John and Mary Doe,* U.S. Supreme Court (1986)

NO: Harry A. Blackmun, from Dissenting Opinion, *Michael J. Bowers, Attorney General of Georgia, v. Michael Hardwick, and John and Mary Doe,* U.S. Supreme Court (1986)

ISSUE SUMMARY

YES: Supreme Court justice Byron R. White, arguing the majority opinion, claims that, unlike heterosexuals, homosexuals do not have a constitutional right to privacy when it comes to engaging in oral or anal sex, even in the privacy of their homes, because of the traditional social and legal condemnation of sodomy.

NO: Supreme Court justice Harry A. Blackmun, dissenting from the majority opinion, argues that since the right to be left alone is the most comprehensive of human rights and the one most valued by civilized people, the state has no right or compelling reason to prohibit any sexual acts engaged in privately by consenting adults.

On August 3, 1982, when Michael Hardwick's friend answered a knock at the door, a police officer said he was there to serve Michael with a warrant because he had not paid a fine for carrying an open can of beer in public. The friend invited the officer in and said Michael was somewhere in the house. When the officer peered into the bedroom, he saw Michael Hardwick engaging in oral sex with another man. Hardwick was arrested for violating Georgia's antisodomy laws, but he was not prosecuted. Even so, Hardwick challenged the seldom-enforced law under which he was arrested. When a federal appellate court in Atlanta held that the Georgia law, enacted in 1816, "infringes upon the fundamental *constitutional* rights of Michael Hardwick" to engage in private sexual relations, his case went to the U.S. Supreme Court.

In July 1986, a divided Court ruled 5 to 4 that the Georgia law prohibiting all people from engaging in oral or anal sex could be used to prosecute such conduct by homosexuals. Contrary to tradition, the dissenting opinions (the opinions of the justices who disagreed with the final verdict) were read along with the majority opinion.

The majority opinion draws a sharp line between those choices that are fundamental to heterosexual life—whether and with whom to marry, whether to conceive a child, and whether to carry the pregnancy to term—and the decision to engage in sexual acts considered to be homosexual. The Court did not rule on whether or not the Constitution protects heterosexual couples from laws against oral or anal sex.

The majority opinion cited history as a reason why the constitutional boundary on privacy does not extend to homosexual acts. They noted a traditional condemnation of oral and anal sex with deep roots in English common law reaching back to the days of King Henry IV. All 13 colonies outlawed sodomy, as did all 50 states until 1961. Since 1961, however, 26 states have removed their laws against oral and anal sex between consenting adults.

The four dissenting justices took a different view of what was the issue at hand. Justice Harry A. Blackmun said the issue is more profound than merely the choice of a sexual act. It encompasses the "fundamental interest individuals have in controlling the nature of their intimate associations with others." He offered a strongly worded plea for expanding the zone of privacy to include human sexuality in all its forms, traditional or not, approved by society or not, as long as the parties involved are consenting adults. "The right of an individual to conduct intimate relationships in the intimacy of his or her own home seems to me to be the heart of the Constitution's protection of privacy."

Hardwick and his defenders argued that, given the importance of every citizen's freedom to choose the nature of the intimate associations he or she has within the privacy of his or her home, a homosexual's right to private consensual sexual relations is part of American society's "ordered liberty." The majority of the Court said this claim is "at best, facetious." Yet, a *Newsweek*-sponsored Gallup poll conducted at the time of the decision found that 47 percent of Americans disapproved of the Court's decision, while 41 percent approved of it. Fifty-seven percent opposed laws that prohibit private sexual acts between consenting adult homosexuals, while 34 percent approved of such laws. The vote for "ordered liberty" was even stronger when people were asked about laws prohibiting certain sexual acts between consenting heterosexual men and women: 74 percent opposed such laws, while only 18 percent supported such laws.

The question, as expressed in the opinions by Byron R. White and Harry A. Blackmun, is whether or not the force of history and tradition is stronger than one's constitutional right to privacy.

YES

Byron R. White

STATES HAVE A CONSTITUTIONAL RIGHT TO PROHIBIT CERTAIN SEXUAL CONDUCT

This case does not require a judgment on whether laws against sodomy between consenting adults in general, or between homosexuals in particular, are wise or desirable. It raises no question about the right or propriety of state legislative decisions to repeal their laws that criminalize homosexual sodomy, or of state court decisions invalidating those laws on state constitutional grounds. The issue presented is whether the Federal Constitution confers a fundamental right upon homosexuals to engage in sodomy and hence invalidate the laws of many states that still make such conduct illegal and have done so for a very long time. The case also calls for some judgment about the limits of the court's role in carrying out its constitutional mandate.

We first register our disagreement with the Court of Appeals and with respondent that the Court's prior cases have construed the Constitution to confer a right of privacy that extends to homosexual sodomy and for all intents and purposes have decided this case. Three cases were interpreted as construing the Due Process Clause of the 14th Amendment to confer a fundamental right to decide whether or not to beget or bear a child.

Accepting the decisions in these cases and the above description of them, we think it evident that none of the rights announced in those cases bears any resemblance to the claimed constitutional right of homosexuals to engage in acts of sodomy that is asserted in this case. No connection between family, marriage, or procreation on the one hand and homosexual activity on the other has been demonstrated, either by the Court of Appeals or by respondent. Moreover, any claim that these cases nevertheless stand for the proposition that any kind of private sexual conduct between consenting

From *Michael J. Bowers, Attorney General of Georgia, v. Michael Hardwick, and John and Mary Doe,* 478 U.S. 186, 92 L. Ed. 2d 140, 106 S. Ct. 2841 (1986).

adults is constitutionally insulated from state proscription is unsupportable.

WHAT RESPONDENT SEEKS

Precedent aside, however, respondent would have us announce, as the Court of Appeals did, a fundamental right to engage in homosexual sodomy. This we are quite unwilling to do. It is true that despite the language of the Due Process Clauses of the Fifth and 14th Amendments, which appears to focus only on the processes by which life, liberty, or property is taken, the cases are legion in which those clauses have been interpreted to have substantive content, subsuming rights that to a great extent are immune from Federal or state regulation or proscription. Among such cases are those recognizing rights that have little textual support in the constitutional language.

Striving to assure itself and the public that announcing rights not readily identifiable in the Constitution's text involves much more than the imposition of the Justices' own choice of values on the states and the Federal Government, the Court has sought to identify the nature of the rights qualifying for heightened judicial protection. In *Palko v. Connecticut*, (1937), it was said that this category includes those fundamental liberties that are "implicit in the concept of ordered liberty," such that "neither liberty nor justice would exist if (they) were sacrificed." A different description of fundamental liberties appeared in *Moore v. East Cleveland*, (1977) (opinion of Powell, J.), where they are characterized as those liberties that are "deeply rooted in the nation's history and tradition." See also *Griswold v. Connecticut*.

ANCIENT ROOTS OF PROSCRIPTIONS

It is obvious to us that neither of these formulations would extend a fundamental right to homosexuals to engage in acts of consensual sodomy. Proscriptions against that conduct have ancient roots. Sodomy was a criminal offense at common law and was forbidden by the laws of the original 13 states when they ratified the Bill of Rights. In 1868, when the 14th Amendment was ratified, all but 5 of the 37 states in the Union had criminal sodomy laws. In fact, until 1961, all 50 states outlawed sodomy, and today, 24 states and the District of Columbia continue to provide criminal penalties for sodomy performed in private and between consenting adults. Against the background, to claim that a right to engage in such conduct is "deeply rooted in this nation's history and tradition" or "implicit in the concept of ordered liberty" is, at best, facetious.

Nor are we inclined to take a more expansive view of our authority to discover new fundamental rights imbedded in the Due Process Clause. The Court is most vulnerable and comes nearest to illegitimacy when it deals with judge-made constitutional law having little or no cognizable roots in the language or design of the Constitution. That this is so was painfully demonstrated by the face-off between the Executive and the Court in the 1930s, which resulted in the repudiation of much of the substantive gloss that the Court had placed on the Due Process Clause of the Fifth and 14th Amendments. There should be, therefore, great resistance to expanding the substantive reach of those clauses, particularly if it requires redefining the category of rights deemed to be fundamental.

Otherwise, the judiciary necessarily takes to itself further authority to govern the country without express constitutional authority. The claimed right pressed on us today falls far short of overcoming this resistance.

PRIVACY OF THE HOME

Respondent, however, asserts that the result should be different where the homosexual conduct occurs in the privacy of the home. He relies on *Stanley v. Georgia* (1969), where the Court held that the First Amendment prevents conviction for possessing and reading obscene material in the privacy of his home: "If the First Amendment means anything, it means that a state has no business telling a man, sitting alone in his house, what books he may read or what films he may watch."

Stanley did protect conduct that would not have been protected outside the home, and it partially prevented the enforcement of state obscenity laws; but the decision was firmly grounded in the First Amendment. The right pressed upon us here has no similar support in the text of the Constitution, and it does not qualify for recognition under the prevailing principles for construing the 14th Amendment. Its limits are also difficult to discern. Plainly enough, otherwise illegal conduct is not always immunized whenever it occurs in the home. Victimless crimes, such as the possession and use of illegal drugs do not escape the law where they are committed at home. *Stanley* itself recognized that its holding offered no protection for the possession in the home of drugs, firearms, or stolen goods. And if respondent's submission is limited to the voluntary sexual conduct between consenting adults,

it would be difficult, except by fiat, to limit the claimed right to homosexual conduct while leaving exposed to prosecution adultery, incest, and other sexual crimes even though they are committed in the home. We are unwilling to start down that road.

Even if the conduct at issue here is not a fundamental right, respondent asserts that there must be a rational basis for the law and that there is none in this case other than the presumed belief of a majority of the electorate in Georgia that homosexual sodomy is immoral and unacceptable. This is said to be an inadequate rationale to support the law. The law, however, is constantly based on notions of morality, and if all laws representing essentially moral choices are to be invalidated under the Due Process Clause, the courts will be very busy indeed. Even respondent makes no such claim, but insists that majority sentiments about the morality of homosexuality should be declared inadequate. We do not agree and are unpersuaded that the sodomy laws of some 25 states should be invalidated on this basis.

Accordingly, the judgment of the Court of Appeals is reversed.

BY CHIEF JUSTICE BURGER, CONCURRING

I join the Court's opinion, but I write separately to underscore my view that in constitutional terms there is no such thing as a fundamental right to commit homosexual sodomy.

As the Court notes, the proscriptions against sodomy have very "ancient roots." Decisions of individuals relating to homosexual conduct have been subject to state intervention throughout the history of Western civilization. Condemnation of those practices is firmly rooted in Judeo-Christian moral and ethical standards. Homosexual sodomy was a capital crime under Roman law. See Code Theod. 9.7.6; Code Just 9.9.31. See also D. Bailey, Homosexuality in the Western Christian Tradition 70-81. During the English Reformation when powers of the ecclesiastical courts were transferred to the King's Courts, the first English statute criminalizing sodomy was passed. 25 Hen. VIII, c.6. Blackstone described "the infamous crime against nature" as an offense of "deeper malignity" than rape, an heinous act "the very mention of which is a disgrace to human nature," and "a crime not fit to be named." Blackstone's Commentaries *215. The common law of England, including its prohibition of sodomy, became the received law of Georgia and the other colonies. In 1816 the Georgia Legislature passed the statute at issue here, and the statute has been continuously in force in one form or another since that time. To hold that the act of homosexual sodomy is somehow protected as a fundamental right would be to cast aside millennia of moral teaching.

This is essentially not a question of personal "preferences" but rather of the legislative authority of the state. I find nothing in the Constitution depriving a state of the power to enact the statute challenged here.

BY JUSTICE POWELL, CONCURRING

I join the opinion of the Court. I agree with the Court that there is no fundamental right—i.e., no substantive right under the Due Process Clause—such as that claimed by respondent, and found to exist by the Court of Appeals. This is not to suggest, however, that respondent may not be protected by the Eighth Amendment of the Constitution. The Georgia statute at issue in this case authorizes a court to imprison a person for up to 20 years for a single private, consensual act of sodomy. In my view, prison sentence for such conduct—certainly a sentence of long duration—would create a serious Eighth Amendment issue. Under the Georgia statute a single act of sodomy, even in the private setting of a home, is a felony comparable in terms of the possible sentence imposed to serious felonies such as aggravated battery, first degree arson, and robbery.

In this case, however, respondent has not been tried, much less convicted and sentenced. Moreover, respondent has not raised the Eighth Amendment issue below. For these reasons this constitutional argument is not before us.

NO

Harry A. Blackmun

GOVERNMENT HAS NO COMPELLING REASON TO MAKE LAWS REGULATING PRIVATE SEXUAL ACTS

This case is no more about "a fundamental right to engage in homosexuality sodomy," as the court purports to declare, than *Stanley v. Georgia* (1969) was about a fundamental right to watch obscene movies, or *Katz v. United States* (1967) was about a fundamental right to place interstate bets from a telephone booth. Rather, this case is about "the most comprehensive of rights and the most valued by civilized men," namely "the right to be let alone." *Olmstead v. United States* (1928) (Brandeis, J., dissenting).

The statute at issue, Ga. Code Ann. section 16-6-2, denies individuals the right to engage in particular forms of private, consensual sexual activity. The Court concludes that section 16-6-2 is valid essentially because "the laws of many states still make such conduct illegal and have done so for a very long time." But the fact that the moral judgments expressed by statutes like section 16-6-2 may be "natural and familiar ought not to conclude our judgment upon the question whether statutes embodying them conflict with the Constitution of the United States." *Roe v. Wade* 410 U.S. 113, 117 (1973).

Like Justice Holmes, I believe that "(i)t is revolting to have no better reason for a rule of law than that so it was laid down in the time of Henry IV. It is still more revolting if the grounds upon which it was laid down have vanished long since, and rule simply persists from blind imitation of the past." Holmes, The Path of the Law (1897). I believe we must analyze respondent's claim in the light of the values that underlie the constitutional right to privacy. If that right means anything, it means that, before Georgia can prosecute its citizens for making choices about the most intimate aspects of their lives, it must do more than assert that the choice they have made is an "abominable crime not fit to be named among Christians." *Herring v. State* 119 Ga. 709, (1904).

From *Michael J. Bowers, Attorney General of Georgia, v. Michael Hardwick, and John and Mary Doe,* 478 U.S. 186, 92 L. Ed. 2d 140, 106 S. Ct. 2841 (1986).

DISTORTION IS DISCERNED

In its haste to reverse the Court of Appeals and hold that the Constitution does not "confe(r) a fundamental right upon homosexuals to engage in sodomy," the Court relegates the actual statute being challenged to a footnote and ignores the procedural posture of the case before it. A fair reading of the statute and of the complaint clearly reveals that the majority has distorted the question this case presents.

First, the Court's .almost obsessive focus on homosexual activity is particularly hard to justify in light of the broad language Georgia has used. Unlike the court, the Georgia Legislature has not proceeded on the assumption that homosexuals are so different from other citizens that their lives may be controlled in a way that would not be tolerated if it limited the choices of those other citizens. Rather, Georgia has provided that "(a) person commits the offense of sodomy when he performs or submits to any sexual act involving the sex organs of one person and the mouth or anus of another." Ga. Code Ann. section 16-6-2(a).

The sex or status of the persons who engage in the act is irrelevant as a matter of state law. In fact, to the extent I can discern a legislative purpose for Georgia's 1968 enactment of section 16-6-2, that purpose seems to have been to broaden the coverage of the law to reach heterosexual as well as homosexual activity. I therefore see no basis for the Court's decision to treat this case as an "as applied" challenge to section 16-6-2, see *ante*, at 2, n. 2, or for Georgia's attempt, both in its brief and at oral argument, to defend section 16-6-2 solely on the grounds that it prohibits homosexual activity.

Michael Hardwick's standing may rest in significant part on Georgia's apparent willingness to enforce against homosexuals a law it seems not to have any desire to enforce against heterosexuals. But his claim that section 16-6-2 involves an unconstitutional intrusion on his privacy and his right of intimate association does not depend in any way on his sexual orientation.

DISAGREEMENT OVER LAW

Second, I disagree with the Court's refusal to consider whether section 16-6-2 runs afoul of the Eighth or Ninth Amendments or the Equal Protection Clause of the 14th Amendment. I need not reach either the Eight Amendment or the Equal Protection Clause issues because I believe that Hardwick has stated a cognizable claim that section 16-6-2 interferes with constitutionally protected interests in privacy and freedom of intimate association. But neither the Eighth Amendment nor the Equal Protection Clause is so clearly irrelevant that a claim resting on either provision should be peremptorily dismissed. The Court's cramped reading of the issue before it makes for a short opinion, but it does little to make for a persuasive one.

"Our cases long have recognized that the Constitution embodies a promise that a certain private sphere of individual liberty will be kept largely beyond the reach of government." *Thornburgh v. American Coll. of Obst. & Gyn.* (1986). In construing the right to privacy, the Court has proceeded along two somewhat distinct, albeit complementary, lines. First, it has recognized a privacy interest with reference to certain decisions that are properly for the individual to make. *E.g., Roe v. Wade* (1973). Second, it has recognized a privacy interest with reference to certain places without regard for the particular activities in which the individuals who occupy them are engaged. The case before us implicates both the decisional and the spatial aspects of the right of privacy.

The Court concludes today that none of our prior cases dealing with various decisions that individuals are entitled to make free of governmental interference "bears any resemblance to the claimed constitutional right of homosexuals to engage in acts of sodomy that is asserted in this case." While it is true that these cases may be characterized by their connection to protection of the family, the Court's conclusion that they extend no further than this boundary ignores the warning in *Moore v. East Cleveland*, (1977) (plurality opinion), against "Clos-(ing) our eyes to the basic reasons why certain rights associated with the family have been accorded shelter under the 14th Amendment's Due Process Clause."

WHY RIGHTS ARE PROTECTED

We protect those rights not because they contribute, in some direct and material way, to the general public welfare, but because they form so central a part of an individual life. We protect the decision whether to marry precisely because marriage "is an association that promotes a way of life, not causes; a harmony in living, not political faiths; a bilateral loyalty, not commercial or social projects." *Griswold v. Connecticut*. We protect the decision whether to have a child because parenthood alters so dramatically an individual's self-definition, not because of demographic considerations or the Bible's command to be fruitful and multi-

ply. And we protect the family because it contributes so powerfully to the happiness of individuals, not because of a preference for stereotypical households.

Only the most willful blindness could obscure the fact that sexual intimacy is "a sensitive, key relationship of human existence, central to family life, community welfare, and the development of human personality," *Paris Adult Theatre I v. Slayton*, (1973). The fact that individuals define themselves in a significant way through their intimate sexual relationships with others suggests, in a nation as diverse as ours, that there may be many "right" ways of conducting those relationships, and that much of the richness of a relationship will come from the freedom an individual has to choose the form and nature of these intensely personal bonds.

In a variety of circumstances we have recognized that a necessary corollary of giving individuals freedom to choose how to conduct their lives is acceptance of the fact that different individuals will make different choices. For example, in holding that the clearly important state interest in public education should give way to competing claims by the Amish to the effect that extended formal schooling threatened their way of life, the Court declared: "There can be no assumption that today's majority is 'right' and the Amish and others like them are 'wrong.' A way of life that is odd or even erratic but interferes with no rights or interests of others is not to be condemned because it is different." *Wisconsin v. Yoder* (1972). The Court claims that its decision today merely refuses to recognize a fundamental right to engage in homosexual sodomy; what the Court really has refused to recognize is the fundamental interest all individuals have in controlling the nature of their intimate associations with others.

PRIVACY OF THE HOME

The behavior for which Hardwick faces prosecution occurred in his own home, a place to which the Fourth Amendment attaches special significance. The Court's treatment of this aspect of the case is symptomatic of its overall refusal to consider the broad principles that have informed our treatment of privacy in specific cases. Just as the right to privacy is more than the mere aggregation of a number of entitlements to engage in specific behavior, so too, protecting the physical integrity of the home is more than merely a means of protecting specific activities that often take place there.

The Court's interpretation of the pivotal case of *Stanley v. Georgia* (1969), is entirely unconvincing. *Stanley* held that Georgia's undoubted power to punish the public distribution on constitutionally unprotected, obscene material did not permit the state to punish the private possession of such material. According to the majority here, *Stanley* relied entirely on the First Amendment, and thus, it is claimed, sheds no light on cases not involving printed materials. But that is not what *Stanley* said. Rather, the *Stanley* Court anchored its holding in the Fourth Amendment's special protection for the individual in his home. The right of an individual to conduct intimate relationships in the intimacy of his or her own home seems to me to be the heart of the Constitution's protection of privacy.

First, petitioner asserts that the acts made criminal by the statute may have serious adverse consequences for "the general public health and welfare," such as spreading communicable diseases or fostering other criminal activity. Nothing in the record before the Court provides any justification for finding the activity forbidden by section 16-6-2 to be physically dangerous, either to the persons engaged in it or to others.

The core of petitioner's defense of section 16-6-2, however, is that respondent and others who engage in the conduct by section 16-6-2 interfere with Georgia's exercise of the "right of the nation and the states to maintain a decent society." Essentially, petitioner argues, and the Court agrees, that the fact that the acts described in section 16-6-2 "for hundreds of years, if not thousands, have been uniformly condemned as immoral" is a sufficient reason to permit a state to ban them today.

THE FREEDOM TO DIFFER

I cannot agree that either the length of time a majority has held its convictions or the passions with which it defends them can withdraw legislation from this Court's scrutiny. As Justice Jackson wrote so eloquently for the Court in *West Virginia Board of Education v. Barnette* (1943), "we apply the limitations of the Constitution with no fear that freedom to be intellectually and spiritually diverse or even contrary will disintegrate the social organization. (F)reedom to differ is not limited to things that do not matter much. That would be a mere shadow of freedom. The test of its substance is the right to differ as to things that touch the heart of the existing order." It is precisely because the issues raised by this case touches the heart of what makes individuals what they are that we should be especially sensitive to the rights of those whose choices upset the majority.

The assertion that "traditional Judeo-Christian values proscribe" the conduct involved, cannot provide an adequate justification for section 16-6-2. That certain, but by no means all, religious groups condemn the behavior at issue gives the State no license to impose their judgments on the entire citizenry. The legitimacy of secular legislation depends instead on whether the State can advance some justification for its law beyond its conformity to religious doctrine. Thus, far from buttressing his case, petitioner's invocation of Leviticus, Romans, St. Thomas Aquinas, and sodomy's heretical status during the Middle Ages undermines his suggestion that section 16-6-2 represents a legitimate use of secular coercive power. A state can no more punish private behavior because of religious intolerance than it can punish such behavior because of racial animus.

PEOPLE AND MORALITY

Nor can section 16-6-2 be justified as a "morally neutral" exercise of Georgia's power to "protect the public environment," *Paris Adult Theatre I*, 413 U.S., at 68-69. Certainly, some private behavior can affect the fabric of society as a whole. Reasonable people may differ about whether particular sexual acts are moral or immoral, but "we have ample evidence for believing that people will not abandon morality, will not think any better of murder, cruelty and dishonesty, merely because some private sexual practice which they abominate is not punished by the law." Petitioner and the Court fail to see the difference between laws that protect public sensibilities and those that enforce private morality. Stat-

utes banning public sexual activity are entirely consistent with protecting the individual's liberty interest in decisions concerning sexual relations; the same recognition that those decisions are intensely private which justified protecting individuals from unwilling exposure to the sexual activities of others. But the mere fact that intimate behavior may be punished when it takes place in public cannot dictate how states can regulate intimate behavior that occurs in intimate places.

This case involves no real interference with the rights of others, for the mere knowledge that other individuals do not adhere to one's value system cannot be a legally cognizable interest, let alone an interest that can justify invading the houses, hearts, and minds of citizens who choose to live their lives differently.

I can only hope that the Court soon will reconsider its analysis and conclude that depriving individuals of the right to choose for themselves how to conduct their intimate relationships poses a far greater threat to the values most deeply rooted in our nation's history than tolerance of nonconformity could ever do. Because I think the Court today betrays those values, I dissent.

POSTSCRIPT

Does Government Have a Constitutional Right to Prohibit Certain Kinds of Sexual Conduct?

So-called blue laws prohibiting sodomy, oral and anal sex, fornication, and adultery may sound silly and Victorian in today's world, but they have, in recent years, become a concern for many Americans.

Today, antiquated, little-used, and almost forgotten blue laws are being imposed less and less to harass and punish homosexual men. But as selective enforcement against gays fades, these same laws are now being used by jealous or angry spouses to embarrass and harass their partners, to save faltering marriages, or to defend against impending divorces. In 1990, several men and women in Connecticut filed formal charges against their unfaithful spouses. One husband who charged his wife with adultery said, "I'm fighting for the rights of the American family and marriage." In several states, men have been charged with and found guilty of engaging in consensual oral sex. Newspaper headlines about the revival of blue laws may have little or no effect on infidelity or the practice of oral and anal sex, but they do give a lot of people reason to be nervous. Michael Hardwick was not prosecuted, he paid no fine, and he spent no time in prison. But some wandering spouses and some heterosexuals engaging in consensual sodomy may, in the 1990s, find themselves in prison or on probation.

Legislators commonly agree that laws prohibiting fornication, adultery, and sodomy between consenting adults are totally out of touch with today's world. But it is one thing for a legislator to wink about a law in private and quite another to publicly call for its removal from the books on the floor of the state legislature. As one lawmaker admitted, a lot of people are leery about being perceived as pro-adultery or as supportive of any traditionally forbidden sexual behavior.

SUGGESTED READINGS

"Father, Daughter Lawmakers Clash Over Opposing Bills to Change Oral Sex Laws of Georgia," *Jet* (February 5/March 12, 1990).

E. Kolbert, "Using Blue Laws to Keep Spouses from Scarlet Life," *New York Times* (September 21, 1990).

A. S. Leonard, "Report from the Legal Front," *The Nation* (July 5, 1990).

N. A. Lewis, "Rare Glimpses of Judicial Chess and Poker," *The New York Times* (May 25, 1993).

A. Press, "A Government in the Bedroom," *Newsweek* (July 14, 1986).

D. Y. Rist, "Homosexuals and Human Rights," *The Nation* (April 9, 1990).

ISSUE 12

Do Parental Notification Laws Benefit Minors Seeking Abortions?

YES: Focus on the Family and Family Research Council of America, from *Amicus Curiae, State of Ohio, Appellant, v. Akron Center for Reproductive Health et al.,* U.S. Supreme Court (1990)

NO: Fran Avallone, from *Parental Consent and Notification Laws* (Right to Choose Education Fund, 1990)

ISSUE SUMMARY

YES: Focus on the Family, a publishing and broadcasting organization "dedicated to the maintenance of traditional values," and the Family Research Council of America, a conservative, profamily lobbying organization, argue that the state has many legitimate and compelling reasons to require parental notification and consent for teenagers seeking abortions. Such laws permit parents to deal with issues underlying adolescent pregnancy and to provide emotional and psychological support for whatever decision the pregnant minor makes.

NO: Fran Avallone, state coordinator for Right to Choose of New Jersey, favors parental involvement in a minor's abortion decision but opposes laws requiring parental notification or consent. She argues that the only real effect of such laws is to delay abortions and further traumatize pregnant minors, especially among the poor.

The question of whether or not unemancipated minor females have a right to privacy in their sexual activities and in deciding the outcome of a pregnancy brings the rights and responsibilities of parents into conflict with the newly recognized rights of their sexually active teenage children. But this issue is also part of a much larger social and legal process in which the rights of children and both single and married women have been expanding rapidly throughout the latter half of this century.

In 1873, Anthony Comstock managed to get enacted a broadly worded law that prohibited mailing any "obscene" material. Many states followed suit, passing laws that prohibited distribution of any obscene material—meaning any information about sexual matters, contraceptives, and abortion (which had already been outlawed). These laws also prohibited the sale of contraceptives, leaving women with little control over their reproductive processes.

The sexual revolution greatly changed this situation. In 1966 the U.S. Supreme Court struck down laws prohibiting the sale of contraceptives to married women. Similar laws prohibiting contraceptive sales to single women were struck down in 1972. As the birth control pill became popular, the courts also began to recognize the rights of teenagers to obtain information about contraceptives and to be treated for sexually transmitted diseases without obtaining their parents' consent.

In the 1970s, after recognizing women's right to privacy in seeking abortions and the rights of minors to contraceptive information and services, the courts were forced to consider the right of unemancipated pregnant females to seek abortions. Although several court decisions have supported the right of a teenager to have an abortion without notifying her parents or obtaining their consent, a 1981 Supreme Court decision upheld the so-called squeal laws, which require doctors to notify the parents of "immature teenagers" seeking abortions. In recent years, parental notification and consent laws have become a major issue in state legislatures because the Supreme Court refused to overturn *Roe v. Wade*, the landmark case that established women's right to abortion.

In a *Time*/CNN survey conducted by Yankelovich Clancy Shulman, 38 percent of the adult Americans surveyed supported the privacy of teenagers seeking abortions, while 57 percent supported parental notification and consent laws. More revealing is the 1992 Alan Guttmacher Institute survey of 1,500 teenage girls who had abortions in 1991 while living in states that did not have any parental notification or consent laws. This study found that 61 percent of the parents were told about the abortion in advance. Younger girls were more likely to have talked about abortion with at least one parent. Only 10 percent of those aged 14 or younger had an abortion without their parents knowing beforehand, while 74 percent of those 16 or 17 years old did not inform their parents.

The Guttmacher study also found that 43 percent of the teens told their mothers themselves, 10 percent of the parents were told by someone else with the minor's consent, and 6 percent of the parents found out in some other way. Twelve percent of the girls had told their fathers directly, and another 12 percent of the fathers had been told by someone else. Of the girls who did not tell either parent, 73 percent said they did not want to disappoint their parents, 55 percent feared parental anger, and 32 percent said they did not want their parents to know they were sexually active.

Opponents of notification laws cite the Guttmacher study and similar surveys as evidence that laws requiring minors to discuss an abortion decision with their parents are unnecessary. Supporters of parental notification and consent laws obviously disagree. The following selections by Focus on the Family and the Family Research Council of America and by Fran Avallone highlight these differing views and their consequences.

YES

Focus on the Family and Family
Research Council of America

PARENTAL NOTIFICATION/CONSENT
LAWS PROTECT VULNERABLE
ADOLESCENTS AND FAMILIES
FROM HARM

SUMMARY OF THE ARGUMENT

Courts and state legislatures remain uncertain about whether parental consultation laws are constitutional, and if so, within what specific legal parameters. Presently, sixteen parental consultation laws have been enjoined. Only five such statutes have been found constitutional. A clear enunciation that reasonable parental notification and consent laws do not unconstitutionally limit the right to an abortion is needed to permit states to protect minors and their families. Because state legislatures are best suited to provide these protections, the Court should limit its review to whether a statute or regulation is supported by a rational relationship to legitimate state interests.

Many legitimate, if not compelling, state interests are involved in parental consultation laws, particularly when a pregnant teenager is making the difficult and traumatic abortion decision. The courts recognize at least three state interests for parental consultation laws: (1) the peculiar vulnerability of children; (2) minor's inability to make critical decisions in an informed, mature manner; and (3) the importance of the parental role in child rearing. In light of the growing body of scientific evidence about the adverse physical and psychological effects of abortion, parents and the state have an additional and heightened interest in ensuring that the pregnant adolescent is protected from rash, ill-informed or pressured decisions on this traumatic question.

The initial state and parental interest in adolescent pregnancy and abortion is to reduce or eliminate medical and psychological problems of the

From *State of Ohio, Appellant, v. Akron Center for Reproductive Health et al.*, 110 S. Ct. 2972 (1990). Notes and some references omitted.

pregnant minor. Negative medical consequences from abortion include hemorrhage, perforated uterus, subsequent fetal malformation, cervical trauma, ectopic pregnancies, infection, menstrual disturbances, infertility, Pelvic Inflammation Disease (PID), miscarriage and high-risk prematurity in subsequent pregnancies. Since adolescents generally have immature cervixes, researchers have concluded that adverse physical health effects are more common and severe in teenage abortions. Young women who have abortions have also been found to be more predisposed to adverse outcomes in future, planned pregnancies than their sexually mature adult counterparts.

Compared to adults, adolescents appear to also have more negative emotional and psychological responses following abortion. The immediate negative psychological responses include severe guilt, anxiety, depression and psychosis. The long-term adverse psychological effects, which include denial, depression, isolation, alienation, suicide attempts and a family of psychiatric symptoms called Post Abortion Stress (PAS), appear to be more problematic and more devastating for the adolescent aborter.

Parental consultation also enhances a legitimate state interest to help adolescents make better, well-informed decisions about their pregnancy. Parents who have knowledge of a pending abortion can help their daughter assess the medical and psychological risks involved. After consultation, if she still decides to abort, they can relate important medical and psychological information to the abortionist. If adverse complications result, the parents will be aware of the cause and can give important medical information to the subsequent treating physician.

Family involvement in the abortion decision promotes important state interests of family unity and parental control in three ways: (1) it permits the parents to deal with issues underlying adolescent pregnancy; (2) it helps avoid the compounding problems of alienation, isolation and depression, which secret abortions frequently entail; and (3) it provides emotional and psychological support for whatever decision the minors make.

Parental consultation laws clearly have a rational relationship to these legitimate state interests. In addition, consultation laws with a waiting period and a judicial bypass provision cannot be said to unduly burden the minor's abortion right because parents do not have arbitrary, absolute veto power over her decision. After sixteen years, the Court should return to the constitutional principles historically employed in reviewing state health and safety laws, adopt the rational basis standard of review in the parental consultation requirements and jettison the conflicting, intricate set of abortion-related rules that are unrelated to Constitutional doctrine.

ARGUMENT

A. Parental Consultation Promotes Maternal Health in the Pregnant Adolescent by Reducing the Physical and Psychological Risks of Abortion.
The decision to terminate pregnancy involves one of the most complex and difficult decisions of a woman's life. *Planned Parenthood of Central Missouri v. Danforth*, 428 U.S. 52, 67 (1976) ("Danforth"). Medical and psychological risk factors are often overlooked or unknown, and her decision involves other

multiple social, economic and moral factors which are further confused by the physiological and psychological changes produced by pregnancy. Minor women, in particular, are often ill-informed about abortion and its serious ramifications and unable to make mature, rational decisions in their own best interest.

1. Physical Risks from Abortion.

The serious physical complications which have been associated with abortion specifically include: hemorrhaging, cervical trauma, infection, Pelvic Inflammatory Disease (PID), ectopic pregnancy, infertility and subsequent fetal malformation, miscarriages and high risk premature birth in later planned pregnancies and death. *See Amicus Brief* of Focus on the Family in *Turnock v. Ragsdale*, No. 88–790, Appendix, Table 1. Researchers who analyze data collected under the auspices of the Centers for Disease Control on Teen Abortion Morbidity and Mortality concluded that women under age eighteen who obtain abortions were more susceptible to physical injury than were older women: "[T]hese finding cause concern because cervical injury in initial, unplanned pregnancies may predispose young women to adverse outcomes in future planned pregnancy. . . . [S]ome of the most catastrophic complications occur in teenagers." Cates, Schultz and Grimes, *Risk Associated With Teenage Abortion*, 309 NEW ENGLAND JOURNAL OF MEDICINE 621, 624 (1983). Hence, one abortion decision can impact the entire childbearing potential of a teenage patient.

One abortionist reported on his post-abortion follow up, ranging from two to twelve years, of fifty teenage mothers whose pregnancies he had aborted: "The cervix of the young teenager pregnant for the first time is invariably small and tightly closed and especially liable to damage on dilation." Russel, *Sexual Activity and Its Consequences in the Teenager*, 3 CLINICS IN OB AND GYN 683–698 (1974); *see also* J. Wilke, ABORTION QUESTIONS AND ANSWERS 108–109 (rev. 1988) (hereinafter "ABORTION QUESTIONS"). In fifty-three subsequent pregnancies, he found that six had another induced abortion, nineteen had spontaneous miscarriages, one delivered a stillborn baby at six months, and six babies died between birth and two years. Only twenty-one babies survived. Two-thirds of the teenagers subsequently experienced miscarriage or high-risk premature birth of their second wanted pregnancies. *Id.*

2. Mortality Risks from Abortion.

A truly irreversible complication of teenage abortion is death of the mother. Unfortunately, tragic accounts of teenagers dying after an abortion, like the daughter of *amicus* Ann Marie Lozenski, are all too common. *See* Reardon at 109–113, and Appendix A. While statistics are difficult to obtain, it has been reported that in the United States alone, from 1972 to 1981, there were 175 maternal deaths caused by legal abortions, a figure which does not include ectopic pregnancy deaths. Like other post-abortive complications, however, deaths are also grossly underreported. According to one estimate, less than 10% of deaths from legal abortion are reported as such. HANDBOOK ON ABORTION at 80, 98–99.

A 1974 random survey of 486 obstetricians (6% of the total 21,700 in the U.S. in 1979) about their experience with complications resulting from legal abortion revealed that: 91% treated patients for complications; 87% had to hospitalize one or more patients; and 6% reported one or more patients having died from a legal abortion. A. Saltzenberger, EVERY WOMAN HAS THE RIGHT TO KNOW THE DANGER OF LEGAL ABORTION 51 (1982) (hereinafter "EVERY WOMAN"). The Center for Disease Control admits that the reported rate of deaths due to legal abortion may be deliberately kept low through selective underreporting. *Id.*

3. *Emotional and Psychological Harms from Abortion.*

In addition to the mortality and physical risks of abortion, the risks to the emotional and psychological well being of adolescent mothers are profound. *See* Focus on the Family *Amicus Brief* in *Turnock v. Ragsdale*, No. 88–790, Appendix, Table 2. "Compared with adults, adolescents appear to have somewhat more negative responses on the average following abortion." Adler & Dolcini, *Adolescent Abortion: Psychological Issues in Abortion For Adolescents,* in ADOLESCENT ABORTION: PSYCHOLOGICAL AND LEGAL ISSUES 84 (G. Melton Ed., 1986) (hereinafter "Adler & Dolcini"); Freeman, *Abortion: Subjective Attitudes and Feelings,* 10 FAMILY PLANNING PERSPECTIVES 150 (1978).

B. Parental Consultation Substantially Benefits the Minor's Decision Making Process.

There is substantial evidence that adolescents change markedly as they progress through adolescence, and differ significantly from adults, in at least five ways, in how they make decisions on whether to abort or carry to baby to full term:

1. Adolescents consider fewer and different factors in pregnancy decisions and in potential childrearing decisions;

2. Adolescents consider future solutions and goals less than adults;

3. Adolescents delay their decision more than adults;

4. Adolescents differ from adults in consideration of future consequences in hypothetical dilemmas; and

5. Adolescents have been found to differ from adults in their ability to understand aspects of moral decisions from the viewpoint of others.

Worthington at 134–135 (citations omitted).

The foregoing differences in decision making between adolescents and adults suggest that parental involvement helps adolescents, especially younger ones, make better decisions about how to react to her pregnancy in at least five ways.

First, parental notification requires the adolescent, through the waiting period provision of parental notification laws, to take 24 to 48 hours to consider the decision to abort, rather than respond immediately to the often demand-laden situation of finding that she is pregnant while at a clinic that does abortions. One study suggests that pregnant adolescents are particularly vulnerable to immediate situational cues in making pregnancy resolution decisions. Cobliner, *Pregnancy and Single Adolescent Girls: The Role of Cognitive Functions,* 3 JOURNAL OF YOUTH AND ADOLESCENTS 17–29 (1974).

Second, notifying parents allows them to give her balance and support in the decision making. While the initial response to learning about the pregnancy may be stressful for the parents, and they may consider their own wishes and fears in addition to their daughter's, parents will generally have more experience in making decisions under emotional strain and will be more likely to carefully consider a variety of options than will the adolescents. Worthington, *The Benefits of Legislation Requiring Parental Involvement Prior to Adolescent Abortion* in

VALUES AND PUBLIC POLICY 221, 226–227 (G. Regier Ed., 1988) (hereinafter *Parental Involvement*).

While the decision to abort is difficult, even for an adult woman, teenage girls are particularly subject to ambivalence and confusion regarding the abortion decision. Horowitz at 557. One study found that almost one third of young women (31.8%) changed their minds once or twice about continuing the pregnancy or having the abortion, and 18% changed their minds even more frequently.

Third, parents are also able to correct any misapprehensions that their daughter might have and to challenge her erroneous beliefs. Miracheck, *Counseling Adolescents with Problem Pregnancies*, 42 AMERICAN PSYCHOLOGISTS 84–88 (1987). One frequent erroneous belief that would be corrected is that parents will reject the adolescent because of her pregnancy. In fact, parents usually react less negatively than adolescents anticipate. There is substantial evidence that most parents will support their daughters during an adolescent pregnancy. Barglow, Bornstein, Etsome, Wright and Visodsky, *Some Psychiatric Aspects of Illegitimate Pregnancy During Early Adolescence*, 37 AMERICAN JOURNAL OF ORTHOPSYCHIATRY 226, 267 (1967).

After a preliminary period of disequilibrium (anger, disappointment, disgust), there appears to be a more stable problem solving and acceptance process when both the mother and daughter take steps toward resolving these problems in the pregnancy. *Parental Involvement* at 230. In numerous studies, over two-thirds of the families reported that members strongly support each other, participate with the pregnant adolescent, and demonstrate attachment to the new child prior to birth. *Id.* In one study, young women felt

that 67% of their mothers and 74% of their fathers would have negative reactions toward abortion. Among those minor women who did finally inform their parents of their decision to have an abortion, reported reaction to the news expressed by both parents were overwhelmingly positive. Few negative responses were reported. Clary, *Minor Women Obtaining Abortion: The Study of Parental Notification in Metropolitan Areas*, 72 AM. J. PUB. H. 283–284 (1982) (hereinafter "Clary").

Fourth, parents supply the real life experience in autonomy and problem solving which adolescents often lack— young women rely on less analytic approaches to the problem such as following the normative behavior of their peers in basing their decisions on romantic, unrealistic scripts. Ramsey, *Representation of a Child in Protection Proceedings: The Determination of Decision Making Capacity*, 17 FAMILY LAW QUARTERLY 315, 344–345 (1983) (hereinafter "Ramsey"):

> The ability to reason abstractly and foresee consequences which is so important [in] making a good decision of such magnitude [i.e., pregnancy resolution] is lacking in most teenagers.

Eisen, Zellman, Liebonitz, Chow and Evans, *Factors Discriminating Pregnancy Resolution Decisions of Unmarried Adolescents*, 108 GEN. PSYCH. MON. 69, 94 (1983). "Minors often lack the experienced perspective and judgment to avoid choices that could be detrimental to them." Clary at 284.

Fifth, parental involvement tends to moderate the emotional upheavals of adolescents which often impact heavily upon their ability to make sound judgments. "Teenagers may tend to be egocentric and to make irrational and emotional decisions about themselves and others. A particular fourteen year old may have been more capable of making a certain decision when she was younger, before the emotional upheavals of adolescence interfered with her judgments." Ramsey at 315.

This Court has recognized the significance of parents in the minor's decision making process:

> There can be little doubt that the state furthers a constitutionally permissible end by encouraging an unmarried, pregnant minor to seek the help and advice of her parents in making the very important decision whether or not [to] bear a child. That is a grave decision and a girl of tender years under emotional stress may be ill-equipped to make it without advice and emotional support. It seems unlikely that she will obtain adequate counsel and support from the attending physician at the abortion clinic.

Danforth, 428 U.S. at 91 (Stewart, J., concurring). *See Bellotti, II*, 443 U.S. at 637. A consistent thread in these cases and others is a recognition of the profound significance to the minor's well being of parental participation in the abortion decision.

C. Parental Consultation Helps Protect Vulnerable, Immature Minors from Exploitation.

Pregnant teenage girls are "particularly vulnerable" to abortion clinics which offer immediate answers to an unwanted pregnancy, and to the influence of their peers and boyfriends. *See Bellotti II*, 443, U.S. at 634. "There is no logical relationship between the capacity to become pregnant and the capacity for mature judgment concerning the wisdom of an abortion." *Matheson*, 450 U.S. at 407. In a 1980 survey of abortion clinics, it was found that less than half require parental notice even for teenagers fifteen years of age or younger; and even fewer require parental notification before performing abortions on minors aged sixteen and above. *Telling Parents* at 285 (Table 1). Almost half (45%) of the 1170 teenage abortion patients interviewed admitted that their parents had no knowledge of their intended abortion. *Id.* at 289 (Table 5). Over 90% of these teenagers were living with their parents, with only 4% living with relatives or friends. *Id.* at 287.

The bottom line is that vulnerable adolescents are exploited either consciously by abortion providers or unknowingly by the teenage peers who are equally uninformed, misinformed or emotionally and experientially unable to render rational, objective advice on abortion or childbirth. Thus, parental consultation provides the people who are most interested in the ultimate well being of pregnant adolescents the opportunity to protect them against false, misleading, prejudicial or harmful advice from their abortion "counselor" and their equally uninformed peers.

STATE NOTIFICATION AND CONSENT LAWS ARE RATIONALLY RELATED TO LEGITIMATE INTERESTS AND DO NOT "UNDULY BURDEN" A MINOR'S RIGHT TO HAVE AN ABORTION.

The federal courts' deference to state legislatures on the parental consultation question is a function of the standard of review adopted: strict scrutiny, rational basis or some intermediate standard. "A woman's ability to choose an abortion is a species of 'liberty.'" *Thornburgh v. American College of Obstetricians and Gynecologists*, 476 U.S. 747, 790 (1986)

(White, J., dissenting) ("*Thornburgh*") *see also Roe v. Wade*, 410 U.S. at 113 (Rehnquest, J., dissenting). The presence of such a liberty interest, however, ordinarily means only that state regulation affecting that liberty interest must be procedurally fair and must bear a *rational relation* to valid state objectives. *See Williamson v. Lee Optical Co.*, 348 U.S. 483, 486 (1955).

State regulation will only be subjected to the higher standard of strict scrutiny, if it *substantially interferes* with a fundamental constitutional right. *City of Akron v. Akron Center for Reproductive Health*, 462 U.S. 416, 462 (O'Connor, J., dissenting) ("*Akron I*").

The appropriate standard to review state notification and consent laws should be whether the laws are *reasonably related* to promote or further *legitimate state interests*. The countervailing protected right to abortion is "qualified," *Roe*, 410 U.S. at 154, and thus, where the state interests directly impact its ability to protect its citizens, this Court should defer to state legislative authority. In the parental consultation context, the Court has recognized many legitimate and compelling state interests: (1) to protect the mental and physical well being of pregnant minors; (2) to promote informed, rational decision making and family unit; and (3) to protect potential human life—all of which notification and consent laws promote and permissibly further.

NO

Fran Avallone

PARENTAL CONSENT AND NOTIFICATION LAWS

BACKGROUND

Anti-abortion legislators always pick on the weakest group when they want to restrict access to abortion, groups that either do not or cannot vote. The first laws that passed after the 1973 Supreme Court ruling in *Roe v. Wade* denied federal and state funding for abortions for poor women through the Medicaid programs. Now they are targeting the young and laws mandating parental consent or notification for minors seeking abortions have passed in many states.

One million teenagers get pregnant every year—one out of ten aged 15–19 and studies show that 50% of the pregnancies are unintended. Forty percent of the teens have abortions and 16–17 year olds make up the great majority of minors seeking abortions. Girls who have babies before they are 16 years old are more likely to have another baby before they are 20 years old. Only 50% of sexually active teenagers use contraception at first intercourse.

Parental consent requirements make the receipt of services conditional upon parental agreement. Parental notification requirements provide only that parents be informed that their daughters are receiving services. Notification laws usually have waiting periods—typically 48 hours—so that the abortion provider has time to notify the parent(s) by mail or in person. When the word "minor" is used it means an unemancipated minor—one who is under 18 years of age, usually living at home and dependent on her parents.

In July 1976 the U.S. Supreme Court decided the cases of *Planned Parenthood of Central Missouri v. Danforth* and *Bellotti v. Baird.* Based on previous decisions which granted minors the right to privacy, they ruled that parents cannot veto a minor's decision to obtain an abortion.

In July 1979 the Court reaffirmed that decision in *Bellotti v. Baird II* and indicated that neither consent nor notification may be required without allowing the minor to obtain, promptly and confidentially, a waiver of the consent or notification requirements, from a judge or other independent person, in order to determine if she is mature enough to make the decision and, if not, if the abortion is in her best interests. The Court said, *". . . considering her probable education, employment skills, financial resources, and emotional maturity, unwanted motherhood may be exceptionally burdensome for a minor."*

And in June 1983, the Court again reaffirmed that position and struck down a law requiring all minors to have the consent of a parent or the approval of a judge. They upheld a law requiring that immature minors must have the consent of a parent or a court but allowing them the opportunity to prove to a court that they are mature enough to consent to the abortion.

The situation in the states changes so often that it is hard to keep track of what is happening where but, as of June 1990, consent laws were in effect in 9 states and notification laws were in effect in 3. However, 33 states have laws on the books, some have been enjoined and some are not being enforced.

MASSACHUSETTS

After the Supreme Court's 1979 decision, the state of Massachusetts put into effect a law which requires both parents to consent to their minor daughter's abortion decision. If one or both parents refuse or if the minor chooses not to go to them, she can go before a judge, prove herself mature and obtain a court order for an abortion.

According to data, fully one-third of Massachusetts teenagers who want an abortion go out-of-state to obtain one. The decline in minors' abortions in that state has been matched by a rise in abortions performed on Massachusetts teens in the six surrounding states. When Rhode Island enacted a parental consent law, the number of Massachusetts teenagers seeking an abortion in that state went down and the number of abortions to Massachusetts minors went up in the other neighboring states. Studies also show that one-third of the young women are being referred to attorneys who will help them with the court procedure.

During the first year that the law was in effect, judges saw 647 teenagers and none were refused permission for the procedure. Some of the judges have stated that they are opposed to implementing a law which they believe imposes needless trauma on pregnant teens. Two dozen judges interviewed by a Boston newspaper felt they could not imagine forcing a minor to have a baby. Superior Court Judge Paul Garrity, who is morally opposed to abortion stated, *"What's happened here is the Legislature has given half a loaf to the anti-abortion forces and dumped the other half on us. The court is a pure rubber stamp. All the law does is to harass kids. It sets up a barrier to abortion."*

MINNESOTA

On June 25, 1990, the United States Supreme Court issued two decisions, 5–4, on a Minnesota law. First, they struck down the part of the law that requires two parent notification without judicial bypass. Then, they upheld the two parent notification with judicial bypass. Justice Sandra Day O'Connor switched sides in each vote.

Justice Thurgood Marshall wrote a separate opinion in which he said, *"Neither the scope of a woman's privacy right nor the magnitude of a law's burden is diminished because a woman is a minor. . . . The disclosure of a daughter's intention to have an abortion often leads to a family crisis, characterized by severe parental anger and rejection . . . the statute . . . does not require parental notification where the minor seeks medical treatment for pregnancy, venereal disease or alcohol and other drug abuse. Are we to believe that Minnesota parents have no interest in their children's well-being in these other contexts?"*

Minnesota's law requires notification of both parents, regardless of circumstances such as separation and divorce or even if the teenager's father had caused the pregnancy. Only 50% of Minnesota's minors live with both biological parents, 33% live with only one parent and 9% live with neither parent. There is a 48 hour waiting period before the physician can perform the abortion.

More than one-third of the minors who sought abortions in 1984 chose to use the judicial bypass procedure. During the five years that the law was in effect there were 3,573 cases of judicial bypass.

A study done at 4 clinics in the state found that no minor aged 13–14 used the bypass procedure, 36% of 15 year olds did, 45% of 16 year olds and 56% of 17 year olds. The study found that teenagers from low income families were less likely to go to court and minors who had frequently attended church were less likely to tell their parents. All but 15 of the minors were granted the right to have an abortion without notifying their parents. The judges who dealt with 90%

of the cases testified that they could see no positive effect of the law. The District Court found that in many cases there was a delay of a week or more which increased the medical risk associated with later abortion. The state has seen a rise of 26.6% in second trimester abortions performed on minors. The birth rate for teenagers 15–17 years old rose 38.4%, but for teenagers not affected by the law, those 18–19 year olds, the birth rate rose only .3%.

The Minnesota law was enacted in 1981 and was struck down after being in effect for five years. The District Court Judge, Donald Alsop, found that *". . . five weeks of trial have produced no factual basis upon which the court can find that the statute on the whole furthers in any meaningful way the state's interest in protecting pregnant minors or assuring family integrity. . . . Notification of the minor's pregnancy and abortion decision can provoke violence, even where the parents are divorced or separated. . . ."* The District Court also found that the law indicated that legislators desired to deter and dissuade minors from choosing to terminate their pregnancies.

OHIO

The Supreme Court also decided an Ohio law on June 25, 1990. They upheld, 6–3, a requirement that one parent be notified. They said the law *"does not impose an undue, or otherwise unconstitutional, burden on a minor seeking an abortion."* The Ohio law was enacted in 1985 and was overturned by the U.S. Court of Appeals for the 6th Circuit.

Ohio's law prohibits any person from performing an abortion on an unmarried, unemancipated, minor without notifying one parent or getting an order of approval from a court. The physician, as an alternative, may notify a minor's adult brother, sister, step-parent or grandparent if the minor and the relative each file an affidavit with a juvenile court stating that the minor fears physical, sexual, or severe emotional abuse from one of her parents.

The doctor has to give 24 hours notice, in person or by telephone, and if he/she cannot contact the parents, the physician may perform the abortion 48 hours after sending a notice by registered and certified mail.

If the minor chooses not to have her parents notified, she is required to file a complaint in juvenile court stating that she has sufficient maturity and information to make an intelligent decision whether to have an abortion or that she is the victim of physical, sexual or emotional abuse or that notifying her parents is not in her best interests. The court has five days to schedule a hearing.

All of these situations can cause delays of many weeks.

JUDICIAL BYPASS

Going before a judge is not easy for anyone and certainly traumatic for young pregnant teenagers. In courtrooms there are guards, court clerks, court reporters, not to mention the people who are always around a courthouse—police officers, newspaper reporters and attorneys.

Pregnant minors are frightened. They don't want anyone to find out about their situation. By being forced to seek a judge's approval for their abortion, they are denied their right to confidentiality.

In urban areas there are usually many facilities providing abortion services and public transportation is often available.

Rural areas have few, if any, abortion clinics and minors who cannot get someone to drive them to a city cannot get to the courthouse. Courthouses can be extremely far from a rural teenager. In Minnesota, minors may have to travel 250 miles each way to get to a judge. The national abortion statistics for 1987, published by the Centers for Disease Control, show that the number of abortions per 1,000 women varies greatly depending on whether it is an urban or rural state. New York's abortion ratio was 35 per 1,000 women, South Dakota's ratio was 9 per 1,000 and Wyoming's was 3 per 1,000.

Courts are only open from Monday to Friday, from 9 A.M. to 5 P.M. and some courtrooms and judges are only available between 10 A.M. and 4 P.M. Teenagers are in school on those days and during those hours. Many schools call the home if the student does not show up for class. Will school personnel get involved in covering for the teenager so that her parents don't find out she is in court, trying to convince a judge, who has never met her before, that she is mature enough to decide for herself whether or not to have an abortion? A typical court hearing lasts less than 15 minutes.

Court calendars are crowded and judges are overworked, their time is very limited. Does a state have enough money to assign several judges to the task of hearing the petitions of teenagers seeking abortions? Even if parental consent/ notification laws require pro-judicial action, there can be a delay of weeks before the teenager gets to see a judge. If the judge denies the minor the right to an abortion without parental involvement, the minor has the right to appeal which can add more weeks of delay.

The minor should have an attorney with her when she faces a judge. In Massachusetts, abortion clinics have a rotating list of lawyers, willing to work without a fee, who will accompany the minor to court. But what will happen if free attorneys are not available? Will a state provide funding to cover this expense?

PSYCHOLOGICAL AFTER-EFFECTS

The anti-abortionists try to use the argument that abortion causes psychological harm to women. However, when the American Psychological Association commissioned a panel of experts to study the effect of abortion on a woman's mental health, they reported, in the April 1990 issue of Science magazine, that legal, voluntary abortion does not cause emotional distress. The panel surveyed 200 studies that have been published over the last 20 years.

Their report said that though some women may feel regret, sadness or guilt, *"the weight of the evidence from scientific studies indicates that legal abortion of an unwanted pregnancy in the first trimester does not pose a psychological hazard for most women. Severe negative reactions after abortions are rare and can best be understood in the framework of coping with a normal life stress."*

Three studies which investigated the effects of abortions on teenagers also show no harmful psychological effects of abortions. Teenagers who have abortions show more adaptive, healthier functioning than those who carry to term. Negative responses to abortion are more likely when the teenager has not been actively involved in the decision or when abortion was not the first choice.

Another study found that the U.S. Supreme Court, in upholding parental involvement laws, ignored the possibility of psychological harm as a result of intrusions upon privacy and of decisions to carry a pregnancy to term. Further, a 1973 study found the most common reaction to abortion among both minors and adults is one of relief.

Indeed, a 1986 study found that the psychological trauma of full term pregnancy, birth and becoming a teenage parent is substantially greater than the psychological risks of adolescent abortion.

A minor's most common reason for not talking to her mother is to avoid hurting her mother's feelings and 30% of the young women, in a study published in the American Journal of Public Health in 1982, did not inform either parent because of fear of retaliation or physical punishment.

THE EFFECTS

For most young women there is no difference between consent and notification laws. Their only concern is that their parents not know that they are sexually active. Many of them express the desire not to disappoint their parents.

One study in Michigan found that 57% of adolescents involved their parents in their decision to have an abortion. The younger the patient, the more likely she is to talk to a parent. Young minors who do not work or drive need their parents to pay for the abortion and to take them to the clinic. Some young girls do talk to an older sibling or grandparent.

In Indiana in 1988, 17 year old Becky Bell, faced with an unintended pregnancy, went to a family planning clinic seeking an abortion. She was told she needed her parents' consent or she could go to a judge and try to convince him that she was mature enough to make her own decision. She refused to ask her parents for permission and, when she was told the judge she would see was against abortion, she rejected judicial bypass. She could have gone to Kentucky for the procedure but she had no way of getting there.

Two months after her visit to the family planning facility, she told her parents she was going to a party but she went somewhere (no one knows where) and tried to self-abort. She came home feeling ill and her parents suspected the flu. The next day she was taken to the hospital where the doctors determined she had pneumonia. A few hours later she was in a coma, and three hours later she died. Becky had told her best friend that she couldn't tell her parents. *"I can't hurt Mom and Dad. I love them too much,"* she said. Her parents are now making public appearances and they believe that the consent law in Indiana caused their daughter's death.

In Michigan several years ago, an 11 year old was raped by her mother's boyfriend. When the case was brought to court because her mother refused permission for an abortion, the decision was delayed by the judge for so long that it became too late to perform the procedure. After her mother was charged with abuse, the girl was placed in a foster home and she stayed there after she gave birth. The state subsequently took the baby away from her and she was charged with abuse and neglect of her child.

In Idaho last year, a 12 year old was raped by her father who was ordered to stay away from her. Her pregnancy was discovered at 14 weeks and that state has no facility that will perform an abortion after 12 weeks. Contacts were made with pro-choice groups and a physician was found in Oregon who would do the abortion without cost. Money was raised for bus fare and food and a place to stay was arranged for the girl and her mother. At 6:30 AM on the day they were to leave for Oregon, the girl's father entered the house and shot the 12 year old in the head, killing her instantly. He then turned the gun on himself and is now in a coma.

These three cases are extreme and out of the ordinary. But they happened and they could happen again. Studies show that 50% of teenagers faced with an unintended pregnancy and wanting an abortion do talk to their parents. If you visit an abortion clinic you will see many girls who arrive with their parents, especially those under 16.

I will always remember the 16 year old who came to a Planned Parenthood where I was working. She said she was 22 weeks pregnant and her father would kill her if he found out. When she was examined by the nurse practitioner, she was found to be at least 28 weeks pregnant and she was told she could not have an abortion; it was too late. She cried that she couldn't be 28 weeks pregnant and that she had to have an abortion. She was sent to the hospital for a sonogram which showed her to be 32 weeks pregnant, just weeks away from delivery. She was referred to the Division of Youth and Family Services to get help in dealing with her family. She did not look pregnant and could not have weighed more than 90 pounds dripping wet. She had stopped eating in order to hide the pregnancy. Her baby was born with a low birth weight because she had not only malnourished herself through the pregnancy, she had malnourished her fetus.

ALTERNATIVES TO CONSENT/NOTIFICATION LAWS

Several states have passed bills that are alternatives to restrictive consent and notification laws. In July 1989, the Governor of Maine signed a bill which requires the written consent of the minor and one parent, guardian or adult family member and the minor must receive counseling from one of the following persons: psychiatrist, psychologist, social worker, clergyperson, physician's assistant, nurse practitioner, guidance counselor or practical nurse.

The counseling has to include information on prenatal care and the alternatives to abortion and information about family planning agencies. The counseling session must explain to the minor that she can change her mind about the abortion up to the last minute and they must discuss with the teenager involving her parents or other adult family members.

If the minor does not want to involve a parent, guardian or family member, she may petition a court to grant her the right to an abortion. The court can only deny the petition if it finds that the minor is not mature enough to make her own decision and that the abortion is not in her best interest. If the court does deny the petition, an appeal is available. The law appropriated over $25,000 for the 1990–1991 fiscal year to provide attorneys for minors.

A Wisconsin law requires abortion providers to encourage parental notification unless they determine that the minor has a valid reason for not telling her parents.

The most recent law was passed in Connecticut and signed by the Governor on April 30, 1990. It is similar to the Maine law and also repeals the criminal statutes on abortion which have not been in force since the *Roe v. Wade* decision. The law requires that counseling be given to a minor, under 16 years of age, by either a psychiatrist, a psychologist, a social worker, marriage and family counselor, clergyperson, physician's assistant, guidance counselor, nurse-midwife, registered or practical nurse.

The minor has to be told that she may change her mind at any time prior to the procedure; alternative choices available to her must be explained; lists of public and private agencies which provide birth control information must be given to her; and the counselor must discuss the possibility of involving her parents or other adult family members in the decision. The minor must have adequate opportunity to ask any questions concerning the pregnancy, abortion, child care and adoption. After the counseling, the minor is required to sign a form stating that all of the above has been discussed with her. The counseling is not required if a medical emergency exists.

CONCLUSIONS

Pro-choice organizations favor parental involvement in a teenager's decision to have an abortion but are opposed to any law mandating such involvement. You cannot legislate family communication, especially if it didn't exist prior to the pregnancy.

No one is pro-abortion and no one wants teenagers to be sexually active, especially at a young age. Everyone would like every family to be loving and kind and everyone would hope that teenagers who are going to be sexually active would be responsible enough to use birth control. But the birth control must be safe, affordable and accessible.

Anti-abortionists contend that parental consent and notification laws bring families closer together. But they can have the opposite effect and can be very dangerous for young girls. The teenage years are the most difficult, for parent and child.

The way to deal with the issue of teenage sexual activity and teenage pregnancy is not to mandate parental consent or notification but to educate young people about contraception and sexual responsibility.

Most states allow minors to receive treatment for drug and alcohol abuse and sexually transmitted diseases without parental knowledge. Medical authorities know that teenagers will delay getting medical treatment if they fear that their parents will find out. This is doubly true when a young girl is pregnant.

Many health organizations oppose parental consent/notification laws, including the American College of Obstetricians and Gynecologists and the American Association of Pediatrics.

Anti-abortionists claim that teenagers are not mature enough to make the decision to have an abortion. But, if that is true, are they mature enough to care for a baby?

Those who oppose abortion say that minors may not know about medical conditions they may have. What kind of parents do not talk to their children about their medical condition or allergies they may have, especially allergies to medications? Family life education should be required in every school in every state. Right now there are only 12 states that have such a requirement. Most parents do not talk to their children about sex. Classes should be mandatory for parents of teenagers to instruct them on how to discuss sexuality and contraception with their children.

School based health clinics could provide detailed information to students and help prevent teenage pregnancy. Studies show that teens in schools with health clinics are more likely to use birth control. For many children in urban areas, a school based health clinic is their only source of medical care, even for sore throats and flu.

Anti-abortionists oppose school based health clinics because some of them provide information on contraception and referrals to family planning agencies.

Many parents of pregnant minors want their daughter to have an abortion. No court has ever ruled that a parent can force a minor to undergo the procedure but if courts and states insist on consent or notification laws, might not a court or physician agree with a parent that an abortion is in the best interest of the teenager and force her to have the abortion against her will? We read every day about a baby being left on a doorstep or in a trash bin and sometimes we read horror stories of young women who have given birth and killed the baby. Would a court, faced with such a teenager who was pregnant again, order an abortion on the grounds that she was unfit?

In the video "Abortion Denied," Becky Bell's mother says, "*I want everybody to remember Becky and what happened to us and I have the graveyard now.*" Dr. Kenneth Edelin, in the film, says, "*Women, at some time during their lives, will be so desperate when they find themselves pregnant and don't want to be pregnant, will put their lives and their health on the line to terminate a pregnancy."*

Parental consent and notification laws can kill. They will not bring families closer together. They will drive families further apart. We must not deny young women the right to make their own decisions, decisions that can affect the rest of their lives. Parental consent/notification laws must be opposed and defeated or we will see many more Becky Bells.

POSTSCRIPT

Do Parental Notification Laws Benefit Minors Seeking Abortions?

U.S. Supreme Court justice Thurgood Marshall described the dilemma of parental notification and consent laws in his dissent in the 1989 *Webster v. Reproductive Health Services* decision (which upheld a Missouri law giving states new authority to restrict abortions): "This schema forces a young woman in an already dire situation to choose between two fundamentally unacceptable alternatives: notifying a possibly dictatorial or even abusive parent or justifying her profoundly personal decision in an intimidating judicial proceeding to a black-robed stranger." In another case, Justice Sandra Day O'Connor indicated that her decision had been influenced by the large number of minors who do not live with both biological parents, a fact that makes laws requiring notification of both parents impractical.

How do we weigh the often conflicting interpretations of pro-choice and pro-life advocates on the mortality risks, and the physical, emotional, and subsequent fertility consequences of teenage abortions? What does the alternative of judicial bypass really accomplish? Do parental notification and consent laws exist to "harass these kids," as former Massachusetts Superior Court judge Paul Garrity asserts? Or do they really promote communication between sexually active teenagers and their parents and reduce the number of teen abortions? Do they promote the health and future fertility of teenagers?

Although the Clinton administration has committed itself to opening up access to abortions and providing medical coverage for all women seeking abortions under some kind of national health care insurance, it is likely that Congress will require some kind of parental notification as part of any legislation broadening access to abortion. But what kind of parental notification and consent laws would work best?

SUGGESTED READINGS

L. Blumberg, "Why Fetal Rights Must Be Opposed," *Social Policy* (Fall 1987).
M. Carlson, "Abortion's Hardest Cases," *Time* (July 9, 1990).
S. Henshaw and K. Kost, "Parental Involvement in Minors' Abortion Decisions," *Family Planning Perspectives* (September/October 1992).

T. J. Joyce and N. H. Mocan, "Impact of Legalized Abortion on Adolescent Childbearing in New York City," *American Journal of Public Health* (March 1990).

L. Tribe, *The Clash of Absolutes* (W. W. Norton, 1990).

Webster v. Reproductive Health Services (Excerpts from the decisions of the justices), in R. M. Baird and S. E. Rosenbaum, eds., *The Ethics of Abortion* (Prometheus Press, 1989).

E. L. Worthington et al., "The Benefits of Legislation Requiring Parental Involvement Prior to Adolescent Abortion," *American Psychologist* (December 1989).

S. Yates and A. J. Pliner, "Judging Maturity in the Courts: The Massachusetts Consent Statute," *American Journal of Public Health* (June 1988).

ISSUE 13

Should the Policy Banning Gays from the Military Be Lifted?

YES: Randy Shilts, from "What's Fair in Love and War," *Newsweek* (February 1, 1993)

NO: Eugene T. Gomulka, from "Why No Gays?" *Proceedings* (December 1992)

ISSUE SUMMARY

YES: Randy Shilts, national correspondent for the *San Francisco Chronicle*, argues that the military's handling of the homosexual issue in World War II, the Korean War, the Vietnam War, and the Gulf War documents the hypocrisy of the policy that embraces gay men and lesbians in times of war and discharges them in times of peace.

NO: Eugene T. Gomulka, a commander in the U.S. Navy Chaplain Corps, argues that the ban must be maintained, because of "widespread sexual compulsion," a high rate of suicide, and high rates of alcoholism, STDs, and HIV infection among gays, as well as "behavioral problems" and tensions that come with housing gay and heterosexual personnel together in tight quarters.

The military has always been a major cultural institution in American society. Traditionally, for men, being a marine, an army sergeant, an air force fighter pilot, a battleship gunner, or a submarine torpedo man is the hallmark and crucial test of masculinity. It is little wonder, then, that the issue of recognizing and accepting the presence of homosexuals (to whom some attribute unmasculine traits) in the U.S. military has stirred such emotional reactions on every side.

Fourteen of the 16 nations in NATO (North Atlantic Treaty Organization) either have laws protecting homosexuals from discrimination, including in the military, or follow policies that make no distinction between homosexuals and nonhomosexuals, even for highly sensitive, special security military duty. In October 1992 Canada eliminated all barriers to gays in its military. Australia is expected to do the same in the near future. In NATO, only the United States and Great Britain maintain a ban on gay men and lesbians in the military.

Opponents of the ban on homosexuals cite the success of Holland, Denmark, Switzerland, Norway, Sweden, Spain, Italy, and (to a lesser extent) France, where gays have already been integrated into the armed forces. Supporters of the ban argue that whether or not any of these nations allow gays into their militaries is irrelevant, because most of these nations have never had a topnotch army, and those that did ceased to be major powers long ago.

Opponents of the ban counterattack by citing the experience of the German and Israeli militaries. Germany maintains a ban on sexual relations between military personnel while on duty but is not concerned with what goes on off duty and off base. In Israel, mandatory service requirements mean that every 18-year-old man and woman enlists without exception. One Americanized Israeli soldier recalled: "I had thought Israel was less tolerant than the United States, but when I enlisted, I never witnessed any moral problems caused by homosexuals and didn't hear any homophobic talk. . . . There were openly gay soldiers I encountered, but no one seemed to resent it. It's not even an issue. I don't know why it is in America." Traditionalists, in response, emphasize the perils of mixing soldiers and sailors who may become sexually attracted to one another.

There is also a practical problem to consider: Recently, the U.S. government's General Accounting Office (GAO) pointed out that enforcing the ban on homosexuals in the military wastes about $27 million in training costs every year. Calling the ban too costly, the GAO argued that "experts believe the policy is unsupported, unfair and counterproductive; has no validity according to current scientific research and opinions; and appears to be based on the same type of prejudicial suppositions [once] used to discriminate against blacks and women."

Despite the costs of maintaining the ban, congressional hearings have highlighted one pragmatic issue in defense of the ban; namely, the close quarters and lack of privacy in much of military life—on board ship and submarine and in barracks, for example. Some argue that maintaining such close quarters with gay men and lesbians causes undue discomfort to heterosexual personnel.

In the following selections, Randy Shilts argues that history has shown that gays can work effectively in the military and that the ban should be lifted. Eugene T. Gomulka maintains that the ban should remain in place to avoid compromising the military's effectiveness.

YES

Randy Shilts

WHAT'S FAIR IN LOVE AND WAR

A chronicler of the gay-rights movement argues that the military actually eases up on its anti-homosexual rules when it needs people to fight.

On the first night of the Scud missile attacks on American troops in the Persian Gulf, an army specialist fourth class with the 27th Field Artillery found himself cramped in a foxhole with three other men. Like many young enlisted men, the specialist (who asked that his name not be used) had previously confided to the other men, his friends, that he was gay.

During that night in the foxhole, they huddled together in their suffocating suits meant to protect them from chemical and biological warfare agents. They could not see one another, but to reassure themselves that they were still there, still alive, each man kept one hand on the other. Nobody seemed to mind that one reassuring hand belonged to a homosexual, the soldier recalls—there were more important things to think about.

Defense Department policy contends that the purpose of excluding gays from the armed forces is to preserve the "good order, discipline and morale" of the military, because no heterosexual soldier would want to serve with, take orders from or share a foxhole with a homosexual. America's experience in its past three wars suggests otherwise. The behavior of military officials in accepting gays during these wars also suggests that the generals themselves know their arguments are fallacious. At no time is good order, discipline and morale more crucial for a fighting unit than in time of combat; at no time have the military's regulations against gays been more roundly ignored than in periods when troops were sent out to fight.

President Clinton's intention of integrating acknowledged lesbians and gay men into the armed forces has raised a great cry from opponents of reform, most of whom question how soldiers will respond to sharing a foxhole with a gay soldier. These arguments belie the fact that gay soldiers have served in U.S. military foxholes since the days of Valley Forge, some openly.

From the first days of the Defense Department's anti-gay regulations in the early 1940s, the government was willing to waive the for-heterosexuals-only requirement for military service if barring gays interfered with manpower exigencies. In 1945, just two years after the regulation was adopted, and during the height of the final European offensive against the Third Reich, Secretary of War Henry Stimson ordered a review of all gay discharges in the previous two years, with an eye toward reinducting gay men who had not committed any in-service homosexual acts. At the same time, orders went out to "salvage" homosexuals for the service whenever possible.

The Korean War saw a dramatic plunge in gay-related discharges. In the late 1940s, the navy meted out 1,100 undesirable discharges a year to gay sailors. In 1950, at the height of the Korean War, that number was down to 483. But in 1953, when the armistice was signed at Panmunjom, the navy cracked down again with vigor, distributing 1,353 gay-related undesirable discharges in that year alone.

The Vietnam War provides some of the most striking examples of the military's tacit acceptance of homosexuality in times of war. When Air Force Sgt. Roberto Reyes-Colon was seen leaving his base near the demilitarized zone with his Marine Corps boyfriend, military police brought him before his commanding officer the next day. The commander listened to the MPs complain that they had seen Reyes-Colon kiss the Marine, but once they left the room, the commanding officer ripped up the report they had written on the incident. Reyes-Colon's defense was that "there's a war going on," and the officer agreed.

Marine Corps Lt. Ben Dillingham, assigned to lead a reconnaissance platoon in Vietnam in 1970, was surprised to discover that two of his enlisted men were lovers, inseparable, patrolling together, even sleeping together under the same blanket. All the other soldiers in the tightly knit platoon were aware of the relationship, and no one cared. It seemed to Dillingham that with a war going on, and everyone's life depending on the others, no one had time to quibble about gay soldiers.

Discharges for homosexuality still occurred, but Pentagon statistics themselves bear out that the armed forces became strangely uninterested in enforcing their regulations against homosexuals during this period. Between 1963 and 1966, the navy, which at the time was the only branch of the military to keep detailed statistics of gay discharges, "separated" between 1,600 and 1,700 enlisted members a year for homosexuality. From 1966 to 1967, as the Vietnam buildup began in earnest, the number of gay discharges dropped from 1,708 to 1,094. In 1969, at the peak of the escalation, gay discharges dropped to 643. A year later, only 461 sailors were relieved of duty for being gay.

These dramatic reductions occurred during a period of some of the service's highest membership since World War II. It was not that there were any fewer gays in the navy; by all appearances there were many more. But the navy had effectively stopped enforcing regulations against homosexuality. Draftees who announced themselves to be homosexual at their induction centers frequently were told by army doctors that they were welcome in the army just the same. In at least three circumstances in the early 1970s, gay activists had to go to federal court to force the government to observe its own policies regarding the exclusion of gays.

History repeated itself two years ago during Operation Desert Storm when numerous military personnel, most serving in the reserves, tried to escape mobilization by telling their reserve commanders they were gay—and many reserve commanders responded that gay soldiers could serve anyway. When a lesbian officer in a Western medical-support group told her commander that she was a lesbian, he replied, "That's all right. We wouldn't have a medical service without gays." When army reservist Donna Lynn Jackson told her commander she was a lesbian, she says he told her bluntly that she would go to Saudi Arabia, and be discharged for homosexuality at the end of the war. Jackson went to the newspapers, and an embarrassed Pentagon discharged her quickly, insisting that such cases were aberrations and that the Defense Department had an ironclad ban on gays in the military.

Despite the public pronouncements, military commanders made it as difficult as possible to separate gay personnel for the duration of the conflict. Decade-old Defense Department regulations demanded that anyone who even intimated that he or she was gay—or had the "intent" to commit gay sexual acts in the future—must be discharged, with no exceptions allowed. In the days before the ground war in the gulf started, however, the staff judge advocate's office of the Marine Corps Reserve Support Center instructed a lesbian who had acknowledged her homosexuality that "claimed sexual preferences do not constitute an exemption from the mobilization process."

At the 40th Aeromedical Evacuation Squadron at McChord Air Force Base in Washington, another gay reservist seeking to avoid mobilization by announcing she was gay was told that she would not be certified as a homosexual by the air force unless she produced a marriage license listing another woman as a spouse. No jurisdiction in the United States allows gays to marry. Demanding that the woman produce a marriage license was like insisting she produce a piece of Mars.

Once stationed in the gulf, many of the gay military personnel found a remarkably accepting environment. When officers supervising a navy corpsman stationed with a Marine Corps unit on the front lines of Kuwait became concerned that his Marines all knew he was gay, the corpsman was transferred to another unit. The Marines in the new unit soon heard the rumors that he was gay, but befriended him anyway, and even jokingly nicknamed him "Precious," after the miniature poodle in the movie "The Silence of the Lambs."

The acceptance of gays in some quarters does not mean that lesbians and gay men will be easily integrated into every fighting unit. As with African-Americans and with women, the ability of the tradition-bound institution to accommodate gay members will take years, if not decades. The travails of gays in the military will not stop with a new president's executive order—they will just begin.

Still, animosity toward gays in the armed forces is not nearly so ingrained as opponents of the change would have us believe. For the past several years, some navy ship commanders have been privately candid with their crews about no longer having any intention of enforcing the ban on homosexuals. In 1990, the reluctance of ship commanders to pursue lesbians led Vice Adm. Joseph Donnell, commander of the U.S. Atlantic fleet, to order all his commanding officers to enforce regulations more aggressively against lesbians. The memorandum acknowledged why many commanders were reluctant to do this: because, Donnell wrote, "the stereotypical female homosexual" was "hardworking, career-oriented, willing to put in long hours on the job and among the command's top professionals."

Tens of thousands of gay military personnel, particularly those in the enlisted ranks, serve with some degree of openness in the military today, informing their co-workers, though not the press or their officers, that they are gay. Over the past five years, many more officers have served openly as well, though they do not tempt fate by allowing their names to be released publicly. Typical of stories from the new military is the tale I heard of an air force major serving in Florida whose colleagues threw him a 40th birthday party, and enlisted the major's lover to organize it.

THIS BRINGS US TO THE FUNDAMENTAL truth about the military's policies toward homosexuals. The point is not to eject all gays, but to allow the military to say it does not accept homosexuals. This preserves its image as the upholder of traditional notions of masculinity, the one institution in the nation that claims to take boys and turn them into men. In harsh economic times, this raises the question as to whether the taxpayers grant the Defense Department nearly $300 billion a year to provide the most cost-effective defense for the nation, or whether it is an investment in preserving a club where heterosexual men can assure themselves of their masculinity.

The argument that gays will unalterably subvert discipline and good order in the armed forces is also hard to justify within the context of the history of the U.S. military. History tells us that the man who first instilled discipline in the ragtag Continental Army at Valley Forge was the Prussian Baron Frederick William von Steuben. It was he who took what were essentially 13 different colonial militias and molded them into one army.

Von Steuben at first had declined Benjamin Franklin's offer of the job, because the Continental Congress could not pay him. But when von Steuben learned that ecclesiastical authorities were planning to try him for homosexuality, he renegotiated with Franklin and was appointed a major general to the Continental Army. When he came to Valley Forge to begin his drills, he appeared with a 17-year-old French interpreter, who must have had other talents useful to the general, because it soon became clear that he had no linguistic skills.

Nevertheless, von Steuben, the army's first inspector general, came to have an incalculable impact on the U.S. military, writing the drill books that would be used for the next 35 years by the fledgling U.S. Army. His plans for a military academy became embodied in West Point. Some military historians have judged von Steuben as one of only two men whose contributions were "indispensable" toward winning the Revolutionary War; the other was George Washington.

It is a crowning irony that anti-gay policies are defended in the name of preserving the good order and discipline of the U.S. military, when that very order and discipline was the creation of a gay man.

NO

Eugene T. Gomulka

WHY NO GAYS?

Secretary of Defense Dick Cheney and other governmental and military leaders have been under pressure to change the long-standing policy that excludes homosexuals from military service.[1] Critics liken the policy to the past exclusion of blacks and women and call for an end to the "discrimination." The *News Tribune* of Tacoma, Washington, for example, published a story on 5 June 1992 concerning Seattle Mayor Norm Rice's criticism "equating the military's ban on homosexuals with racial segregation." In a written response to Mayor Rice, General Colin Powell distinguished between race—as an uncontrollable factor relating to personhood—and homosexual behavior—as a controllable factor relating to conduct. General Powell wrote, "Skin color is a benign, nonbehavioral characteristic. . . . Comparison of the two is a convenient but invalid statement."

Even if it is shown that some homosexuals have not "chosen" their orientation, it is fair to state that homosexual behavior is a choice; one that most people do not view as normal conduct, in or out of the military.[2]

A fundamental flaw in the argument for allowing homosexuals to serve in the military is the failure to recognize the link between "nonthreatening" sexual orientation and sexual behavior. More frequently today, practicing homosexuals do not consider their orientation a private matter, but are inclined to seek public affirmation for their lifestyle. It can be argued that the deliberate manifestation by word or deed of one's homosexual orientation marks the beginning of behavioral change because the announcement itself is the demand for a social infrastructure to support the behavior.[3]

The military believes for a number of sound reasons that many persons with a homosexual orientation would experience difficulty controlling their behavior in the unique circumstances of military life.[4] Unlike living conditions in most civilian circumstances, private moments on board ship or while deployed are few or nonexistent. As Secretary Cheney has noted on previous occasions, the line between public and private for those who wear the uniform is very small indeed.[5]

SERIOUS QUESTIONS TO CONSIDER

Critics of the Department of Defense (DoD) policy question the validity of the arguments used by the military to justify the exclusion of homosexuals from its ranks. These same critics (many of whom are civilian), who downplay the behavioral aspects of homosexuality, should be prepared to discuss some concerns that might be raised by the military personnel whose lives would be affected by a change in the current policy.

• Given the uniquely close living conditions of military life, would forcing heterosexuals to compromise their privacy and be looked upon as sexual objects by some homosexuals impact recruitment and retention?

• Without the current exclusion, couldn't the military service, with its predominantly young male population, be an attractive occupation for homosexuals who see no reason to restrict their behavior?

• In light of what some would argue is an innate orientation, would it be wise for a liquor store manager to hire an alcoholic who does not see that condition as a problem and who may abuse his situation?

• How might we expect a heterosexual to behave while sharing a small room with an attractive person of the opposite sex in a ship deployed at sea for six months?

• If homosexuals were allowed to serve in the military and occupy the same quarters, wouldn't it be discriminatory for an unmarried heterosexual couple to be denied permission to share quarters in barracks, base housing, or even at sea?[6]

• It is ironic that some lawmakers who have been outspoken in regard to sexual harassment in the military also endorse homosexuals serving in those same armed forces. Would any of these lawmakers be comfortable having a 17-year-old son billeted in a three-man barracks room with two homosexuals, for a four-year tour of duty?

Unfortunately, these are but a few questions that opponents of the current DoD policy do not wish to consider.

STATISTICS

A recent General Accounting Office (GAO) report, *Defense Force Management: DoD's Policy on Homosexuality*, notes statistics regarding the number of homosexuals who have been discharged from the military.[7] Opponents of the current DoD policy like to quote this report in regard to the amount of money expended in discharging homosexuals. They give the impression that homosexuals are separated simply because of a discovered nonthreatening orientation. However, many separation cases involve instances of homosexual behavior, which will only increase if known homosexuals are allowed to enlist. Consequently, the amount of money expended on separating people because of homosexual behavior actually could increase if homosexuals were admitted. The GAO report should persuade those concerned with finances to think twice before endorsing a policy that could result in separation costs far greater than today's.

There are a number of other statistics that the GAO report did not include. Here are a few others that should be considered:

• There is evidence of widespread sexual compulsion among homosexual men. A recent University of Chicago survey revealed that, for the U.S. population as a whole, the estimated number of sex partners since age 18 is 7.15 (8.67 for those never married).[8] These numbers stand in striking contrast to the results of a major study by the Kinsey Institute that revealed that 43% of the homosexual men surveyed estimated they had sex with 500 or more partners; 28% with 1,000 or more partners.[9] In the same study, 79% of the white male homosexuals surveyed said that more than half of their partners were strangers; 70% said more than half of the sexual partners were men with whom they had sex only once.[10] Since the onset of the AIDS epidemic, there does not appear to be a significant decrease in homosexual partnering behavior. In one study, the number of different partners reported fell from 70 to 50 per year; in another study, the number went from 76 to 47 per year.[11]

- Homosexual men are six times more likely to have attempted suicide than are heterosexual men.[12]
- Studies indicate that between 25% and 33% of homosexual men and women are alcoholics.[13]
- In a survey by the American Public Health Association, 78% of the gay respondents reported they had been infected with a sexually transmitted disease at least one time.[14]
- The latest figures available from the Centers for Disease Control show that two thirds of all AIDS cases are directly attributable to homosexual conduct.[15] Admitting homosexuals into the military surely would bring about an increase in the number of AIDS cases and would put additional financial and personnel demands on an already strained military medicine program.[16]

CONCLUSION

American society is experiencing increasing sensitivity with respect to human rights, accompanied by a growing rejection of sexual morality. The movement to approve homosexual conduct as an acceptable lifestyle is not surprising in today's permissive society. Military leaders are in a position to influence the attitudes of their subordinates—by their words and their example (lifestyle)—and can profoundly affect the direction and lives of those they lead. This fact was articulated by General John Lejeune, the 13th Commandant of the Marine Corps, who noted that "a large portion of those enlisting are under 21 years of age" and "are in a very formative period of their lives. We owe it to them, to their parents, and to the nation, that when discharged from the services they should be far better physically, mentally, and morally than they were when they enlisted." Military personnel themselves and the parents of young service men and women cannot help but be concerned about this matter. Legislators and military leaders have a legitimate role to play in providing positive, acceptable role models, especially for young people whose minds and characters are in formative stages.

In summary, the DoD homosexual-exclusion policy is designed to preserve, promote and protect legitimate military interests, including the personal privacy rights of service members. Discussions with active-duty personnel whose lives would be affected by a policy change give evidence that recruitment of avowed homosexuals could erode morale and have a negative impact on recruitment and retention. Heterosexual military personnel should not be forced to interface with homosexuals without recourse to other living arrangements, as would be available to most civilians. Just as the military excludes persons because of physical handicap or age for the good of the service, so too is it justified in excluding homosexuals from its ranks.

While opponents of the current DoD policy prefer to discount behavioral aspects, in favor of presenting homosexuality as a nonthreatening orientation, the fact is that lifelong, or even career-long celibacy among those with a homosexual orientation is a rare exception rather than the rule. Today—when militant homosexuals not only reveal their liaisons and lifestyles, but also actively and articulately promote the homosexual relationship as a morally acceptable alternative to marriage—legislation that would require the military to accept homosexuals would do much more to violate the rights of heterosexual military personnel than it would to promote the rights of homosexuals. Consequently, legislation that would threaten the rights of military personnel by allowing acknowledged homosexuals into the military should not be enacted.

NOTES

1. Colbert I. King, "Debunking the Case Against Gays in the Military," *The Washington Post*, 7 July 1992, p. 19. The argument in this and so many other articles attempts to define the DoD ban as primarily concerned with sexual orientation. The article cites presidential candidates who are swayed by this attempt to portray the military as preoccupied with orientation vice the negative effects that homosexual behavior would have upon military good order, morale, and discipline. "Bill Clinton has already said . . . if denied the right [to serve in the military], it should be on the basis of behavior, not status." Given the high degree of sexual compulsion on the part of male homosexuals, the defective presumption is that people with a homosexual orientation (status) will remain celibate on ships, in barracks, etc., and not actualize their orientation through homosexual behavior.

2. Henry Robinson, "They Came to Reclaim Asheville," *Asheville Citizen Times*, 27 June 1992, p. 5B. When 1,500 people participated in a Gay Pride March, a counter demonstration was organized the following week that drew more than 20,000 marchers. Current DoD policy mirrors the fact that most Americans strongly disapprove of homosexual behavior, which they do not view as an acceptable alternative to marriage and family life.

3. Steve Scott, "Gay Church Wants Its Clergy to be Chaplains," *Dallas Morning News*, 3 July 1992, p. 36. This article demonstrates a provision for a "social infrastructure" in a religious body that does not perceive the behavior as morally or socially reprehensible.

4. The numerous reasons for excluding homosexuals from military service are contained in DoD Directive 1332.14 H(1), which reads: "Homosexuality is incompatible with military service. The presence in the military environment of persons who engage in homosexual conduct, or who, by their statements, demonstrate a propensity to engage in homosexual conduct, seriously impairs the accomplishments of the military mission. The presence of such members adversely affects the ability of the military services to maintain discipline, good order and morale, foster mutual trust and confidence among service members, to ensure the integrity of the system of rank and command, to facilitate assignment and worldwide deployment of service members who frequently must live and work under close conditions affording minimal privacy, to recruit and retain members of the military services, to maintain public acceptability of military service, and to prevent breaches of security."

5. In *Steffan v. Cheney*, the United States District Court for the District of Columbia ruled on 19 December 1991 in favor of the Secretary of Defense. The judge noted that, "in the military establishment . . . the policy of separating men and women while sleeping, bathing, and using the bathroom seeks to maintain the privacy of officers and the enlisted when in certain cases of undress. The embarrassment of being naked as between the sexes is prevalent because sometimes the other is considered a sexual object. The quite rational assumption in the Navy is that with no one present who has a homosexual orientation, men and women alike can undress, sleep, bathe, and use the bathroom without fear or embarrassment that they are being viewed as sexual objects."

6. Charles Moskos, "Why Banning Homosexuals Still Makes Sense," *Navy Times*, 30 March 1992, p. 27. Rather than drawing an analogy between homosexuality and racism, the writer argues that the more correct analogy is between homosexuality and heterosexuality. He writes, "Anybody who wants to allow homosexuals into the military must make the same argument for breaking down the barrier between the sexes."

7. U.S. General Accounting Office, "Defense Force Management: DoD's Policy on Homosexuality" (Washington, D.C.), 12 June 1992, pp. 16–26.

8. Tom W. Smith, *Adult Sexual Behavior in 1989: Number of Partners, Frequency, and Risk,* presented to the American Association for the Advancement of Science, February 1990, published by NORC, University of Chicago.

9. Alan P. Bell and Martin S. Weinberg, *Homosexualities: A Study of Diversity Among Men and Women* (New York: Simon and Schuster, 1978), p. 308.

10. Ibid., p. 308.

11. S. A. Stewart, *USA Today,* 21 November 1984; L. McKusick, et al., "AIDS and Sexual Behavior Reported by Gay Men in San Francisco," *American Journal of Public Health,* 1985, pp. 493–496.

12. Ibid., Table 21.12.

13. Robert J. Kus, "Alcoholics Anonymous and Gay American Men," *Journal of Homosexuality,* Volume 14, No. 2 (1987), p. 254.

14. Enrique T. Rueda, *The Homosexual Network* (Old Greenwich, CT: The Devin Adair Company, 1982), p. 53.

15. "The HIV/AIDS Surveillance Report," Department of Health and Human Services, Public Health Service, Centers for Disease Control, National Center for Infectious Diseases, Division of HIV/AIDS, January 1992, p. 9.

16. *Steffan v. Cheney,* op. cit., p. 28. The threat of AIDS was a factor in ruling in favor of the current DoD policy. The judge wrote, "There is another justification for the policy of excluding homosexuals from service in the U.S. armed forces . . . Far and away the highest risk category for those who are HIV-positive, a population who will with a high degree of medical certainty one day contract AIDS, is homosexual men."

AUTHOR'S NOTE

The purpose of this paper is to help focus the current discussion on the issue of homosexuality and military service. It is not a criticism or an attack on homosexual persons as individuals or as a group. Personally, I know and care very much for persons who have confided in me that they have a homosexual orientation. I am pastorally aware of problems and challenges they experience, and I pray that God may help them to experience a happy, healthy, and full life.

Although critics of the current DoD policy on homosexuality attempt to frame the discussion of this issue along the lines of sexual orientation, many homosexuals are separated from the military because of their behavior—and a change in the current policy may well result in more behavior problems.

This paper's arguments in defense of the current DoD policy are not primarily religious. They are based upon the commonly accepted belief in American society that homosexual activity is not an acceptable alternative to marriage and family life. The issues of family values and heterosexual and homosexual rights lie at the heart of this matter. I hope this paper will help stimulate a rational and profitable discussion of the issue.

POSTSCRIPT

Should the Policy Banning Gays from the Military Be Lifted?

By mid-1993, after a year of heated debate in Congress and in the news media and television, it seemed likely that the ban on homosexuals in the military would eventually be lifted but that this would be a gradual process involving compromises along the way.

In 1993, Senator Sam Nunn (D-Georgia), head of the Armed Services Committee, advocated a "don't ask, don't tell" compromise that could allow homosexuals to serve in the military "if they're dedicated to that purpose, as long as they keep their private life private." Congressman Barney Frank (D-Massachusetts), who is gay, stated that he would prefer completely lifting the ban, but he admitted, "We don't have the votes for that in Congress." His compromise was to allow gay men and lesbians to serve in the military and to be open about their sexual orientation off duty, so long as they keep quiet about their orientation while on duty. Under Frank's proposal, if someone reported seeing a sailor or a soldier going to a gay bar or a gay support meeting in civilian clothes during his or her off-duty hours, the military's response should be, "None of your business or ours."

That this debate will continue for some time was evident in the various responses to Frank's proposal: Congressman Gerry E. Studds (D-Massachusetts), who is also gay, accused his colleague of "prematurely raising the white flag on this issue." Thomas Stoddard, coordinator of the Campaign for Military Service, a gay rights group, found Frank's proposal "a creative gambit which, while preferable to the deeply offensive policy now, perpetuates the underlying policy of discrimination."

Meanwhile, Congressman Robert Dornan (R-California), Senator Orrin G. Hatch, (R-Utah), and some religious leaders support the military's opposition to any change in the current ban. For these leaders, homosexuality is an immoral aberration that government policy must not condone.

SUGGESTED READINGS

D. Jackson, "I Just Don't Want To Go," *Time* (July 6, 1992).

E. Konigsberg, "Gays in Arms," *Washington Monthly* (November 1992).

T. Morganthau, "Gays and the Military," *Newsweek* (February 1, 1993).

R. Shilts, *Conduct Unbecoming: Gays and Lesbians in the U.S. Military* (St. Martin's Press, 1993).

J. Steffan, *Honor Bound: An American Fights Against Prejudice and for the Right to Serve His Country* (Villard Publishers, 1992).

J. M. Wall, "Gays and the Armed Forces," *Christian Century* (December 2, 1992).

ISSUE 14

Should Prostitution Be Decriminalized?

YES: Norma Jean Almodovar, from "Prostitution and the Criminal Justice System," *The Truth Seeker* (Summer 1990)

NO: Charles Winick, from "Debate on Legalization of Prostitution," *Medical Aspects of Human Sexuality* (September 1979)

ISSUE SUMMARY

YES: Norma Jean Almodovar, a prostitutes' rights activist and the author of *Cop to Call Girl*, argues that the real problem with prostitution lies not with some women's choice to exchange sexual favors for money but with the consequences of laws that make this exchange illegal.

NO: Charles Winick, coauthor of the *The Lively Commerce: Prostitution in the United States*, argues that prostitution serves no function except to exploit women and to encourage other illegal activities and that it should therefore be eliminated entirely.

In maintaining prostitution's criminal status, the United States has ignored two alternatives adopted by many other countries: legalization and decriminalization.

Prostitution, although not socially acceptable, was tolerated to a limited extent in the United States prior to the Civil War, and few states had specific laws making prostitution a crime. After the Civil War, however, some states passed laws to segregate and license prostitutes operating in "red-light" districts. In 1910, in an attempt to eliminate the importation of young women from Asia and South America for purposes of prostitution, Congress passed the Mann Act, which prohibited any male from accompanying a female across a state border for the purpose of prostitution, debauchery, or any other immoral purpose. During World War I, concern for the morals and health of U.S. soldiers led the surgeon general to close down all houses of prostitution near training camps, especially the famous whorehouses of the French Quarter and Storyville, New Orleans. By 1925 every state had enacted an antiprostitution law.

The effectiveness and the social and economic costs of criminalizing prostitution have been continually questioned. The sexual revolution and the women's movement have added new controversies to the debate. Some advocates of women's rights and equality condemn prostitution as male exploitation of women and their bodies. Others champion the rights of women to control their own bodies and engage in prostitution. Increasing social problems confuse the issue further: the growing concern over drug use, the risk of human immunodeficiency virus (HIV) infection among street prostitutes, and the exploitation of teenage girls and boys.

Prostitution has been addressed in a variety of ways around the world. In Germany, where prostitution is legal and regulated, there are efficient, convenient drive-in motels, often owned and run by women, where customers can reserve the services of prostitutes. Italy and France, long considered the bastions of regulated prostitution, have abandoned this approach because of organized efforts of women to abolish it and evidence that other approaches could reduce the spread of venereal diseases more effectively than legalization and regulation.

In Great Britain, since 1959, solicitation *on the streets* has been a crime, but prostitution per se is no longer against the law. The British authorities have concluded that prostitution cannot be controlled simply by making it a crime.

In the Soviet Union in the 1920s, the government provided job training, employment, housing, and health care for former prostitutes. Unfortunately, in the 1930s, the government's attitude changed to intolerance when it became apparent that other working women were turning to prostitution as a way of achieving a higher standard of living than they would otherwise have.

Several approaches have been suggested for dealing with the "world's oldest profession":

1. Outlaw prostitution and throw all available resources into a legal campaign to eliminate it entirely.

2. Outlaw some aspects of behavior, primarily solicitation; this, however, raises the question, What is overt solicitation and when does flirtation become illegal solicitation?

3. Legalize prostitution and control it by licensing prostitutes, requiring regular medical checkups, and setting aside specific areas where prostitutes can ply their trade.

4. Decriminalize all sexual activities between consenting adults, whether or not money changes hands. Advertising and solicitation can be limited by social properiety, and minors can be protected against recruitment and exploitation by age of consent and child abuse laws currently in effect.

In the following selections, Norma Jean Almodovar argues that prostitution laws should focus on regulation, not prosecution, while Charles Winick argues that prostitution should be eliminated entirely.

YES

Norma Jean Almodovar

PROSTITUTION AND THE CRIMINAL JUSTICE SYSTEM

It is often said that nothing ever changes, and that history repeats itself. Nothing could be truer for the world's oldest profession! In Los Angeles, California, where the name of the game is sex for play, prostitution has seen many different players, but the game never changes. In the 1920's and 30's, the major players were the cops, politicians, and a madam named Lee Francis. In the 1940's and 50's, it was the cops, politicians and a madam named Brenda Allen. In the 80's, it was the cops, politicians, and a madam named Alex. (And in 1983, let's not forget a former L.A. Traffic Officer turned Call Girl.)

In every decade, sex scandals and police corruption surface, politicians are exposed, and the Madam (or major prostitute) is arrested. Behind each scenario is a greedy cop or two, an ousted or retiring politician, and/or the memoirs of a prostitute or madam about to be published. It happens . . . in every major city and small town throughout the United States. It has become so common that it barely makes the news anymore, unless it involves celebrities.

No one seems to be quite sure what was the original intention of the prostitution law, other than the moral (and therefore political) climate that existed at the time they were passed. Some say it was to stop the spread of venereal diseases among the armed forces during the first world war. Some say it was protectionist legislation because young women were the victims of white slavery and because many feminists felt prostitution was exploitive of all women. Many say it is because it is immoral to sell one's body.

Because laws regulating adult human sexuality are so difficult to enforce without using selective prosecution, many states have repealed most so called moral laws against sodomy, oral copulation, etc., that are considered private consenting adult acts—as long as no coercion is involved. Yet, we as a society irrationally cling to our "sex for money or other consideration" laws, and incarcerate women for daring to charge for that which they may give away—free. Although the California Constitution explicitly grants an "absolute right to privacy," the concept "absolute" is obliterated when it comes to acts of prostitution. Why and how the government can both be out of one's bedroom when there is no commercial transaction involved in a consenting adult act and yet jump out of the closet when money appears is a bit puzzling. How do they do it?

When pressed for a reason that these laws are enforced, law enforcement officials state that prostitutes are victims and that prostitution is worse on the "victim" (i.e. the prostitute) than rape or robbery. Thus, the solution to a voluntarily made choice to prostitute one's self is obviously incarceration to prevent further victimization!

Apparently, indiscriminate sexual intercourse without the exchange of money or other consideration has no significant impact upon the victim, but money and sex equals shame and degradation for the woman brazen enough to charge for it. Give it away for free and there is no problem and no crime! The government cares not if a woman loses her reputation. Let her charge for it, and the government will be right there to take it away from her in the form of fines and jail sentences and give her a criminal record to boot! This will absolve the shame from her act? And though the law applies equally to the prostitute and her 'john' or client, it is almost always the woman who is prosecuted, fined and imprisoned. . . . There is no prostitute without a client!

This kind of reasoning involves the irrational belief that all women are inherently incapable of self determination, and need "big brother" protection, not from men who would exploit her for "free"—but from men who know her value and pay her accordingly. This pro-

tection comes not in the form of incarceration for the man who supposedly exploits her, but in taking away her freedom! (Can you imagine the outrage from feminists groups around the country if it was suggested that women who have been raped should be incarcerated instead of the rapist? It could be argued, using the same logic that now locks up prostitutes for being victims, that since rape is illegal, both parties to the crime are culpable.)

Whatever the alleged reasons are for the laws against prostitution, the time is long overdue for its abolition. Not only are the laws inherently irrational, discriminatory and in blatant violation of the Fourteenth Amendment, they waste an enormous amount of taxpayers' money and valuable police resources. As I will attempt to show, there are no rational reasons for these laws to continue to exist, other than to increase the statistical average of closed by arrest cases for law enforcement agencies, and to serve as extortion tools for these same law enforcement agencies.

The issues concerning the spread of sexually transmitted diseases, are brought up in a report called "The Challenge of Crime in a Free Society" which states, *"Of course, a state has an interest in protecting the health of its citizens, and the spread of venereal diseases is a serious health problem. In light of the statistics which show that prostitution contributes very little to the problem, however, a general prohibition of prostitution on that basis is overboard to achieve the legislative purpose, and should be reevaluated."*

Dr. Charles Winick, a member of the American Social Health Association and Professor of Sociology, City College of the City University of New York, has stated, *"We know from many different studies that the amount of VD attributable to prostitution is remaining fairly constant at a little under 5%, which is a negligible proportion to the amount of VD that we have."*

Later studies indicate that VD from prostitutes is now about 3%. About 75% of sexually transmitted diseases come from high school and college age young people, and the remainder from non-commercial sexual encounters, by women at bars who wouldn't dream of charging for their favors!

The statistics for AIDS are similar, in that because prostitutes have lower overall incidents of STDs, they also have a lower percentage of testing positive for the HIV II. Unless a woman who is a prostitute is an IV drug user, or has a bisexual partner, she is not at a higher risk than other women in the community who are not engaging in commercial sex. To date, in the United States, *in terms of contact tracing,* there has not been one documented case of a man becoming infected through contact with a specific prostitute.

However, this does not mean that prostitution is not a *link* in the chain of STD transmission. The issue is not prostitution, *per se,* but rather the health status of safe sex practices of the prostitute. Equally relevant are these same issues for the male who rarely is given focused attention on the spread of STDs. Males infect prostitutes and prostitutes infect males. This is particularly true for HIV infections where the HIV is heavily represented in the male ejaculate but is poorly represented in the otherwise healthy normal vaginal tract. Women, including prostitutes, are at much greater risk of being infected from an HIV positive male than is the male becoming infected from an HIV positive female, other fac-

tors being equal. And it is equally in error to use the term "prostitutes," as if all prostitutes are the same. There is an enormous difference between street prostitutes, massage prostitutes, call-out service prostitutes and high-class call girls. Also, the role of "prostitution" in the spread of STDs varies substantially between countries.

The reason that organized crime has been able to get involved at all with prostitution is because of the illegal status of the profession. Just as during Prohibition, the Mafia was able to gain control over the sale and distribution of alcohol, not because of its nature, but because of its illegality and the corruptible nature of human beings. So too, it is the illegal status of prostitution that allows any organized criminal element to move in and control areas of prostitution. But for the most part, because prostitutes are highly independent, they are hard to organize. Most men and women operate independently of organized crime, although many do end up paying for police protection, which is equally 'organized crime' even though the extortion is carried out by a governmental agency.

Plummer and Ngugi (1990) . . . make the following observation about prostitution and crime:

"The legal approach to prostitution assumes that prostitution is an undesirable activity. Moral reasons or the association of prostitution with other crime is often the motivation for the legal approach. It would seem that at least part of the association of prostitution with other crime is begotten by the criminality of prostitution."

In a memorandum filed by Hon. Gerald Adler in the case of *Cherry v. Koch, et al.* Kings County, New York, Hon. Adler says, *"It has long been recognized that com-*

mercial sex has many attendant evils." Quoting from *Commonwealth v. Dodge*, he asserts, " *'Prostitution is a source of profit and power for criminal groups who commonly combine it with illicit trade in drugs and liquor, illegal gambling and even robbery and extortion. Prostitution is also a corrupt influence on government and law enforcement machinery. Its promoters are willing and able to pay for police protection; unscrupulous officials and politicians find them an easy mark for extortion. . . .' "*

Looking at this, it seems clear that it is the "illegal" status of prostitution that causes these problems, not the act of prostitution itself. Although police corruption will always exist, its connection to prostitution would be eliminated if prostitution were decriminalized, since there would be no need for the prostitute or madam to pay off police officers, in money, sex or information, in order to remain in business.

Los Angeles Police Officer Alan Vanderpool, a long-term undercover vice cop, stated during the Trial of Mary Ellen Tracy, so called "High Priestess of Sex," that in his professional opinion, when there was an increase in prostitution arrests, there was a corresponding decrease in other criminal activity. (What criminal activity, he didn't say.) There is direct evidence that this is untrue; not only does the *incidence* of other crimes *increase*, but *arrests* for violent crimes *decrease* significantly. . . .

From 1976 to 1985, the *Reports* of Violent Crimes increased 32%; *Arrests* for Violent Crimes increased 3.7%; while *Arrests* for Prostitution *increased* 135%. Additionally, *Arrests* for Homicide and Robbery *declined* 15% and *Arrests* for Property Crimes *declined* 3% for this same time period. Clearly, time and resources spent arresting prostitutes sig-

nificantly interferes with the prevention and control of violent crimes and property crimes.

The Hastings Law Journal Report cites the "Times Square Action Plan Interim Six Month Report," *"In Manhattan in 1978–79, the Times Square Action Plan succeeded in nearly doubling the prostitution arrest rate of the previous year. During that same period of time, and within the same midtown area, complaints of rape, robbery, burglary, and felonious assault rose by as much as 40%. A 30% increase in rape complaints was not accompanied by any increase in arrests; reported incidents of burglary rose by 22%, while the arrest rate plummeted 40%. For these results, the New York City Police Department deployed almost twice the number of patrol units used in Times Square a year earlier."*

The Hastings Law Journal report notes further, that *"Faced with far more threatening crime, and the statistic that 90% of arrested prostitutes escape judicial sanction, one wonders why police departments devote so much of their resources to enforcing prostitution laws. A possible explanation is that prostitution cases raise the 'closed by arrest' rate' for total crime indices. Prostitution is one of the only offenses for which nearly 100% of 'reported incidences' result in arrest. To the extent that total arrest rate indices are elevated by the inclusion of this high percentage for prostitution, they engender a false account of overall police protection."* . . .

In a major study on the differential "arrest" efforts of law enforcement involving violent crimes and prostitution in six large cities and 10 small cities for the year 1985, . . . "cleared by arrest" increased only 27% for violent crimes, [while] such arrests remained at 100% for prostitution. "Cleared by arrest" means that at least one person has been arrested, charged and turned over to court for prosecution. Of special significance from this study is the finding of the disproportionate effort of law enforcement in arresting prostitutes vs. perpetrators of violent crime. Specifically, prostitution arrests equaled 51% of the arrests made for violent crime for the large cities and equaled 102% of the arrests made for violent crime for the small cities. For all cities combined prostitution "cleared arrests" equaled 64% of the "cleared arrests" made for violent crimes. In other words, for the small cities, greater effort and resources were expended arresting prostitutes than were expended for arresting violent criminals (102%); and for the large cities this figure is 51%. No wonder that violent crime is out of control!

Going back to Vice Officer Alan Vanderpool's professional assessment of the results of his activities, one wonders what "criminal activities" he meant decrease when there is an increase in prostitution arrests? Perhaps what he meant was, "criminal arrests decrease," because that is the only conclusion one can come to, given the statistics!

The disproportionate and excessive law enforcement efforts against prostitution is, of course, reflected in the costs of these efforts. . . . [In] the estimated annual average costs for prostitution control in the 6 large and 10 small cities . . . total average law enforcement costs (includes police costs, corrections costs and court costs) was $12 million dollars for the large cities and $5 million dollars for the small cities. . . . If prostitution was eliminated as a criminal activity there would be available an additional average of $12 million dollars for each large city and $5 million dollars for each small city to fight violent crimes without any

tax increase to support this budgetary "increase"!

This message is reinforced . . . [by] the average number of police hours spent enforcing prostitution laws in the 6 large and 10 small city study for 1985. Specifically, the daily average police hours spent arresting prostitutes was 324 hours for the large cities and 146 hours for the small cities. This translates into 46 additional police officers to prosecute prostitution for the large cities and 21 additional police officers to prosecute prostitution for the small cities for an average of 30 additional police officers for the combined cities. Again, if prostitution was eliminated as a criminal offense there would be available an additional 46 police officers for the large cities and 21 additional police officers for the small cities without any increase of taxes/budget for these "additional" police officers to fight violent crime! What police chief would not welcome such a significant increase in his police force to fight violent crime?

In a decriminalized system, prostitution activity could still be limited in the time and place that it occurred. Generally, when prostitution is decriminalized, the women tend to work off the street. Those who wished to remain on the street, could be given an area (such as near adult motels) and time periods (i.e. evenings, not during rush hour traffic, or while school is letting out). Those who wished to find the services of men or women on the street would know where to look. Those who wished not to be disturbed by the sight of sex-peddlers could avoid those areas where they work.

Finally, there is the argument that if prostitution were legalized or decriminalized, that many young people would be forced into a life of prostitution.

It is and still would be illegal to engage in sexual activities with minors. Decriminalization of prostitution would not change those laws. Because the laws against prostitution and related activity makes no distinction between coercive and non-coercive activity, a person who is willing to use force is at no more risk than a person who does not use force. The result is that law enforcement is spread thin, trying to entrap men and women who are engaging in consensual adult behavior, rather than going after men and/or women who are using force against others.

Decriminalization would leave the police with more time and manpower to go after those who would hire underage girls/boys. Men and women in the profession would be able to report acts of violence or force used against them to the police without being subjected to ridicule or the threat of imprisonment themselves.

Most people involved with the prostitute's rights issues are in favor of a decriminalized system rather than a legalized one. Legalization is a system whereby the state regulates, taxes, and licenses whatever form of prostitution is legalized, and often involves the establishment of special government agencies to deal with prostitution. It means that the government enacts new laws which put the control of prostitution in the hands of the police, or the state. The police department (or the criminal justice system) has no business running or regulating prostitution, anymore than it should run restaurants or grocery stores or the movie industry. These are all businesses, subject to business regulations, and under civil authority. Prostitution is a business, a service industry. It should be run as a business, subject only to the same kinds of business laws and regulations as other businesses.

Decriminalization would allow this to happen. It would repeal all existing criminal codes from non-coercive adult commercial sex activity, and related areas, such as management and personal relationships. It would involve no new legislation to deal with prostitution per se, because there are already plenty of laws which cover problems of fraud, force, theft, negligence, collusion, etc. Those laws could be enforced against anyone who violated them, just as they are now, when force or fraud is used in any other profession. As Priscilla Alexander points out in "California NOW, Working on Prostitution," *decriminalization offers the best chance for women who are involved in prostitution to gain some measure of control over their work. It would also make it easier to prosecute those who abuse prostitutes either physically or economically, because the voluntary, non-abusive situations would be left alone.*

Prostitution is the same issue for feminists (and others) as abortion. It is the right to choice. The right for a woman to control her own sexuality; whom she will have sex with, when and under what circumstances. (It goes without saying that the same right applies to men and their bodies.)

A Woman's BODY belongs to HER and to HER alone and not to ANY governmental institutional entity: city, state or federal; not to ANY religious institutional entity: Jewish, Christian, Islamic or any other religious institutions of the East.

The U.S. Constitution is the supreme law of the land, and the Constitution protects the individual's rights to own, use and enjoy his/her body in any manner that he/she deems appropriate, as long as he/she does not violate the rights of others. Everyone has a right to make moral decisions for his/her life and property (including his/her body) that others may find disagreeable, disgusting, or immoral.

Even the government (or at least those who write the law books) is conceding the issue. According to the California Criminal Law Manual prostitution may not even be a crime. It notes, *"In view of the legislature's recent repeal of certain sex laws which previously made certain sex acts a crime, some legal scholars feel that prostitution may also no longer be a crime. They submit that if the performance of certain sex acts by male and/or female consenting adults in private is no longer a crime, prostitution (which is performed by consenting adults in private) may be a noncriminal act."*

In the past few years, several cities and states, faced with shortages of financial resources and police manpower, have considered alternatives to the criminalization of prostitution. In 1985, the New York Bar Association, Committee on Revision of the Criminal Law, held hearings in New York City. A panel of witnesses, from ministers to johns and ex-prostitutes, judges and police officers, testified before the committee. The end result of the hearings was a strong recommendation for the immediate repeal of all penalties for discreet and private prostitution, and the repeal of penalties for prostitutional loitering (and patronizing) at specified locations and times (and to increase such penalties at all other locations and times).

NO

Charles Winick

DEBATE ON LEGALIZATION OF PROSTITUTION

Since prostitution has always been with us, it is often argued that it is an exercise in futility to try to control it. However, the argument that something has existed for a long time and meets human needs is a very questionable one. Merely because something has existed does not make it in any way socially desirable. For centuries slavery was in existence and it appeared to be a very important service in many different countries. However, we now recognize that slavery is unacceptable. . . .

Prostitution has been described as a crime without a victim, but I say the women are victimized. First of all, the call girl, however attractive she may be to writers and movie-makers, represents a very small part of the prostitution population. It's also the part of prostitution which is of least concern to the public, since call girls operate away from where they offend the citizenry.

I've interviewed over 2,000 prostitutes in the United States during the last ten years. It's not a very good job, by and large. The gross income is about what a good secretary might earn, of which they keep a very small percentage.

And while a good secretary may look forward, as her career develops, to various kinds of upward mobility, the prostitute is in one of the very few occupations where the mobility is all downward. She does not become more valuable and more sought after as she becomes older. Her most important asset is her youth.

Furthermore, whether or not it is legal, any business in which there is a large flow of cash invites the attention of a variety of elements connected in some way with the criminal world. There's a large group of people eager to take away her money, and a large group of people that she may be eager to give money to, such as pimps, because of the barrenness of her emotional life.

So we have a situation where the income is relatively low, where a lot of people are interested in taking away much of what money there is, and where the working life, in terms of years, is relatively brief. The prostitute is clearly a "victim."

As she gets older, a prostitute will find herself essentially without friends, surrounded by exploiters who have been living off her but who want nothing to do with her once her income begins to decline. She will not have a salable occupation or vocation; she will not have an experience on which she can build, she does not have the opportunity for putting aside money in a conventional way by pension benefits or unemployment insurance or workmen's compensation and the like.

Where is this woman at the age of 30? It's hardly any wonder that every study of prostitutes has reported an enormously high suicide attempt rate. This hardly seems a desirable career line that society should encourage. . . .

Pimps and other persons profiting from prostitution have existed and do exist whether or not prostitution is legal or decriminalized. In Germany, Holland, and England today, where prostitution is accepted, pimps and procurers flourish. In fact, no twentieth century community has experienced prostitution without an array of third persons who profited from it. It is chimerical to suggest that legalization of prostitution can eliminate exploiters.

Another chimera is that prostitutes can effectively organize themselves into a guild or other regulatory apparatus that will exclude amateurs and freelancers. Whether in London, Paris, Hamburg, or Honolulu, no such machinery has worked. It is too easy for outsiders to find clients, and enforcement of restrictions on client activity is next to impossible.

At one time, up to the 1940s, pimps were indeed necessary for protection from violent clients, for provision of bail and legal assistance, and other supportive services. Today, they seldom carry out such functions. Pimps are seldom available near where prostitutes are working, unless they appear to urge her to greater efforts or check to see if she has slipped into a coffee shop or is otherwise taking a break. The pimp is not a social but an emotional necessity because of the thorough demoralization and psychological incapacitation of prostitutes. . . .

I think it would be extremely foolhardy to base public policy on the temporary or neurotic needs of a very small element of the population. There has never been any society where regulated prostitution has worked. Prostitution has never been a completely aboveboard transaction. Many women prostitutes are drug-dependent and enter the vocation in order to get money for drugs. A substantial proportion of other prostitutes use drugs in order to deal with the difficulties and problems of their vocation, often seeking to anesthetize themselves while they are working. Such needs would exist whether or not prostitution were legal. Indeed, legalizing prostitution would foster such tragic adaptations. Furthermore, I would suggest that at the very time that sexual attitudes in general are apparently becoming more liberal, our attitudes toward prostitution should be hardening because of our increasing concern with equality. There is a desire not to encourage people to enter into exploitative and degrading relationships, and prostitution is an exploitative relationship.

Why should we have laws regulating it? Very simply, where you have laws which are enforced reasonably there is a minimum amount of prostitution; it is minimally offensive to the citizens and there is a minimum amount of police corruption and graft in connection with prostitution. Where the laws are on the books but not enforced, there is the most overt streetwalking, with thousands of people accosting persons at all hours of the day and night. . . .

We have a recurrent theme—the difference between what we might deem desirable and what is humanly possible to achieve. If we could get prostitutes to testify against pimps and other exploiters in the courts, that would be very good. Then we could address ourselves to implementing the laws against abuses such as blackmail, forced labor, and the like rather than regulating the mere sale of sex. But in fact because of the emotional ties which prostitutes have with pimps and similar persons, it is almost impossible to get a prostitute to testify against a pimp even after he has rejected her, beat her up, thrown her out, taken all her money, and will not even talk to her.

So, in principle, we should have laws regulating the exploitation of these women, but we know that such laws would not be enforceable because it is important to the woman to be beaten, assaulted, have her money taken away, be supplied with heroin, and so forth. These are part of her complicated emotional relationship with her pimp. So if we eliminated the laws against prostitution and encouraged police to implement the laws against exploitation, nothing would happen. . . .

Prostitution is so emotionally freighted that it seems to me very unlikely that it will ever become an ordinary service occupation like barbering or being a beautician or anything like that. The stigma attracts a type of personality that is often prone to criminality.

There has always been a predatory attitude among many prostitutes toward their clients which legalization is not likely to alter. For decades there's been the "Murphy game," where the customer hands his money over to an intermediary who guarantees to hold it for him while he is with the woman, and then disappears with the money. There's the long history of the "creeper," the person who creeps in while the prostitute is engaged in sexual activity with the client, and goes through his pockets. During sexual activity most men's sensory apparatus is functioning minimally and hearing and vision are severely depressed. We don't as yet have an occupation of providing sexual pleasure to others in an altruistic, devoted spirit. Given the values of our culture, this strikes me as an impossibility. . . .

The contention that some men *need* prostitutes is like the old argument that prostitution is the sewer that the city needs in order to remain clean. We have several studies of what happened to communities before and after prostitution was eliminated. The closing of the brothels had no particular effect on anything, except that the general level of law enforcement increased. The incidence of all crimes appeared to go down, because the existence of prostitution carries with it a certain amount of acceptance of other illegal activity. Therefore, when prostitution ceased many other forms of illegal activity also ceased. As for increases in sex crime—promiscuity, availability of pornography, rape, and so forth—none of that happened. So I don't think we can say that prostitution is a necessary outlet for needs that are not being met in other ways.

Current enforcement of laws against prostitution is indeed hypocritical by being selective and chauvinistic. In 24 states, "customer amendments" make the client as guilty as the prostitute. In most such states, however, the law is not enforced. The woman is arrested, tried, and convicted, but the client is usually set free. Were such laws enforced properly, our ability to control prostitution would be substantially enhanced.

I agree that "social control and rehabilitation" should be the foci of our policy toward prostitution. It is particularly disturbing that rehabilitation is so generally unavailable for those women who wish to leave prostitution. Countries like England have been able to mount and develop dignified and effective programs of resocialization of prostitutes. In this country, "rescue" operations often imply the sinfulness and guilt of the woman and are not set up toward realistic goals. We possess knowledge to conduct thoughtful programs of resocialization, but community ambivalence over such programs has led to their generally being moralistic and underfunded, and of low priority.

The reason for a prostitute's downward mobility is that customers prize youth. As a woman grows older, she is less desirable to customers and less able to earn money. The typical prostitute working in a legal context in Nevada is in her 20s because clients do not want older women. Organization into guilds or unions is not going to force customers to take what they do not want.

POSTSCRIPT
Should Prostitution Be Decriminalized?

Some years ago, a United Nations study team came up with a sophisticated list of arguments for and against the treatment of prostitution as a crime. It is interesting to examine the study team's arguments as we conclude this issue. The arguments in support of the prohibition of prostitution were: (1) It is the responsibility of the government to regulate public morals in the interest of the public good and, therefore, to declare prostitution a punishable offense; (2) If prostitution per se is not made a punishable offense, the abolition of the regulation of prostitution will merely replace controlled prostitution with clandestine prostitution; (3) It will be difficult to enforce strictly legal provisions proscribing the exploitation of the prostitution of others when prostitution itself is not considered a punishable offense; (4) Many women and girls on the borderline may be encouraged to take up prostitution if the law does not proscribe such a calling; (5) The absence of any legal provision against prostitution may be interpreted by the public as meaning that the government tolerates commercialized vice as a "necessary evil."

The arguments for decriminalization were: (1) To make prostitution a crime requires defining this activity; (2) Laws against prostitution, even when written to include both parties, in practice penalize only one party, the woman; (3) There is only a difference of degree between prostitution and other sexual relations outside wedlock, and it is unjust to limit the penalty only to persons who meet the arbitrary criteria set forth in the legal definition of prostitution; (4) While laws are needed to maintain public order and protect minors, penal law should not take cognizance of all adult moral violations nor single out adult prostitution for punishment apart from other adult moral violations; (5) Criminalization of prostitution does not reduce or eliminate it. Instead it promotes a ruthless underworld organization that increases exploitation and crime; (6) The prohibitionist policy depends for its effectiveness on a system of police espionage and entrapment that is itself harmful to society.

SUGGESTED READINGS

M. Freund, T. L. Leonard, and N. Lee, "Sexual Behavior of Resident Street Prostitutes With Their Clients in Camden, New Jersey," *Journal of Sex Research* (November 1989).

D. French, *Working: My Life as a Prostitute* (E. P. Dutton, 1988).

H. Moody and A. Carmen, *Working Women: The Subterranean World of Street Prostitution* (Little, Brown, 1985).

F. A. Plummer and E. N. Ngugi, "Prostitutes and Their Clients in the Epidemiology and Control of Sexually Transmitted Diseases," in K. K. Holmes et al., eds., *Sexually Transmitted Diseases* (McGraw-Hill, 1990).

ISSUE 15

Should Society Recognize Gay Marriages?

YES: Brent Hartinger, from "A Case for Gay Marriage: In Support of Loving and Monogamous Relationships," *Commonweal* (November 22, 1991)

NO: Dennis O'Brien, from "Against Gay Marriage: What Heterosexuality Means," *Commonweal* (November 22, 1991)

ISSUE SUMMARY

YES: Brent Hartinger, a free-lance writer, argues that "domestic partnership" legislation and other legal strategies used by gay men and lesbians to protect their relationship rights are inadequate and actually weaken the traditional institution of marriage. Society, he argues, has a clear interest in committed, long-lasting relationships and strong family structures, whether these are heterosexual or same-gender. Legalizing gay marriages, Hartinger concludes, would promote social stability and enhance heterosexual marriage.
NO: Dennis O'Brien, president of the University of Rochester, defends deep and abiding homosexual relationships, but he is not convinced that legally recognizing these unions as marriages would accomplish anything that cannot be accomplished equally as well with existing legal strategies. The religious or moral meaning of marriage, he contends, poses an even more substantial argument against recognizing gay unions as marriages.

For a quarter of a century there has been a growing debate over whether or not gay men and lesbians should seek the right to marry and, in turn, whether or not the state should recognize such marriages. In 1993 this debate took on a new urgency when the Hawaii Supreme Court ruled on a case brought by a gay male couple and two lesbian couples. The three couples claimed that a ban on gay marriages violates the state constitution, which prohibits any discrimination based on sex.

In the majority opinion, Justice Steven Levinson wrote that "marriage is a basic civil right" and that "on its face and as applied [Hawaii may be prohibited by its own constitution from denying] same-sex couples access to the marital status and its concomitant rights and benefits." The majority opinion relied heavily on a 1967 U.S. Supreme Court ruling that overturned all state laws prohibiting mixed-race marriages. If it is unconstitutional to deny interracial couples the right to marry, is it constitutional to deny gay couples that same right?

Legal experts expect the case to be decided by a trial court review without going to the U.S. Supreme Court. Since the Hawaii Supreme Court found that the ban on homosexual marriages probably does violate the state's constitutional ban on sex discrimination, the state must now demonstrate a "compelling state interest" to justify such a prohibition. If the state of Hawaii cannot provide a "compelling interest" to support its ban, the trial court could force legal recognition of homosexual marriages. This would set a legal precedent with national consequences because, since the American Revolution, individual states have recognized all marriages performed in other states. Thus, other states would have to recognize lesbian and gay male couples married in Hawaii and their rights to tax, health, and survivor benefits anywhere in the United States.

Until recently, Jewish and Christian traditions were unanimous in condemning homosexual relationships. In 1989, however, the United Church of Canada voted to recognize and accept any relationship that was based on "commitment," including gay male and lesbian relationships.

Also in 1989, Denmark became the first country to legally recognize gay marriages. In the same year, the board of directors of the Bar Association in San Francisco asked the state of California to make gay marriages possible. Several large cities across the country have since passed laws extending minimal benefits to unmarried "domestic partners."

The growing debate among members of lesbian and gay civil rights organizations across the country raises questions about the political and philosophical implications of the institutions of marriage and family that should concern all men and women, whatever their sexual orientation.

In the following selections, Brent Hartinger maintains that recognizing gay marriages would benefit the marital institution and promote strong family structures. Dennis O'Brien argues that the meaning of marriage is not compatible with homosexuality.

YES

Brent Hartinger

A CASE FOR GAY MARRIAGE:
IN SUPPORT OF LOVING AND
MONOGAMOUS RELATIONSHIPS

In San Francisco this year, homosexuals won't just be registering for the draft and to vote. In November 1990, voters approved legislation which allows unmarried live-in partners—heterosexual or homosexual—to register themselves as "domestic partners," publicly agreeing to be jointly responsible for basic living expenses. Like a few other cities, including New York and Seattle, San Francisco had already allowed bereavement leave to the domestic partners of municipal employees. But San Francisco lesbians and gays had been trying for eight years to have some form of partnership registration—for symbolic reasons at least—ever since 1982 when then-mayor Diane Feinstein vetoed a similar ordinance. A smattering of other cities provide health benefits to the domestic partners of city employees. In 1989, a New York court ruled that a gay couple is a "family" in that state, at least in regard to their rent-controlled housing (the decision was reaffirmed late last year). And in October of 1989, Denmark became the first industrialized country to permit same-sex unions (since then, one-fifth of all marriages performed there have been homosexual ones).

However sporadic, these represent major victories for gay men and lesbians for whom legal marriage is not an option. Other challenges are coming fast and furious. Two women, Sandra Rovira and Majorie Forlini, lived together in a marriage-like relationship for twelve years—and now after her partner's death, Rovira is suing AT&T, Forlini's employer, for refusing to pay the death benefits the company usually provides surviving spouses. Craig Dean and Patrick Gill, a Washington, D.C., couple, have filed a $1 million discrimination suit against that city for denying them a marriage license and allegedly violating its human rights acts which outlaw discrimination on the basis of sexual orientation; the city's marriage laws explicitly prohibit polygamous and incestuous marriages, but not same-sex ones.

From Brent Hartinger, "A Case for Gay Marriage: In Support of Loving and Monogamous Relationships," *Commonweal*, vol. 118, no. 20 (November 22, 1991). Copyright © 1991 by The Commonweal Foundation. Reprinted by permission.

Legally and financially, much is at stake. Most employee benefit plans—which include health insurance, parental leave, and bereavement leave—extend only to legal spouses. Marriage also allows partners to file joint income taxes, usually saving them money. Social Security can give extra payment to qualified spouses. And assets left from one legal spouse to the other after death are not subject to estate taxes. If a couple splits up, there is the issue of visitation rights for adopted children or offspring conceived by artificial insemination. And then there are issues of jurisprudence (a legal spouse cannot be compelled to testify against his or her partner) and inheritance, tenancy, and conservatorship: pressing concerns for many gays as a result of AIDS.

In terms of numbers alone, a need exists. An estimated 10 percent of the population—about 25 million Americans—is exclusively or predominantly homosexual in sexual orientation, and upwards of 50 percent of the men and about 70 percent of the women are in long-term, committed relationships. A 1990 survey of 1,266 lesbian and gay couples found that 82 percent of the male couples and 75 percent of the female ones share all or part of their incomes.

As a result, many lesbians and gays have fought for "domestic partnership" legislation to extend some marital and family benefits to unmarried couples—cohabitating partners either unwilling or, in the case of homosexuals, unable to marry. In New York City, for example, unmarried municipal workers who have lived with their partners at least a year may register their relationships with the personnel department, attesting to a "close and committed" relationship "involving shared responsibilities," and are then entitled to bereavement leave.

But such a prescription is inadequate; the protections and benefits are only a fraction of those resulting from marriage—and are available to only a small percentage of gays in a handful of cities (in the above-mentioned survey, considerably less than 10 percent of lesbian and gay couples were eligible for any form of shared job benefits). Even the concept of "domestic partnership" is seriously flawed. What constitutes a "domestic partner"? Could roommates qualify? A woman and her live-in maid? It could take an array of judicial decision making to find out.

FURTHER, BECAUSE THE BENEFITS OF "DO-mestic partnership" are allotted to couples without much legal responsibility—and because the advantages of domestic partnership are necessarily allowed for unmarried heterosexual partners as well as homosexual ones—domestic partnership has the unwanted consequence of weakening traditional marriage. Society has a vested interest in stable, committed relationships—especially, as in the case of most heterosexual couples, when children are concerned. But by eliminating the financial and legal advantages to marriage, domestic partnership dilutes that institution.

Society already has a measure of relational union—it's called marriage, and it's not at all difficult to ascertain: you're either married or you're not.

Yet for unmarried heterosexual couples, marriage is at least an option. Gay couples have no such choice—and society also has an interest in committed, long-lasting relationships even between homosexuals. An estimated 3 to 5 million homosexuals have parented children within heterosexual relationships, and at least 1,000 children were born to lesbian or gay couples in the San Francisco area alone in just the last five years. None of the recent thirty-five studies on homosexual parents has shown that parental sexual orientation has any adverse effect on children (and the children of gays are no more likely to be gay themselves). Surely increased stability in the relationships of lesbians and gay men could only help the gays themselves and their many millions of children.

Some suggest that legal mechanisms already exist by which lesbian and gay couples could create some of the desired protections for their relationships: power-of-attorney agreements, proxies, wills, insurance policies, and joint tenancy arrangements. But even these can provide only a fraction of the benefits of marriage. And such an unwieldy checklist guarantees that many lesbian and gay couples will not employ even those available.

There is a simpler solution. Allow gay civil marriage. And throw the weight of our religious institutions behind such unions.

In 1959, Mildred Jeter and Richard Loving, a mixed-race Virginia couple married in Washington, D.C., pleaded guilty to violating Virginia's ban on interracial marriages. Jeter and Loving were given a suspended jail sentence on the condition that they leave the state. In passing the sentence, the judge said, "Almighty God created the races white, black, yellow, Malay, and red, and he placed them on separate continents. And but for the interference with his arrange-ments, there would be no cause for such marriages. The fact that he separated the races shows that he did not intend for the races to mix." A motion to overturn the decision was denied by two higher Virginia courts until the state's ban on interracial marriage was declared unconstitutional by the United States Supreme Court in 1967. At the time, fifteen other states also had such marital prohibitions.

Clearly, one's sexual orientation is different from one's race. While psychological consensus (and compelling identical and fraternal twin studies) force us to concede that the homosexual *orientation* is not a choice, (nor is it subject to change), homosexual behavior definitely is a choice, very unlike race. Critics maintain that gays can marry—just not to members of their same sex.

But with regard to marriage, whether homosexual behavior is a choice or not is irrelevant, since one's marriage partner is *necessarily* a choice. In 1959, Richard Loving, a white man, could have chosen a different partner to marry other than Mildred Jeter, a black woman; the point is that he did not. The question is whether, in the absence of a compelling state interest, the state should be allowed to supersede the individual's choice.

Some maintain that there are compelling state interests to prohibiting same-sex marriages: that tolerance for gay marriages would open the door for any number of unconventional marital arrangements—group marriage, for example. In fact, most lesbian and gay relationships are probably far more conventional than most people think. In the vast majority of respects, gay relationships closely resemble heterosexual ones—or even actually improve upon them (gay relationships tend to be more egalitarian than heterosexual ones). And in a society where most cities have at least one openly gay bar and sizable gay communities—where lesbians and gays appear regularly on television and in the movies—a committed relationship between two people of the same sex is not nearly the break from convention that a polygamous one is. More important, easing the ban on same-sex marriage would make lesbians and gays, the vast majority of whom have not chosen celibacy, even more likely to live within long-term, committed partnerships. The result would be more people living more conventional lifestyles, not more people living less conventional ones. It's actually a conservative move, not a liberal one.

SIMILARLY, THERE IS LITTLE DANGER THAT giving legitimacy to gay marriages would undermine the legitimacy of heterosexual ones—cause "the breakdown of the family." Since heterosexuality appears to be at least as immutable as homosexuality (and since there's no evidence that the prevalence of homosexuality increases following the decriminalization of it), there's no chance heterosexuals would opt for the "homosexual alternative." Heterosexual marriage would still be the ultimate social union for heterosexuals. Gay marriage would simply recognize a consistent crosscultural, transhistorical minority and allow that significant minority to also participate in an important social institution. And since marriage licenses are not rationed out, homosexual partnerships wouldn't deny anyone else the privilege.

Indeed, the compelling state interest lies in *permitting* gay unions. In the wake of AIDS, encouraging gay monogamy is simply rational public health policy. Just as important, gay marriage would reduce the number of closeted gays who marry heterosexual partners, as an estimated 20 percent of all gays do, in an effort to conform to social pressure—but at enormous cost to themselves, their children, and their opposite-sex spouses. It would reduce the atmosphere of ridicule and abuse in which the children of homosexual parents grow up. And it would reduce the number of shameful parents who disown their children or banish their gay teen-agers to lives of crime, prostitution, and drug abuse, or to suicide (psychologists estimate that gay youth comprise up to 30 percent of all teen suicides, and one Seattle study found that a whopping 40 percent of that city's street kids may be lesbian or gay, most having run away or been expelled from intolerant homes). Gay marriage wouldn't weaken the family; it would *strengthen* it.

The unprecedented social legitimacy given gay partnerships—and homosexuality in general—would have other societal benefits as well: it would dramatically reduce the widespread housing and job discrimination, and verbal and physical violence experienced by most lesbians and gays, clear moral and social evils.

Of course, legal and religious gay marriage wouldn't, as some writers claim, "celebrate" or be "an endorsement" of homosexual sexual behavior—any more than heterosexual marriage celebrates heterosexual sex or endorses it; gay marriage would celebrate the loving, committed relationship between two individuals, a relationship in which sexual behavior is one small part. Still, the legalization of gay marriage, while not making homosexual sexual behavior any more prevalent, would remove much of the stigma concerning such behavior, at least that which takes place within the confines of "marriage." And if the church sanctions such unions, a further, moral legitimacy will be granted. In short, regardless of the potential societal gains, should society and the church reserve a centuries-old moral stand that condemns homosexual sexual behavior?

We have no choice; the premises upon which the moral stand are based have changed. Science now acknowledges the existence of a homosexual sexual *orientation*, like heterosexuality, a fundamental affectional predisposition. Unlike specific behaviors of, say, rape or incest, a homosexual's sexual behavior is the logical expression of his or her most basic, unchangeable sexual make-up. And unlike rape and incest, necessarily manifestations of destruction and abuse, sexual behavior resulting from one's sexual orientation can be an expression of love and unity (it is the complete denial of this love—indeed, an unsettling preoccupation with genital activity—that make the inflammatory comparisons of homosexual sex to rape, incest, and alcoholism so frustrating for lesbians and gays).

Moral condemnation of homosexual sexual behavior is often founded on the belief that sex and marriage are—and should be—inexorably linked with child-rearing; because lesbians and gay men are physiologically incapable of creating children alone, all such sexual behavior is deemed immoral—and gays are considered unsuitable to the institution of marriage. But since moral sanction is not withheld from infertile couples or those who intend to remain childless, this standard is clearly being inconsistently—and unfairly—applied.

SOME CITE THE PROMISCUITY OF SOME MALE gays as if this is an indication that all homosexuals are incapable or undeserving of marriage. But this standard is also inconsistently applied; it has never been seriously suggested that the existence of promiscuous heterosexuals invalidate all heterosexuals from the privilege of marriage. And if homosexuals are more likely than heterosexuals to be promiscuous—and if continual, harsh condemnation hasn't altered that fact—the sensible solution would seem to be to try to lure gays back to the monogamous fold by providing efforts in that direction with some measure of respect and social support: something gay marriage would definitely provide.

Human beings are sexual creatures. It is simply not logical to say, as the church does, that while one's basic sexual outlook is neither chosen nor sinful, any activity taken as a result of that orientation is. One must then ask exactly where does the sin of "activity" begin anyway? Hugging a person of the same sex? Kissing? Same-sex sexual fantasy? Even apart from the practical impossibilities, what about the ramifications of such an attempt? How does the homosexual adolescent formulate self-esteem while being told that *any* expression of his or her sexuality *ever* is unacceptable—or downright evil? The priest chooses celibacy (asexuality isn't required), but this *is* a choice—one made well after adolescence.

Cultural condemnations and biblical prohibitions of (usually male) homosexual orientation requires that there be some acceptable expression of it. Of course, there's no reason why lesbians and gays should be granted moral leniency over heterosexuals—which is why perhaps the most acceptable expression of same-sex sexuality should be within the context of a government sanctioned, religiously blessed marriage. But before we can talk about the proper way to get two brides or two grooms down a single church aisle, we have to first show there's an aisle wide enough to accommodate them.

NO

Dennis O'Brien

AGAINST GAY MARRIAGE: WHAT HETEROSEXUALITY MEANS

My firmest conviction on this debate is that it will end with no conviction. To reach some common view would require an agreement on the meaning of *marriage*—no easy subject; an agreement on whether homosexuality has a meaning—or is it just a natural fact; finally, we would have to find a tone of "sexual wisdom" for the discussion—we are usually too passionate about our passions for wise dispassion.

The very day that *Commonweal* asked me to comment on the subject, I happened to read a personality squib in the local paper about the movie actors Kurt Russell and Goldie Hawn. It seems that they are "together" after previous unhappy marriages. They now have a four-year-old son and they would consider marriage if their current arrangement proved difficult to the youngster. Since Hollywood is usually the avant-garde of the culture, it may be that marriage of any kind is a charming anachronism. I assume that the reluctance to enter marriage is that it destroys the honesty and commitment of "true love." Genuine commitment does not need the sanctions of judge or priest. In fact, it shows a weakening of ardor to rest fidelity on formality.

I have no doubt that there are deep and abiding homosexual commitments. What would formal marriage add? Legal marriages do help in divorce proceedings because there is a known system for dissolution and disposition of claims. If legal rights are an issue, they can, of course, be settled by (non-marriage) civil contracts. Should Kurt and Goldie break up this side of marriage, there are "palimony" settlements and similar suits have been brought for homosexual partnerships.

If the sole meaning of "marriage" is legal, then marriage of any sex may become a matter of "indifference." Perhaps truly loving couples should be as "indifferent" to marriage as our Hollywood pair. That there have been homosexual palimony cases would suggest that the law already brings homosexual partners into some sort of "coupled" network of legal restriction. It seems a short step from palimony to matrimony.

From Dennis O'Brien, "Against Gay Marriage: What Heterosexuality Means," *Commonweal*, vol. 118, no. 20 (November 22, 1991). Copyright © 1991 by The Commonweal Foundation. Reprinted by permission.

If there is an *issue* regarding homosexual marriage, it must rest on some deeper political or "religious" concerns. I do not mean what the newspapers think of as "political": who has the clout to carry the day. I am interested in the basic values of the American *polis*. What does our society express about itself and the human condition through its sanctioned institutions?

One might believe that the American *polis* avoids deep value issues; America is a debating society of opposing philosophies and life styles. Arguments are settled, if necessary or at all, by clout not cultural commitment. On the other hand, it is doubtful that any *polis* can exist at all without a cultural sense, however suppressed. American democracy rests on a powerful set of assumptions about human nature and society which legitimate the character of its institutions. Would homosexual marriage harmonize with our underlying values? I am not certain I can answer that question, but it is worth pointing out that "nonnormal" marriages have previously received constitutional scrutiny. The most famous are "the Mormon cases" which ruled on the legitimacy of polygamy (as a religiously protected right). The Supreme Court struck down polygamous marriage in part on *democratic* grounds. "Poligamy leads to the patriarchal principle ... which, when applied to large communities, fetters the people in stationary despotism, while that principle cannot long exist in connection with monogamy" *Reynolds v. United States* 98 US 145 (1879).

I am not overwhelmed by the sociology of the Court's opinion, but the justices were correct in attempting to connect marriage customs with the deeper values of the society. If homosexual marriage were to be seriously advanced, similar large concepts should be brought into play.

Are there potential problems for this *polis* if homosexual marriage becomes a legally sanctioned institution? There are some obvious social concerns. Heterosexual arrangements remain the mainstay for creating the next generation—which is not an incidental issue for any continuing social body. Surrounding heterosexual arrangements with political blessing and legal structures could be judged to have special social utility on that ground alone. Giving heterosexual marriage a positive place in the legal structure does not, however, imply that homosexual relations need suffer from negative legal stricture. What consenting adults do, and so forth—but the state is not obliged to bless every bedroom. (The Athenian *polis*, while it practiced a form of sanctioned homosexuality, did not amalgamate that practice to marriage.)

A *religious* position on homosexual marriage would go beyond the merely legal and the larger political values. (I believe that homosexuality should not be discussed as a straightforward *moral* issue; *moral* issues generally deal with specific acts but the concern here is a life choice. The church has thought traditionally that a religiously celibate life choice was more exalted than marriage. For all that, marriage did not thus become "immoral.")

Is the *meaning of marriage* (as religious sacrament) consonant with *the meaning of homosexuality*? The latter meaning may be even less recoverable than the former. To the extent that superficial accounts of homosexuality treat it as a direct expression of a biologically determined appetite, they displace it from the web of cultural development that would assay the worth of homosexual life patterns. If all there is to homosexuality (or heterosexuality) is natural determinism, we could remove it from the human spiritual agenda.

I would like to believe that sex is a human artifact for all that it has a biological base. (Human eating habits are not just feeding behavior. The prevalence of fantasy in sex certainly suggests heavy human seasoning of an essential appetite.) Assuming that sex has a human meaning, it seems plausible that homosexual life patterns differ from heterosexual if for no other reason than that male bodies and female bodies are different. If we were only accidentally related to our bodies (angels in disguise, ghosts in a machine), then how these mechanisms got sexual kicks might not *fundamentally* invade our sense of person and human value. *Playboy* and Puritanism both assume the triviality of bodies; they are for playful/sinful distraction only. Catholics seem more stuck with incarnation—and somewhere along that line would be a Catholic answer to the question posed.

I AM NO FAN AT ALL OF THE "NATURAL law" arguments about procreative sexuality as presented in *Humanae vitae*. These arguments assume that one can read the moral law off the book of nature. Social Darwinist argued that because humans are naturally aggressive, war was morally desirable. (The same mistake occurs when someone argues from a natural urge for hetero/homosexuality to the moral obligation to carry forward the urge.) But for all that nature gives no dogmas, nature presents an ur-text for human meaning. Heterosexual marriage is a deep story developed from the ur-text of genital biology.

What difference could thee possibly be in homosexual relations? Well, perhaps homosexual relations are better sex. After all, one knows one's own sex's response better than the heterosexual response. "It takes one to know one!" (As Oscar Wilde said about masturbation: "cleaner, more efficient, and you meet a better class of people.") The sexiness of homosexuality may or may not be the case, but I believe that reflection on hetero/homosexual embodiments would reveal quite different erotic story lines. It seems eminently plausible that bedding with an other (strange?) sex is as different as travel abroad can be from staying at home.

One could conclude that the homosexual story line was valuable—perhaps more valuable than the heterosexual. But not all things are possible in either variation. There are distinct spiritual problems with homosexual "marriage" in the Jewish and Christian traditions. Franz Rosenzweig states a deep truth when he attempts to explicate Jewish "faith": "the belief of the Jew is not the content of a testimony, but rather the product of reproduction. The Jew, engendered a Jew, attests his belief by continuing to procreate the Jewish people."

Underneath all the heated argument about artificial contraception, abortion, population control, family planning and the lot, the traditional Jewish *mitzvah* for procreation expresses human solidarity with the Creator God. The Christian claim for an embodied God moves in the same spiritual territory. (I do not imply that family size scales one up in blessedness.)

Kierkegaard regarded marriage as spirit's proper synthesis of recollection and hope. Without getting into deep theological water, it is certainly the case that heterosexual marriage normally carries with it the meaning of recollection and hope. Normative heterosexual marriage recollects parents in the act of parenting and literally embodies hope in the bringing forth of children. Homosexuals may, of course, recall parents and be hopeful for the future but they do not, of course, embody a family history. In so far as these Judaic faiths are not finally enacted in the realm of attitudes, they seem destined to give a special place to embodiment. Procreative "marriage" seems to me to be a special and irreplaceable central symbol of the tradition.

POSTSCRIPT

Should Society Recognize Gay Marriages?

In April 1993, 1,500 homosexual couples gathered on the White House lawn to participate in a massive "wedding," complete with ministers and rice. The vows were not legally binding, but the political and social message was clear.

Although attitudes toward gay rights have become more liberal in recent years, a 1993 *Washington Post* poll found that 70 percent of Americans oppose same-sex marriage. Yet, only 53 percent oppose homosexual relations between consenting adults, down from 57 percent in 1990.

Some gay rights activists argue that broadening laws to recognize same-gender marriages will force the transformation of marriage and family into a more flexible and egalitarian life-style. Others argue that the very idea of marriage runs contrary to the primary goals of the lesbian and gay movement, namely, the affirmation of a gay identity and culture and the validation of a rich pluralism in our life-styles and relationships. Conservatives argue that societies privilege heterosexual marriage principally because it creates enduring mother–father–child-rearing units. Homosexual marriages, they assert, do not serve that purpose.

The visibility of gay and lesbian couples in American society and their efforts to achieve equal legal status with heterosexual couples is likely to increase in the years ahead. Pioneering legal cases, such as the Hawaiian lawsuit, take years to reach a precedent-setting conclusion. Typical is the federal suit filed by Sandra Rovira in late 1990 against AT&T, one of the first lawsuits of its kind. Sandra and Marjorie Forlini, a lesbian couple, had lived together in a marriage-like relationship for 12 years while Marjorie worked as an AT&T manager. In a 1977 ceremony for friends and family, Sandra and Marjorie formalized their relationship and exchanged rings and vows. Sandra maintained in the suit that her life with Marjorie was as much of a marriage as any heterosexual union. However, when Marjorie died of cancer in 1988, AT&T refused to acknowledge the relationship. "She died in my arms. But when I called AT&T [to inquire about family survivor benefits], they treated me like I was nothing and our whole relationship was nothing. It was so humiliating. We were a family like any other family, and we deserved to be treated like one." AT&T said its family benefits are for legal spouses only.

The number of court cases and legal challenges like Rovira's will likely increase as more and more people seek an extension of marital benefits to their unconventional relationships. While New York's highest court has recognized a gay couple's rights as domestic partners in a rent-controlled apartment, gay teachers are suing for health insurance for their domestic partners. Municipal employees in several cities are now entitled to sick leave to care for a domestic partner and to bereavement leave for a partner's funeral.

Debate over the legalization of gay marriages raises questions about how society defines and privileges marriage and the family. It raises questions about our most fundamental social structures. And that, as would be expected, means the debate will likely continue to be heated and not easily resolved.

SUGGESTED READINGS

J. Elshtain, "Against Gay Marriage: Accepting Limits," *Commonweal* (November 22, 1991).

P. L. Ettelbrick, "Since When Is Marriage a Path to Liberation?" *OUT/LOOK* (Fall 1989).

"Gay Rights: Happy Families," *The Economist* (November 18, 1989).

W. Isaacson, "Should Gays Have Marriage Rights?" *Time* (November 20, 1989).

J. Leo, "Gay Rights: Gay Marriages," *U.S. News & World Report* (May 24, 1993).

D. Y. Rist, "Homosexuals and Human Rights," *The Nation* (April 9, 1990).

R. Sherman, "Gay Law No Longer Closeted: Family Issues Face Courts and Lawmakers," *National Law Journal* (October 26, 1992).

T. B. Stoddard, "Why Gay People Should Seek the Right to Marry," *OUT/LOOK* (Fall 1989).

ISSUE 16

Is Sexual Harassment a Pervasive Problem?

YES: Catharine R. Stimpson, from "Over-Reaching: Sexual Harassment and Education," *Initiatives* (vol. 52, no. 3)

NO: Gretchen Morgenson, from "May I Have the Pleasure," *National Review* (November 18, 1991)

ISSUE SUMMARY

YES: Catharine R. Stimpson, graduate dean at Rutgers University, claims that sexual harassment is epidemic in American society and will remain epidemic as long as males are in power and control. Although some significant progress has been made in creating resistance to sexual harassment, she believes the only way to create a harassment-free society is to redefine the historical connections between sexuality, gender, and power.
NO: Gretchen Morgenson, senior editor of *Forbes* magazine, argues that statistics on the prevalence of sexual harassment are grossly exaggerated by "consultants" who make a good livelihood instituting corporate anti-harassment programs. She argues that, in reality, the problem of sexual harassment has and will continue to become less of a problem.

In the fall of 1991, stories of sexual harassment began splashing daily across the front pages of newspapers and opening nearly every television news broadcast. For example, Anita F. Hill, a law professor, charged that Judge Clarence Thomas had sexually harassed her when she worked for him at the Equal Employment Opportunity Commission. This charge came close to derailing Thomas's nomination to the U.S. Supreme Court. In the sports world, three members of the New England Patriots football team (and the team itself) were fined nearly $50,000 for making lewd gestures and remarks to *Boston Herald* reporter Lisa Olson in their locker room.

Sexual harassment charges have also been leveled at America's political leaders. The majority leader of Florida's House of Representatives lost his position for allowing an "offensive, degrading and inappropriate" atmosphere of sexual innuendo among his staff. Senator Bob Packwood (R-Oregon) faced a more personal attack, as a congressional ethics committee investigated charges that he had regularly sexually harassed female colleagues.

In late 1991 and through most of 1992, the infamous Tailhook Association convention of U.S. Navy and Marine Corps pilots made national news. After interviewing more than 1,500 officers and civilians, investigators implicated more than 70 officers in sexual harassment and assault incidents against at least 26 women and several men (including 14 officers), either directly or in covering up the affair. The 70 officers were referred for disciplinary reviews and possible dismissal from the service. Top admirals were charged with tacitly approving such behavior for years, and major promotions for two admirals were lost because of sexual harassment questions.

In 1993, the American Association of University Women Education Foundation polled 1,632 teenagers in grades 8 to 11 on sexual harassment. They found that 76 percent of the girls and 56 percent of the boys reported receiving unwanted sexual comments or looks; 65 percent of the girls and 42 percent of the boys said they were touched, grabbed, or pinched in a sexual way. Some questioned whether all the behaviors included in the survey can legitimately be considered sexual harassment. Christina Hoff Sommers, at Clark University, said, "They're committed to finding gender bias everywhere, behind every door, in every hallway, and they find it. What this is going to invite is we're going to begin litigating high-school flirtation. In order to find gender bias against girls, they had to ask questions so broad that they invited complaints from boys." Countering this criticism, Maryka Biaggio, at Pacific University in Oregon, defended the broad, inclusive nature of the questions: "We know that people in general tend to underreport or minimize occurrences of sexual harassment, so in order to get a good sense of an individual's experience, you have to put forth a fairly inclusive definition."

Billie Dziech, coauthor of *The Lecherous Professor*, says, "We need clear definitions. We need to recognize that they are not hard and fast. They will differ for different individuals. This is slippery terminology." Dziech suggests we distinguish among what we consider normal flirting and "horseplay between men and women," a "sexual hassle," and "sexual harassment." But even that distinction will likely differ with different people and with the same person in different situations. This problem is compounded in a multiethnic society; behavior that is acceptable between two persons from the same culture may be unacceptable when the two parties are from different cultures. Still, the distinction might help separate the lewd comment from the funny sexual joke, and it may better define raunchy, suggestive, seductive, complimentary, and leering comments, looks, and gestures. When, for example, should the comment "You look great today" be interpreted as a sexist remark?

In the following selections, Catharine R. Stimpson and Gretchen Morgenson explore some of the complex questions raised by sexual harassment.

YES

Catharine R. Stimpson

OVER-REACHING: SEXUAL HARASSMENT AND EDUCATION

Sexual harassment is an ancient shame that has become a modern embarrassment. Largely because of the pressure of feminism and feminists, such a shift in status took place during the 1970s. Today, the psychological and social pollution that harassment spews out is like air pollution. No one defends either of them. We have classified them as malaises that damage people and their environments. For this reason, both forms of pollution are largely illegal. In 1986, in *Meritor Savings Bank v. Vinson,* the Supreme Court held an employer liable for acts of sexual harassment that its supervisory personnel might commit.

Yet, like air pollution, the psychological and social pollution of sexual harassment persists. In the stratosphere, chlorofluorocarbons from aerosol sprays and other products break apart and help to destroy the ozone layer. Well below the stratosphere, in classrooms and laboratories sexual louts refuse to disappear, imposing themselves on a significant proportion of our students.[1] As the graduate dean at a big public university, I experience, in my everyday life, the contradiction between disapproval of sexual harassment and the raw reality of its existence. I work, with men and women of good will, to end harassment. We must work, however, because the harassers are among us.

Inevitably, then, we must ask why sexual harassment persists, why we have been unable to extirpate this careless and cruel habit of the heartless. As we know, but must continue to repeat, a major reason is the historical strength of the connections among sexuality, gender, and power. But one demonstration of the force of these connections, sexual harassment, floats at the mid-point of an ugly, long-lasting continuum. At the most glamorous end of the continuum is a particular vision of romance, love, and erotic desire. Here men pursue women for their mutual pleasure. That promise of pleasure masks the inequities of power. "Had we but world enough, and time," a poet [Andrew Marvell] sings, "This coyness, Lady, were no crime." But for the poet, there is not enough world, not enough time. The lady, then,

From Catharine R. Stimpson, "Over-Reaching: Sexual Harassment and Education," *Initiatives,* vol. 52, no. 3, pp. 1–5. Copyright by The National Association for Women in Education. Reprinted by permission.

must submit to him before " . . . Worms shall try/That long preserv'd Virginity." At the other end of the continuum is men's coercion of women's bodies, the brutalities of incest and of rape, in which any pleasure is perverse.

In the mid-nineteenth century, Robert Browning wrote a famous dramatic monologue, "Andrea Del Sarto." In the poem, a painter is using his wife as a model. As he paints, he speaks, muses, and broods. He is worried about his marriage, for his model/wife is apparently faithless, a less than model wife. He is worried about his art, for his talents may be inadequate. He is, finally, worried about his reputation, for other painters may be gaining on and surpassing him. In the midst of expressing his fears, he declares, "Ah, but a man's reach should exceed his grasp/Or what's a heaven for. . . ." Traditional interpretations of his poem have praised Browning for praising the necessity of man's ambitions, of man's reaching out for grandeur. Indeed, Del Sarto, in an act of minor blasphemy, casts heaven not as God's space but as man's reminder that he has not yet achieved his personal best. Unhappily, these interpretations go on, women can hurt men in their noble quests. Fickle, feckless, the feminine often embarks on her own quest, a search-and-destroy mission against male grandeur.

A revisionary interpretation of "Andrea Del Sarto," however, can find the poem a different kind of parable about sexuality, gender, and power. In this reading, a man has at least two capacities. First, he can reach out and move about in public space and historical time. Del Sarto goes after both canvas and fame. Next, he can define a woman's identity, here through talking about her and painting her portrait. Del Sarto literally shapes the image of his wife. Iron-

ically, he wants to believe that he is a victim. He exercises his powers in order to demonstrate that he is powerless. A man, he projects himself as a poor baby who cannot shape up his mate.

A sexual harasser in higher education reveals similar, but more sinister, capacities. The hierarchical structure of institutions sends him a supportive message: the arduous climb up the ladder is worth it. The higher a man goes, the more he deserves and ought to enjoy the sweetness and freedoms of his place.[2] First, a man reaches out for what he wants. He makes sexual "advances." His offensive weapons can be linguistic (a joke, for example) or physical (a touch). He warns the powerless that he has the ability to reach out in order to grasp and get what he wants. He also demonstrates to himself that he is able to dominate a situation. As the psychoanalyst Ethel Spector Person has pointed out, for many men, sexuality and domination are inseparable. To be sexual is to dominate and to be reassured of the possession of the power to dominate (Person, 1980).[3]

Usually, women compose the powerless group, but it may contain younger men as well, the disadvantages of age erasing the advantages of gender. One example: a 1986 survey at the University of Illinois/Champaign-Urbana found that 19 percent of the female graduate students, 10 percent of the undergraduates, and 8 percent of the professional school students had experienced harassment. So, too, had 5 percent of the male respondents. In all but one incident, the harasser was another man (Allen & Okawa, 1987).

Second, the harasser assumes the right to define the identity of the person whom he assaults. To him, she is not mind, but body; not student, not professional, but sexual being. She is who and what the harasser says she is. Ironically, like Andrea Del Sarto, many academics project their own power onto a woman and then assert that she, not he, has power.[4] He, not she, is powerless. Her sexuality seduces and betrays him. This psychological maneuver must help to explain one fear that people express about sexual harassment policies—that such policies will permit, even encourage, false complaints against blameless faculty and staff. A recent study found 78 percent of respondents worried about loss of due process and about the fate of innocent people who might be accused of misconduct. Yet, the study concluded, less than 1 percent of all sexual harassment complaints each year *are* false. The deep problem is not wrongful accusations against the innocent, but the refusal of the wronged to file any complaint at all. In part, they believe they should handle sexual matters themselves. In part, they hope the problem will go away if they ignore it. In part, they fear retaliation, punishment for stepping out of line (Robertson, Dyer, & Campbell, 1988).

The unreasonable fear about false complaints is also a symptom of the blindness of the powerful to the realities of their own situation. They enjoy its benefits but are unable to see its nature and costs to other people. They are like a driver of an inherited sports car who loves to drive but refuses to learn where gas and oil come from, who services the car when it is in the garage, or why pedestrians might shout when he speeds through a red light. In a probing essay, Molly Hite (1988) tells a story about a harasser on a United States campus, a powerful professor who abused his authority over female graduate students. He damaged several women, psycho-

logically and professionally. Yet even after that damage became public knowledge, he survived, reputation intact, although he did discreetly move to another campus. Hite inventories the responses of her colleagues to this event. Men, no matter what their academic rank, tended to underplay the seriousness of his behavior. They thought that he had acted "normally," if sometimes insensitively, that the women had acted abnormally and weakly. Women, no matter what their academic rank, tended to sympathize with the female victims. They could identify with powerlessness. Hite writes, "The more the victim is someone who could be you, the easier it is to be scared. By the same reasoning, it's possible to be cosmically un-scared, even to find the whole situation trivial to the point of absurdity, if you can't imagine ever being the victim" (p. 9).

So far, higher education has participated in building at least four related modes of resistance to sexual harassment. First, we have named the problem *as a problem.* We have pushed it into public consciousness as an issue. The Equal Employment Opportunity Commission guidelines, in particular, have provided a citable, national language with which to describe harassment, a justifiable entry in the dictionary of our concerns. Next, we have learned how much administrative leadership has mattered in urging an institution to address this concern. Not surprisingly, faculties have not moved to reform themselves. Next, workshops that educate people about the nature of harassment do seem to reduce its virulence. Finally, we have created grievance procedures with which we can hear complaints, investigate them, and punish harassers.[5] The most carefully designed in themselves help to empower women. The process does not itself perpetuate her sense of self as victim (Hoffman, 1986).

These modes of resistance, good in themselves, have also done good. They have shown an institution's commitment to a fair, non-polluting social environment. They have warned potential harassers to stop. They have offered some redress to the harassed. Resistance will, however, be of only limited good unless a rewriting of the historical connections among sexuality, gender, and power accompanies it. Similarly, putting up traffic lights on crowded streets is a good. Lights are, however, of only limited good unless drivers believe in the rights of other drivers, in safety, and in the limits of their machines.

In such a rewriting, an act of "over-reaching" will be interpreted not as aspiration and desire, but as an invasion of another person's body, dignity, and livelihood. No one will feel the approaching grasp of the harasser as a welcome clasp. Over-reaching will be a sign not of grace but of disgrace, not of strength but of callousness and, possibly, anxiety, not of virility but of moral and psychological weakness. It will not be a warm joke between erotic equals, but a smutty titter from an erotic jerk. The rhetoric of neither romance nor comedy will be able to paint over the grammar of exploitation.[6]

One consequence of this rewriting will be to expand our modes of resistance to include a general education curriculum, not simply about harassment as a phenomenon, but about power itself, which harassment symptomizes. This will mean teaching many men to cut the ties among selfhood, masculinity, and domination. It will mean teaching many women to cut the ties among self, femininity, and intimacy at any price, including the price of submission. Occasionally, reading a sexual harassment complaint from a young woman, I have asked myself, in some rue and pain, why she has acted *like a woman.* By that, I have meant that her training for womanhood has taught her to value closeness, feeling, relationships. Fine and dandy, but too often, she takes this lesson to heart above all others.

The first part of the curriculum, for women, will remind them of their capacity for resistance, for saying no. Telling a harasser to stop can be effective.[7] Speaking out, acting verbally, can also empower an individual woman. Less fortunately, these speech acts reconstitute the traditional sexual roles of man as hunter, woman as prey. Unlike a rabbit or doe, she is responsible for setting the limits of the hunt, for fencing in the game park. If the hunter violates these limits, it is because she did not uphold them firmly enough. Moreover, saying no to the aggressor also occurs in private space. Because of this location, both harasser and harassed can forget that these apparently private actions embody, in little, grosser structures of authority.

The second part of the curriculum will be for men and women. Fortunately, women's studies programs are now developed enough to serve as a resource for an entire institution that chooses to offer lessons about gender and power. These lessons will do more than anatomize abuses. They will also present an ethical perspective, which the practices of colleges and universities might well represent. This ethic will cherish a divorce between sexuality and the control of another person, an unbridgeable distance between a lover's pleasure and a bully's threat. This ethic will also ask us to cherish our capacities to care for each other, to attend to each other's needs without manipulating them.[8] We will reach out to each other without grasping, hauling, pushing, mauling.

The struggle against sexual harassment, then, is part of a larger struggle to replant the moral grounds of education. Our visionary hope is that we will, in clear air, harvest new gestures, laws, customs, and practices. We will still take poets as our prophets. When we do so, however, we might replace the dramatic monologue of a fraught, Renaissance painter with that of a strong-willed, late twentieth-century feminist. In 1977, in "Natural Resources," Adrienne Rich spoke for those who stubbornly continue to believe in visionary hope:

> "My heart is moved by all I cannot save:
> so much has been destroyed.
> I have to cast my lot with those
> who age after age, perversely,
> with no extraordinary power,
> reconstitute the world."

NOTES

1. The authors of a survey of 311 institutions of higher education, conducted in 1984, estimate that one woman out of four experiences some form of harassment as a student (Robertson et al., 1988). A survey of a single institution, a large public research university, found that 31 percent of the more than 700 respondents had been subjected to "sex-stereotyped jokes, remarks, references, or examples" ("Survey documents," 1988, pp. 41–42).

2. As Robertson et al. comment, "individuals in positions of authority . . . (are) used to viewing professional status as expanding privilege rather than increasing responsibility and obligation" (p. 808). An anecdote illustrates this generalization. Recently, I was chairing a meeting of the graduate faculty of my university. Our agenda item was a proposal to conduct a periodic review of faculty members, program by program, to help insure they were still qualified to be graduate teachers. A professor, well-known for his decency, stood up in opposition. He said, "When I got tenure, I became a member of a club, and no one is going to tell me what to do. If I don't want to publish, that's my business."

3. Not coincidentally, most of the sexual harassers whom I have had to investigate as graduate dean have had streaks of arrogance, flare-ups of vanity. In contrast, the men who have been most sympathetic to the necessity of my investigations have had a certain ethical poise, a balance of standards and stability.

4. An obvious parallel is a traditional response to rape, in which women are held culpable for being raped. Moreover, like versions of Jezebel, they are thought only too likely to cry rape in order to cover up their own sins.

5. I am grateful to Robertson et al. (1988) for their description of various modes of resistance to harassment. Their study also explores the reasons why public institutions have been more sensitive than private institutions. More specifically, Beauvais (1986) describes workshops that deal with harassment for residence hall staff at the University of Michigan.

6. Disguising the language of harassment as humor has several advantages. First, it draws on our old, shrewd assessment of much sexual behavior as funny and comic. Next, it simultaneously inflates the harasser to the status of good fellow, able to tell a joke, and deflates the harassed to the status of prude, unable to take one.

7. Allen and Okawa (1987) say that this worked for two-thirds of the respondents in their study of harassment at the University of Illinois.

8. Tronto (1987) suggestively outlines a theory of care that educational institutions might adopt.

REFERENCES

Allen, D., & Okawa, J. B. (1987). A counseling center looks at sexual harassment. *Journal of the National Association for Women Deans, Administrators, and Counselors, 51*(1), 9–16.

Beauvais, K. (1986). Workshops to combat sexual harassment: A case study of changing attitudes. *Signs, 12*(1), 130–145.

Hite, M. (1988). Sexual harassment and the university community. Unpublished manuscript.

Hoffman, F. L. (1986). Sexual harassment in academia. *Harvard Educational Review, 56*(2), 105–121.

Person, E. (1980). Sexuality as the mainstay of identity. In C. R. Stimpson & E. S. Person (eds.), *Women: Sex and sexuality.* Chicago: University of Chicago Press.

Robertson, C., Dyer, C. C., & Campbell, D. A. (1988). Campus harassment: Sexual harassment policies and procedures at institutions of higher learning. *Signs, 13*(4), 792–812.

Survey documents sexual harassment at U Mass. (1988). *Liberal Education, 74*(2), 41–2.

Tronto, J. C. (1987). Beyond gender differences to a theory of care. *Signs, 12*(4), 644–663.

NO

Gretchen Morgenson

MAY I HAVE THE PLEASURE

On October 11 [1991],in the middle of the Anita Hill/Clarence Thomas contretemps, the *New York Times* somberly reported that sexual harassment pervades the American workplace. The source for this page-one story was a *Times*/CBS poll conducted two days earlier in which a handful (294) of women were interviewed by telephone. Thirty-eight per cent of respondents confirmed that they had been at one time or another "the object of sexual advances, propositions, or unwanted sexual discussions from men who supervise you or can affect your position at work." How many reported the incident at the time it happened? Four per cent.

Did the *Times* offer any explanation for why so few actually reported the incident? Could it be that these women did not report their "harassment" because they themselves did not regard a sexual advance as harassment? Some intelligent speculation on this matter might shed light on a key point: the vague definitions of harassment that make it easy to allege, hard to identify, and almost impossible to prosecute. Alas, the *Times* was in no mood to enlighten its readers.

It has been more than ten years since the Equal Employment Opportunity Commission (EEOC) wrote its guidelines defining sexual harassment as a form of sexual discrimination and, therefore, illegal under Title VII of the Civil Rights Act of 1964. According to the EEOC there are two different types of harassment: so-called *quid pro quo* harassment, in which career or job advancement is guaranteed in return for sexual favors, and environmental harassment, in which unwelcome sexual conduct "unreasonably interferes" with an individual's working environment or creates an "intimidating, hostile, or offensive working environment."

Following the EEOC's lead, an estimated three out of four companies nationwide have instituted strict policies against harassment; millions of dollars are spent each year educating employees in the subtleties of Title VII etiquette. Men are warned to watch their behavior, to jettison the patronizing pat and excise the sexist comment from their vocabularies.

Yet, if you believe what you read in the newspapers, we are in the Stone Age where the sexes are concerned. A theme common to the media,

From Gretchen Morgenson, "May I Have the Pleasure . . . ," *National Review* (November 18, 1991). Copyright © 1991 by National Review, Inc., 150 East 35th Street, New York, NY 10016. Reprinted by permission.

plaintiff's lawyers, and employee-relations consultants is that male harassment of women is costing corporations millions each year in lost productivity and low employee morale. "Sexual harassment costs a typical Fortune 500 Service or Manufacturing company $6.7 million a year" says a sexual-harassment survey conducted late in 1988 for *Working Woman* by Klein Associates. This Boston consulting firm is part of a veritable growth industry which has sprung up to dispense sexual-harassment advice to worried companies in the form of seminars, videos, and encounter groups.

But is sexual harassment such a huge problem in business? Or is it largely a product of hype and hysteria? The statistics show that sexual harassment is less prevalent today than it was five years ago. According to the EEOC, federal cases alleging harassment on the job totaled 5,694 in 1990, compared to 6,342 in 1984. Yet today there are 17 per cent more women working than there were then.

At that, the EEOC's figures are almost certainly too high. In a good many of those complaints, sexual harassment may be tangential to the case; the complaint may primarily involve another form of discrimination in Title VII territory: race, national origin, or religious discrimination, for example. The EEOC doesn't separate cases involving sexual harassment alone; any case where sexual harassment is mentioned, even in passing, gets lumped into its figures.

Many of the stories depicting sexual harassment as a severe problem spring from "consultants" whose livelihoods depend upon exaggerating its extent. In one year, DuPont spent $450,000 on sexual-harassment training programs and materials. Susan Webb, president of Pacific Resources Development Group, a Seattle consultant, says she spends 95 per cent of her time advising on sexual harassment. Like most consultants, Miss Webb acts as an expert witness in harassment cases, conducts investigations for companies and municipalities, and teaches seminars. She charges clients $1,500 for her 35-minute sexual-harassment video program and handbooks.

UNFELT NEEDS

Corporations began to express concern on the issue back in the early Eighties, just after the EEOC published its first guidelines. But it was *Meritor Savings Bank v. Vinson*, a harassment case that made it to the Supreme Court in 1985, that really acted as an employment act for sex-harassment consultants. In *Vinson*, the Court stated that employers could limit their liability to harassment claims by implementing anti-harassment policies and procedures in the workplace. And so, the anti-harassment industry was born.

Naturally, the consultants believe they are filling a need, not creating one. "Harassment is still as big a problem as it has been because the workplace is not integrated," says Susan Webb. Ergo, dwindling numbers of cases filed with the EEOC are simply not indicative of a diminution in the problem.

Then what do the figures indicate? Two things, according to the harassment industry. First, that more plaintiffs are bringing private lawsuits against their employers than are suing through the EEOC or state civil-rights commissions. Second, that the number of cases filed is a drop in the bucket compared to the number of actual, everyday harassment incidents.

It certainly stands to reason that a plaintiff in a sexual-harassment case would prefer bringing a private action against her employer to filing an EEOC claim. EEOC and state civil-rights cases allow plaintiffs only compensatory damages, such as back pay or legal fees. In order to collect big money—punitive damages—from an employer, a plaintiff must file a private action.

Yet there's simply no proof that huge or increasing numbers of private actions are being filed today. No data are collected on numbers of private harassment suits filed, largely because they're brought as tort actions—assault and battery, emotional distress, or breach of contract. During the second half of the Eighties, the San Francisco law firm of Orrick, Herrington, and Sutcliffe monitored private sexual-harassment cases filed in California. Its findings: From 1984 to 1989, the number of sexual-harassment cases in California that were litigated through a verdict totaled a whopping 15. That's in a state with almost six million working women.

Of course, cases are often settled prior to a verdict. But how many? Orrick, Herrington partner Ralph H. Baxter Jr., management co-chairman of the American Bar Association's Labor Law Committee on Employee Rights and Responsibilities, believes the number of private sexual-harassment cases launched today is greatly overstated. "Litigation is not as big a problem as it's made out to be; you're not going to see case after case," says Mr. Baxter. "A high percentage of matters go to the EEOC and a substantial number of cases get resolved."

Those sexual-harassment actions that do get to a jury are the ones that really grab headlines. A couple of massive awards have been granted in recent years—five plaintiffs were awarded $3.8 million by a North Carolina jury—but most mammoth awards are reduced on appeal. In fact, million-dollar sexual-harassment verdicts are still exceedingly rare. In California, land of the happy litigator, the median jury verdict for all sexual-harassment cases litigated between 1984 and 1989 was $183,000. The top verdict in the sate was just under $500,000, the lowest was $45,000. And California, known for its sympathetic jurors, probably produces higher awards than most states.

Now to argument number two: that the number of litigated harassment cases is tiny compared to the number of actual incidents that occur. Bringing a sexual-harassment case is similar to filing a rape case, consultants and lawyers say; both are nasty proceedings which involve defamation, possible job loss, and threats to both parties' family harmony.

It may well be that cases of perceived harassment go unfiled, but is it reasonable to assume that the numbers of these unfiled cases run into the millions? Consider the numbers of cases filed that are dismissed for "no probable cause." According to the New York State human-rights commission, almost two-thirds of the complaints filed in the past five years were dismissed for lack of probable cause. Of the two hundred sexual-harassment cases the commission receives a year, 38 per cent bring benefits to the complainant.

What about private actions? No one keeps figures on the percentage of cases nationwide won by the plaintiff versus the percentage that are dismissed. However, the outcomes of private sexual-harassment suits brought in California from 1984 to 1989 mirror the public figures from New York. According to Orrick, Herrington, of the 15 cases litigated to a verdict in California from 1984 to 1989, slightly less than half were dismissed and slightly more than half (53 per cent) were won by the plaintiff.

Are California and New York anomalies? Stephen Perlman, a partner in labor law at the Boston firm of Ropes & Gray, who has 15 years' experience litigating sexual-harassment cases, thinks not: "I don't suppose I've had as many as a dozen cases go to litigation. Most of the cases I've seen—the vast majority—get dismissed. They don't even have probable cause to warrant further processing."

WHAT IS HARASSMENT?

A major problem is the vague definition of harassment. If "environmental harassment" were clearly defined and specifiable, lawyers would undoubtedly see more winnable cases walk through their doors. Asking a subordinate to perform sexual favors in exchange for a raise is clearly illegal. But a dirty joke? A pin-up? A request for a date?

In fact, behavior which one woman may consider harassment could be seen by another as a non-threatening joke. The closest thing to harassment that I have experienced during my 15-year career occurred in the early Eighties when I was a stockbroker-in-training at Dean Witter Reynolds in New York City. I had brought in the largest personal account within Dean Witter's entire retail brokerage system, an account which held roughly $20 million in blue-chip stocks. Having this account under my management meant I had a larger capital responsibility than any of my colleagues, yet I was relatively new to the business. My fellow brokers were curious, but only one was brutish enough to walk right up to me and pop the question: "How did

you get that account? Did you sleep with the guy?"

Instead of running away in tears, I dealt with him as I would any rude person. "Yeah," I answered. "Eat your heart out." He turned on his heel and never bothered me again. Was my colleague a harasser, or just practicing Wall Street's aggressive humor, which is dished out to men in other ways? Apparently, I am in the minority in thinking the latter. But the question remains. Whose standards should be used to define harassment?

Under tort law, the behavior which has resulted in a case—such as an assault or the intent to cause emotional distress—must be considered objectionable by a "reasonable person." The EEOC follows this lead and in its guidelines defines environmental harassment as that which "unreasonably interferes with an individual's job performance."

Yet, sexual-harassment consultants argue that any such behavior—even that which is perceived as harassment only by the most hypersensitive employee—ought to be considered illegal and stamped out. In fact, they say, the subtler hostile-environment cases are the most common and cause the most anguish. Says Frieda Klein, the Boston consultant: "My goal is to create a corporate climate where every employee feels free to object to behavior, where people are clear about their boundaries and can ask that objectionable behavior stop."

Sounds great. But rudeness and annoying behavior cannot be legislated out of existence; nor should corporations be forced to live under the tyranny of a hypersensitive employee. No woman should have to run a daily gauntlet of sexual innuendo, but neither is it reasonable for women to expect a pristine work environment free of coarse behavior.

Susan Hartzoge Gray, a labor lawyer at Haworth, Riggs, Kuhn, and Haworth in Raleigh, North Carolina, believes that hostile-environment harassment shouldn't be actionable under Title VII. "How can the law say one person's lewd and another's nice?" she asks. "There are so many different taste levels. . . . We condone sexual jokes and innuendos in the media—a movie might get a PG rating—yet an employer can be called on the carpet because the same thing bothers someone in an office."

But changing demographics may do more to eliminate genuine sexual harassment than all the apparatus of law and consultancy. As women reach a critical mass in the workforce, the problem of sexual harassment tends to go away. Frieda Klein says the problem practically vanishes once 30 per cent of the workers in a department, an assembly line, or a company are women.

Reaching that critical mass won't take long. According to the Bureau of Labor Statistics, there will be 66 million women to 73 million men in the workplace by 2000. They won't all be running departments or heading companies, of course, but many will.

So sexual harassment will probably become even less of a problem in the years ahead than it is today. But you are not likely to read that story in a major newspaper anytime soon.

POSTSCRIPT

Is Sexual Harassment a Pervasive Problem?

For many women, the high cost of fighting sexual harassment often makes suffering in silence more appealing. As feminist Naomi Wolf points out, "Many strong, successful professional women have made conscious decisions to ignore sexual harassment in their offices because they know that as soon as they complained, there would be 50 other [women] waiting to take their jobs." Camille Paglia, author of *Sexual Personae*, counters, "Women allow themselves to become victims when they don't take responsibility. If getting the guy to stop means putting a heel into his crotch, then just do it. Don't complain about it 10 years later." Yet, Deborah Tanner, author of *You Just Don't Understand: Women and Men in Conversation*, says, "Women have learned that confrontation is to be avoided and they don't have the verbal tools to attack this kind of problem head-on as a man would."

This issue may have some chilling effects on everyday male-female relations, on dating and courtship, in the workplace, on college campuses, and even in high schools. Anthropologist Lionel Tiger predicts a "return to a kind of Victorian period" in which some men will be reluctant to try developing a relationship with any woman who initially seems aloof.

The Tailhook Association incident, which has made headlines around the world, seems to have had some global influence: the Belgian and Dutch governments have launched public information campaigns; the Spanish and French governments have recently passed laws making sexual harassment a crime; and the European Commission, the administrative arm of the 12-nation European Community, has issued a code defining sexual harassment.

Sexual harassment is fast becoming a global issue that will likely continue to have reverberations in the ways women and men relate for years to come.

SUGGESTED READINGS

F. Barringer, "School Hallways as Gantlets of Sexual Taunts," *The New York Times* (June 2, 1993).

B. W. Dziech and L. Weiner, *The Lecherous Professor: Sexual Harassment on Campus* (Beacon Press, 1984).

M. Lawton, "Survey Paints 'Picture' of School Sexual Harassment," *Education Week* (March 31, 1993).

A. N. LeBlanc, "Harassment at School: The Truth Is Out," *Seventeen* (May 1993).

P. Sharpe and F. Mascia-Lees, " 'Always Believe the Victim,' 'Innocent Until Proven Guilty,' 'There Is No Truth': The Competing Claims of Feminism, Humanism, and Postmodernism in Interpreting Charges of Harassment in the Academy," *Anthropological Quarterly* (April 1993).

N. Wolf, *The Beauty Myth: How Images of Beauty Are Used Against Women* (William Morrow, 1991).

ISSUE 17

Has the Federal Government Spent Enough on AIDS Research?

YES: Michael Fumento, from "Are We Spending Too Much on AIDS?" *Commentary* (October 1990)

NO: Timothy F. Murphy, from "No Time for an AIDS Backlash," *Hastings Center Report* (March/April 1991)

ISSUE SUMMARY

YES: Michael Fumento, a former AIDS analyst for the U.S. Commission on Civil Rights, is disturbed that the Public Health Service spent more money in 1990 for AIDS research and education than it allocated for any other fatal disease. He points out that each year many times more Americans die of heart disease and cancer than of AIDS, and he asserts that the time has come to stop spending so much money and time on the disease.

NO: Assistant professor of philosophy Timothy F. Murphy maintains that the massive funding for AIDS research and prevention is justified. He argues that a communicable, lethal disease like AIDS ought to receive priority over noncommunicable diseases like cancer and heart disease, both of which can be medically managed to allow patients to live to old age.

AIDS (acquired immunodeficiency syndrome) and the many controversies that surround it may best be understood in the context of the ongoing conflict between humans and pathogens.

In the past, epidemics have ravaged the land, killing thousands or even millions in a few days, months, or years. In the late 500s bubonic plague—the Black Death—spread from Asia to Europe in less than 50 years, killing 100 million people, or one out of every two people in Southwest Asia, Africa, and Europe. Between 1347 and 1351, the Black Death again killed between two-thirds and three-quarters of all Europeans—25 million people—in only five years. Worldwide, the plague of the 1300s killed an estimated 43 million people. Several more outbreaks of the plague occurred over the next 200 years, culminating in the Great Plague of London (1665), which decimated that city within a few weeks.

Widespread death can demolish the social structure and order of whole nations and continents. With the first plague, Justinian's Byzantine Empire collapsed, allowing the followers of Mohammed to sweep out of the Middle East, conquer North Africa and Spain, and threaten all of Europe. A second major plague, in the 1300s, wiped out the feudal world of the Middle Ages and the Holy Roman Empire. In the wake of this devastation, the Renaissance was born in Florence, and a whole new social order emerged. Over the course of 200 years, the Renaissance spread across most of Europe, sparking Europe's exploration of the Americas, the Far East, and the Pacific, and igniting the Industrial Revolution.

In 1916, polio (infantile paralysis) struck 27,000 Americans and killed over 7,000. Polio resurfaced in 1949 to infect 42,000 and kill 2,720, and again in 1952 to cripple 58,000 and kill 3,300. In 1918, an influenza epidemic killed 500,000 Americans in eight months. It is easy to see how the threat of another epidemic in the United States may frighten some people.

Between June 1981 and March 1993, the human immunodeficiency virus (HIV, the AIDS virus) infected an estimated 1 million Americans and produced 285,000 cases of full-blown AIDS. AIDS has killed 170,000 adults and adolescents and 4,500 children. With no cure in sight, it is probable that all of the 1 million HIV-infected Americans will eventually die of AIDS. By the year 2000, the World Health Organization (WHO) estimates that, worldwide, 30 to 40 million people will be infected, about the same number of people who died of the plague in the 1300s.

One main difference between the plague and HIV is that the plague was caused by a bacteria transmitted by fleas and other vermin. HIV, however, is a virus that is mainly contracted through preventable behaviors, such as sexual contact with an infected person and intravenous drug use.

In the following selections, Michael Fumento argues that too much money is being spent on trying to find a cure for this behaviorally controllable disease at the cost of reduced funding for research for other, more widespread diseases. Timothy F. Murphy believes that the epidemic spread of AIDS warrants the amount of money being spent on the disease, and he urges the federal government to allocate even more to the cause.

YES

Michael Fumento

ARE WE SPENDING TOO
MUCH ON AIDS?

If there is one thing Americans seem to agree upon about AIDS, it is that we are not spending enough on the disease. "The government has blood on its hands," reads a bumper sticker that is ubiquitous in major cities, "one AIDS death every half hour." AIDS activists, who are fond of asserting that AIDS is "not a homosexual disease," tell us in the same breath that the failure to spend more on it constitutes genocide against homosexuals. A recent public-opinion poll shows, indeed, that most Americans favor increasing spending on AIDS.

But consider. This past year, reported cases of AIDS in the U.S. increased only 9 percent over the previous year's tally. The federal Centers for Disease Control (CDC) of the Public Health Service (PHS) has been forced to lower greatly both its estimate of current infections and its projections of future cases. The World Health Organization, similarly, has lowered its original estimate of as many as 100 million infections by 1990 to a current eight to ten million. New York City, AIDS capital of the nation, has lowered its estimate of current infections from 500,000 to about 150,000.

Nor has the long-expected "breakout" of AIDS into the heterosexual middle class shown any sign of occurring. Former Surgeon General C. Everett Koop, who probably coined the expression "heterosexual AIDS explosion," now claims he knew "from the very beginning" that such a thing would never happen; Gene Antonio, author of *The AIDS Cover-Up?* (300,000 copies in print), which predicted as many as 64 million infections by this year [1990], now denies having made such a prediction. At the recent international AIDS conference in San Francisco, Dr. Nancy Padian put another nail in the coffin of the "breakout" theory when she reported the results of her study of 41 couples among whom the woman was originally infected and the man was not: over a period of years, only one man became infected, and that only after both he and his partner had experienced penile and vaginal bleeding on over 100 occasions.

This year, AIDS dropped from being the 14th biggest killer of Americans to number 15. Heart disease this year will kill about 775,000 Americans, a figure perhaps 20 times as high as the number of Americans who will die of AIDS in the next twelve months. In the next two months cancer will kill almost as many people as have died of AIDS in the course of the entire epidemic.

Nevertheless, the *current* PHS allocation of about $1.6 billion for AIDS research and education is higher than that allocated for any other cause of death. In 1990, the CDC will spend $10,000 on prevention and education for each AIDS sufferer as opposed to $185 for each victim of cancer and a mere $3.50 for each cardiac patient. Total federal research expenditures on AIDS this year will be more than 100 percent of nationwide patient costs; in the case of cancer, the corresponding ratio of research-and-development spending to patient costs is about 4.5 percent, in the case of heart disease about 2.9 percent, and in the case of Alzheimer's disease, less than 1 percent.

AIDS ACTIVISTS HAVE ANSWERS TO THESE statistics. Since AIDS strikes most often in the prime of life, they urge us to consider the years of lost productivity as a cost that could be avoided by more spending now on AIDS research. Yet every year cancer and heart disease *each* kills more than 150,000 Americans below the age of sixty, while this year AIDS will kill around 30,000 persons of all ages. Nor do the calculations of years lost take account of the fact that intravenous drug abusers, who make up a growing portion of those affected by the disease, have a very low life expectancy and an even lower expectancy of productivity.

But, say AIDS activists, the disease is overwhelming the nation's health-care system, and this alone justifies increased spending on research. A figure repeated often in the media has been the Rand Corporation's estimate that by 1991, direct medical costs for AIDS (that is, medical expenses only, with lost wages not included) could be as high as $133 billion, with up to $38 billion in 1991 alone. *U.S. News & World Report* flatly declared, "What is now becoming clear to an array of leaders—in medicine, business, government, and academia—is that AIDS not only threatens untold death and suffering but could bankrupt America's health system as well." In fact, however, a typical AIDS case costs approximately the same as a terminal cancer case, about $40,000 to $50,000, which means that the 35,000 reported AIDS cases last year will end up costing the nation something less than $2 billion, or considerably less than 1 percent of this year's total U.S. medical costs of approximately $650 billion.

Of course, localized emergencies can exist. New York City's hospital system, running poorly even before AIDS, is clearly in a state of crisis even though cases in that city have peaked. The reason New York, San Francisco, Los Angeles, and other such cities have been hit so hard by AIDS is that they are refuges for homosexuals and drug abusers. With that in mind, the House and Senate are seeking to authorize $2.9 billion and $4 billion, respectively, over the next six years, mostly for these hard-hit cities and states. (Ironically, the bill has been cast as emergency relief for *rural* areas, apparently in the belief that voters have more sympathy for the problems of Peoria than for those of San Francisco or New York.) This special allocation for

AIDS, which comes on top of an earlier special allocation to subsidize the drug AZT, is almost without precedent. There is nothing similar for people with heart disease or cancer or diabetes or lupus or any number of other potentially fatal diseases (with the exception of end-stage renal disease).

WHAT ABOUT THE ASSERTION THAT AIDS deserves more funding because it is contagious, while heart disease and cancer are not? In fact, AIDS is contagious almost exclusively through behavior, and modification of that behavior could in theory reduce future AIDS cases virtually to zero without another penny spent on research and without a single medical breakthrough. An as-yet uninfected homosexual who avoids high-risk behavior will almost certainly never contract AIDS; but his chance of dying of cancer remains one in five. Indeed, male homosexuals outside of such high-incidence areas as San Francisco, Los Angeles, and New York, and whose HIV status is unknown, currently have less chance of getting AIDS than of dying of either heart disease or cancer.

It is said that even if research on AIDS does not yield a cure, spin-offs from that research could lead to cures and treatments for other diseases. In line with this idea, Congressman Ted Weiss (D.-NY) requested the Office of Technology Assessment (OTA) to prepare a report titled, "How Has Federal Research on AIDS/HIV Contributed to Other Fields?" The reviewer in the British medical journal *Lancet*, struck by the contrast between this tiny report and OTA's customary "behemoth, exhaustive" efforts, noted that it was comprised of nothing more than opinions from an "unspecified organization of 'distinguished biomedical and social scientists,' " and that "For policy or polemics, this OTA production is a bust."

Nevertheless, Dr. Anthony Fauci, the director of the National Institutes of Allergies and Infectious Diseases (NIAID), a branch of the National Institutes of Health (NIH), and long an advocate of increased spending on AIDS, declared that "There's positive spin-offs already and certainly in the next decade or two you'll see more," adding that these included cancer. In fact, no life has ever been saved, no disease ever ameliorated, by AIDS spin-offs. As former NIH director Donald Fredrickson has pointed out, most AIDS research is far too narrowly targeted to lead to significant spin-offs. Indeed, most of the money spent by the PHS on AIDS (including for advertisements on late-night television like the one featuring a man who resolves not to go out on the town and "bring back AIDS to my family") does not involve clinical research at all.

This is not to say that no spin-offs are ever possible. After all, no one knew that the space program would end up introducing the world to velcro. But we did not embark on the space program because we wanted a new kind of fastener. If it is a cure for cancer we seek, we should spend money on cancer research, not on another disease entirely. As it happens, increasing spending on cancer at the expense of spending on AIDS might do more for both diseases: of the first three drugs approved for treatment of AIDS or its conditions, two—AZT and alpha interferon—were spin-offs of cancer research.

Among the deleterious effects of disproportionate spending on AIDS have been inevitable boondoggles, as great a problem in medicine as in national defense. In December 1988, NIAID announced two grants totaling $22.8 million to study non-drug-using heterosexuals in order, as the Associated Press put it, to "prevent a huge new epidemic." Speaking on condition of anonymity, one prominent federal epidemiologist said of the study, "I think it's complete bullshit." He added, "My sense was that a huge amount of money got dumped on NIAID and that by the time they got around to awarding the money a lot of good institutions had already been funded and all that was left was schlock."

CONCENTRATION ON AIDS HAS IN GENERAL prompted a de-emphasis of other medical diseases like Alzheimer's, a cruel, debilitating malady that will continue to exact an ever-higher yearly toll unless medical intervention becomes possible. Nobody is more conscious of this than researchers themselves. It takes up to a decade to put a high-school graduate through medical school; thus, for now and for the immediate future AIDS researchers are being drawn from other research areas, primarily cancer, and the rumblings from traditionally nonpolitical laboratories are growing louder and louder. Some are calling it "AIDS Resentment Complex," a play on "AIDS Related Complex." Dr. Vincent T. DeVita, Jr., just before stepping down from his position as director of the National Cancer Institute (NCI), said that AIDS "has been an extraordinary drain on the energy of the scientific establishment." In fact, AIDS research has now weakened cancer research to the point where NCI's ability to fund promising new proposals is lower than at any time in the past two decades.

Two top doctors left NCI in late 1988, partly out of frustration over this state of affairs. According to one of them, Dr. Robert Young, now president of the American Society of Clinical Oncology, "the superstructure of cancer research is being dismantled." Indeed, for non-AIDS work, NIH lost almost 1,100 employees between 1984 and 1989. At the same time, according to *Science* magazine, the number of NIH employees engaged in AIDS work increased by more than 400 to 580 workers or their full-time equivalents.

The most vocal opposition to spiraling federal AIDS expenditures has probably come from women concerned about breast cancer, which kills about 44,000 a year; every two years as many women die of breast cancer alone as the number of men and women who have died of AIDS over the course of the entire epidemic. True, Congress is now considering bills that would appropriate funds for cancer screening in women, but the total to be allocated for both breast cancer and cervical cancer—the latter kills 6,000 women a year and is virtually always preventable if caught early enough—is only $50 million, as contrasted with the $3 to $4 billion which Congress wants to spend for AIDS treatment programs over the next six years and which will probably not save a single life, from AIDS or anything else.

THE BLUNT FACT IS, THEN, THAT A GREAT many people will die of other diseases because of the overemphasis on AIDS. We will never know their names and those names will never be sewn into a giant quilt. We will never know their exact numbers. But they will die nonetheless.

Is this right? Should a compassionate society allocate funds and research on the basis of media attention, on the basis of whoever makes the loudest noise? Or should it, rather, put its appropriations where they can do the most good for the greatest number of people?

NO

Timothy F. Murphy

NO TIME FOR AN AIDS BACKLASH

Writing in *Time*, Charles Krauthammer described the May 1990 protests by AIDS activists at the National Institutes of Health as a most misdirected demonstration: "The idea that American government or American society has been inattentive or unresponsive to AIDS is quite simply absurd." On the contrary, "AIDS has become the most privileged disease in America," this since Congress continues to allocate an enormous amount of money for research and for the treatment of people with HIV-related conditions. Except cancer research, HIV-related disease now receives more research funding than any other illness in the United States, a priority Krauthammer maintains is all out of proportion to its significance since AIDS kills fewer people each year than many other diseases. The privilege of AIDS even extends to access to certain experimental drugs—access others do not share.

Chicago Tribune columnist Mike Royko has also challenged the view that there is government indifference regarding AIDS. "That might have been true at one time. But it no longer is. Vast sums are being spent on AIDS research. Far more per victim than on cancer, heart disease and other diseases that kill far more people." In his view, some AIDS education posters have far more to do with the "promotion" of homosexuality than with the prevention of disease. Views of this kind reflect a movement that would assign AIDS a lesser standing in the social and medical priorities of the nation.

This view is not new in the epidemic; the sentiment that homosexuals with AIDS were being treated as a privileged class had surfaced as early as 1983. What is new, though, is the increasing prominence of this view in public discourse and the extent to which the view is defended. In *The Myth of Heterosexual AIDS*, Michael Fumento mounts a full-scale defense of the proposition that the AIDS epidemic has achieved national and medical priority all out of proportion to its dangers, especially since the disease will make few inroads against white, middle-class heterosexuals. Fumento writes in self-conscious sound-bites: "Other than fairly spectacular rare occurrences, such as shark attacks and maulings by wild animals, it is difficult to name any broad category of death that will take fewer lives than heterosexually transmitted AIDS." He also says that the mass mailing of the Surgeon General's report on AIDS to every household "makes every bit as much sense as sending a booklet warning against the dangers of frostbite to every home in the nation, from Key West, Florida, to San Diego, California." Because there is no looming heterosexual epidemic and because the nation has neglected other medical priorities by siphoning off talent and money for AIDS research, Fumento concludes that "the ratio of AIDS research and development spending to federal patient costs is vastly out of proportion to other deadly diseases." Fumento also believes that the priority assigned to AIDS will endanger the lives of other people: "The blunt fact is that people will die of these other diseases because of the overemphasis on AIDS. We will never know their names, and those names will never be sewn into a giant quilt. We will never know their exact numbers. But they will die nonetheless."

Not only the priority of AIDS on the national agenda but also the tactics used to put it there and keep it there have found their critics. Krauthammer concedes that the gains made by AIDS activists are a tribute to their passion and commitment, but he believes that such gains have been won by ingenuous strategy. He charges that the "homosexual community," to advance its own interests, first claimed that AIDS was everyone's problem because everyone was at risk and its solution required universal social urgency. As it became clear that people would not fall at random to the disease, he says activists changed their tactics and began to prey on social guilt:

how dare a society let its gay men, needle-users, their partners and their children get sick and die? But this guilt is unwarranted, Krauthammer believes, since for the most part HIV-related disease is the consequence of individual choices that ignore clear warnings.

Also objecting to activist tactics, the *New York Times* criticized the ACT-UP [AIDS Coalition to Unleash Power] disruption that made it impossible for the Secretary for Health and Human Services to be heard during his remarks at the 1990 international AIDS conference in San Francisco. "It is hard," that paper of record wrote, "to think of a surer way for people with AIDS to alienate their best supporters." The action was characterized as a pointless breakdown in sense and civility. "ACT-UP's members had no justification for turning a research conference into a political circus," especially since, in the standard refrain, society has not only not turned its back but has committed extravagant effort and resources to the HIV epidemic. The disruption, moreover, was all out of proportion to the matters protested: immigration restrictions (since lifted) for people with HIV infection and President Bush's absence from the conference by reason of an event important to the re-election of North Carolina Senator Jesse Helms.

In a different vein, Bruce Fleming suggests in *The Nation* that Americans have come to hype AIDS because of a distorted sense of what it means to be sick and dying. Westerners, he says, assume that absence of disease is the normal state of human being, and that disease thereby becomes a divergence to be named, isolated, and eliminated. Thus can there be the fury and anger he found in a presentation at a Modern Language

Association convention, an AIDS address full of Susan Sontag, Harvey Fierstein, and laments about the lost golden age of free sex. Accepting sickness and death as an integral part of life, he thinks, would free us from the frenetic feeling that AIDS and all disease was unfair treatment amenable to moral and medical control—control it is in any case impossible to achieve.

For all the good intentions here, intentions to remember people sick and dying with other conditions, intentions to keep priorities and discourse rational, intentions to recall the inevitable mortality of human beings as an antidote to their hubris, there is little good reason to shift the priority now devoted to the HIV epidemic, to smear the tactics that have made that priority possible, or to alter the view that sickness and dying with HIV-related disease are evils to be resisted.

Fumento's book makes the most direct claim that people are dying from neglect because the nation has chosen to worry about people with HIV-related conditions. For this reason he thinks AIDS needs to be put into perspective, but he offers not a word about what priority an infectious, communicable lethal disease should receive as against, for example, diabetes or certain heart conditions, which are noncommunicable and can be successfully managed by medicine throughout life. There is not a word, indeed, on how priorities ought to be set at all. Surely an infectious, communicable, lethal disease ought to receive priority over diseases that can currently be medically managed in a way that permits people to live into old age, a prospect not enjoyed by people with HIV-related disease. It is not even clear that funding should be allocated according to the number of persons affected by a particular disease, since such allocation would effectively orphan certain diseases altogether. Moreover, many of the diseases that do now kill people in numbers greater than AIDS have a *long* history of funding, and the expenditures made on behalf of AIDS research and treatment should be measured against that history, not against current annual budget allocations. It may be that AIDS is only now catching up with comparable past expenditures.

Perhaps it is the seemingly voluntary nature of infection that invites the notion that enough has been done for HIV-related conditions. After all, if only people refrained from behavior known to be associated with HIV infection, they wouldn't be at any risk of sickness and death. But HIV-related disease is simply a matter of individual failure to heed clear warnings. Many cases of AIDS were contracted *before any public identification* of the syndrome. Even after the identification of the syndrome, there was no clear identification of its cause or how to avoid it altogether. Early on, there were no efforts to protect blood used in transfusions even when certain screening tests were available. Even after the discovery of the presumptive causal virus and development of blood-screening tests, educational efforts to reach persons most at risk were inadequate and in any case no one knew what forms of education were capable of effecting behavioral change. What educational programs there were failed, then and now, to reach drug-users, their sexual partners, and persons in rural areas. Some persons were infected by means altogether beyond their control: by rape, by transfusion, by Factor VIII used in control of hemophilia, through birth to an infected mother, by accidental needle infection while providing health care or using drugs, through artificial insemination. Because of ambiguities and delays (culpable or not) in biomedicine, education, and public policy, it is not evident for the majority of people with AIDS that there were "clear warnings" that went unheeded.

Even now, when HIV-related disease is well known, it does not follow automatically that those people who contract an HIV infection do so in any morally culpable sense. Over ten years will soon have passed since the CDC [Centers for Disease Control] first reported the occurrence of rare diseases in gay men and drug-using persons. Since that time, ten years of new gay men and drug-users have come along, persons who may not have been educated about the dangers of HIV, young persons who will not yet have maturity of judgment in sexual and drug matters, persons who may not have access to clean needles or drug rehabilitation programs, who may not have the personal and social skills necessary to avoid risk behavior altogether. In some cases there may be cultural and social barriers to protection from risk as well, such as resistance to condom use. It is important to remember, too, that as regards the enticements of sex and drugs, people are weak and not always capable of protecting themselves even from those risks they know and fear. It is not surprising then that a considerable portion of *all* human illness is self-incurred, brought about through one's life choices. This is to vary the principle of double effect: what is chosen is not illness but sex, food, alcohol, drugs, and so on. Their aftermath, unchosen if inevitable, may be illness. But it is telling in this society that those whose heart or lung

disease, for example, is related to their life choices are not asked to wait for research and treatment while those whose disease is accidental or genetic are served first.

It is odd that critics see misplaced privilege in the priority and attention AIDS has won where they might instead see a paradigm for other successes. Should the priority accorded to AIDS research and care be seen as an indictment of the wiles of AIDS activists or should it be required study in schools of public health? AIDS activists are not trying to bleed the government dry, and neither are they blind to the nation's other needs. They are merely trying to insure that government and medicine work together to achieve important goals. If other disease research and care is being neglected, the question is not whether activists have rallied the Congress or the American Medical Association into questionable priorities. The relevant question is why other health care research services cannot be delivered with the urgency and high profile that the HIV epidemic has received. In this sense, the HIV epidemic is an opportunity for critical thinking about the nature of health care in the United States: is it the nature of the disease itself or the design of the health care system that makes the HIV epidemic so formidable? Is it the transmissibility of the disease or social attitudes toward sexuality and drug use that make prevention so difficult?

But all this talk of the priority given to the HIV epidemic is likely to be misleading. It is important to remember that AIDS is no privilege. A diagnosis of AIDS amounts to a virtually unlimited onslaught against an individual's physical, emotional, familial, and economic resources. In addition, there is the burden of stigmatization, given that the disease has sometimes been seen as a punishment or deserved consequence of immoral behavior. For example, a 1988 report showed that, depending on the social category of the respondent, some 8 to 60 percent of persons surveyed considered AIDS to be God's punishment for immoral sexual behavior. A minority of Americans is prepared to tolerate considerable discrimination against people with HIV-related conditions. Varying but significant numbers of persons surveyed report that they would refuse to work alongside people with AIDS, would take their children out of school if a child with AIDS were in attendance, would favor the right of landlords to evict people with AIDS, and so on. Perhaps most tellingly, the majority of people in one survey believed health professionals should be warned if patients have an HIV infection, and a third would allow physicians to decide whether to treat such patients.

This last observation would be benign by itself except that medical students and faculty express a great deal of apprehension in working with people with AIDS and there is some evidence that some of them are choosing specialties and geographies that will keep them at a distance from such patients. Some physicians have even taken to the pages of the *New York Times* to announce that they will refuse to treat any patients with an HIV infection. Nursing recruitment has become difficult for hospitals that care for large numbers of people with HIV-related disorders. There are still places in the United States where hospital food trays are left at the doors of people with AIDS because the nutrition staff will not go into the rooms.

All the money thus far spent in the HIV epidemic has not by itself insured adequate medical care for all people with HIV-related conditions. This is most especially true for the homeless who have HIV-related illness. Neither have the dollars spent on HIV research produced any medical panacea. Treatment with zidovudine (AZT) has proved important for some people but not for all, and there are still many unresolved questions about its long-term ability to extend the lives of all people with HIV infection or to guarantee the quality of life. Zidovudine notwithstanding, as Larry Kramer has pointed out, there continues to be one HIV-related death every twelve minutes in the United States. Is it therefore surprising that ACT-UP now chants, "One billion dollars . . . one drug . . . big deal"?

As Charles Perrow and Mauro F. Guillén point out in *The AIDS Disaster*, it is of course hard to "prove" that funding for AIDS research and care has been inadequate. But as they also point out, a broad array of highly credible reports have each drawn attention to government and philanthropic failures to respond to the epidemic. These reports have come from the Office of Technology Assessment, the Congressional Research Service, the General Accounting Office, the Institute of Medicine, and the Presidential Commission on the Human Immunodeficiency Virus Epidemic. Whatever funding has occurred, it is hard to see that one can object to the amounts per se that need yet to be spent. The money called for by, for example, the Presidential Commission on the Human Immunodeficiency Virus Epidemic or the Institute of Medicine and the National Academy of Sciences is not an invented figure pulled out of the air as a way of keeping scientists and bureaucrats in fat salaries. The figures represent estimates made in good faith about the extent of funding needed. It was clear early on that billions would be required, and that estimation has not changed merely because headlines have moved on to other subjects.

Perhaps the public is used to thinking in terms of billions only for military budgets, but the medical expenditures of the nation are measured in billions as well. The research carried out by the National Institutes of Health has always been enormously expensive, as has been the provision of medical benefits to veterans, the elderly, and the poor. The federal funding of dialysis for end-stage renal disease alone, for example, provides life-saving therapy for only some seventy thousand people, yet its costs have been measured in the billions since Congress decided to pick up the bill for such services. If this kind of funding is any precedent, neither high cost nor small number of affected persons serve as a convincing rationale for limiting the funding now accorded to AIDS research and treatment.

Budget requests based on what should be done are one thing, of course, and budgets actually produced in government legislatures are another. The question at issue in discussions about the "privilege" of AIDS is the question of what priority should be assigned to AIDS funding given all the other funding needs that face the nation. Richard D. Mohr has argued that AIDS funding exerts a moral claim insofar as the disease is associated with gay men; in many of its most significant aspects, the HIV epidemic is the consequence of prejudicial social choices and arrangements. Because its rituals, laws, educational sys-

tem, and prevailing opinion fail to offer gay men any clear or supportive pathway to self-esteem or any incentives to the rewards of durable relationships, society has effectively forced some gay men into promiscuous behavior. Neither does society permit gay men the opportunity to form families that could shoulder at least part of the care their sick need. Patricia Illingworth has fleshed out this argument and extended it to drug users as well. These are powerful arguments; it is hard to think, for example, of a single public ritual in family life, education, the media, religion, or the law that dignifies the love of one man for another, that supports any abiding union there. It is also hard to see that society has protected its needle-users where it cannot prevent drug use or offer successful drug rehabilitation programs. American society's enthusiasm for wars on drugs has not, after all, been translated into action capable of helping any but a fortunate few stop their drug use. Needle-exchange programs have been rejected out of fear that such action will appear to "condone" drug use—a fear that is odd given the de facto acceptance of drug use at every stratum of American culture from Supreme Court justice nominees on down.

It is not surprising then, that left to their own devices, many gay men, drug users, their sexual partners and children find themselves at the mercy of an indifferent virus as they try to lead what lives they can. Victims of disease rarely "just happen." More often than not society's choices permit them to happen, indeed make them inevitable. Robert M. Veatch has observed that it is fair to permit inequality of outcome where opportunities have been equal, but such a conclusion as regards health care would "not apply to persons who are truly not equal in their opportunity because of their social or psychological conditions. It would not apply to those who are forced into their health-risky behavior because of social oppression or stress in the mode of production." Because many of the persons who have contracted HIV-related conditions have done so under circumstances implicating prejudicial social arrangements, there is a substantial claim that priority for HIV research and care is required for reasons of compensation.

But it is not compensation alone that frames the moral imperative about how a society should act here. Moral philosophy also avails itself of the supererogatory, those burdens we undertake beyond the call of formal obligation. Seen from this perspective, the society worth praising, the society worth *having* is the one that will find ways to care and to research, even though there is no formal obligation to do so and for no other reason than that its citizens are ill and dying. The care of those who contracted HIV infection through blood transfusions would be relevant in this regard, as would be women whose HIV risk was a secretly sexually active husband. The morally admirable society would do what it could to protect such persons from infection and care for them when they are sick whether or not society specifically *owes* them this concern and care as a form of compensation.

Cost alone should not be any obstacle for keeping AIDS research and care a national priority. The research is as important as any other research being conducted in the United States today. Delaying this research will not only impede therapy and vaccine development, but it will also subject the eventual costs to inflation; AIDS research will only get more expensive the longer it is delayed. Delays in researching treatments and vaccines will also increase the number of people who may be potentially at risk of HIV-related disease. It is worth remembering that only one disease (smallpox) has ever been entirely eliminated. HIV-related disease is a problem for our time, and it will be a problem for future generations. It is not something that one can throw a fixed sum of money at before moving on. Even when fully effective vaccines and treatment become available, there will be people who will fail to benefit from either by reason of social deprivation, geography, choice, and chance. HIV-related disease therefore needs to be treated as a disease that is here to stay and not one that has already had its share of the limelight and public coffers.

Objections to ACT-UP disruptions of traffic and speech seem to share the view that quiet discourse, argued in mannerly fashion by legislators consulting with medical boards is enough to insure that the nation will set appropriate medical goals. But this view of rationally framed public policy is not entirely true to history. There are few important social reforms that did not require the abandonment of polite discourse and the disruption of business as usual. It is important to remember that government and policy in this country are as much a product of protests, strikes, and civil disobedience as of reasoned debate. It is wrong to pretend that civil disobedience and social disruption are not part and parcel of this nation's political techniques, and it is wrong to blame AIDS activists for using these techniques as others have used them. Perhaps we have forgotten that the United States owes its very origin to acts of rebellion that the

New York Times might have found easy to condemn as breakdowns in sense and civility.

Without protests, moreover, it is hard to see how the battle against AIDS would ever have gotten off the ground. In the early years of the epidemic, the sickness and death of small numbers of gay men did not lend itself to the advocacy of important legislators and medical commissions. It was necessary then that impolite discourse be used in order to be heard. That need continues to this day. Most of the many recommendations of the 1988 Presidential Commission Report on the Human Immunodeficiency Virus Epidemic, for example, are already collecting dust. If an analysis with the stature of a Presidential Commission report cannot spur action on important goals, what other recourse is there than the tried and true methods of protest that are as much a part of American democracy as its parliamentary rules of order? It is odd that where people do not see conspiracy behind AIDS activism, they see irrationality and impropriety when what they might see is a standard of urgency and passion by which to evaluate and improve the entire health care system in the United States.

It is hard to see moreover that an acceptance of disease and dying, in the way Fleming has urged, is anything but an invitation to quietism. If disease and dying are inevitable, what incentive is there to resist their damages? Granted, some Americans may have lost the sense of their mortality, but it is hard to see that much is gained by restoring it. On the contrary, it may be the perception of disease as "excrescence" that is the very spur to its control and eradication. There is no point in glorifying disease and dying; the lessons they teach are easily learned and do not require advanced instruction. There is a point at which sickness and dying cease to offer insights into the human condition or opportunities for strength and become instead unbearable, unredeemable absurdity. This is most often how AIDS appears to those who know it. To his credit, Fleming does say that hesitation by the U.S. government to carry out necessary HIV research would be criminal. But if this is so, then it's unclear that the change in the perception of death he counsels would make any practical difference in regard to the responsibility of government and medicine to resist the epidemic as much as it can with all the resources it can muster.

The sentiment nevertheless grows that AIDS is getting more than its share of media attention, resources, and social indulgence. But there really hasn't been any change in the status of the epidemic to warrant a change in the scope of intensity of research and treatment programs. HIV remains a highly lethal, communicable virus. Despite better medical management, the number of HIV-related deaths continues to increase. More and more hospital resources have to be directed to the care of people with HIV-related conditions. What accounts for the sentiment, then, that AIDS has gotten more than its share? From the onset of the epidemic, there have been many dire prophesies about the toll of the epidemic, predictions that millions to billions would die. Is it possible that critics can say that AIDS has gotten more than its share because it has not yet killed *enough* people? Is the same epidemic at the margins of national attention now inspiring the claim that enough has been done? The sentiment that enough has been done for AIDS has primarily been argued in the press or journalistic accounts and not in professional journals of medicine, bioethics, or public policy. Could it be that this sentiment belongs to those who do not know the epidemic at first hand?

If HIV research and therapy are relegated to a lesser rank in the nation's priorities, it will be gay men, needle-users, their sexual partners and their children who will continue to pay the price of neglect, and the epidemic will become again the shadow killer that it was in the beginning. In view of the people who are still sick, who are dying, who bear the costs of this epidemic, it is too early and shameful to say that enough has been done. In an epidemic not yet ten years old, it is too early for a backlash.

POSTSCRIPT

Has the Federal Government Spent Enough on AIDS Research?

In her book *AIDS and Its Metaphors*, Susan Sontag describes a classic pattern in the way people have considered plagues over the centuries. Plagues, she notes, always have three characteristics: First, plagues are unexplainable epidemics that affect everyone. They strike the innocent and the bad, the naive, and those who try futilely to protect themselves. Second, plagues are seen as a punishment from God, usually a punishment for the people's immorality, decadence, and sexual promiscuity, especially if the disease is spread sexually. Third, plagues demand an exotic, primitive, and foreign origin.

In parallel with this classic belief that plagues always have some exotic and foreign origin, some people initially thought that AIDS originated in the jungles of Africa, where people ate or had sexual intercourse with green monkeys. The people of Africa and the Caribbean recently proposed that AIDS is the result of biological warfare designed by the United States. AIDS, some have claimed, was brought to the United States by promiscuous homosexuals who engaged in anal sex. Many Americans have repeated the claim that AIDS is God's punishment on homosexuals for their "unnatural" promiscuity.

As Sontag clearly shows, the classic metaphor of the plague is still being played out. People feel the need to blame someone for this devastating new disease. Heterosexuals and people who do not use intravenous drugs often find homosexuals and drug users to be handy scapegoats. Theories of exotic origins and the futility of safe sex prevention are widespread. How we use this classic metaphor can influence the way we respond to the question, "Have we spent enough on AIDS?"

In the 1940s, Americans "declared war" on polio and invested millions in the March of Dimes to finally control this disease that killed innocent children. In the 1930, "wars" on cancer and heart disease were launched. For over half a century, Americans have supported the American Cancer Society and the American Heart Association with billions of dollars' worth of federal and private funds. But none of these diseases are connected with sex, and we must ask how our knowledge that the HIV virus is spread mainly through sexual contact influences our response to it. In the early 1980s homosexual sexual activity and the use of contaminated drug needles were the main vehicles of HIV transmission. By the year 2000, heterosexual vaginal intercourse will likely be the main source of HIV infections in the developing nations. Whether or not this pattern will follow in the United States and Europe will be determined by several unpredictable variables.

Does this possibility affect whether the federal government should spend more or less on AIDS research?

SUGGESTED READINGS

G. Antonio, *The AIDS Cover-Up? The Real and Alarming Facts About AIDS* (Ignatius Press, 1986).

E. Fax, "Committee Report Scores Federal AIDS-Prevention Efforts," *Education Week* (April 15, 1992).

M. Fumento, *The Myth of Heterosexual AIDS* (Basic Books, 1990).

M. Fumento, "Magic's Gone," *National Review* (October 19, 1992).

M. Gladwell, "A Real AIDS Cure: Only Select," *The New Republic* (June 21, 1993).

R. Massa, "The Other War," *Village Voice* (February 12, 1991).

R. Massa, "Unfair Share," *Village Voice* (May 26, 1992).

C. Perrow and M. F. Guillen, *The AIDS Disaster: The Failure of Organizations in New York and the Nation* (Yale University Press, 1990).

R. Shilts, *And the Band Played On: Politics, People and the AIDS Epidemic* (St. Martin's Press, 1987).

S. Sontag, *AIDS and Its Metaphors* (Farrar, Straus & Giroux, 1989).

CONTRIBUTORS
TO THIS VOLUME

EDITOR

ROBERT T. FRANCOEUR has taught human sexuality at colleges and high schools for over 20 years. He is currently a professor of biological and allied health sciences at Fairleigh Dickinson University in Madison, New Jersey, and the author of 7 books on human sexuality, including *Hot and Cool Sex: Cultures in Conflict* (Harcourt Brace Jovanovich, 1974); *Becoming a Sexual Person* (Macmillan, 1989), a human sexuality textbook; *A Descriptive Dictionary and Atlas of Sexology* (Greenwood, 1992); and *An International Handbook of Sexuality* (Greenwood, 1994). He has contributed to 53 handbooks and readers on human sexuality, and he has 47 technical papers and over 110 popular articles on sexual issues to his credit. A guest lecturer on sexual topics at over 250 colleges and universities, he is also a fellow of the Society for the Scientific Study of Sex. He holds a doctorate in embryology and master's degrees in Catholic theology and biology, and he is a charter member of the American College of Sexology.

STAFF

Marguerite L. Egan   Program Manager
Brenda S. Filley   Production Manager
Whit Vye   Designer
Libra Ann Cusack   Typesetting Supervisor
Juliana Arbo   Typesetter
David Brackley   Copy Editor
David Dean   Administrative Assistant
Diane Barker   Editorial Assistant

AUTHORS

NORMA JEAN ALMODOVAR is a former Los Angeles police department traffic officer who later became a prostitute. She is now a prostitutes' rights activist, and she is the author of *Cop to Call Girl.*

FRAN AVALLONE is the state coordinator for Right to Choose of New Jersey. She is a former president and member of the board of directors for the Planned Parenthood League of Middlesex County, and she has received the 1992 Women of Achievement Award, presented by Douglass College and the New Jersey State Federation of Women's Clubs, and the 1993 Mary Philbrook Award, presented by the Women's Political Caucus of New Jersey.

JANET BENSHOOF is an attorney with the Center for Reproductive Law and Policy in New York City.

H. JEAN BIRNBAUM, currently retired, was a clinical psychologist at the Treatment Center for Sexually Dangerous Persons in Bridgewater, Massachusetts. She is the coauthor, with A. Nicholas Groth, of *Men Who Rape: The Psychology of the Offender* (Plenum Press, 1979).

HARRY A. BLACKMUN is an associate justice of the U.S. Supreme Court. He received an LL.B. from Harvard Law School in 1932 and then worked in a law firm in Minneapolis, Minnesota, where he specialized in taxation, litigation, wills, trusts, and estate planning. He was nominated to the U.S. Court of Appeals by President Eisenhower in 1959, and he served in that capacity until his nomination to associate justice by President Nixon in 1970.

JANET CALLUM is a former director of administrative services for the Feminist Women's Health Center in Atlanta, Georgia.

PATRICK CARNES is the primary architect of an inpatient program for sexual dependency at the Golden Valley Health Center in Minneapolis, Minnesota. He is the author of *Out of the Shadows: Understanding Sexual Addiction* (CompCare, 1985) and *Counseling the Sexual Addict* (CompCare, 1986). He received a Ph.D. from the University of Minnesota.

CENTER FOR POPULATION OPTIONS works to increase the opportunities for and abilities of youth to make healthy decisions about sexuality. Since 1980, it has provided information, education, and advocacy to youth-serving agencies and professionals, policymakers, and the media.

REBECCA CHALKER is a women's health advocate and an author who speaks internationally on women's health care and sexuality. Her publications include *The Complete Cervical Cap Guide* (Harper & Row, 1987); *Overcoming Bladder Disorders* (HarperCollins, 1990), coauthored with Kristene Whitmore; and *A Woman's Book of Choices: Abortion, Menstrual Extraction, RU-486* (Four Walls Eight Windows, 1992).

EDWIN J. DELATTRE is the dean of the School of Education and a professor of education and philosophy in the College of Liberal Arts at Boston University in Boston, Massachusetts. His publications include *Education and the Public Trust: The Imperative for Common Purposes* (Ethics and Public Policy, 1988) and *Character and Cops: Ethics in Policing* (American Enterprise Institute, 1989). President emeritus of St. John's College, he is well known nationally for his work on ethics in daily public and private life.

JAMES C. DOBSON is the founder and president of Focus on the Family, an organization dedicated to preserving traditional family values. He is a former member of the U.S. Attorney General's Commission on Pornography, which delivered its final report to the public and to then-president Ronald Reagan in June 1986, and the author of *Love for a Lifetime* (Multnomah, 1987).

LYNETTE DUMBLE is a research fellow in the Department of Surgery at the University of Melbourne in Parkville, Victoria, Australia.

FAMILY RESEARCH COUNCIL OF AMERICA, founded in 1981 and formerly the Family Research Group, is a conservative, profamily lobbying organization in Washington, D.C., that provides information on such issues as parental autonomy and responsibility, the effects of the tax system on families, adolescent pregnancy, and teenage suicide to government agencies, members of Congress, and the public. Its president is Gary Bauer.

SANDRA C. FINZI is a clinical psychologist practicing in Washington, D.C. Trained in psychodynamic, behavioral, and systemic theories and techniques, her research intersts focus on psychotherapy integration.

FOCUS ON THE FAMILY is an organization dedicated to preserving traditional family values. It was founded by James C. Dobson, a former member of the U.S. Attorney General's Commission on Pornography.

MICHAEL FUMENTO, a former AIDS analyst and attorney for the U.S. Commission on Civil Rights, is the science and economics reporter for *Investor's Business Daily*. He is the author of numerous articles and two books on AIDS, including *The Myth of Heterosexual AIDS* (New Republic Books, 1990) and *Science Under Siege* (William Morrow, 1993). He received a J.D. from the University of Illinois College of Law in 1985.

EUGENE T. GOMULKA, a commander in the U.S. Navy Chaplain Corps, is currently serving as deputy chaplain for the U.S. Marine Corps. He received a B.A. in philosophy from Saint Francis College and a licentiate in sacred theology from the Pontifical University of Saint Thomas Aquinas in Rome, Italy. He has received two Meritorious Service Medals, the Navy Commendation Medal, and the Navy Achievement Medal.

A. NICHOLAS GROTH is a clinical psychologist and the director of the Sex Offender Treatment Program at the Wyoming State Honor Farm in Riverton, Wyoming. Recognized nationally and internationally as an expert on sexual assault, he is the coauthor, with H. Jean Birnbaum, of *Men Who Rape: The Psychology of the Offender* (Plenum Press, 1979).

BRENT HARTINGER is a free-lance writer based in Seattle, Washington.

DOREEN KIMURA is a neuropsychologist and a professor in the Department of Psychology at the University of Western Ontario in London, Ontario, Canada. Her research interests focus on the brain and hormonal bases of human intellectual abilities. A fellow of the Royal Society of Canada, she is the author of *Neuromotor Mechanisms in Human Communication* (Oxford University Press, 1993).

MARTY KLEIN is a California-licensed marriage and family therapist and a nationally certified sex educator. He serves on the national board of the Society for the Scientific Study of Sex, and he is the author of a book, a textbook chapter, and 150 articles about sexuality.

RENATE KLEIN is a senior lecturer in the School of Humanities at the Deakin University in Geelong, Victoria, Australia.

KNIGHTS OF COLUMBUS is a national fraternal organization of Roman Catholics that works to promote Catholic interests by providing social activities, sponsoring

athletic events, and contributing to various charitable and educational projects. Its headquarters are in New Haven, Connecticut.

GRETCHEN MORGENSON is a senior editor of *Forbes* magazine.

MONICA B. MORRIS is an independent sociologist and a former professor of sociology at California State University, Los Angeles, whose research interests focus on love relationships in later life. She is the author of *An Excursion into Creative Sociology* (Columbia University Press, 1977) and *Last-Chance Children: Growing Up With Older Parents* (Columbia University Press, 1988).

TIMOTHY F. MURPHY is an assistant professor of philosophy in the Department of Biomedical Sciences at the University of Illinois College of Medicine in Chicago, Illinois. His publications include *Writing AIDS: Gay Literature, Language, and Analysis* (Columbia University Press, 1993), coedited with Suzanne Poirier.

ERIC NADLER, a senior editor of *Forum,* is a journalist based in New York City whose work has appeared in many national publications, including *Harper's Magazine, The Nation,* and *Mother Jones.*

RICHARD JOHN NEUHAUS has been the director of the Rockford Institute Center on Religion and Society since 1984. He is the editor in chief of *This Word* and an editor of *Forum Letter* and *The Religion and Society Report.* His publications include *The Naked Public Square: Religion and Democracy in America* (W. B. Eerdmans, 1984) and *The Catholic Moment: The Paradox of the Church in the Postmodern World* (Harper & Row, 1987).

PHILIP NOBILE is a free-lance writer based in Scarsdale, New York. He studied for the Catholic priesthood, and he has graduate degrees from Boston University and the Higher Institute of Philosophy at Louvain, Belgium.

DENNIS O'BRIEN, a former president of Bucknell University, has been the president of the University of Rochester in Rochester, New York, since 1981. A former professor at both Princeton University and Middlebury College, he is the author of five books and several articles on philosophy, religion, and modern art that have appeared in professional and popular publications. He is a member of the board of directors for LaSalle University and a member of the Business–Higher Education Forum and the Salzburg Seminar.

CRAIG T. PALMER is a professor in the Department of Sociology at Arizona State University in Temple, Arizona.

FRANK PITTMAN is a psychiatrist and family therapist in Atlantá, Georgia, a clinical assistant professor of psychiatry at Emory University School of Medicine, and an adjunct professor of psychology at Georgia State University. He is a charter member of the American

Family Therapy Academy, a fellow and an approved supervisor of the American Association for Marriage and Family Therapy, and a former director of psychiatric services at Grady Memorial Hospital in Atlanta. His publications include *Private Lies: Infidelity and the Betrayal of Intimacy* (W. W. Norton, 1989) and *Man Enough: Fathers, Sons, and the Search for Masculinity* (G. P. Putnam's Sons, 1993).

JANICE RAYMOND is a professor of women's studies and medical ethics at the University of Massachusetts–Amherst.

KATIE ROIPHE is a doctoral candidate in English literature at Princeton University in Princeton, New Jersey, and the author of *The Morning After: Sex, Fear and Feminism on Campus* (Little, Brown, 1993).

RANDY SHILTS is an author and a journalist for the *San Francisco Chronicle*, where he has been reporting full-time on the AIDS epidemic and homosexuals since 1983. He is the author of *And the Band Played On: Politics, People, and the AIDS Epidemic* (St. Martin's Press, 1987), which has been translated into seven languages and released in 14 nations, and *Conduct Unbecoming: Gays and Lesbians in the U.S. Military* (St. Martin's Press, 1993).

CATHARINE R. STIMPSON is the dean of the graduate college at Rutgers University and a former president of the Modern Language Association. Her publications include *Where the Meanings Are* (Methuen, 1988).

CAROL TAVRIS is a social psychologist and an author based in Los Angeles, California. Her publications include *The Longest War: Sex Differences in Perspective*, 2d ed. (Harcourt Brace Jovanovich, 1984), coauthored with Carole Wade, and *Anger: The Misunderstood Emotion* (Simon & Schuster, 1989). She is a member of the American Psychological Association.

ROBIN WARSHAW is a free-lance journalist based in Pennsauken, New Jersey, and a victim of acquaintance rape.

BYRON R. WHITE is a former associate justice of the U.S. Supreme Court. He received an LL.B. from Yale University in 1946 and, upon graduating, served as a law clerk to Supreme Court chief justice Frederick M. Vinson. In 1948, he joined a law firm in Denver, Colorado, where he stayed until he was appointed deputy attorney general of the United States in 1961. He served as an associate justice of the Supreme Court for 31 years, from his appointment by President Kennedy in 1962 until his retirement in 1993.

CHARLES WINICK is a professor in the Department of Sociology at City College, City University of New York. He is a member of the American Social Health Association, the editor of *Deviance and Mass Media* (Sage Publications, 1978), and the coeditor, with Leon Brill, of *Yearbook of Substance Use and Abuse* (Human Science Press, 1985).

INDEX